Situating Portfolios

Situating Portfolios

Four Perspectives

Kathleen Blake Yancey and Irwin Weiser, editors

UTAH STATE UNIVERSITY PRESS
Logan, Utah
1997

Utah State University Press
Logan, Utah 84322-7800

Library of Congress Cataloging-in-Publication Data
Situating portfolios : four perspectives / edited by Kathleen Blake Yancey and Irwin Weiser.
p. cm.
Includes bibliographical references.
ISBN 0-87421-220-0
1. Portfolios in education–United States. 2. Grading and marking (Students)–United States. 3. English language–Composition and exercises–United States–Ability testing. I. Yancey, Kathleen Blake, 1950- . II. Weiser, Irwin.
LB1029.P67.S58 1997
371.2'7–dc20 96-45774
CIP

Contents

Part II: Pedagogy

Part III: Teaching and Professional Development

Part IV: Technology

Situating Portfolios
An Introduction

Kathleen Blake Yancey
Irwin Weiser

WHEN TEACHERS BEGAN DEVELOPING PORTFOLIOS OVER A DECADE AGO, we knew that what we were about—with process writing and collaborative pedagogies and, not least, portfolios—was pretty ambitious: it was, in fact, nothing short of changing the face of American education.

College and University Portfolio *Assessment*

At the postsecondary level, the efforts were initiated more often than not by a demand for accountability, an insistence that students demonstrate they could write well enough to move to the next level or to graduate. Portfolios, then—as documented by Pat Belanoff, Peter Elbow, and William Condon—comprised a creative response to that demand for accountability. At the same time, portfolios also became the resolution to the widespread perception of a mismatch between, on the one hand, what writers did in class and on the other, the way students were asked to demonstrate they could write. In the classroom, they were asked to write on topics of interest them, to share that writing, and to revise and/or rewrite on the basis of that response. When asked to *demonstrate* they could write, however, students found the conditions radically different: assigned topics, limited times for writing (typically, thirty to forty-five minutes), and a demand for editing above all else. Portfolios provided a way to bridge classroom and test, and most of the early work in collegiate portfolios (e.g., Belanoff and Dickson 1991) focused, not surprisingly, on the assessment strand of portfolio assessment.

Portfolio Assessment in K-12 Schooling

In the K-12 context, unlike the postsecondary context, the motivation for portfolios was provided, typically, not by an external demand for testing or accountability, but by the teachers themselves, by *their* sense that there was something missing in their classrooms, that there had to be a better way to invite students to show what they had learned. Across the country—sometimes quietly and alone, sometimes in groups and quite deliberately—teachers in elementary and middle and high schools introduced portfolios to their students, with results that are now well-documented (e.g., Graves and Sunstein 1992; Yancey 1992b). Given this freedom, they designed diverse models—writing portfolios and literature portfolios and reading portfolios and journalism portfolios and literacy portfolios—all of them sensitive to their local communities, to their educational contexts, and perhaps most important, to their students' needs. The fact that teachers are still engaged in this conversation, and expanding it as well, testifies to the ability of portfolios to link and to showcase multiple variables: student growth, student achievement, commentary about learning, rich curricula, and innovative teachers and administrators. In the K-12 context, then, the portfolio strand motivated the primary interest in portfolio assessment.

Portfolio Assessment

Currently, both threads of the phrase portfolio assessment—portfolio and assessment—inform work in portfolios in educational contexts ranging from early childhood to graduate school. And in the intervening years between the time the first portfolio volumes were published—1991 to 1992—and now, much has changed: the situations described above have almost reversed themselves. In colleges and universities, portfolios are currently situated within classrooms as often as within programs and institutions. Current questions regarding portfolios in this context focus not on portfolios' legitimacy, but rather on issues both pragmatic and theoretical, and frequently on learning: what new portfolio models can we develop; how does reading a set of portfolios help us understand our own curriculum; how might one develop an electronic portfolio, and how might one assess it? In contrast, as we hear from Sandra Murphy and Susan Callahan particularly, teachers in the kindergarten through twelfth context have found themselves more constrained and increasingly under pressure as states—from Vermont to Kentucky to Connecticut—have designed statewide portfolio models used for assessment—models often imposed from state capitals, often by administrators with little understanding of what is involved in daily teaching and learning.

Not that these changes should surprise us. Catharine Lucas predicted them several years ago. In an essay outlining her cautions about portfolio use, she identifies three factors that the portfolio movement, should it be successful, needs to address:

> 1) the weakening of effect through careless imitation, 2) the failure of research to validate the pedagogy, and 3) the co-option by large-scale external testing programs. (Lucas 1992, 3)

It is our purpose here to consider these cautions as a frame for introducing the current volume and for commenting on the status of portfolios today: what we know, what we understand, what we need to learn about portfolio—a set of texts whose intent is purposeful, whose audience is specific, and whose metacommentary, or reflection, makes sense of the portfolio.

Weakening of Effect

The Classroom Portfolio, The Bridge Portfolio

Lucas locates her concern about weakening of effect with a single question: "Can this spirit of exploration remain central to the use of portfolios as they become more commonplace?" (Lucas 1992, 6) The chapters here suggest that the answer to this question is yes: portfolio models have moved beyond the writing classroom to other classrooms and programs, beyond print literacy into electronic literacy, have expanded in multiple, complex, and interesting ways. Classroom versions, for example, from the early developmental model for preschoolers to "bridge" portfolios—those whose purpose and/or contents are explicitly intended to create links between and among students' diverse experiences—demonstrate new iterations, raise new questions, help us understand in new ways what and how our students learn.

Specifically, we see in Mary Ann Smith's chapter the interaction between classroom culture and the portfolio model. Addressed briefly in earlier portfolio texts (Graves and Sunstein 1992; Yancey 1992b) the classroom context, as Smith outlines it, is perhaps the central factor related to portfolios that promote learning; a point to which Sandra Murphy, among others, will return. Classrooms hospitable to portfolios center on partnership and collaboration; they foster active construction of knowledge, student reflection and self-evaluation, and community structures in which students and teachers work together as readers, writers, thinkers, researchers, and learners. Sandra Stone likewise explores the value of partnership, of using portfolios to have even very young students show teachers what they are learning; such portfolios both shape curriculum and provide a vehicle for communication with parents as well. Thomas Philion's chapter connects theory with practice in its description of portfolios, arguing that because they can be fluid contexts for growth and learning, portfolios are consistent with what Mihaly Csikszentmihalyi and his colleagues refer to as "flow," an involvement in learning that usually occurs when there are clear goals for learning, immediate feedback, and an opportunity to act on that feedback. At its best, then, the portfolio enacts our understandings about how learners learn.

Others discuss classroom portfolios as well, but their emphasis reveals another quality of this next wave of portfolio: its power to "bridge" across classes, across experiences, between schools, and from school to work. This kind of portfolio, while documented briefly elsewhere (Kneeshaw 1992), is examined as a specific type here by three contributors. Mary Perry, for instance, invites high school students to situate portfolios within rhetorical situations of their own design. In assembling portfolios for employment and for college scholarships, students "bridge" school and work as they are invited to take what is learned in one situation and apply it as they prepare to move on to the next. Perry notes the influence of a real "exigence": when students see practical functions for portfolios, they are much more engaged in developing them than when the portfolio seems to lack a purpose beyond classroom assessment. In "Building Bridges, Closing Gaps," William Condon emphasizes the potential for portfolios to provide continuity for teachers and students; he also comments on the power of the portfolio to shape both educational contexts, high school and college. In her discussion of portfolios in law school courses, Susan R. Dailey discusses a bridging approach: the intersection portfolios can provide between the academic world and the working world.

Overall, what we see in this section both heartens and concerns. We see very different models of portfolios, different not just from institution to institution, but different in their understandings of and response to student needs. And at the same time, we note similar purposes—like those informing Perry's portfolios and Dailey's—beginning to form a coherent pattern across educational contexts. As important, we see bridging portfolios inviting students—from high school to law school—to make a whole text from the fragments of their academic and non-academic experiences, to include in their school work new, real exigence and new, real audiences. We see new partnerships and collaborations; we see teachers and students learning both with and from each other. Over and over and over, we see the importance of classroom culture.

Still, the bridging portfolios, particularly, invite us to issue some cautions ourselves. Bridging portfolios, because they operate in more than one context, seem an especially valuable means of resisting Lucas's weakening of effect, it's true. But at the same time, precisely because they cross disciplines and boundaries and institutions and cultures, there is likely to be a countervailing effect: an invitation to centralize, to standardize, to enable the demands of one context to dictate the text produced in another, and ultimately to make the portfolios crossing those boundaries look alike. Both the University of Michigan and Miami University (see Stygall et al. 1994, for instance) seem to do some of this already; they define a particular type of portfolio which schools prepare students to construct, just in the same way they prepared students for the timed writing placement essay, as Condon points out. This kind of shaping effect could lead, we think, to an undesirable weakening of effect indeed. One way to assure it does not is to follow Mary Perry's lead: to help students themselves understand the theory contextualizing portfolios. Portfolios are texts serving the needs of a particular rhetorical situation, and they can take many forms, can answer many questions, can present many selves.

Electronic Literacy, Electronic Portfolios

And just as writing is changing, so too are writing portfolios: enter a portfolio untreated in the earlier volumes addressing portfolios, the electronic portfolio. This portfolio is a new kind of "literacy portfolio," an e-literacy portfolio perhaps, one characterized more by Cynthia Selfe's notion of layered literacy than by print discourse. Print documents may well be included in such a portfolio (see, e.g., Mayers 1996), but the electronic portfolio can take another form: completely electronic. And it can be multiply formed, multiply linear: hypertextual. Clearly, this is no weakening of effect, and clearly, the questions generated by this kind of portfolio are numerous and go to the heart of what it is we think we mean when we use the word literacy.

Gail Hawisher and Cynthia Selfe begin answering these questions by showing us, in a thoughtful reflection, how the two technologies—computers and portfolios—offer opportunities that can only be realized if we theorize our work, and if we begin to include work in electronic literacy and in portfolios with our prospective colleagues as well as with our colleagues already practicing. Greg Wickliff and, then, Katherine Fischer introduce us to different versions of hypertext portfolios—one for a professional writing class, the other for a creative writing class—showing us how, again, each serves the specified and appropriate needs of students, course, and institution. As they describe their practice, Wickliff and Fischer also theorize about what they experienced so that those of us who have yet to develop such a model have one we might adapt, but one whose limits we also understand. And again, as they describe each iteration of portfolio, we see partnerships: students and teacher together negotiating a portfolio model very much under construction.

Pam Takayoshi and Kristine Blair also describe a hypertext portfolio, but their focus serves more to illustrate the evaluation issues an electronic portfolio raises. Given the shifting roles of writer and reader in hypertext, as well as the different kinds of thinking animating the text, how do we read this kind of portfolio, how do we evaluate it, and how do we grade it? Finally, six members of "Portnet," a group of college faculty from across the country, discuss their on-line reading and evaluation of a single WAC portfolio, showing in the process how similar readers construct and interpret the same texts differently, how expectations we bring to text shape our reading processes, and how a listserver discussion group might be used by others—not for large-scale scoring of portfolios and ranking and numbering of students, but for uncovering assumptions, for creating new hypotheses, and for another kind of testing—seeing if what we claim to practice and reward is indeed what we do practice and reward.

Hawisher and Selfe are correct, we think, in their understanding of both the opportunities and the dangers that a wedding of portfolios and electronics presents. There is a party line, advocated in each camp, that insists that each technology necessarily brings with it desired ends: student empowerment, new collaboration, and indeed new education. Practice simply does not bear this out, as Susan Callahan, Sandy Murphy, and Pam

Takayoshi (Takayoshi 1994) make clear. Each opportunity is just that: an opportunity that has quite possibly equal potential to do harm (and worse, because it's in the name of good). To make good use of the opportunity the electronic portfolio offers and to prevent a weakening of even this portfolio's effect, we must commit to three actions:

1. continue to describe our practices fully, including in those descriptions accounts of what didn't work and of what issues remain;
2. begin to answer, no matter how incompletely, the questions raised by Takayoshi and Blair; and
3. use collaborative groups like Portnet to serve students, not to provide new sites for the same evaluation practices.

Teacher Portfolios

All portfolios, of course, are not writing portfolios, though it is the writing portfolio that is often credited with generating this newer model, the teacher portfolio, and in this volume, the student-teacher portfolio as well. The teacher portfolio also suggests strengthening rather than weakening of effect, and it too—like the writing portfolio—is often prompted by a need to address that which is perceived as inadequate or even wrongheaded in the current system.

Robert P. Yagelski links portfolios explicitly to reflective practice and examines some of the difficulties teacher educators face in preparing preservice English teachers for such practice. His portfolio, of course, is intended as one piece of an effort to address those difficulties. Kathleen Blake Yancey reads with us three of her students' portfolios, finding in them grounds for a new understanding of the intersection between the articulated curriculum and the experienced curriculum; the former planned and perhaps delivered by the faculty member, and the latter perceived and experienced by the student. Working more quantitatively and from a still different model of teacher portfolio, C. Beth Burch details the findings of her investigation of the documents secondary English education students chose to place in their course portfolios. Her findings argue that secondary English education programs frequently shortchange students, who are too often inadequately prepared to teach writing and language and whose understanding of literature is frequently limited to a very narrow canon and to a literary-historical approach to texts. For undergraduates, then, teacher portfolios provide one way to encourage professional identity, one means for us to understand the processes contributing to that identity.

Pearl and Leon Paulson use the portfolio for a similar purpose, for faculty development, though the faculty they work with are already practicing teachers. Paulson and Paulson explain how teachers in continuing education classes planned and prepared their own portfolios as a means of learning how to implement portfolios with their students. Through this process, teachers—like Mary Perry's students—learned of the complexity of choosing appropriate material according to the purpose of the portfolio, of organizing it effectively, and of determining their own evaluative standards for their work. Irwin Weiser focuses on graduate students, describing how teacher portfolios are situated within a practicum for students-who-are-becoming-teachers. These student-teachers are learning to teach at the same time they are learning about portfolios, the practicum and the portfolio providing a safe place for learning about process pedagogy and successful writing.

Here we see no weakening of effect, but again, we have concerns. That teacher educators have moved so quickly to incorporate portfolios into the curriculum, we think, is commendable. To put the point directly, teacher education is in the process of being rescripted by portfolios. We can use them for a variety of tasks: to learn about the curriculum as it is experienced by our students and to help our students apply for teaching jobs. We are developing alternative models for graduate students and for practicing teachers. At the same time, a theme sounded in Yagelski, in Yancey, and in Burch—student resistance—is one we resist at our peril. It's interesting, but perhaps not surprising, that even beginning teachers resist portfolios. Learning is, after all, culture-bound, and the students going into teaching right now are those who have done well with the old game in the old culture. Based on their own experience, they may have less rather than more reason to change practice, especially when the new practice of resisting fixed answers poses so many risks and uncertainties. If we don't acknowledge that resistance, seek to understand it on its own terms, and respond to it in appropriate ways, we may well lose the chance to affect education as we have hoped (Bishop 1991; Yancey 1994).

Failure of Research

A second concern articulated by Catharine Lucas is research-based: "The danger here is that those who cling to the illusion that only what can be measured or counted is worth doing will find the effects of portfolios . . . not only resistant to measurement but initially resistant even to definition" (Lucas 1992, 7). As an alternative, Lucas recommends "Ethnographic research that 'looks into' the portfolios rather than attempts to prove them worthwhile" (Lucas 1992, 7) and "reporting in" before reporting out.

Lucas's concern here is almost prescient. Not two years later, we began hearing such calls for research, first from Brian Huot, and then from Sandra Stotsky. Huot calls the early work in portfolios "show-and-tell," suggesting now that practice is defined, we need research; since we have now described the "show-and-tell" of practice, we should move ahead to the next stage which is research and/or theory. Sandra Stotsky, then editor of *Research in the Teaching of English* (*RTE*), relies on the same understanding of how we will know about portfolios when she calls for *research* that will confirm or disconfirm what has been claimed for portfolios in practitioner accounts. In the introduction to the October 1992 issue of *RTE*, Stotsky calls for such knowledge. There is, she says, "a conspicuous absence of research studies on portfolio assessment and other alternative forms of assessment. Portfolio assessment has increased markedly in the past six years . . . and it is truly puzzling to me why *RTE* has so far received *no empirical studies* in this area" (italics added, Stotsky 1992, 246). The claim, then, in this view of how we know what we know is that we need to move *beyond* accounts of practice.

But the teachers, administrators, and assessment specialists working with portfolios have constructed this "how we learn" process another way, as the editors of the most recent text on portfolios, *New Directions in Portfolio Assessment*, make quite clear. This understanding of the research that has helped us *know* about portfolios is arguably the major contribution this volume makes to the conversation about portfolio assessment. Black, Daiker, Sommers, and Stygall define the accounts in their edited collection as "well-theorized reflective practice" grounded in a "felt experience," which they define by specific reference to Nancy Baker's May 1993 *RTE* article on portfolios. In that study, Baker used the methodology of positivism, through matching an experimental group of students with a control group, to test the idea that portfolios would help students produce better writing. Although the results did not confirm her hypothesis, Baker argues, "in its result the experiment was incomplete." It failed to account for her "felt experience" that the students were writing better. Using this example of research as a point of departure, the *New Directions* editors articulate a different kind of research connected to portfolios:

> The felt knowledge of writing teachers, the one that says portfolios adequately address the connection between classroom and writing, is tenacious. In spite of a number of calls for experimental and positivistic research to "prove" that

> portfolios do a better job of teaching or assessing writing, the discipline has resisted this specific call. Instead, the research on portfolios has been more classroom-based, more reflective, and more qualitative in nature. Even when the traditional educational research paradigm is invoked and presented, the researcher can still "feel" that somehow such research couldn't capture what portfolios were about. (Stygall et al. 1994, 2)

Their aim in creating the *New Directions* text was to honor this "felt experience," to learn from it what it had to teach: "In order to reflect teachers' felt experience, we present essays that closely examine individual classrooms, problematize particular practices, and isolate sites rich for portfolio evaluation" (Stygall et al. 1994, 3).

Discussing their research method directly in the same collection, contributors Liz Hamp-Lyons and William Condon move from practice to theory to practice again:

> We can describe a kind of research spiral; reader protocols turned up problems in readers' behaviors; discussions followed about what measures might assure that readers would attend to more of the writing in each portfolio; these discussions led to changes that not only improved the quality of the assessment, but had a positive impact on the teaching/learning environment in the course as well; finally, changes in the purpose and structure of the portfolio reading groups produced the desired result, as the later protocols demonstrated. (Stygall et al. 1994, 283)

Hamp-Lyons and Condon are working from a reflective, practice-based understanding of how we know, not from the stage-model linear mode with show-and-tell followed by confirming empirical research. They articulate practice, analyze reflectively, change practice, and reflect anew in what they call *spiral-like* development. The articulation and the reflective analysis work together, the one informing the other.

On this basis, like Hamp-Lyons and Condon before us, we have grounds for changing practice, for describing it anew. In other words, the chapters here not only extend and differentiate earlier practice, but talk back to it, refine it, problematize it: help us understand it and ask other good questions of it. In Donald Schon's terms, the writers about portfolios—all these reflective writers—are involved in what he calls "making" something, improvisationally. He compares such reflective practitioners—the makers—to jazz musicians:

> . . . the participants are making something. Out of the musical materials or themes of talk, they make a piece of music or a conversation, an artifact with its own meaning and coherence. Their reflection-in-action is a conversation with the materials of a situation—"conversation," now, in a metaphorical sense. Each person carries out his own evolving role in the collective performance, listens to the surprises—or, as I shall say, "back talk"—that results from earlier moves, and responds through on-line production of new moves that give new meanings and directions to the development of the artifact. (Schon 1987, 31)

The writers in this volume thus take their places in the collective portfolio performance and through that joining contribute to the development of portfolio, knowing that the next generation of writers will take their turn talking back to the descriptions and insights in this volume.

Rather than our learning about portfolios proceeding as a spiral, then, we might instead think of it as developing in waves, with one wave of practice preparing the next wave of theorizing about that practice, with an intermediate wave extending new practice. By such reflective "wave action" is knowledge created. A knowledge that is responsive to and incorporates "felt sense," a knowledge that is grounded in reflective analysis, a knowledge that always returns to practice as a source for knowing.

And in particular, we see different kinds of research, all of which contribute to what we know about portfolios:

First, we see a kind of historical research in the work from Pat Belanoff and Peter Elbow, both an account of what happened with this early version of portfolio and an interpretation of what it signifies and what questions are raised in such a history. It's axiomatic, of course, that without a sense of where we have been, we cannot know where we are heading. Pieces like this one help us do both.

Second, we are beginning to develop qualitative studies of reading portfolios, as we see in the Portnet chapter: how do we construct these texts, how do we value them, what is the role between general expectations and local norms? We see hints of this as well in texts like Katherine Fischer's; focused on practice, it nonetheless raises important issues about how we—students and teachers—are learning to read hypertext portfolios.

Third, we are beginning to understand, through portfolios, both curriculum and students. In Beth Burch's account, we see our own curriculum reflected back to us; its inadequacies can be catalogued and only then addressed. In Kathleen Yancey's account, we see the multiple curricula that always comprise a course, and we see how students' articulations fit, or not, within what it is we have designed. And we are also, through including students' own words, beginning to understand what they have learned. Historically, of course, we have asked students not what they have learned, but *whether they have learned what it is that we expected them to learn.* As Frank Smith makes all too clear, however, students are learning all the time; with portfolios, we are finally beginning to hear from them *what it is they have learned.* This is good news on two fronts: 1) it means we can reward them for learning, and 2) it means we can create a curriculum that is more responsive to the students we actually teach.

Fourth, we have developed enough models now, and they have been used in sufficiently different enough contexts, that we can talk about what the portfolios can and cannot accomplish. Studies like Sandra Murphy's and Susan Callahan's show us that portfolios are no panacea, that they will function within a context in predictable ways, and that we must take such contexts into account before we can talk about their effects. Callahan, Murphy, and Gerilee Nicastro and Cheri Ause also show us the professionalism that portfolios can motivate, and they suggest the variables that assure such a benefit.

Fifth, theory is increasingly being brought into our accounts of practice, into our questions, into our "felt sense" of what happened. We see this in Tom Philion's discussion of flow, in Robert Leigh Davis's application of literary theory, in Brian Huot's and Michael Williamson's theory of writing assessment and its (always) political implications.

We share Lucas's concern about the need for research to validate practice, and we agree with her, as with the editors of *New Directions in Portfolio Assessment*, that the research we are thinking of is more qualitative, more reflective, based in a new methodology that includes multiple voices, that is more interpretive in nature (Moss 1994b). Moreover, unless we continue reporting in—telling our own histories, listening in on our students and interpreting with them what we hear, linking practice with theory, investigating the effects of larger cultural forces on portfolio and the ways those forces situate portfolios as well as students and teachers—our story, sooner or later, will be appropriated by others; it's too attractive to resist.

We're encouraged, therefore, by the accounts we have; we would wish for more, and we would wish for those, like the accounts here, to build on, contradict, even refute what has come before. Certainly, all the news will not be good (e.g., Murphy; Burch, both this volume). But it is in qualifying our claims about portfolios and in testing those claims against practice that we bring understanding to what we do and create knowledge about portfolio. And it is that knowledge that enables us, in successive waves, to revisit our practice, to revise it, and to critique it anew.

Co-option by Large Scale Assessment

Catharine Lucas's final concern is that portfolios will become merely the newest vehicle to perform the old task, with the result that portfolios will become standardized—with "common assignments" and "clearly defined criteria" and restrictive conditions governing the writing of the texts in the portfolio. Should this happen, Lucas says, portfolios "will be just as likely as other standardized tests to limit learning by restricting curriculum to what is most easily and economically measured" (Lucas 1992, 9).

Unfortunately, what Lucas foresaw—that portfolios are a better measure of what students can do—has been seen by more than teachers and parents and students; it has been seen by those who exercise authority for large-scale assessment. The problem isn't that the portfolio isn't a better sampling device; it is. The problem is that once identified as a means of large-scale testing, the very features that made a portfolio a means of learning—the freedom to write multiple kinds of texts, to frame rhetorical situations that speak to different kinds of students, to include the context of the class in the portfolio, to allow in "messy data"—are the very features to be *excluded* from the portfolio test.

So we return to the assessment strand of portfolio assessment, with special reference to the K-12 context. Peter Elbow and Pat Belanoff, among the earliest advocates of portfolio use, offer several important cautions about the current wide interest in portfolios and about their uses for assessment particularly: that portfolios may be viewed as a cure-all for all assessment problems; that portfolio assessment may be driven by mandates rather than in response to specific local needs; and that portfolio systems, once in place, lose their vitality.

These cautions are also echoed and then extended and elaborated by the authors of the seven pieces which complete this section. Robert Leigh Davis argues that portfolio practice is not only consistent with current composition practices, but with literary theory as well, which also insists on the inseparability of language from context. Brian Huot and Michael Williamson, Susan Callahan, and Sandra Murphy take as their focus the portfolios of large-scale assessment programs. Huot and Williamson explain how the need to standardize assessment procedures to achieve reliability, validity, or some common standard can also be seen merely as an exercise in power—the power to impose others' standards on large numbers of teachers and students. They argue that as portfolio systems are developed and implemented, teachers need to maintain as much power as possible over how these systems work if portfolios are to deliver on their potential to create important connections among teaching, learning, and assessing. Susan Callahan's year-long ethnographic study of a high school English department's response to a state-imposed portfolio system shows the effects of a statewide mandated portfolio assessment on the teachers who are charged not as teachers so much as agents of the state. Sandra Murphy delineates the conditions that must obtain if portfolios and large-scale assessment programs are to work together: including teachers as consultants, creating flexible criteria that are congruent with the aims of portfolio, and resisting the standardization characteristic of mass testing.

The last three chapters in this section focus more specifically on how individuals have used portfolios to exercise some control over evaluation procedures. Gerilee Nicastro and Cheri Evans Ause describe their work in developing "demonstration portfolios" that their junior high school students take with them to the high school and that serve as a writer's introduction for their new teachers. Like William Condon, Nicastro and Ause seek to close gaps between institutions; their portfolio is also a bridge. And at the same time their portfolio, like Mary Perry's, is based on the decisions about purpose and assessment which were part of the planning for this project. Charlotte O'Brien describes how portfolio concepts and methodology can be used to invigorate and then considerably alter a district-wide, holistically scored timed writing sample, how the messiness of classroom portfolios *can* be included in assessment activity, how a district can honor learning and still be accountable. Finally, Janice Heiges describes how she negotiated the substitution of a portfolio for the traditional doctoral candidacy examination at George Mason University, chronicling the path from the inception of the idea to translating its criteria into terms more conventionally understood to final recommendation for advancement to candidacy.

These victories, if victories they are, may be but small steps, but they are important ones. From its inception, the portfolio has assumed that its composer could exercise some agency, would have something to say worth hearing and an audience who wished to hear. And from its inception, the school portfolio has assumed a student's teacher who exercised the same kind of agency, based in this case on a knowledge of writing and reading, a knowledge about students and about their development and about how to use formative assessment to help students learn, and a willingness, often an eagerness, to learn more. As Lucas tells us, and Murphy and Callahan repeat, and Heiges and Nicastro and Ause embody, the best form of resistance to efforts to undermine these assumptions of portfolios is the "increasingly aware" teacher.

It is with him and her, too, that we also place our hopes.

* * *

At the 1996 American Association for Higher Education (AAHE) conference on Faculty Roles and Rewards, Lee Shulman gave a plenary, "Course Anatomy: The Dissection and Transformation of Knowledge," whose purpose was to extend and elaborate Ernest Boyer's scholarship of teaching, with particular reference to the course portfolio as a public document. Briefly, Shulman's thesis is that one way of knowing, particularly when it is practice we examine, comes through a two-step reflective process: 1) we *stop* the activity in which we are engaged; and 2) we *explain* it to others, since what we know lies in that explanation, that making public.

We offer this volume in that spirit as well. Each contributor here has stopped the flow of work: teaching. Each contributor has sought to *explain* to others what they do, what it means, how it connects with other work, and why it matters. In the area of assessment, we see contributors who focus particularly on the power relationships that obtain in any rhetorical situation, but which in an assessment context seem particularly difficult, but perhaps not impossible, to change. In the area of the classroom, we see contributors who have moved away from only teaching through the portfolio toward learning with learners from their learners' portfolios. In the teacher portfolio chapters, we see through portfolios opportunities for reflective analysis of both quantitative and qualitative varieties, and through that analysis a means of apprehending and then changing our curricula. In the technology section, we see what happens when two "technologies"—the portfolio and the computer—are brought together: how they complicate but also enrich how students learn, how teachers learn with students, how teachers learn with other teachers.

And across contexts, we see five themes we'd like to stress:

First, we see the kinds of collaborations that portfolios have invited: between students and students, as Mary Ann Smith shows us; among teachers and students, as Katherine Fischer explains; and across contexts, as William Condon explains. To our knowledge, no other vehicle for assessment, nor technique for teaching and learning, has proven so powerful in its ability to showcase learning.

Second, we see how important portfolio models are as well as the relationship between them and the culture they operate in. Those who claim that portfolios can transform education are only partly correct: how much of a transformation portfolios can engender—and in fact whether or not there is any transformation at all—is largely a function of the design of the model and its place, its situation in a given culture.

Third, in all the portfolio models, and particularly in the bridging model, we recognize the opportunity that students may have for bringing disparate parts of their experiences together in the portfolio to compose a whole learning and to explain that to others—because what Lee Shulman says is true for teachers is, of course, also true for students. In portfolios, students, like teachers, *stop* and *explain* to others, and like teachers, these students have both something worth learning and something worth sharing.

Fourth, if students do have something worth sharing, then we should listen. They do exhibit a kind of expertise: they *know* how they write, how they read, how they understand, what is going on in their other classrooms and their other schools and their other lives. It's not too soon to start learning about those other experiences, to begin to take what they can share and use it to make what we do better—in our classrooms, in our curricula, in our schools, in our understanding.

Fifth, the portfolios we learn about within this volume have much to say about how literacy is changing before our eyes—partly as a function of how reflection in the portfolio asks students to describe and narrate and analyze their own learning, and partly as a function of the electronic media. It's a truism that literacy doesn't any longer mean just reading or just writing; what it is in the process of meaning is illustrated in the pages within.

* * *

Together, the twenty-four essays collected in these pages are themselves a kind of portfolio; one prepared for others through interruption, a portfolio whose significance we understand ourselves only as we explain it to others. Like the portfolios written by single authors, these essays demonstrate a range—of voices, of perspectives, and of contexts, unified not by one author-subject, but by a common interest in exploring, extending, and critiquing our use of a rich and complex teaching and evaluation tool.

We hope that the ways portfolios have been situated in these essays will offer teachers at many levels and in a variety of institutional settings stimulus for their own reflection and practice and collaboration.

I

Theory and Power

1

Reflections on an Explosion

Portfolios in the '90s and Beyond

Peter Elbow
Pat Belanoff

KATHLEEN YANCEY INVITED US TO REFLECT ON WHAT WE NOTICE AS WE LOOK at the portfolio explosion that has gained steady strength since we started our experiment in 1983 at Stony Brook.

First, we note that we are not assessment specialists. We have not mastered the technical dimensions of psychometrics. That doesn't mean we don't respect the field; we agree with Ed White that one of the greatest needs is for practitioners and theorists like us to talk to psychometricians. But we don't feel comfortable doing that so long as they continue to worship numbers as the bottom line. We think teaching is more important and more interesting than assessment. (Yes, teaching involves internal, informal assessment, but not external, formal assessment.) The reason we felt impelled to get deeply involved in assessment was that it began to impinge so powerfully upon teaching. The most important lesson we've learned is that people can do useful work in assessment without being on top of technical psychometrics.

The portfolio explosion has brought conferences, journal articles, essay collections, diverse experiments, research reports, and more. Portfolios are currently being used at all educational levels: kindergarten to graduate to returning adult programs. And they are being used in a wide variety of contexts: within individual classrooms, across grade levels, and within citywide and statewide assessment programs. The bulk of this activity has developed within the last eleven years. Perhaps the first thing to say is that we can't "look back" on all of this: it's too much to see—to keep up with.

Nevertheless we are excited and bemused—and proud too.

Why the Portfolio Explosion?

The proliferation itself suggests, first, that what looks on the surface like a miraculous increase is not so miraculous after all. It makes us think of the down-to-earth interpretation of the biblical miracle of the loaves and fishes: a lot of members of the crowd had stuffed their pockets with a lot of bread and fish when they realized they were going to walk out into the desert. When it was time to eat, a lot of pockets were opened. We've discovered that many teachers, especially at the elementary level, had been using portfolios in their own quiet ways for years before we did. When we listen at the ubiquitous portfolio conferences, we hear teachers start off, "Well, in 1965, here's how I did it." We whisper to each other, "We never dreamed of portfolios that long ago!"

In short, our two essays in 1986 (and Chris Burnham's in the same year and Roberta Camp's a year earlier) brought a process and a principle to wider attention that had already existed in scattered ways. Apparently, we provided a wider conceptual scheme for an activity already underway in scattered sites. We managed to frame thinking about portfolios more consciously in terms of assessment—particularly external large-scale assessment. This process makes us think of the history of freewriting. Ken Macrorie made freewriting prominent and Peter managed to publicize it more, but as Macrorie pointed out in his historical essay (Macrorie 1991), it's an idea that had been kicking around in various forms for years and years. (For striking examples, see William Carlos Williams 1964 and S. I. Hayakawa 1962.) We can see the same thing with writing groups. Anne Ruggles Gere showed that what looked like innovation in the classroom twenty years ago was hardly news to many writers. What all of this makes us realize is that startling practical and ideological movements seldom spring from nowhere. Some catalyst draws together, foregrounds, and provides a useful conceptual framework for the growth of already existing or incipient ideas.

But if the idea of portfolios had been kicking around for so many years, what was it about 1986 and the years just following that somehow made it a catalytic situation? In retrospect, what was striking was the urgent and growing pressure for assessment, assessment, assessment; test everything and everyone again and again; give everything and everyone a score; don't trust teachers. (This distrust was perversely reinforced at the college level in English because so many teachers were adjuncts, part-timers, or temporary.) School, district, and state administrators turned more and more to outside testing, psychometricians, and large testing agencies to ascertain and validate student learning in order to evaluate the effectiveness of teachers and programs. People began to believe that without an outside-derived number and a grade it was impossible to trust that any learning had taken place. It was in this era of growing distrust and suspicion that the steamroller movement for standards started gathering momentum. In writing, this was the era of more and more holistic testing and norming.

This greater than usual pressure for testing and bottom line, single-dimensional numbers was the matrix for a greater than usual hunger for an alternative way to assess student writing and learning. Teachers have always given grades—and no doubt will continue to do so. But never before had so many teachers and programs had to give so many single number scores for performances that are as hard to quantify as writing. For teachers who already knew how problematic such assessment was, the pressure for more of it drove them to seek assessment that was more compatible with their classroom practices. We see, in short, a dialectic process: too much pressure for X creates a striking growth of Y.

Thus the events at Stony Brook were a paradigm of the times. The faculty senate had decided several years earlier not to trust the grades given by first year writing teachers (especially graduate-assistant teachers), and therefore mandated a proficiency exam that overrode course grades: no one could satisfy the writing requirement without passing the exam—even if they got an A in the course itself. The exam was a typical, holistically scored affair. Because we so strongly resisted this system—because it made a mockery of strategies we advocated in the classroom—we were driven to find an alternative.

We were surprised and even pleased to discover that our own hunger for a different way to evaluate writing ability was echoed in so many colleagues in the widest variety of institutional settings: "You mean we don't have to do it this way? You mean grades on individual papers and writing exams are not built into the universe like gravity? You mean we're not stuck with holistic scoring?" This fertile soil led to the proliferation of portfolio evaluation. And we were lucky enough to have a forum from which to speak to a growing audience. Peter had managed to get a reputation by this time, and the discipline of composition and rhetoric had begun to establish itself as an important field that other disciplines were beginning to listen to.

A New Emphasis on Collaboration and Negotiation

Portfolios have always been useful and productive for individual teachers, but we added a new emphasis on collaboration and negotiation. What was central to our experiment was to move portfolios outside the individual classroom so that they would be read by someone else in addition to the classroom teacher. We wanted a situation where teachers had to work together and negotiate a judgment. Once we got this kind of collaborative talk going, we came to understand even more fully than before how inadequate traditional proficiency testing can be. Collaboration prompts teachers to have to articulate for others (and thus for themselves) the basis for their judgments. In the course of such articulation, we came to understand how subjective all evaluation is. No one in our program could close a door and just give grades without being influenced by other teachers.

We think we learned something important about the negotiation process. Negotiation and collaboration often break down when participants are working under too many rigid constraints. Stony Brook teachers do not have to use the conventional range of holistic scores from one to four or one to six; they just score portfolios satisfactory or not satisfactory. In addition, teachers are not obliged, in the end, to agree. What they must do is engage in the collaborative and negotiating process and listen to any differences between their judgment and that of their peers. For the vast majority of portfolios, readers do manage to agree. For a few they do not. The point is that collaboration and negotiation (and, most important, the ability actually to change your mind) work best when the situation isn't too rigid or coercive. (For more about the specifics of our Stony Brook system, see Belanoff and Elbow 1991; Elbow and Belanoff 1991.)

Collaboration and negotiation, once initiated, have a way of permeating a whole program. The evaluative process spills back into the classroom and leads to more collaboration and negotiation in teaching. If teachers have to negotiate about the end-of-semester portfolios produced by each other's students, they have a powerful incentive to collaborate and negotiate about what and how they will teach.

The collaborative dimension of portfolio assessment seems to want to spread further. Pat is currently engaged in a nationwide project in which portfolios from a variety of institutions are being read by those who are geographically quite separated (see chapter 24, this volume). Such a project engages her and her colleagues in negotiation at a much broader level. We do not yet know what the outcome of this project will be, but we already see the value of moving collaboration and negotiation to other sites. But, since collaboration and negotiation have become such sunny words in our field these days, it is important not to forget how difficult they are and how often they fail. (For a vivid and helpful account of a problematic collaboration between a university and a school system over portfolio assessment, see Roemer 1991.)

The Effects of Portfolio Assessment on Holistic Scoring and Assessment Theory

We are excited that portfolios haven't turned out to be just another tool in the testing cabinet. Portfolios have kicked back at testing itself—helping people rethink some central assumptions and practices.

This process started when portfolios helped testers face up to a problem they had been ignoring (probably because the problem was so intractable till portfolios came along): any writing exam is inherently untrustworthy if it calls for only one piece of writing. That is, we cannot get a trustworthy picture of writing ability unless we look at various kinds of writing done on various occasions. Otherwise the sample is skewed by the genre, the prompt, the student's mood, health, and so on. Portfolios, by providing different samples written under different conditions, finally went some way towards solving this problem—giving us a better picture of what we are testing for. (This means better validity—though people now argue over different meanings for that technical term.)

But when portfolios brought this improvement, they also brought a new problem. You'd think that better pictures would lead to better rating of those pictures, but these better pictures seem to lead to more disagreement among scorers. (This is a reliability problem.) This disagreement isn't really surprising once you think about it. When scorers only have to score single samples written under exam conditions—all on the same topic and in the same genre—they have a much easier time agreeing with each other than when they score the mixture of pieces in a portfolio. In one portfolio, some pieces are stronger than others, some dimensions of writing are better than others (e.g., ideas, organization, syntax, mechanics), and in fact single dimensions or aspects of the writing may be strong in one piece and weak in another. Even one reader of a portfolio tends to get into fights with herself trying to settle on a single number score she can trust for this mixed bag. The disagreements escalate when we ask several readers with different values to agree.

Of course there is a traditional assessment technology that handles disagreement among scorers: readers are "trained" to agree in training sessions where the leaders use scoring rubrics and "range-finder" sample papers. But it turns out that this training doesn't work so well on portfolio readers. They are more ornery in their disagreements. When portfolio scorers see multiple pieces by one student, they tend to put more trust in their sense of that student, and so tend to fight harder for their judgment. In conventional, single-sample tests, they are more liable to feel, at least unconsciously, "Why fight for my judgment, when I have no evidence that this text is typical of the student's other writing—especially the writing she does in more natural writing situations." (For three recent and vivid studies of actual scoring sessions that illustrate this remarkable difficulty in trying to train portfolio scorers to agree, see Broad 1994; Despain and Hilgers 1992; Hamp-Lyons and Condon 1993. Vermont is being asked to rethink its statewide portfolio assessment procedures because the testers themselves got such low scores on inter-reader reliability.) In short, portfolios seem to kick back when people try to pin single numbers on them.

Thus portfolios have put the assessment process in a pickle. They finally give more trustworthy pictures of ability (making us realize how little we could trust those old conventional single-sample pictures), but in the same stroke they undermine any trust we might want to put in the scoring of these pictures. Of course people have been calling into question holistic scoring, grading, and single-dimension-ranking for a long time. But portfolios have finally made this critique stick better.

Still, sometimes we need a single number on a single dimension—a single "bottom line" verdict or holistic score. That is, in certain situations, we need to decide which students should be denied a place in our course or institution if we have limited resources—or denied credit, or made to repeat a course, or required to take a preparatory course. Sometimes we also want to exempt students from a course or pick students for an award or scholarship. We don't need most of the scores we normally get from holistic scoring, but occasionally we need some, and we can't just beg off and say, "Our readers won't agree because they finally see that ability is not monodimensional."

Portfolios turn out to suggest a way to deal with this problem. What about a full and rich portfolio where readers agree that most of the pieces are unsatisfactory? Are we not more than usually justified in giving this portfolio a score of unsatisfactory or failing or notably weak for this population? Similarly, what if most readers agree that most of the pieces are excellent? Are we not more than usually justified in giving a score of excellent or notably strong, or some such label? In short, portfolios have led to the concept of minimal or limited holistic scoring.

At first glance, this procedure seems odd. For one thing it might seem theoretically scandalous to give holistic scores to portfolios at the margins and no scores at all to the rest. The process is liable to yield an unsettlingly large group of portfolios in a middle, more or less acceptable, default range. In our view, however, the real theoretical scandal comes from continuing to make all those fine-grained distinctions across the middle range: these are scores about which readers tend to disagree, and so they are simply the accident of compromise and of the value judgments unilaterally decreed by test administrators.

We are not trying to pretend that minimal or limited holistic scoring—picking out the best and worst portfolios—is truly or completely trustworthy. There is always an element of subjectivity in any evaluation process—in some cases a large element. We defend the process only because it involves making far fewer dubious judgments and making only those judgments that are most needed. In short, the principle here is the same as for surgery: since every operation carries a risk of genuine harm, we should perform surgery only when there is genuine need and a likely chance of success. Most holistic writing scores are neither necessary nor trustworthy.

Now just as it's cheaper to avoid surgery, it is cheaper to avoid all those unnecessary and untrustworthy holistic scores. Thus minimal holistic scoring recoups much of the extra cost of going from single sample assessment to portfolio assessment. With minimal scoring, most portfolios can be read in just a couple of minutes: they soon establish themselves as too good for unsatisfactory and too flawed for excellent. Scoring is faster and cheaper still if we don't need to identify top-rated portfolios. So if portfolios are used as an exit test—or if they are used for a placement procedure where students are not exempted—only poor portfolios need to be identified.

Most large-scale writing assessments are designed to sort students, not give feedback. But what if we do want to give students some feedback? What if we want to use assessment to increase learning? Portfolios come to the rescue again and show us how to give more sophisticated and useful feedback on an exam. Since portfolios are mixed bags, they invite us, by their nature, to notice differences: strengths and weaknesses within a portfolio—whether between different papers or between different writing skills or dimensions.

Once we get interested in differences rather than just single numbers, we realize that it's not so hard to communicate these differences in scoring so that the student at last gets a bit of substantive feedback from the assessment process. For this feedback we don't need traditional analytic scoring—that elaborate process in which various writing dimensions or features are scored on a scale of four or six and these subscores are added up into a holistic score. No, it's much more feasible and trustworthy to use something simple and minimal: readers score a writing trait or dimension or paper only if they feel it is notably strong or weak. Thus there are only two scores, strong and weak, along with a third default middle range. The traits might be traditional ones, such as ideas, details, organization, clarity of syntax, voice, mechanics; or rhetorical features like finding a subject, or making contact with readers; scorers might even note individual papers in a portfolio as particularly strong or weak. (See Broad 1994, Figure 20-2 for a long list of features that readers can quickly check off as notably strong or weak while they read a portfolio—features that Broad derived from actual scoring sessions.)

Obviously, we are no longer saving time and money if we decide to give this kind of feedback to portfolios. But there is a compromise that we used at Stony Brook: we gave this kind of analytic feedback only to failing portfolios. This didn't take much time—since readers already had to read failing portfolios more carefully. And of course the failing students need this feedback most.

All of this, then, is a story of how portfolios have highlighted problems with assessment that have been lurking there all along. In particular, portfolio assessment has finally brought wider attention to the problems of holistic scoring that a number of us have been calling attention to for a long time.[1] Portfolios kick back not only at conventional holistic scoring but even at grading in general. That is, once portfolios force us to reflect on what should be obvious—namely that no complex performance can be accurately summed up in a single number because it almost always has stronger and weaker aspects or dimensions—we can see all the more clearly that conventional grades, whether on papers or for a whole course, also don't make sense. Trying to give a course grade is very much like trying to give a portfolio grade. In both cases one is trying to pin a single number on a mixed bag of performances. And so the obvious solution suggests itself: minimal or limited grading—using terms such as outstanding, satisfactory, and unsatisfactory—and adding differential notations that describe where the student did particularly well or badly. The debate about grading has tended to be binary and oversimple as though we had to choose between conventional grading and no grading (such as at Evergreen or Hampshire College). The example of portfolios shows us how feasible it is to use some kind of minimal holistic grading—along with some markers of strengths and weaknesses.

To summarize this section: portfolios have helped more people involved in assessment to acknowledge how untrustworthy it is to rank multidimensional performances along a monodimensional scale. When testing is only for placement or for identifying students who have reached a satisfactory, mere minimal holistic scoring will do. This saves money and means fewer dubious judgments. But because portfolios are mixed bags and thus invite evaluators to notice differences (things done well and not so well), they have come to suggest the possibility of scoring strengths and weaknesses.

Effects of Portfolio Assessment on Teaching

We got involved in portfolio experimentation in 1983 because of the threat to teaching posed by proficiency exams, but we had no idea of the teaching potential of the portfolio process itself. It's true that Peter, because of his three-year stint in a competence-based research project, did have a sense of some of the theoretical implications in assessment—particularly evidenced in the move from norm-referenced to criterion-referenced models of testing (see Elbow and Belanoff 1991; McClelland 1973). And Pat, during her years at NYU, had been involved in a portfolio project created by Lil Brannon as an alternative way of satisfying the writing requirement for those who failed NYU's proficiency exam. She had an opportunity to experience the difference between "scoring" a proficiency exam and evaluating a portfolio. But neither of us had any sense of how widely adaptable this portfolio creature was. And most of all we had no idea of how deeply it would reflect back on the teaching process.

Portfolios wormed themselves into everything we did. They seem to do that in many settings. They have a fruitful and supportive effect on the individual classroom, both on teachers and students. We continue to see how portfolios help teachers negotiate the conflict between the role of supportive, welcoming helper and the role of critical, skeptical evaluator. On the one hand, portfolios help separate the two roles. That is, portfolios help teachers stay longer and more productively in the supportive role, but then in turn, help them move more cleanly but less frequently into the critical role. Indeed, in a system where teachers collaborate with each other for portfolio assessment, the teaching and testing roles are separated even more since the teacher brings in an actual outside evaluator who occupies only the role of critic.

But on the other hand, portfolios help teachers unite or integrate these conflicting roles of teacher and evaluator. That is, portfolios permit us to avoid putting grades on individual papers, and thereby help us make the evaluations we do during the semester formative, not summative. (Of course, grades on papers in a conventional course are supposed to be formative rather than summative, but because they are single number grades that go down in the grade book, both teacher and student tend to experience them as summative. This undermines the learning process.) And when teachers evaluate portfolios together at the end of the semester for summative verdicts, the fruits of their discussions tend to become internalized and help shape ongoing classroom strategies, conversation, and feedback. When all goes well, this consciousness also then seeps into students' conversations about theirs and their peers' writing. After all, self-evaluation is the strongest force for successful revision.

The important issue here for all of us in education is the way practice and theory interact and enrich one another. Our desire to replace Stony Brook's proficiency exam grew out of our acceptance of certain theories inadequately summed up as the "process movement" in composition and rhetoric. This movement led us to change our own teaching; the resulting changes in our classrooms led us to challenge a proficiency exam that contradicted how we taught the course—a course that was supposed to prepare students for the exam. By asking ourselves why portfolios seem to help our practice, we feel we can enrich our own (and we hope others') theoretical awareness of developments within the field. We will just mention here in a summary way the larger theoretical points that strike us as most important:

- Grades undermine improvement in writing because they restrict and pervert students' naturally developing sense of audience awareness.
- Writing is its own heuristic; it doesn't have to be graded to lead to learning.
- Portfolios lead to a decentralization of responsibility which empowers everyone involved.
- Teacher authority needs to be shared if writers are to have genuine authority.
- All evaluation exists within a context of literacy defined by a multitude of factors, not all of which are products of the classroom.
- Knowledge, whether of grades or of teaching strategies or of theoretical underpinnings, is a product of discussion among community members.
- Evaluation, judging, liking,and scoring are inextricably bound up together and need to be thoughtfully examined.

What's important is not so much whether we are right in these thumbnail theoretical points (and our list is not meant to be exhaustive), but the process through which practice and theory come together. Our practice led to theoretical reflections and conclusions which in turn enriched practices at many levels and sites. These enriched practices have led and will continue to lead to greater exploration of theories to explain the success (and failure) of whatever the new practices are. All of this supports our conviction that theory and practice when separated become stunted. All of us need to be both practitioners and theorists or philosophers of practice.

Potential Problems with Portfolio Use

We worry that portfolios have become a fad. Some people have jumped on this bandwagon in order to convince the public or their administrators that they're on the cutting edge. Others have trivialized or short-circuited the whole process of designing and implementing a portfolio system and thus robbed it of its peculiar ability to create a sense of ownership among those who do this planning. One way of doing this is to mandate from above procedures designed by administrators. The usual result of such short-circuiting is that those "ordered" to use portfolios just go through the motions and miss the enriching, empowering potentialities. (Again, there is an instructive comparison with freewriting: "Yes, I love to use freewriting in my teaching. My students get good grades on their freewriting, and I enjoy reading it.")

Portfolio assessment is sometimes felt as a cure-all. Indeed, because portfolio assessment is better than conventional assessment, teachers and administrators sometimes slide into treating it as desirable in itself, absolutely—thereby fueling the impulse for more assessment. So, ironically, whereas we think of portfolios as a way to hold back the assessment steamroller a bit, some people advocate and use portfolios in such a way as to accelerate that steamroller. Portfolios can actually be used in such a way as to make students feel as though every scrap of writing they ever do in a course might be evaluated—can make them feel the search-light of official evaluation shining into every nook and cranny of writing they do for any purpose.

Another uncomfortable realization: once a portfolio system is in place, it's sometimes difficult to change. If the participants have expended a lot of ingenuity, effort, and even risk, they have a big investment and may well be reluctant to change "their baby." Also, portfolio users do not always acknowledge the inherent problems of any portfolio system. None of us should dismiss as non-serious the issues of cost effectiveness, time spent reading, the potential for abuse, and the need for constant attention to developing problems. We do not win skeptics to our side by treating these issues as easily resolved.

But one of the inherent potentialities of portfolio assessment is to invite change. For the portfolio brings more of the writing process and the teaching process—with all their idiosyncrasy and variability—right into the center of the assessment process. Teaching needs to be the dog that wags the tail of assessment rather than vice versa.

Despite the inherent potentiality for change, portfolio assessment can be administered and experienced as rigid, especially for those who come into a portfolio system after its initial creation. Currently at Stony Brook, we need to constantly prod graduate students to criticize the system and suggest new and better strategies; they look upon it as carved in stone because it was in place when they arrived. We know many resist or misunderstand the system. As one graduate student put it: "Portfolios are just the department's way of getting into our classrooms and dictating what we do." We're certain that this phenomenon is not limited to Stony Brook. We all need to seek ways for keeping portfolios vital, and up to now, a large part of their vitality is a product of the fact that those who use them are the same as those who designed them. We need to keep stressing that those who continue to use them have the power to redesign them.

For portfolios are simply the best system we currently have to assess writing while still trying not to disrupt or undermine the teaching and learning process. Surely something better will come along—perhaps an outgrowth of portfolio use. We all need to keep an open mind and welcome new developments. We cannot be chauvinistic about our baby. The many uses of portfolios described in this book are evidence of the power of portfolios to modify both thinking and practice.

Notes

1. In addition to the fact that holistic scoring is not trustworthy, it has these other problems. It gives nonsubstantive feedback: it's only a reading on a yea/boo applause meter. Worst of all, holistic scoring fuels the biggest enemy of thoughtful evaluation: judgment based on global or holistic feelings ("I like it"/"I don't like it"), rather than judgment that tries to describe and to discriminate between strengths and weaknesses. And it also feeds the pervasive hunger in our culture to rank complex performances with simple numbers—the pervasive assumption that evaluation isn't trustworthy, hardheaded, or honest unless it consists of single numbers along a single

dimension or a bell curve. Portfolios are helping more and more people realize that, as professionals, we need to convince people that evaluation isn't trustworthy unless it avoids the distortion of single numbers. Because portfolios get us to think in a more sophisticated way about the assessment of writing, more people are finally acknowledging that even a single short essay is a complex performance, and that giving it a single number is usually a distortion. (See Appendix A of Elbow, "Writing Assessment," for a long list of works criticizing holistic scoring.)

2

The Lunar Light of Student Writing

Portfolios and Literary Theory

Robert Leigh Davis

IN THE UPPER BEDROOM OF HIS HOUSE ON MICKLE STREET IN CAMDEN, NEW Jersey, Walt Whitman wrote a literary retrospective in 1888 entitled "A Backward Glance O'er Travel'd Roads." Looking back at his life as a writer, Whitman proposes this theory of literary interpretation:

> Also it must be carefully remember'd that first class literature does not shine by any luminosity of its own; nor do its poems. They grow of circumstances, and are evolutionary. The actual living light is always curiously from elsewhere—follows unaccountable sources, and is lunar and relative at the best. . . .
>
> Just as all the old imaginative works rest, after their kind, on long trains of presuppositions, often entirely unmention'd by themselves, yet supplying the most important bases of them, and without which they could have had no reason for being, so "Leaves of Grass," . . . is the result of such presupposition. I should say, indeed, it were useless to attempt reading the book without first carefully tallying that preparatory background and quality in the mind. (Whitman 1982, 660)

It's a strange metaphor: the text as a reflective surface, a lunar landscape bending back a light that comes "curiously from elsewhere." Rejecting a myth of creative autonomy, the myth of the artist laboring alone in that upper bedroom, Whitman views his work as a reflection or reconstruction of historical contexts: Emersonian self-reliance, radical democracy, literary sentimentality, and, perhaps most important of all, the lingering terror of the American Civil War. "The unnamed lost," he once remarked, "are ever present in my mind." These are the "preparatory background[s]" of the poet's writing—the lunar light playing over the surface of his page.[1]

Rejecting the Autonomous Text

Much current teaching and research in literary studies is based on this idea: texts cannot be read in isolation. Writing, however formal, cannot be understood apart from the local, shaping environments in which it's produced. "Indeed, I believe that the most important effect of contemporary theory upon the practice of literary criticism," Stephen Greenblatt writes, "and certainly upon *my* practice, is to subvert the tendency to think of aesthetic representation as ultimately autonomous, separable from its cultural context and hence divorced from the social, ideological, and material matrix in which all art is produced and consumed" (Greenblatt 1988, 102).

This, arguably, is the most important single change in liberal studies in the past thirty years. Rejecting the notion of an autonomous text—language as a freestanding artifact, a verbal icon—philosophers, social scientists, historians, and literary critics insist on reading and writing in context.[2] Understanding the circumstances out of which writing emerges becomes as important as knowing what's on the page itself. Naming this commitment "reconstructive criticism," David Reynolds identifies it with the emergence of a new "era": "In a more general sense, I trust that we are leaving the period of hermetic close readings, based on the myth of textual autonomy, and are entering the era of reconstructive close readings, based on the reality of socioliterary dialogism" (Reynolds 1988, 564).

However it's named, contextual thinking has radically changed the profession of English, altering the way we read, teach, and write about literary texts. But the implications of this change for composition are less clear. According to Janet Emig, the assessment of writing remains entrenched in what she calls "a positivistic point of view"; that is, a point of view that denies the role of context in human meaning and behavior. Emig cites as evidence of this view writing assignments that do not emerge from a student's prior learning as well as writing assessments that presume to judge writing ability from a single sample. "To summarize," she writes, "the whole notion and enactment of a monolithic writing sample operates out of a set of positivistic assumptions" (Emig 1983, 164)—a set of assumptions deeply discredited in literary theory but just as deeply institutionalized in single-sample assessments.

Contextual Assessments

Are there alternatives? Are there assessments that support the movement in liberal studies toward contextual rather than positivistic theories of reading? If context is a crucial component for understanding language, isn't it also a crucial component for assessing it? Proponents of portfolio assessment insist that it is, and this premise provides a way of integrating literary theory and composition practice. It provides a foundational claim about language itself, and it applies to student texts the key principle in the interpretation of all texts: language is inseparable from human situations.[3] Portfolios thicken and specify those situations. They allow student writers to acknowledge the cultural and intellectual settings of their work and to make those settings an integral part of interpretation itself. Knowing as much as we can about student writers—their backgrounds, their interests, their reflections on their own writing, the range and expectations of their courses—does not compromise assessment. It does not contaminate interpretation with what we once called "extrinsic evidence." It makes interpretation possible.

Portfolios thus support changes in reading theory taking place since the New Criticism. Wimsatt and Beardsley put it this way in a famous passage from "The Intentional Fallacy":

> There is a gross body of life, of sensory and mental experience, which lies behind and in some sense causes every poem, but can never be and need not be known in the verbal and hence intellectual composition which is the poem. For all the objects of our manifold experience, for every unity, there is an action of the mind which cuts off roots, melts away context—or indeed we should never have objects or ideas or anything to talk about. (Wimsatt and Beardsley 1954, 12)

Writing teachers have long resisted any action of mind which "cuts off roots, melts away context" and reconceives language as mere product. The importance of context is a central theme in composition theory, and it provides a key premise for many writing handbooks and anthologies.[4] "In this book, I have persistently asked students to think about the origins and effects of reading and writing, both their own and others'," Susan Miller writes in the introduction to her anthology, *The Written World*:

> [Students] are invited to appreciate how diverse and complex the reasons for writing can be.
>
> Consequently, *The Written World* works against a flatly textual approach that removes the selections from their own contexts and purposes. It doesn't suggest

> that students simply receive a text as an example of "good writing." Instead, it encourages them to see the cultural and individual energies that produced a text and to realize how these are at work in its words. (Miller 1989, xvii)

The flatly textual approach of much writing assessment, however, flatly contradicts this commitment. Impromptu and quantitative assessments present readers with an anonymous piece of language—a note in a bottle—detached from specific uses and situations. Such exams undercut firmly held convictions about how to read and comprehend writing. The emphasis on a de-contextualized product does not correspond with the pedagogical and interpretive models most teachers actually hold: models that encourage students, as Miller says, "to see the cultural and individual energies that produced a text and to realize how these are at work in its words" (Miller 1989, xvii). Neutralizing that energy with decontextualized assessments places writing instructors in the compromised position of welcoming the end of "hermetic close readings" (Reynolds, 564) in their teaching, only to witness the return of such readings in their assessments. They demonstrate to students that when interpretation matters most, as it does in a proficiency exam, when our readings have something serious and significant at stake, we are still New Critics. And our earnest talk about context and circumstance and "long trains of presupposition" (Whitman 1982, 660) fades into so much white noise.

"Tallying That Preparatory Background"

A portfolio approach resolves this contradiction by providing a bridge between literary theory and composition practice. It directs attention to that "gross body of life" standing apart from and illuminating the text with its own reflected light. We cannot read without that light. We can neither comprehend nor assess writing without a sense of context. "I should say, indeed, it were useless to attempt reading the book," Whitman claims, (and one could add—the essay, the journal, the lab report, the letter), "without first tallying that preparatory background. . . ." Portfolio assessment allows writing instructors to do just that: to read student writing according to the same interpretive lights they use to read and judge all writing—brilliant as well as opaque, accomplished as well as marginal, student as well as professional.

It's worth pausing for a moment to note how a commitment to the contexts of writing draws together literary theorists who would otherwise have little in common. The culture wars of higher education threaten to engulf the entire landscape of literary studies. But there is at least one neutral ground in these culture wars, at least one Geneva Convention where nearly everyone is willing to gather for a while and lay aside their differences. That neutral ground is historical context. Robert Scholes, for example, claims that "the supposed skill of reading is actually based upon a [prior] knowledge of the codes that were operative in the composition of any given text and the historical situation in which it was composed." Ross Chambers writes that "meaning is not inherent in discourse and its structures, but contextual, a function of the pragmatic situation in which the discourse occurs." Jonathan Culler believes that "the problem of interpreting the poem is essentially that of deciding what attitude the poem takes to a prior discourse which it designates as presupposed." E. D. Hirsch argues that "every writer is aware that the subtlety and complexity of what can be conveyed in writing depends on the amount of relevant tacit knowledge that can be assumed in readers" (Graff 1987, 256). Summing up this consensus in literary theory, Graff claims,

> If there is any point of agreement among deconstructionists, structuralists, reader-response critics, pragmatists, phenomenologists, speech-act theorists, and theoretically minded humanists, it is on the principle that texts are not, after all, autonomous and self-contained, that the meaning of any text in itself depends for its comprehension on other texts and textualized frames of reference. (Graff 1987, 256)

Well, that's fine for literature, but what about composition? How do we "historicize" student writing? How do we create "textualized frames of reference" in composition classes and assessments? How, in short, do we perform reconstructive close readings when the text for that reading isn't *Leaves of Grass* but "Why Baseball Should Be Played on Grass," or "How I Learned to Mow the Grass," or—heaven help us—"When I First Smoked Grass"?

We can begin by asking student writers to do with their work what Whitman does with his: write an interpretive introduction. We can create opportunities for student writers to look back over a body of work—an anthology or portfolio—and reflect on the circumstances out of which the anthology emerged, as well as the presuppositions shaping its selection. We can invite student writers, in other words, to take their own "Backward Glance O'er Travel'd Roads." And we can build that backward glance into composition assessment by making such essays an integral part of a writing portfolio, as it is in many writing programs.

But to do this we must base assessment on more than a single sample. The 500-word essay on "Our Responsibility To Others" written in a school gymnasium on a Wednesday afternoon tells us too little about a student's real ability with language. That ability emerges when writing involves sustained intellectual dialogue of some kind. By silencing the voices surrounding the writing task—the voices in the student's reading, the voices of his teachers, the voices of his family, or his enemies, or his friends—by silencing such voices in a decontextualized assessment, we produce writing that is predictably and discouragingly thin. The student writing the responsibility essay is still listening to and incorporating other voices as he writes, but what he hears in that gymnasium is not the voice of his grandmother talking with him on a back porch, nor the voice of Socrates in the Symposium, nor that of Frederick Douglass at the Nantucket Anti-Slavery Convention. What he's likely to hear as he writes his essay is the drone of the schoolmaster: "Never begin a sentence with 'but.' Never end a sentence with a preposition. Never mistake 'which' for 'that.' Never mistake 'lay' for 'lie.' "[5] When we lift student writing out of its intellectual and classroom contexts, we flatten the possibilities of response: not only our own response to student writing but our students' responses to the voices and texts surrounding the writing task. When we lift student writing out of context, we efface what Don H. Bialostosky calls the "virtual space" between texts: the multiple, opposing voices students answer, diminish, refute, co-opt, lionize, or pointedly insult in their prose (quoted in Graff 1987, 257). By having students submit work on a variety of topics they care about—topics they have studied, talked about, read about, and understand—we begin to tally what Whitman calls the "preparatory background" of writing. We begin to recover the cultural conversations out of which student writing emerges. Only then can we judge the skill with which our students join the debate.

Negotiating the Paradigm

To do this, however, we must also change the working paradigm of writing assessment in ways that better reflect the paradigm shift in literary theory. Abandoning a discourse of fixed or universal standards, historically-minded critics like David Reynolds and Stephen Greenblatt adopt a paradigm of *negotiation* to describe the interrelation of writing and context. What's at stake in this change is the myth of the self-contained text. Attacking that myth, Greenblatt presents a view of writing as a cultural transaction, a dynamic set of intellectual and stylistic negotiations. "[T]here is no originary moment," Greenblatt argues, "no pure act of untrammeled creation":

> In place of a blazing genesis, one begins to glimpse something that seems at first far less spectacular: a subtle, elusive set of exchanges, a network of trades and trade-offs, a jostling of competing representations, a negotiation between joint-stock companies. Gradually, these complex, ceaseless borrowings and lendings have come to seem to me more important, more poignant even, than the epiphany for which I had hoped. (Greenblattt 1988, 7)

In Greenblatt's view, the crucial question is not how well or how poorly writers transcend their contexts but how well or how poorly they reflect and transform them, how well or how poorly they negotiate specific cultural demands. The task of interpretation, then, the task of a reconstructive—rather than hermetic—close reading is to recover those demands with rigor and detail.

What goes for literature, in this case, also goes for composition. If a culture's most privileged writing cannot rise above historical contexts, what can? If "first-class literature does not shine by any luminosity of its own," what does? Student and professional writers alike respond to the intricate, shaping pressures of milieu. If anything, student writing is even more responsive to context, even more intimately dependent on setting, than professional or published writing. Thus the success or failure of student texts, precisely like the success or failure of literary texts, depends again on negotiation, that is, on what writers do with what they're given, on how writers assimilate and refashion cultural material close at hand.[6]

Recovering That "Elsewhere"

This premise opens a different and more elusive set of assessment questions: What advice about writing is a student seeking to assimilate or reject? What instructional demands is she trying to fulfill or evade? What cultural or racial or gendered resistance to academic discourse is she trying to mediate, resolve, or even comprehend? Such questions evoke typical negotiations in student writing, some of the "trades and trade-offs" by which writing is produced and understood. Emphasizing the contexts of writing leads us to consider not how a writer measures up to fixed standards of achievement but how she negotiates the local, varied demands of her milieu: how her choice of genre fits her sense of audience, how her strategies of revision match her sense of purpose, how her ideas engage and transform her reading.

Writing portfolios open assessment to include these issues, contextual issues outlawed by formalist literary theory but embraced by virtually every other discipline studying human meaning and behavior. "Context stripping is a key feature of our standard methods of experimental design, measurement, and statistical analysis," Elliot Mishler claimed in 1979. "To test the generality of our hypotheses, we remove the subjects from their natural social settings; their normal roles and social networks are left behind, much as we leave our shoes outside on entering a shrine" (Mishler 1979, 2). It is increasingly difficult to justify this procedure, this reverence. According to Mishler, context-stripping is rapidly giving way to modes of inquiry devoted to the contextual grounding of language, methods that include "thick description" in cultural anthropology, "situated meaning" in learning theory, "indexicality" in sociology, and "reconstructive criticism" in literary studies. Portfolio assessment strengthens this emerging consensus. It builds a bridge between reading theory and assessment practice by affirming, in both cases, the intertextual basis of meaning. Portfolio assessment acknowledges the dialogic quality of student writing—indeed all writing—and it builds assessment on the reality of that dialogue rather than the myth of the text's transcendence, the myth of the verbal icon, the myth of a writer detached from his work like an aloof God, cut off from his creation, coolly paring his fingernails.

The lunar light of student writing may indeed seem alien to us. It does at times seem to come from outer space. But the light of such writing is not pure fancy, pure moonshine. It is instead a light whose energy and inspiration comes, as Whitman says, "curiously from elsewhere." Recovering that "elsewhere"—the haunting, often beautiful otherness of writers who do not share our intellectual worlds—allows us to comprehend student writing, as well as to judge and assess it, with integrity and care.

Notes

1. One of the best studies of the contexts of Whitman's writing is M. Wynn Thomas's *The Lunar Light of Whitman's Poetry*.
2. Elliot G. Mishler provides a useful summary of contextual theories of meaning in the social sciences.

3. Patrick Scott makes this point in "Step by Step: The Development in British Schools of Assessment by Portfolio" page 84. My essay owes much to Scott's analysis of writing assessment.
4. See, for example, Edward White's discussion of how theories of reading affect responses to writing (E. White 1985, 84-99). Providing a cogent critique of what he calls the "formalistic misreading of student writing," White argues that the "author's intentions, the reader's individual associations with words, the reading situation, and all kinds of other matters outlawed by formal criticism can now be considered as part of the total meaning a reader creates from the text" (E. White 1985, 92-93).
5. See Scott's discussion of English language examinations in British schools (Scott 1991, 81).
6. Describing the interpretative practices linking teacher reading and student writing, Louise Wetherbee Phelps articulates "a new attitude toward text" emerging in composition studies (Phelps 1989, 54). "I am not prepared to characterize this new attitude with any authority," Phelps concedes, "and I am even more unsure of its correlates." But it does suggest "that the teacher must 'read' a text—however it appears bounded, temporally or spatially—as embedded in and interpenetrating many other discourses. That is, she or he must read a *situation* as fully as possible, attending to the issues of authorship, the permeability of the student's writing to its context, the embedded mixture of languages that the student is struggling to control" (Phelps 1989, 55). Phelps in fact articulates this new attitude with considerable authority and her emphasis on "negotiation"—what she calls "the negotiations of *situational* meanings" (Phelps 1989, 58)—parallels that of literary theorists like Greenblatt and Reynolds.

3

Rethinking Portfolios for Evaluating Writing

Issues of Assessment and Power

Brian Huot
Michael M. Williamson

Introduction

ISSUES IN WRITING ASSESSMENT HAVE TRADITIONALLY REVOLVED AROUND our ability to construct procedures that represent the ways students write and at the same adhere to the guidelines set down by theories of educational measurement. Moss asserts that this tension between theoretical constraints of literacy education and assessment has been productive in promoting the many new and improved methods for assessing student writing (see Camp 1993a for a discussion of the relationship between the teaching and testing communities in creating writing assessment procedures). Moss also warns, however, that "Proposed solutions often reflect compromises between competing criteria rather than the fundamental rethinking that might push both fields forward" (Moss 1994b, 110). We concur with Moss's admonition about relying solely upon compromises between teaching and testing. While these compromises have been a necessary part of the development of writing assessment, they are also responsible for much of the dissatisfaction educators feel about the continuing importance of interrater reliability and test-type conditions which constrain our ability to develop assessment practices sensitive to the ways people read and write.

To meet Moss's challenge to "rethink" solutions that are more than compromises, we focus in this chapter on portfolios because they are, perhaps, the most popular form of writing assessment ever.[1] As well, portfolios and other forms of performance assessment provide the most rigorous challenges to traditional notions of educational assessment (Moss 1992). Our "rethinking" demands broadening the discussion beyond a consideration of just assessment and pedagogy to include important but often forgotten issues of power. Moss's tension between competing criteria is framed in theoretical terms. We contend that oftentimes issues of power rather than theory drive important assessment decisions. While Moss cites tension between the two disciplines of literacy education and educational measurement, we believe that power is a third, important determinant in crucial decisions about how students will be tested and what impact this testing will have on student learning. To control testing is to control education, to control what will be valued and taught within the schools. Crucial decisions concerning assessment are often made by regulatory agencies and political and educational policymakers based on practical and political concerns of cost, efficiency, and public opinion.

This chapter discusses the relationship between assessment procedures and the underlying power structures which dictate and profit from their use. Examining the various theoretical and political pressures which influence what measurements are chosen and how they are implemented allows us to conceive of assessment procedures as instruments of power and control, revealing so-called theoretical concerns as practical and political. We challenge the notion that concepts like validity and reliability are unquestionable and theoretically necessary. In other words, the need to standardize assessment procedures to achieve reliability, validity, or some common standard can also be seen as a move to impose particular standards on large numbers of teachers and students. Our reconception of the tension Moss describes focuses on who will control assessment and curriculum.

We fear that unless we make explicit the importance of power relationships in assessment, portfolios will fail to live up to their promise to create important connections between teaching, learning, and assessing.

Issues of Assessment

Newer approaches to writing assessment, such as writing portfolios, continue to be subjected to the routine scrutiny of the various theoretical approaches and political pressures all procedures undergo in the fight for control over writing assessment in American schools and colleges (Messick 1989; Moss 1992). No matter what form assessment takes, tradition and accountability dictate a need for standardization. "Standardization refers to the extent to which tasks, working conditions, and scoring criteria are the same for all students" (Moss 1994b, 110). Primarily, standardization is used to compare different educational programs or institutions in terms of their relative effectiveness in student achievement (Moss 1994a).

In writing assessment the need for standardization has been central to its development. The scoring of essays was so unreliable (inconsistent) that writing ability was commonly tested indirectly through the use of multiple choice tests of usage and mechanics.[2] Although the debate between the implementation of direct and indirect measures of assessing writing was often cast in terms of the tension between the teaching and testing communities (White 1993), in fact this debate was always within the field of measurement since it involved the achievement of the psychometric concept of reliability. In direct writing assessment, consistency in scoring is achieved through a set of procedures developed explicitly to ensure agreement of independent raters on the same papers. These procedures which ensure rater consistency in scoring include having students write to common topics in a controlled environment. Readers are trained to agree with one another on scoring guidelines they may or may not have any control over. An acceptable rate of reliability in scoring is crucial because traditionally testing theory dictates it.

Moss (Moss 1994a) challenges the traditional notion that assessment has to be reliable in order to be valid. For Moss, the very concept of reliability as a consistent interchangeable series of judgments on discrete skills or test items privileges standardization, thus limiting the power of local, contextual, performative, and holistic forms of measurement and the curriculum they inform and justify. Moss advocates local, contextual reading of portfolios or other assessment instruments. She offers the example of the procedures commonly used to decide upon the best candidate in a job search, where a committee of colleagues convene and discuss their understanding of each candidate's qualifications based on a full dossier of material. Moss suggests that this discursive, communal, interpretive search for value and meaning makes more sense for performance measures like portfolios. She acknowledges the inability of the psychometric theory of traditional testing to support such procedures but advocates instead the theoretical umbrella of hermeneutics in which the shared search for knowledge and judgment are often considered appropriate. Moss calls for a shift from one conceptual framework to another in order to create practices that are more firmly based on theoretical grounds which support the activity of reading and responding to literate activities. Delandshere and Petrosky invoke a similar switch from psychometrics to poststructuralism in the creation of assessment procedures for teacher performance and certification. Both Moss (Moss 1994a) and Delandshere and Petrosky contend that psychometric theory stipulates a limiting and inaccurate framework for interpretative and judgmental decision-making about complex human behavior.

In current psychometric theories of testing, individual achievement is decontextual and standardized, so that testers can draw generalized inferences about individual performances and compare particular students and groups based upon performance on a particular test. These types of comparisons delete the context of individual learning environments and student populations and assume that the ability to write is a universal, identifiable human trait that can be measured accurately and consistently. The emphasis is on the technical rigor of testing procedures and statistical operations and explanations rather than the complexity of student performance and judgments about that performance. The goal of large group and/or standardized assessment procedures is typically to assess substantial numbers of students and to provide a single numerical index that can be used to compare different groups of students within and among particular settings, assuming that the assigned numbers depict an adequate picture of student achievement and teacher effectiveness across various social, cultural, historical, and geographical contexts.

The losers in the high stakes assessment[3] game made possible by psychometrics are the students and teacher. (See Moss 1994b, "Validity in High Stakes" for a review of the literature on the deleterious effects of large-scale, high stakes testing on students' ability to learn.) Moss notes that large group, standardized assessment procedures present an inherent validity problem (Moss 1994a). Current theories of validity privilege the concept of construct validity in which a test must contain an adequate representation of the ability to be tested and the influence of this test on the teaching and learning of those who take it (Cronbach 1989; Messick 1989). Large-scale, high stakes testing requires standardization and tends to reduce the curriculum to what can be measured. At best, test scores obtained under these conditions are a very poor indicator of the range of learning fostered by a school curriculum. The value of these scores is often affected by the number of students tested and the diversity inherent in such large populations of students. Furthermore, when tests are used for comparisons among students, the procedures have to be standardized. Moss's critique of standardized assessment procedures is that they sacrifice validity for the objectivity of reliability, often resulting in a trivialization of the goals of assessment itself (Moss 1994a). Wiggins contends that this focus on standardization is really a confounding of standards with standardization:

> Standards are never the result of imposed standardization . . . Standards, like good assessment, are contextual. The standards at Harvard have little to do with standards at St. John's College or Julliard; the standards at all our best independent schools and colleges are determined by each faculty, not by policy-maker mandate. (Wiggins 1993a, 282)

Although we recognize the inevitability of assessment driving delivery of curricular goals, we do not see assessment as an inherent evil. If assessment procedures are developed from specific curricular goals, then the assessment will tend to influence teachers and students toward mastering those goals. If, however, the assessment is based upon only those goals that are easily measured, then curriculum will be limited to its assessment procedures (Berlak 1992; Moss 1994b). The crucial element in all these "ifs" and in the ability of assessment to be a positive influence on teaching and learning revolves around the degree of power local stakeholders like principals, teachers, parents, and students have over the many aspects of an evaluation program. Many assessment programs, including those associated with reform movements which advocate site-based decision-making (see Callahan, this volume, for a good review of portfolios and educational reform), mandate certain assessment procedures or euphemistically titled "conceptual frameworks" school districts, principals, and teachers are obliged to implement (Murphy, this volume).

The particular form of assessment creates much of what is considered relevant, valuable, and worthwhile by teachers, students, and parents; assessment is never separate from curriculum. Whether curriculum can drive assessment or whether assessment always drives curriculum is a matter for debate (also an issue upon which we, the authors of this chapter, do not agree). Murphy's recent review of various portfolio programs illustrates that there can be an interactive relationship between assessment and curriculum in which they exist as a dialectic, limiting, affecting, and informing each other (Murphy 1994b). Traditionally, high stakes writing assessment has been handed down, reducing the amount of interaction and creating a situation where, indeed, assessment not only drives curriculum, it "subsumes" it (Elbow and Yancey 1994).

Much has been made about the diverse and individual nature of portfolios to best represent literate behavior in a school setting (Belanoff 1994; Berlin 1994; Graves and Sunstein 1992; and others). However, the move to standardize portfolios is an important aspect of the tradition in educational measurement since assessment instruments have always been standardized in some sense or another. This sets up a conflict, relative to Moss's notion of competing criteria of two disciplines. In fact, the deck is slightly stacked on the side of standardization, for as Moss points out, "we are considerably less knowledgeable about how to design and evaluate nonstandardized assessments and about how to incorporate them into our ongoing assessment practices" (Moss 1994b, 124). What do we do with portfolios as assessment instruments is a legitimate and perplexing question. The problems occur, we believe, when we succumb to the knee-jerk answer "standardize them!" Moss and others would have us look beyond psychometrics to hermeneutics or poststructuralism for theoretical answers to address the tension between the disciplines involved with literacy education and those who assess that education (Moss 1994a). Nonetheless, we think it necessary to also consider issues of power which often appear to exist outside or be invisible within this tension. In fact, issues of control and political expediency ultimately often supply much of the pressure to standardize portfolios and other performance assessments.

Power

If recent history in writing assessment has taught us anything, it has demonstrated that decisions about assessment ultimately involve decisions about where to locate power in educational and political institutions. For instance, the aspects of a writing curriculum that are chosen for evaluation through an assessment program and the procedures of the assessment itself control students' learning and teachers' instruction. The simple truth of educational assessment is that what we choose to evaluate in our students' performances will determine what they attend to in their approach to learning. For example, Resnick and Resnick point to the need to evaluate students' abilities to do independent and self-chosen tasks because they contend that what is not assessed often disappears from the curriculum

(Resnick and Resnick 1992). Those aspects of the curriculum for which we are held accountable will determine what we emphasize in our teaching. Furthermore, our approach to assessment can lead to some unexpected learning on the part of our students when we design an assessment that inadvertently cues them to attend to some aspect of our classroom that we had not intended.

The effects of testing are pervasive and at times surprising. In some instances, poor test results are better than strong ones because this might mean more funding to shore up the valiant but failing efforts of the schools who are seen to be struggling against the inherent problems that certain members of the community bring with them to school. In other instances, notably strong achievement test results can increase the value of property in a specific school district, information which is routinely used by realtors to sell homes to prospective buyers. Test scores can give a school or district the right to claim that it is winning the fight against educational sloth. Clearly, test results can carry with them strong and persuasive outcomes beyond the intended function of the tests themselves.

Another powerful influence of testing on our schools is that assessment often functions as a form of surveillance[4] (Berlak 1992): a way for administrators or other powerful stakeholders to assume and wield their power and influence. Testing in the public schools, for example, allows principals to check up on teachers, who are in turn watched by superintendents and school boards, who are checked up on by state agencies, who are ultimately responsible to the federal government.[5] Linn, in examining the influence of performance assessment instruments on testing practices notes that in the mid-90s we have entered an era of increased testing. Unlike past initiatives, however, "the role of the federal government is much greater than with previous test-based accountability and reform efforts" (Linn 1994, 4). This increased role of the federal government in assessment can also be seen at the postsecondary level in the form of the proposed National Assessment of College Student Learning (NASCL)[6] which will give the federal government more influence over higher education.

Kentucky, which is in the midst of massive and ambitious school reform, provides a good example of the many issues surrounding power, assessment, and portfolios as it moves toward a new statewide curriculum that calls for activity-based instruction and interactive classroom environments. In the Kentucky system, students attend ungraded primary classrooms their first three years in school and are given increased instruction and exposure to computers, and much of the curriculum centers on problem solving and group projects. Also, individual schools have some say over the actual form and rate of change. However, another aspect of the reform is that all fourth, eighth, and twelfth graders are to submit learning portfolios in math and composition to be graded according to the same rubric and anchors generated by the state department of education.

Although there have been efforts by the state to involve teachers in the construction of the assessment program, the program itself has been mandated by the state, and the scores of the portfolios are used to make high stakes decisions. In an ethnographic study of one high school in Kentucky during the second year of the state's mandated assessment program, Callahan (this volume) observes that the use of portfolios increased both the amount of writing students do and the attention teachers give writing in the classroom. "However, since 'portfolio' and 'test' have become synonymous it [will be] difficult for Kentucky teachers to use portfolios for any other purpose . . . [because] they perceive the creation of a portfolio as a stressful activity performed only in response to an external set of demands."

Even though we may use portfolios to assess student writing performance, standardizing their contents and scoring works to locate the power centrally in the hands of the very few who control other sorts of power and decision-making. For example, in the case of portfolio assessment in Vermont, the low interrater reliability coefficients have been enough to raise the call for increased standardizing of the contents of portfolios, even though portfolios are already being viewed as having many positive, though immeasurable, effects on teaching and learning (Koretz et al. 1993). This move to standardize portfolios is based on traditional notions of reliability which claim it "a necessary but insufficient condition for validity" (Cherry and Meyer 1992; and others). In other words, if a measurement system doesn't produce consistent judgments among independent raters, then it cannot be valid. Within the measurement community, however, there is no consensus about the absolute necessity for interchangeable judgments from independent raters. New, emerging theories of assessment point to the problems with rigid and simple conceptions of reliability for measures which include sophisticated judgments about complex activity like that exhibited in a portfolio of student writing. A whole range of assessment specialists are in the process of developing alternative forms of assessment which conceive of reliability as a "critical standard" or "confirmation" (Berlak 1992; Guba and Lincoln 1989; Johnston 1989; Moss 1992, 1994b; and others). At the very least, current conceptions of validity require a consideration of the importance of a test's consequences (Cronbach 1989; Messick 1989).

However, these appeals to less rigid notions of reliability and the positive consequences of portfolio assessment in Vermont are not part of the decision to further standardize writing portfolios to achieve higher interrater reliability coefficients (Koretz 1994). In other words, decisions about portfolios in Vermont are not being based upon the theoretical developments which inform performative assessment procedures like portfolios. If the decision to standardize portfolios in Vermont is being based upon theory, we need to ask whose theory is being used and why?

It is not difficult to see where the power for assessment is located when portfolios or any other measurement instrument is mandated and standardized by a state department of education. The fact that students are compiling portfolios or writing in their classes with their teachers' and classmates' help is secondary. The ultimate authority in these situations has nothing to do with the activity in the classroom which produces the portfolios themselves. Instead, they are being used to generate scores which can support the reform movement. Like all such massive changes, the ones in Kentucky and Vermont require a huge investment from its citizens and politicians, and all of them want some proof that the effort is worth it. While all of this is understandable, we have no assurance that portfolios can encourage a learning environment in which the teachers and students have no say in how they are used, compiled, and scored. In these instances, it appears that the use of portfolios in high stakes assessment scenarios are predicated on political rather than educational rationale. While it is hoped that the wide-scale use of portfolios like that in Kentucky and Vermont can improve student writing ability, surely we increase the chances of this happening when we base decision-making upon educational rather than political premises.

This interweaving and confounding of politics and education is an ongoing dilemma in American schools. Part of the problem stems from the fact that in a very real sense schools are "agents of government to be administered by hierarchical decision-making and controls" (Darling-Hammond 1989, 63). This mixture of political policy and educational theory often creates an odd and ineffective marriage. For example, Berlak talks of how the educational policies of the Reagan and Bush era were contradictory and incoherent because on the one hand they called for increased local control while at the same time they advocated increased use of standardized assessment for increased accountability. According to Berlak, schools cannot attain autonomy when there is an emphasis on standardized assessment which takes the power for curriculum, accountability, and finances away from localities and invests it in centrally located sites controlled by those without knowledge or investment in local contexts.

Alternatives to locating power centrally already exist. In the job search scenario we referred to earlier, Moss offers an example of the way hiring decisions are made at the college level. In her example, the power for judgment rests within the committee itself and the local community from which it is constituted and to which it is responsible. This type of arrangement is considered appropriate for making important decisions about hiring university personnel, and as Wiggins argues, similar localized procedures are used in private and independent institutions to make decisions about students. In discounting traditional notions of reliability as interchangeable consistency, Moss calls for a critical standard by which student performance can be assessed on a local level which honors the importance of contextual and community values necessary for students and teachers to perform at their best within a specific environment (Moss 1994a). Moss's position is similar to Wiggins's, who maintains, "Standards are not fixed or generic. They vary with a performer's aspirations and purpose . . . It is true we use the word standard as if there were a single excellence. But that hides the fact that different criteria and contexts lead to different single excellences" (Wiggins 1993a, 283-284). Citing Sizer, Wiggins maintains that the correct question is not " 'Which Standards?' but 'Whose Standards?' " (Wiggins 1993a, 283), similar in effect to our question about whose theory.

As we see it, ultimately, decisions and discussions about standardization or reliability are political since they are about where to locate the power in an assessment program. Traditionally we have disguised the political character of such issues by referring to the sanctity of technical terms like reliability or validity even though there is little consensus in the measurement community not only about what such terms mean but about their value as meaningful representations. In fact, there have been several calls for dismantling the very notion of validity itself (Berlak 1992; Guba and Lincoln 1989; Johnston 1989).

One way to approach the dilemma we have raised about rethinking the tension between the assessment and educational communities is to "rethink" the notion of accountability. Most initiatives to assess student ability and educational programs are based upon the need for administrators and teachers to be accountable for their programs, practices, and the performances of their students. While we wholeheartedly endorse the importance of education striving for, achieving, and documenting excellence, we wonder how teachers and site-based administrators can be accountable to individuals and organizations who have little understanding of local problems and conditions. The problem, as we see it, is that the concept of accountability often assumes unequal power relations in an inverse relationship to the knowledge and understanding of the salient difficulties in providing a quality education. In other words, the least knowledgeable people often make the most important decisions, many times based upon assessment schemes that are so pared down by standardization that they produce information that has little meaning and importance for local contexts. Programs like those in Kentucky which advocate site-based councils recognize this inherent flaw in the power relationships of accountability. However, as we have already demonstrated, to control curriculum and other important factors in education, you must also control the assessment instruments.

Our "rethinking" of accountability is to replace it with the concept of responsibility. At first glance, there appears little difference between being accountable and being responsible. Like accountability, responsibility also involves providing evidence that local teaching and administrative decisions are based upon the ability of schools to provide quality educational experiences for their students. The difference lies in the relationship of power. Being responsible does not assume that local authorities have to account to higher authorities. The use of assessment for surveillance and other hierarchical functions diminishes as local assessment instruments focus on local programs and actually assist teachers and administrators in being responsible for the spending of public money, the design of educational program, and the education of its students. Changing the power relationships opens up a much more productive set of possibilities for assessment practices.[7]

In Conclusion: Considering Portfolios

As portfolios are continually defined in terms of both their pedagogical value and measurement properties, it is important to remember that an assessment technique itself is not always of primary importance. Although we have some good examples of how portfolios can function in the classroom (see for example Belanoff and Dickson 1991; Paulson, Paulson and Meyer 1991; Yancey 1992a, 1992b), how portfolios are defined by the assessment procedures and how they are used and received by educational regulatory agencies, administrators, teachers, students, and parents will determine their ultimate role in enabling or disabling teaching and learning in writing classrooms.

Although we have no commonly agreed upon definition of portfolios, certain characteristics seem constant. Portfolios contain not only a collection of student work but also the process of how the writing got to be included in the portfolio. Ideally, students learn to make decisions about their writing in terms of what to include and how to improve what they choose to work on. Portfolios can also contain the reflective work students do as they prepare a body of their work not only to be evaluated but to represent them as writers. In this sense each portfolio can be an individual record of a student's journey to understand herself as a writer. Efforts to standardize such a record cut into its ability to help the individual student make sense of herself as a literate person struggling not only to make meaning but to create a context within which she learns to read and write.

As Moss notes, there is an obvious tension between standardized assessment and the highly contextualized, individual nature of communication (Moss 1994b). The power struggle over portfolios is a result of this tension. Any form of assessment which is so individualized as to let students choose their own tasks will be extremely difficult to standardize, unless their individual and self-directed nature is controlled by outside criteria. To do this is to risk reducing portfolios to a specific number of papers on specified topics to enable scoring reliability and standardization that would permit comparisons among different schools. Furthermore, as we have demonstrated, this tension results from the pressure to locate power in a central regulatory agency such as the state education department rather than in the schools and school districts themselves. To preserve the integrity of portfolios and to harness their ability to truly alter the power relationships in assessment, it is necessary to maintain their localized character and to resist any attempts to centrally evaluate them. "Compromises" like statewide scoring guidelines and training sessions are merely disguises to enable standardization.

Many of the initial arguments for portfolio assessment were made in opposition to the standardization required for the reliable scoring of essays. Portfolios are an important juncture in the struggle between educational assessment and political forces. They represent a crossroads, of sorts, at which we need to decide if we will continue along current and traditional lines and standardize their use, so that regulatory agencies can maintain their grip on educational practices. It is important to recognize that this decision is not just about theoretical soundness but about political pressures. We can choose to serve political expedience and create portfolio systems that produce numerical indices and allow for comparability. Or, we can resist such pressures, citing the importance of local control and the power of context in the creation of effective communication.[8] Our position in calling for a reassessment of the way power is located in assessment, especially in the use of writing portfolios, can be viewed, perhaps, as somewhat utopian, unrealistic, or unobtainable. However, there are ways to use portfolios and other assessments which allow them to retain their local character and allow for the kind of assessment which provides rich feedback to inform and enrich teaching and learning. These are already emerging (see Berlak 1992; Johnston 1989; Moss 1994b; and Murphy 1994b for a discussion of such methods). For example, instead of having portfolios compiled by students at various levels and having them read and scored according to mandated guidelines, portfolios could be read by a local board comprised of the teachers themselves, parents, school administrators, and students, who would decide what criteria most relates to their students and school. These portfolios would be discussed and the criteria could change from year to year as student populations and local concerns evolved.[9] Instead of complicated numerical scores, we might think of judging portfolios on the basis of whether a student is on track, ahead of the game, or needs additional help. These numbers could be used to report student progress to the school district or department of education. A central board composed from local constituents would look at a small number of student portfolios either randomly or at particular segments of the school's population, depending upon the purpose. It might be possible, because of the much smaller numbers, to look at portfolios from several grades each year. In terms of the positive effect of assessment on curriculum, this scheme dictates that students compile portfolios every year, and that they are locally read with the potential of being sampled beyond the school. Portfolios have the potential to be more than just what "you do" in certain grades for assessment. Instead, they have the ability to assume a positive role in influencing the curriculum and culture of the school.

Such examples do not, by themselves, provide the necessary reconceptualization we are suggesting; they do, however, acknowledge the critical importance of schools retaining power over their ability to assess and teach. Of course, there are no easy answers to this struggle between locating power for assessment within or outside the schools. Compromises in this struggle have traditionally been resolved in favor of standardization and central authorities, often in the guise of being theoretically sound. It is important that we begin to devise new schemes for assessment which recognize the power relationships within our decisions for assessment and acknowledge the importance of context. It is also vital that individual teachers recognize the power struggles they and their students find themselves in as they attempt to use assessment instruments like portfolios to teach their students.

Notes

1. We base our contention about the popularity of portfolios on the impressive number of volumes (more in the last five years than on all of writing assessment in the last two decades) and the four national conferences held between 1992 and 1994.
2. By the way, these indirect tests are still quite common. In a recent survey on placement practices of colleges and universities, half of the respondents report using indirect measures to place students (Huot 1994).
3. By "high stakes" we borrow a definition from Moss, to include any assessment used for "informing consequential decisions about individuals and programs" (Moss 1994b, 110).
4. There is a long standing concern for government agencies and policies assuming "big brother" roles. See Foucault for an historical review and critical discussion.
5. Although most testing for regulation takes place in the public schools, there is increasing pressure to extend this type of assessment to postsecondary institutions as part of the emerging National Assessment of College Student Learning (NACSL). For a review of the NACSL and its relationship to writing assessment, see Witte and Flach 1994.
6. See Witte and Flach, 1994 for a discussion of the NASCL and its influence on the assessment of writing at the postsecondary level.
7. We are indebted to Patricia F. Carini for discussing with us the differences between accountability and responsibility and their importance in education and educational assessment.
8. The importance of context in language use is arguably the most significant development to come out of the great changes in linguistics, rhetoric, and education during the last three decades. See Witte and Flach, 1994 for a review of the literature on context in communication and its importance to the construction of adequate measures of literacy.
9. Murphy (Murphy 1994b) describes such procedures already in use in her review of school districts and portfolios across the country.

4

Kentucky's State-Mandated Writing Portfolios and Teacher Accountability

Susan Callahan

Mandated Portfolios

AS THEIR USE BECOMES MORE WIDESPREAD, PORTFOLIOS ARE BEING ASKED to function in a variety of ways. In exploring how portfolio design may encourage multiple purposes, though, some of us have begun to suspect that not all purposes are compatible. This suspicion can be seen in the growing tension between those who believe portfolios function best as a highly personalized pedagogy kept deliberately separate from formal assessment and grading and those who see portfolios as a desirable vehicle for assessing individual proficiency. As these two factions have begun eyeing each other with increasing puzzlement and dismay, however, a third perspective has entered the portfolio discussion: Portfolios are being offered as an ideal instrument to provide external accountability.[1]

Of course, designing any portfolio system that provides clear and useful information about a writing program presents a difficult challenge, but Kentucky increased this difficulty by deliberately using portfolios to drive massive school reform. The new portfolio-based accountability system was designed to encourage the benefits we have already identified for students and teachers who use portfolios while at the same time functioning as a test of these benefits. Although a number of states are experimenting with ways portfolios might be used to assess student writing, only Kentucky has abruptly required portfolio assessment as part of a larger education reform effort and factored the resulting portfolio scores into the formula used to hold each individual school accountable for the education it is providing (Reidy 1992). Not surprisingly, the resulting portfolio system has thus far been only partially successful in meeting all the expectations its creators have for it.

My concerns about using portfolios for accountability stem from a year-long study of the way the new state-mandated portfolios are being understood and implemented in one Kentucky high school. Although my study focused on the English teachers' responses to the writing portfolio requirement, I am aware that many of their reactions were colored by other aspects of school reform they were also encountering.[2] Thus, in describing the second year of the portfolio requirement, I am also describing the second year of living with the Kentucky Education Reform Act. Situating accountability portfolios within the emotionally charged atmosphere of education reform makes them particularly vulnerable because it is difficult to examine the portfolio system as a discrete element within the overall reform plan. Nevertheless, I feel the Kentucky experience can be highly instructive for those who are interested in using portfolios for accountability because although the circumstances surrounding the Kentucky portfolio assessment system are unique, the goals of the assessment and the methods the state has used to encourage compliance are not.

A Test Worth Taking

In the fall of 1991 Kentucky began requiring writing portfolios from all its fourth, eighth, and twelfth grade students as one of the first elements of its school reform plan. In using portfolios as a formal test, the state was following the lead of certain theorists who are convinced that since teachers are known to teach to the test, tests should be used to drive curriculum. Having become disenchanted with the ubiquitous standardized test, these theorists are looking for models of what Grant Wiggins calls "an authentic test," a test that is "worth taking" because it reveals how the test taker can actually use knowledge to solve real world problems.[3] Those who follow this line of reasoning believe carefully designed portfolio systems should be authentic tests of writing ability because they encourage students to think and behave like professional writers. According to Tish Wilson, who was the Writing Program Director at the Kentucky Department of Education during the first two years of portfolio assessment, the system is intended to influence classroom instruction in a positive way. In her words, it is expected to "change curriculum to encourage more writing and process-guided instruction."

The contents of the portfolios collected at the three grade levels were carefully stipulated in order to elicit the kind of writing the state wanted to encourage, and the scoring guide was designed to reward writers who succeeded in providing evidence of those writing elements deemed most important in effective communication. During the second year of portfolio assessment the twelfth grade portfolios began with a table of contents, followed by a personal narrative, a short piece of fiction, and three pieces of writing created in response to one of seven "purposes" such as "to predict an outcome," "to defend a position," or "to solve a problem." Two of the pieces in the portfolio had to come from classes other than English because the Department of Education intended portfolio assessment to increase the amount of writing done in all classes. Finally, each portfolio ended with a Letter to the Reviewer reflecting on the pieces in the portfolio and providing some insight into the writer's composing process. (For information about the Letter to the Reviewer, see Appendix B.)

The scoring guide had two sections. The first portion asked readers to evaluate each portfolio holistically, using a rubric that emphasized audience and purpose as the most important feature of the writing and provided a description of the additional factors that should be used to place portfolios in each of the categories described in the rubric. The second portion asked readers to indicate "commendations" or "needs" using an analytic annotation chart keyed in descending order of importance from "purpose/approach," through "idea development/support," "organization," "sentences," and "wording," to "surface features." (See Appendix A for a copy of the scoring guide.)

Building the Boat While Sailing

I spent the 1992 to 1993 school year using basic ethnographic principles to study how a nine-member English department was responding to this requirement and how their responses were affecting their students. The high school, called Pine View for the purposes of my study, fell within the midrange of Kentucky schools in most areas currently documented by the Department of Education (*Profiles*). The nine women who comprised the department were bright, well-educated, articulate, and conscientious. The least experienced teacher had taught six years and the most experienced had been teaching for twenty-seven. All but the youngest teacher had a master's degree in education, and several held Rank I, which requires thirty hours of education beyond the master's. In choosing to focus on the teachers rather than the portfolio system itself, I hoped to discover some needed information about a crucial link between portfolio theory and practice: How are portfolios understood and used by teachers who must implement them as a state-mandated test of their own ability to teach as well as their students' success in learning?

The second year of writing portfolios in Kentucky was, of course, greatly influenced by what had happened during the first year when that initial group of seniors had been told that they must submit a portfolio in order to graduate, and the teachers and administrators had learned that portfolios would count as one sixth of a complex "accountability index" assigned to each school. Once this initial score had been computed, each school was given an individual, numerical target score to reach within two years. Teachers and administrators were told that schools could expect rewards and sanctions based on their performance. In addition to seeing their school's scores published and discussed in the news, teachers knew they could expect financial rewards if their schools showed substantial improvement, while teachers associated with schools with declining scores could find their institutions declared "a school in crisis." If that happened, they could receive additional training, be transferred, or be fired (Foster 1991).

The Department of Education provided information about how they had used the Vermont portfolio system as a model,[4] hired Advanced Systems Testing to provide professional guidance, and involved a number of Kentucky teachers in designing the content requirements and scoring guide. However, most teachers, including those at Pine View, knew nothing about portfolios before they received the requirements for the new fourth, eighth, and twelfth grade writing assessments. The legislative demands for swift implementation of education reform measures meant that the Department of Education had to learn about portfolios, create a large and complex portfolio system, implement it, test it, explain it to all interested parties, and attempt to refine it all at the same time. Within the Division of Performance Testing, the director of the Kentucky Writing Program had the primary responsibility for getting the portfolio system in place. She described the entire process as "building the boat while we are sailing it" (Wilson 1992). The speed with which teachers and administrators were expected to absorb, accept, and administer this new approach to writing assessment naturally intensified the apprehension and confusion that surrounds the implementation of any new teaching method or educational policy.[5] When I began my study in the fall of 1992, the Pine View English teachers were feeling a great deal of tension as they attempted to determine just what their building's first set of portfolio scores might mean for their teaching during the upcoming year. They were also angry and confused because over the summer the state Department of Education had changed the original five-point assessment scale to a four-point scale, and all the portfolio scores had been correspondingly lowered.[6] They felt their hard work during the previous year had been discounted and that many individual students had been evaluated as writing more poorly than their teachers believed they actually did. Their tension was exacerbated by learning the portfolio content requirements for the second year had also been changed to eliminate two categories some teachers had begun to plan writing assignments around. While these new requirements came with reasonable explanations from the state, the teachers saw the changes as evidence that the Department of Education "does not know what it is doing" and felt apprehensive that the requirements might be changed yet again.

Finally, the English teachers were becoming increasingly resentful of bearing the portfolio burden for the entire school. Although they had no real control over the pieces that students had to provide from non-English classes, they felt the principal was holding them responsible as a department for the quality of the resulting portfolios. They also felt it was unfair for them to be expected to give hours of their time to helping students assemble their work and then to reading and scoring schoolwide portfolios while other faculty had no such responsibility. Their discontent was fueled by the knowledge that because the state had left the selection of portfolio readers and the granting of release time and/or stipends for scoring portfolios to the discretion of individual school districts, some of their colleagues in other districts seemed to be receiving more consideration than they were.

In early November, the English department sponsored a workshop by a consultant from the Department of Education who was expected to provide suggestions for ways teachers could incorporate meaningful writing assignments into their various courses. Although the resource teacher did provide an excellent overview of Kentucky's expectations for writing across the curriculum and a theoretical foundation for the roles of assessment and "student-centered classrooms" in curriculum design, the English teachers were disappointed she did not give faculty in social studies, business, and science the opportunity to see or develop some model writing assignments.

In the course of her presentation, the consultant frequently referred to "classroom working folders" and the importance they had in helping students learn to develop portfolios. When I subsequently asked the Pine View English teachers about what they understood these classroom folders to be, they indicated that these folders were intended for storage so that students would have papers to use for their senior portfolios. Consequently, during the year, only one of the teachers experimented with a form of portfolio grading in one of her classes. Her decision to "try" classroom portfolios was based on her own reading, and she received no specific encouragement or assistance in doing so. When I asked her to tell me about her experience, she said she believed it was "a good idea in theory," but that it was making her "suicidal" and she couldn't imagine doing it in all of her classes.

In response to the previous year's experience with portfolios and their understanding of "working folders," the Pine View English Department had begun a central file for students to use to collect potential portfolio pieces. The teachers asked students at all grade levels to give them pieces to put into this file. By February the file mainly contained pieces written in English classes because students frequently forgot to add material written in other content area courses. Consequently, when students in the senior class of 1993 began assembling their portfolios, 52 percent of them believed they had at least six pieces in their central file, but 42 percent said only one or two of these pieces came from non-English classes. The teachers were hopeful, though, that the students who were currently in grades nine, ten, and eleven would have larger and more varied collections by the time they were seniors.

In addition to creating the central file, the English department had made one other response to the first year of portfolio assessment. They had begun to discuss revising the curriculum so that seniors would work with a single English teacher for the entire year rather than moving from one elective course to another, because this structure would make it easier to supervise portfolio assembly which began shortly after the start of the second semester. This curricular change eventually was made, but not without a great deal of regret on the part of several teachers who had developed specialty courses that allowed them to teach areas of particular interest. One teacher agreed to give up a very popular semester-long course comparing Greek mythology and Hebrew Scripture, and another agreed to give up a class in regional writers. At the end of the year, they were still considering whether to provide a single, year-long senior English course or give students a choice of emphases. They were also trying to decide if they could continue offering semester-long courses in creative writing and speech within the new curriculum design.

Although all the teachers understood the necessity for spending more class time on writing, most were uncomfortable with doing so not only because it meant less time for literature, but because only three of the nine teachers had ever received any training in the teaching of writing, two through the Bluegrass Writing Project, and one through a special workshop. Not surprisingly, they all felt very insecure about being viewed as the building experts in this area. Nevertheless, near the end of the second year of portfolio assessment they began to discuss a possible writing in-service they could provide for other faculty and ways they could incorporate more "purposes" writing that was not intended as literary analysis.

In spite of their often professed insecurity, the nine teachers *were* teaching writing, and several were doing it remarkably well. Even before the portfolio requirement, they all had understood and taught some form of process writing and some had begun to make use of peer editing groups. During this second year of portfolio assessment, however, most of them were still struggling with what they saw as "their job" of offering editing suggestions and the time constraints imposed by the increasing amount of writing they were having their students do. As they regularly taught between 80 and 130 students, the time they were willing and able to spend reading student papers influenced the amount of writing they felt they could assign. By the end of the year, a few had begun to use the terminology of the scoring rubric in their classrooms as they discussed writing, but most were too busy helping students understand the various categories of writing the state required to assist them with learning to assess their own work.

As for the responsibility of helping students assemble their senior portfolios, all the teachers spent a tremendous amount of their planning time during the day and before and after school working with individual students, partly to reduce the amount of class time that needed to be devoted to the process. They were also concerned with finding ways to motivate students to work on their portfolios. Some teachers assigned a point value to portfolio work and factored those points into the course grade. Others were reluctant to do this because the portfolios were seen as a compilation of writing from many courses and not an aspect of work done to fulfill the requirements for a specific senior literature course. Most difficult of all was working with students who had completed their required English courses and were not enrolled in English at all during the second semester of their senior year.

Scoring the Portfolios

The teachers viewed their final responsibility, that of scoring the portfolios, with a mixture of apprehension and resignation. The woman who was the designated "cluster leader" for Pine View attended a portfolio scoring workshop provided by the Department of Education and then, in February, led a three-hour workshop one day after school to train the other members of the department to use the four-point scale. This workshop included the Special Education teachers because their students would also be submitting portfolios (even though these teachers would not be involved in the actual scoring of senior portfolios), and the principal, and a curriculum director from the district office. These last two men had been invited by the English teachers, who were hoping to convince the administration that they would need some release time to score the portfolios. During the workshop the teachers worked with the scoring guides and bench-mark portfolios provided by the Department of Education. They spent considerable time translating the terminology of the rubric into their own language, so that, for instance, "minimal awareness of audience" and "purpose" and "limited idea development" came to be understood by the group as "clueless." When one teacher questioned the need for the analytic "commendations" and "needs" evaluations for seniors who would never see the remarks or have another high school class in which the assessment might prove helpful to the teacher, another teacher replied they were needed because "We are being graded, not the students."

As they worked with the new four-point scale, they gradually became more confident of their judgment, but all continued to express a fear that they would be "moderated" by the state and that their building would be "sanctioned" because they had failed to figure out exactly what the state wanted. Their insecurity was intensified by their belief that the inherent subjectivity at the heart of writing evaluation would lead them to "read differently than the state wants us to."

After much time and effort, the department was given a "Professional Development Day" in March to score portfolios and a second half day to complete the suggested double scoring. In response to a Department of Education memo, the portfolios were identified by numbers rather than names, and teachers who recognized familiar work exchanged portfolios until each reader had between twenty-three and twenty-five anonymous portfolios to read as primary scorer. Even after the two days of official portfolio scoring, when each teacher spent about thirteen minutes reading a portfolio and then exchanged portfolios to double score them, several later spent hours rereading the portfolios for which they were the primary scorer and discussing troublesome ones with colleagues in the department. One teacher, the cluster leader, served as tie breaker when primary and secondary scorers disagreed.

During scoring, the teachers frequently voiced complaints that poor quality writing or incomprehensible topics from non-English classes affected the holistic score for the entire portfolio. Most of them felt that many content area teachers either did not know how to create writing assignments or were designing "make work" specifically for the portfolio. One teacher told of a conversation with a student who had said another of her teachers had called the writing assignment he had given "dumb." Several senior English teachers also described conversations with students who had simply created pieces of writing that could have been assigned in a class or redesigned assignments created for English classes so that they appeared to have been done for another class. One also reported that a particularly enterprising student had convinced his science teacher he did not need to do a particular writing assignment because he "already had enough" for his portfolio. The teachers also expressed concern about the authenticity of some of the portfolios they read, but generally they let their suspicions remain suspicions. They knew following up on a suspect portfolio not only would be time consuming but might lower their overall building tally since incomplete portfolios were to be scored "Novice," the lowest possible score. All final scores had to be "bubbled in" on special sheets and signed by the teacher who was the primary scorer.

High Stakes or Authenticity

In the week following the portfolio deadline, I asked all the seniors to complete a questionnaire about their portfolio experience and interviewed sixteen students individually about their portfolios and the assembly process. Most students said they believed that the portfolio requirement had led to their writing more in their classes than they had been asked to do in previous years, and most seemed to feel this writing was done to meet portfolio requirements. Many students, especially those in the lower track English courses, indicated they had taken the portfolio requirement seriously and were very proud of the work they had assembled. Others blithely indicated they had done a perfunctory job while some of the Advanced Placement students complained that doing the portfolio required time they needed for their "real work" and for writing college application essays. One said she did not know why teachers had made it seem like "such a big life or death deal when it really didn't count for anything."[7] The teachers took all these attitudes very much to heart because they felt they were the ones being judged by the quality of the portfolios.[8]

By June of 1993 the word "portfolio" had become firmly embedded at Pine View within the growing lexicon of Kentucky Education Reform Act jargon. And just what does "portfolio" mean in this particular context? It is rapidly acquiring connotations not found in any Department of Education document. Among other things, it is a public performance required of all students every four years. It is a rule-following procedure for students and teachers that takes a great deal of time and energy. It is a reflecting and decision-making experience that teachers believe is good for students to have occasionally, but not as a part of a regular classroom routine. It is a new and stressful responsibility for English teachers. And finally, it is a part of the score that gets published in the paper for parents to see and administrators to attempt to explain. In short, it is "The Test."

At the end of its second year at Pine View, then, the writing portfolio assessment did seem to be meeting part of the state's goal of "encouraging more writing in the classroom" although perhaps not in quite the way the Department of Education had envisioned. Students who wished to graduate were writing and assembling at least six pieces that might have been created in response to classroom assignments. They were spending time revising, or at least recopying, papers they had written at some time preceding the portfolio assembly period or creating new pieces. Finally, some students were, often for the first time, feeling a sense of satisfaction, if not with their writing, then with meeting demanding time, form, and content requirements. By making portfolios a high stakes test for teachers, the state had succeeded in emphasizing the importance of writing and had increased the amount of writing being done. It was no longer acceptable for a senior to graduate having never written more than an occasional paragraph.

On the other hand, the second part of the goal, "encouraging more process-guided instruction," was not faring nearly as well. Within the English department, "the writing process" was seen primarily as a way to insist on at least one revision of a paper, and teachers expected to take an active role in providing topics and in editing. Teachers outside the English department saw writing instruction in terms of providing an appropriate assignment for a potential portfolio piece early enough in the semester for the English department to help students polish it for the assessment portfolio. Finally, at least at Pine View, not all of the effects of the writing requirement on the curriculum were positive. In an effort to "make room" for writing, valuable aspects of the current curriculum were being truncated or discarded, and effective writing assignments were being abandoned because they did not lead to pieces that seemed appropriate for the portfolios.

Further, since portfolios are currently associated with all the emotional baggage that surrounds more traditional state-mandated tests, it will be difficult for teachers to think of portfolios as anything other than a stressful experience. At present, the emphasis on portfolios as an assessment instrument does not encourage Kentucky high school teachers to explore classroom portfolios, but if they decide to do so, they may have a difficult time separating classroom activities from the tension that surrounds compiling the "real" portfolio. In fact, they may have difficulty seeing and communicating the value of any writing assignment that might not eventually be used in the assessment portfolio. Thus, if the portfolio remains, as it currently is, an instrument used to assign a numerical score to materials that have been created expressly for it, then it may succeed in requiring teachers to assign more writing and yet fail as an authentic test of authentic writing.

Notes

1. Sharon Hamilton's article "Portfolio Pedagogy: Is a Theoretical Construct Good Enough?" (*New Directions in Portfolio Assessment*, eds. Laurel Black, Donald A. Daiker, Jeffery Sommers, and Gail Stygall, Portsmouth: Boynton/Cook, Heineman, 1994: 157-67) is perhaps the clearest articulation of the position that portfolios function best as a personalized pedagogy. Some of the others who support a student-centered portfolio approach are Donald Graves, Bonnie Sunstein, and most of the contributors to their volume, *Portfolio Portraits* (Portsmouth: Heinneman; 1992); and Robert Tierney, Mark Carter, and Laura Desai, *Portfolio Assessment in the Reading-Writing Classroom* (Norwood, MA: Christopher-Gordon, 1991).

   Those who advocate portfolios as a vehicle for grading individual proficiency within the classroom often follow the direction set by Christopher Burnham in "Portfolio Evaluation: Room to Breathe and Grow," *Training the New Teacher of College Writing*, ed. Charles W. Bridges (Urbana: NCTE, 1986) while the best-known advocates of using portfolios to assess departmental standards are Pat Belanoff and Peter Elbow who developed the portfolio program at SUNY Stony Brook and William Condon and Liz Hamp-Lyons who developed a similar program at the University of Michigan. Their guiding philosophies can be found in Pat Belanoff and Marcia Dickson, eds., *Portfolios: Process and Product* (Portsmouth: Boynton/Cook, 1991).

   In addition to Grant Wiggins, a number of other theorists are beginning to advocate using portfolio tests as a kind of preemptive strike against reliance on standardized tests. Roberta Camp of ETS suggests portfolios are the logical successors to timed tests of direct writing ("Changing the Model for the Direct Assessment of Writing," *Validating Holistic Scoring for Writing Assessment*, eds. Michael M. Williamson and Brian A. Huot Cresskill, NJ: Hampton P, 1993: 45-78.) And in

"Portfolios and Literacy: Why?" Pat Belanoff describes portfolios as a way to "meet the demand for mandated testing at all levels with systems that do not undercut our teaching" (*New Directions in Portfolio Assessment*, eds. Laurel Black, Donald A. Daiker, Jeffery Sommers, and Gail Stygall, Portsmouth: Boynton/Cook, Heinemann, 1994: 22). Edward M. White, too, sees the value of including portfolios within the dialogue about what large-scale tests can and should do. See, for instance, "Issues and Problems in Writing Assessment," *Assessing Writing* 1 (1994): 11-27.

2. Reform is intended to bring about sweeping changes in curriculum, governance, and finance. Some of these changes include school-based decision making, ungraded primary classes, high school restructuring, and greater use of technology. Portfolios, of course, are not the only kind of assessment being used to change curriculum. Students at the fourth, eighth, and twelfth grades must also sit a battery of "transitional" tests, designed to gradually phase out multiple choice items, and engage in some new performance tasks which test their ability to solve problems and communicate their solution in writing. These test scores, plus factors like attendance rates and retention, all figure into the "accountability index" assigned to each school and become the basis for figuring improvement or lack of improvement. For an explanation of the reform act's provisions, see Legislative Research Commission, *A Citizen's Handbook: The Kentucky Education Reform Act of 1990* (Frankfort, KY: 1994).
3. Grant Wiggins has written extensively about how well-designed tests can enhance teaching and learning. Douglas Archibald and Fred M. Newmann also review the concept of authentic assessment and describe several innovative programs in *Beyond Standardized Testing: Assessing Authentic Academic Achievement* (Reston, VA: National Association of Secondary School Principals, 1988). For a cautionary response to the concept of authentic assessment, see Laurel Black, Edwin Helton, and Jeffery Sommers's article "Connecting Current Research on Authentic and Performance Assessment Through Portfolios," *Assessing Writing* 1 (1994): 247-266.
4. Since so much of the system developed in Kentucky built on the work done in Vermont, Geof Hewitt's "Vermont's Portfolio-Based Writing Assessment Program: A Brief History" (*Teachers and Writers* 24.5 1993: 1-6) provides important background information about Kentucky's hopes for portfolio assessment.
5. Several researchers have written persuasively about the complex processes involved in educational change. See, for instance, Michael Fullan and Suzanne Stiegelbauer, *The New Meaning of Educational Change*, 2nd ed. (New York: Teachers College Press, 1991); Nancy Lester and Cynthia Onore, *Learning Change: One School District Meets Language across the Curriculum* (Portsmouth, NH: Boynton/Cook, 1990); and John Mayher, *Uncommon Sense: Theoretical Practice in Language Education* (Portsmouth, NH: Heinemann, 1990).
6. The original scale used five categories, with a "one" being the lowest possible score and a "five" being the highest. The new scale has four categories, each with a descriptive name rather than a number. All portfolios that received the lowest two scores on the five point scale were automatically reclassified as "Novice" by the state, all the "threes" became "Apprentice," and all the "fours" became "Proficient," while "fives" were called "Distinguished." The Department of Education explained the change was made so that the portfolio evaluations would be compatible with other four-point assessment measures developed after the original portfolio scoring guide. In addition, although each portfolio still would receive a numerical score to be submitted to the state, teachers were urged to discuss and evaluate portfolios using the descriptive terms of the scoring guide.

7. This year's seniors will find that portfolios "count" more because most school districts are encouraging teachers to assign a grade value to the work done for the assessment portfolios, some are discussing "Apprentice" level competency for graduation, and several state universities are exploring ways to use senior portfolios to place incoming freshmen. The writing portfolios themselves are also evolving. Currently, in response to teacher suggestions, the Department of Education has refined the scoring guide and moved the Letter to the Reviewer from the end of the portfolio to the beginning.
8. Administrators, too, are feeling test anxiety. This past spring, newspapers carried accounts of principals providing "perks" to seniors, ranging from free breakfasts to prom tickets, if they took the transitional multiple choice segments and open-ended questions on the general assessment seriously. Portfolio completion was sometimes rewarded with a party.

Appendix A

Kentucky Portfolio Scoring Guide

KIRIS WRITING ASSESSMENT
Holistic Scoring Guide

1992-93

NOVICE	APPRENTICE	PROFICIENT	DISTINGUISHED
• Limited awareness of audience and/or purpose • Minimal idea development; limited and/or unrelated details • Random and/or weak organization • Incorrect and/or ineffective sentence structure • Incorrect and/or ineffective wording • Errors in surface features are disproportionate to length and complexity	• An attempt to establish and maintain purpose and communicate with the audience • Unelaborated idea development; unelaborated and/or repetitious details • Lapses in focus and/or coherence • Simplistic and/or awkward sentence construction • Simplistic and/or imprecise language • Some errors in surface features that do not interfere with communication	• Focused on a purpose; evidence of voice and/or suitable tone • Depth of idea development supported by elaborated, relevant details • Logical organization • Controlled and varied sentence structure • Acceptable, effective language • Few errors in surface features relative to length and complexity	• Establishes and maintains clear focus; evidence of distinctive voice and/or appropriate tone • Depth and complexity of ideas supported by rich, engaging, and/or pertinent details; evidence of analysis, reflection, insight • Careful and/or subtle organization • Variety in sentence structure and length enhances effect • Precise and/or rich language • Control of surface features

Analytic Annotation Guide

CRITERIA	OVERVIEW	COMMENDATIONS		NEEDS	
PURPOSE/ APPROACH	The degree to which the writer • establishes and maintains a purpose • communicates with the audience	P/A-X	clear awareness of audience and purpose	P/A-J	greater sense of audience and purpose
		P/A-Y	original and/or insightful approach and evidence of distinctive voice/tone	P/A-K	more insightful approach and evidence of voice/tone
IDEA DEVELOPMENT/ SUPPORT	The degree to which the writer provides thoughtful, detailed support to develop the main idea(s)	I/S-X	perceptive thinking	I/S-J	more thoughtful investment by author
		I/S-Y	relevant, interesting details	I/S-K	more elaboration of details
ORGANIZATION	The degree to which the writer demonstrates • logical sequencing • coherence • transitions/organizational signals	OX	evidence of planning	OJ	more evidence of planning
		OY	order/sequence easily followed	OK	more logical sequence of ideas and effective transitions
SENTENCES	The degree to which the writer includes sentences that are • varied in structure and length • constructed effectively • complete and correct	SX	variety in structure and length	SJ	greater variety in structure and length
		SY	effectively constructed sentences	SK	more effective sentence construction
WORDING	The degree to which the writer exhibits correct and effective • word choice • usage	WX	successful use of pertinent and/or rich language	WJ	closer attention to effective word choice
		WY	control of conventional usage	WK	greater control of conventional usage
SURFACE FEATURES	The degree to which the writer demonstrates correct • spelling • punctuation • capitalization	SF-X	spelling enhances readability	SF-J	accurate spelling
		SF-Y	capitalization and punctuation aid clarity	SF-K	greater control of punctuation and capitalization

Appendix B

Letter to Reviewer

The Letter to the Reviewer is written by the student to discuss his/her growth as a writer and reflect on the pieces in the portfolio (grades eight and twelve) or "Best Piece" (grade four). In this letter, the student will examine such possibilities as the following:

- a description of himself/herself as a writer including
    - a) goals as a writer,
    - b) progress and growth as a writer through the year,
    - c) who or what has influenced writing progress and growth,
    - d) approaches used by the student when composing, etc.;
- selection of "Best Piece" and /or portfolio pieces including
    - a) how he/she arrived at his/her selections
    - b) role of the writing folder in portfolio selection(s)
    - c) prewriting/thinking about the topic(s)
    - d) revision strategies that were helpful,
    - e) editing strategies that were helpful,
    - d) kinds of changes made and reasons for those changes,
    - g) influence of teacher/peer conferencing;
- any other comments the student wishes to make about this year of writing

From *Kentucky Writing Portfolio: Teacher's Handbook*, Thomas C. Boysen, Commissioner, Kentucky Department of Education, Office of Assessment and Accountability, 1992 to 1993.

5

Teachers and Students

Reclaiming Assessment Via Portfolios

Sandra Murphy

TEACHERS HAVE PROBABLY ALWAYS UNDERSTOOD THE MEANING OF THE phrase "teach to the test." Evidence confirms this, showing that teachers will base instruction on the content and form of tests, especially when high stakes are attached (Corbett and Wilson 1991; Madaus 1988; and M. L. Smith 1991). Now educational reformers want to make use of this tendency by linking "tests" to portfolios. By setting high standards and developing new forms of assessment more closely aligned with current views of learning and good teaching practice, the reasoning goes, we can transform education. Portfolios, especially, seem to provide the ideal recipe for educational reform because they offer new, more individualized modes of instruction, and because they promise to capture information not easily assessed by other methods. We can use portfolios, for example, to assess students' ability to think critically, articulate and solve complex problems, work collaboratively, conduct research, accomplish long-term, worthwhile projects, and set their own goals for learning (Camp 1993b, 1993a; Mitchell 1992; Wolf 1993). We can use portfolios to assess progress over time and to assess performance under a variety of conditions and task requirements.

Yet using portfolios in a reform movement which counts on assessment to drive instruction is problematic. In assessment situations, especially when "high stakes" are attached—regarding important decisions such as "a) graduation, promotion, or placement of students; b) the evaluation or rewarding of teachers or administrators; c) the allocation of resources to schools or school districts; and d) school or school system certification"

(Madaus 1988, 87)—there is pressure to standardize portfolios because traditional statistical kinds of reliability appear easier to achieve when students are asked to submit the same sorts of assignments completed under the same sorts of conditions (see for example, Koretz et al. 1993). However, many teachers believe that some of the benefits from portfolios stem from their power to motivate students to assume responsibility for learning. Portfolios, they say, offer one of the few school opportunities that students have to exercise their own judgment, initiative, and authority. If we standardize portfolios, we will have eliminated that opportunity. The traditional demands of measurement for reliability and validity, then, appear to be in conflict with the very same characteristics of portfolios which motivate students and enhance student learning.

Along with students, teachers are entangled in the reform dilemma. Educational reform demands highly skilled professionals: teachers who are knowledgeable about learning theory, pedagogy, curriculum, assessment, and child development, who accept responsibility for their students' welfare and development, and who plan and evaluate their own work (Darling-Hammond 1989). Yet many programs aimed at reform fail to engage teachers in the kinds of study, investigation, and experimentation required to undertake the multiple challenges of reform, enrolling them instead in "training" programs designed only to expand particular sets of pedagogical practices and skills (Little 1993). What is needed instead are programs which prepare professionals to play informed and active roles in "defining the enterprise of education and the work of teaching," and an educational climate in which teacher-professionals not only consume knowledge, but generate knowledge and assess the knowledge claimed by others (Little 1993, 132).

Certain approaches to assessment may inhibit this kind of professional climate. Scholars argue that prepackaged assessments "frustrate individual initiative and innovation and limit professional prerogative" even when they are explicitly intended to be tools to help the teacher in the classroom (Pearson and Valencia 1987, 1). Research indicates that standardized tests, along with workbooks, canned lessons, drills, and other "teacher-proof" instructional packages, tend to devalue the professional competence of teachers (M. L. Smith 1991). When policymakers mandate highly prescriptive portfolios, then they may revisit an approach to reform which in the past has led not to the professionalization of teachers, but rather to their de-skilling and deprofessionalization (see Darling-Hammond 1989, 1990; McNeil 1988). If portfolios are highly standardized, their effect in the reform movement may be the opposite of what was intended because highly standardized portfolios may restrict opportunities for teachers and students to demonstrate individual initiative and ingenuity—qualities which are essential in any significant, long-lasting reform effort.

To achieve substantial reform, policymakers need to work to create an educational climate which encourages teachers to exercise well-informed professional judgment, and teachers, in turn, need to create a classroom climate which empowers and challenges the student. Key pieces of the reform puzzle, it seems, are the roles played by teachers and students.

The Teacher as Technician

With the growth of bureaucracy in education, teachers in kindergarten through twelfth grade schools are under more pressure than ever to follow policies made at the top of the educational system: policies that are "handed down to administrators, who translate them into rules and procedures (class schedules, curricula, textbooks, rules for promotion and assignment of students, etc.) . . ." (Darling-Hammond 1989, 63). Curriculum is sent "down" to the school, and the adjective "teacher-proof" has become part of the educational lexicon. The teacher's role in this scenario is simply to follow the rules and procedures for transmitting approved curricula, for using particular books, and for administering tests designed by others. In sum, in the bureaucratic model of education, the classroom teacher is viewed as a technician who implements policy decisions and initiatives designed by others—or as Linda Darling-Hammond says, a technician who acts as a "conduit for instructional policy, but not as an actor" (Darling-Hammond 1990, 345).

It seems reasonable to argue that the teacher-as-technician role stems in part from assessment policies. Consider the figure below. Although it oversimplifies very complex issues, the figure highlights contrasting policy decisions underlying different assessment scenarios which can impact teachers' roles.

To say what seems obvious, the assessment policies on the right side of the figure can have ironic consequences in the reform movement because assessments which are mandated by external agencies and developed and evaluated by external experts may constrain the professional authority of teachers. External tests limit teachers' freedom to make decisions about what (and when) to teach and what to assess. Moreover, in "Catch 22" fashion, when teachers are treated as mere assessment-technicians, access to activities

Figure 1
Assessment Policies and Teachers' Roles

Issue: Promoting Teacher Professionalism

Initiated by Teachers	______________	Mandated by External Agencies
Developed by Teachers	______________	Developed by External Experts
Evaluated by Teachers	______________	Evaluated by External Experts

for professional development is curtailed, making it even more difficult for them to assume a professional role (Lucas 1988). Although scoring student writing can be a powerful professional development experience, for instance, relatively few teachers have the opportunity. With few exceptions, scoring of large-scale tests is done by machine, if the tests are of the multiple-choice variety, or by graduate students or groups of "retired and moonlighting" teachers recruited from the vicinity of outside companies (often out-of-state) if actual samples of writing are collected. In 1990, according to Ruth Mitchell, twenty of the twenty-seven states which collected actual writing samples employed outside companies to score them (Mitchell 1992, 39). Thus, even when actual samples of writing are scored, they are typically not scored by the teachers who are involved in helping the students. In the interest of "fairness" as defined by psychometric procedures, or simply in the interest of cost-efficiency, the social consequences of assessment—their impact on students and teachers and schools—has been superseded by statistical considerations (Williamson 1994).

The social consequences of external assessments can be significant. Consider the impact on teachers. This portrait provided by Mary Lee Smith is especially grim:

> . . . if exploration, discovery, [and] integration methods fall out of use because they do not conform to the format of the mandated test, teachers will lose their capacities to teach these topics and subjects, use these methods, or even imagine them as possibilities. A teacher who is able to teach only that which is determined from above and can teach only by worksheets is an unskilled worker. Far from the reflective practitioner or the empowered teachers, those optimistic images of the 1980s, the image we project of teachers in the world after testing

> reform is that of interchangeable technicians receiving the standard curriculum from above, transmitting it as given (the presentation manual never leaving the crook of their arms), and correcting multiple-choice responses of their pupils. (M.L. Smith 1991, 11)

As Lorrie Shepard puts it, externally mandated, standardized tests "reduce both the status and the professional knowledge of teachers" (Shepard 1991, 234). Portfolios too may reduce the professional status of teachers, if contents are narrowly prescribed or if high stakes are attached (see Callahan, this volume; Gomez et al. 1991; and Roe 1991). Like other kinds of external tests, prescriptive portfolios limit teachers' authority to make decisions about what to teach and what to assess.

The Teacher as Professional

Teachers play a very different role, however, in schools where they use portfolios not only as tools for instructional decision-making in their own classrooms, but as focal points for department and schoolwide collective discussions about teaching and learning—in short, for internal accountability. And, when portfolios are systematically analyzed and the results communicated beyond school walls, portfolios serve local external accountability purposes as well. In these schools, teachers are reclaiming responsibility and authority for assessment.

In the mid-eighties, teachers in a junior high school in Oakland, California, were concerned about the writing performance of the students at the school, so they decided to ask their students to create selective collections of their writing from all of their classes (Murphy and Smith 1990). Students filled these portfolios with writing from several subject areas. When the teachers sat down to review the students' portfolios, they worked in pairs. They scored the portfolios along particular dimensions, then traded portfolios and talked. They wrote comments on the portfolios—and talked. They made comments like these:

> "His social studies paper is fine. I wonder why this one in English is so bad."
> "Did you have students cluster here?"
> "Look at how this student was dealing with audience."
> "Maybe it's because of the way this assignment is framed, you don't get those little plot summaries or that awful formula writing."
> "They're not revising. They're just copying the stuff over, making it neat."

The teachers' conversations were one part of their effort to gather and interpret data about what the students at the school were learning about writing, including the extent to which students were revising as opposed to recopying. As the teachers read the students' portfolios, they systematically recorded their observations of students' revision strategies. Along the way, they also made less formal observations about other things they were seeing in the portfolios. And also along the way, they gained a new sense of power and authority because they were doing their own research on problems of immediate relevance to their teaching. Later they discussed their observations as a group and planned action in response to what they had found. Their work benefited both their students and themselves.

While the teachers read the portfolios, and afterwards, they talked about the kinds of activities that helped the students produce engaging writing, about the transformation of dreaded encyclopedia reports into creative journal entries and travel diaries and about the dry lab reports from science which had, thankfully, been recast as letters to friends. They also talked about assignments and activities that didn't work, the tell-not-show assignments that seemed to teach the students little about techniques for engaging audiences and accomplishing purposes. In sum, they talked about what students were learning and what they were not learning and ways to help them learn.

The teachers at this school were engaging in what teachers at Prospect School call reflective conversation (Johnston 1989), the kind of real dialogue through which teachers come to understand the children better and which at the same time engages teachers in reflective evaluation of their teaching activities. Peter Johnston suggests that this kind of activity is likely to produce a community of what Schon has called "reflective practitioners": teachers who "publicly reflect on [their] knowledge-in-practice, and engage in a process of self-education" (Schon, cited in Johnston 1989, 519). It is precisely this kind of collective dialogue which will help teachers become self-educators and make informed and trustworthy judgments about students. But this kind of dialogue is not likely to occur in an environment in which the content and form of the curriculum to be assessed are prescribed in advance. Nor is it likely to occur without institutional support.

Besides talking to each other, the teachers in California talked to parents at open-house, to the school board, and to the PTA. In this way, they created a direct and immediate link between the curricular activities of the school and their community surrounding it. They accomplished some of the accountability purposes usually associated with external assessment, such as communicating important information about student learning and the impact of instruction at the school, but they did it from the inside out (see also, Wolf, LeMahieu, and Eresh 1992). In this way, they assumed responsibility as professionals.

Portfolio Projects in California

In recent years, the kind of collective use of assessment for inquiry and self-evaluation practiced in schools like the California school described above has been institutionalized on a wider scale in a number of alternative assessment projects, including portfolio projects. In such projects, teachers design and research assessments. In short, they take up the role of specialists. Catherine Jamentz describes the new role played by teachers in the California Assessment Collaborative (CAC):

> teachers in CAC . . . projects are inventing a wide range of assessments: projects, exhibitions, open-ended questions and portfolios . . . Typically project participants engage in a recursive series of activities in which they invent tasks or portfolio designs, test them with students and revise them to assure that they assess the full range of what students are expected to know and be able to do. (Jamentz 1994, 1 and 7)

In addition to the CAC projects, large numbers of teachers in California have helped to develop portfolio systems for large-scale assessments. For example, roughly 120 science teachers "representing all regions of California" served as members of the Golden State Examination Development Committees and collaborated to develop guidelines, conduct research, and outline scoring parameters for the pilot of a large-scale portfolio assessment system for science (Martin et al. 1993, 1). As another example, teachers and administrators from participating schools in six districts met to collaboratively develop and experiment with primary-level portfolio assessments in the kindergarten through fourth grade Learning Assessment Project.

The most ambitious of the California portfolio projects was the California Organic Portfolio Pilot Project in English language arts. Until it became a casualty of the governor's budget cuts in the last months of 1994, it showed promise of becoming a particularly enlightened way to deal with statewide assessment in the English language arts. The intent of this project was to find a way to collect and assess evidence of student learning and accomplishment from natural interactions and activities in the classroom. The rationale was that portfolios of student work could provide rich, diverse information about student accomplishments. The policy approach of the California Learning Assessment System (CLAS), of which this portfolio project was a part, was one of "persuasion": an approach very different from that taken in states where sanctions are imposed on staff in schools where students fail to meet specified threshold scores showing improvement (see, for example, Callahan, this volume). As Lorraine McDonnell notes, the assumption behind CLAS was that parents and concerned members of the public would act on reported information by "pressuring for improvement where it is needed" (McDonnell 1994, 405).

In the beginning stages of the California portfolio project, teachers around the state worked with an advisory committee of teachers and other educators, the Portfolio Task Force, to develop a framework for the assessment. The framework was specified at the level of broad dimensions of learning, instead of the content or piece level. That is, instead of submitting a certain number of specified pieces, the idea was that students and teachers would build sets of evidence to demonstrate students' accomplishment in selected dimensions of learning. The plan was that these dimensions would serve as organizing principles for local implementations of portfolio assessment.

The dimensions of learning developed by the Task Force did not encompass everything that students would be expected to know or be able to do. Rather, they represented particular kinds of knowledge and abilities which could not easily be assessed with standardized forms of assessment. The dimensions were framed as processes. For example, one asks teachers and students to show how students "construct meaning," that is, how students

> respond to, interpret, analyze, and make connections within and among works of literature and other texts, oral communication, and personal experiences. Students consider multiple perspectives about issues, customs, values, ethics, and beliefs which they encounter in a variety of texts and personal experiences. They take risks by questioning and evaluating text and oral communication, by making and supporting predictions and inferences, and by developing and defending positions and interpretations. They consider the effect of language, including literal and figurative meaning, connotation and denotation. They reflect on and refine responses, interpretations and analyses by careful revisiting of text and by listening to others. (California Learning Assessment System, Dimensions of Learning in Language Arts, 1)

A second dimension asks teachers and students to show how the students "compose and express ideas," that is, how students

> communicate for a variety of purposes, with a variety of audiences, and in a variety of forms. Their written and oral communication is clearly focused; ideas are coherent, and effectively organized and developed. They use language effectively to compose and express thoughts. They draw on a variety of resources including people, print, and nonprint materials, technology and self evaluation to help them develop, revise and present written and oral communication. They engage in processes, from planning to publishing and presenting; when appropriate, they do substantial and thoughtful revision leading to polished products. Through editing, they show command of sentence structure and conventions appropriate to audience and purpose. (California Learning Assessment System, Dimensions of Learning in Language Arts, 1)

Because the framework was open-ended, it provided for a good deal of flexibility in the ways accomplishment might be demonstrated.

The New Standards Project Portfolio

A collaborative, open-ended approach was also adopted in the portfolio pilot of a partnership of a number of states and school districts collaborating to develop performance assessments called the New Standards Project (NSP, 1993). The New Standards assessment system included on-demand tasks, but the part most relevant to this discussion is the work that was done to develop frameworks for assembling and assessing portfolios. The development process in the New Standards Project was similar to the one adopted in California: that is, teachers were brought together to discuss and reach consensus about the dimensions of learning to be assessed in the portfolios (See Myers and Pearson 1996). In addition, there was a concerted attempt to build on the expertise and success of existing portfolio projects around the country. Representatives of many of these projects collaborated with teachers and other members of the educational community to define the dimensions, to select exemplary portfolios, and to explore approaches to assessing the portfolios.

Not surprisingly, in the first New Standards pilot, dimensions of learning were called "standards." In the 1994 to 1995 pilot, separate standards were expressed for reading, writing, and oral performance (speaking and listening). Students who met the draft standards for writing were expected to: 1) "communicate clearly, effectively and without errors," 2) "write for different kinds of readers using different writing styles," and 3) "evaluate [their] own work" (NSP, Student Portfolio Handbook, High School English Language Arts, 1994).

The standards provided the initial, open-ended framework for the first pilot portfolio. (Later versions were somewhat more prescriptive.) In the initial plan, each piece in the portfolio was to be accompanied by a foreword written by the student explaining which standards were represented in the piece. Any single piece could provide information about more than one standard, and any single standard was usually represented by more than one piece. Many different kinds of evidence might be offered then, as long as the particular standard was demonstrated, allowing students some freedom to decide how to represent their work. Because it was open-ended, the system also addressed a particular challenge faced by NSP: "to design a system that would not intrude on whatever state, district, school, or classroom program was already in place and that would represent primarily a reconfiguration of portfolios that students were already keeping" (Spaulding 1995, 220).

The open-ended portfolio design offered other advantages. For one, it required students to provide information about important dimensions of performance which have not easily been tapped by more traditional methods of assessing writing. For example, information about the scope of a student's ability to "write for different kinds of readers using different writing styles," has not been available in traditional, single-sample approaches to assessing writing. Portfolios, however, invite students (and evaluators) to observe how performance varies from occasion to occasion, how particular strategies and techniques can be adapted for different writing situations, and how writing varies across genre, audience and purpose (Murphy and Smith 1992; Murphy 1994a). In an attempt to capture information about this dimension of accomplishment in writing, teachers in the New Standards Portfolio pilot drafted a rubric for assessing students' "range and versatility." It included the following description of a level four performance on a one to four scale:

- Provides evidence of an awareness of diverse audiences; the writer's attention to public and private audiences matches his/her varied purposes for writing
- Demonstrates the ability to communicate for a variety of purposes; there is ample evidence of the ability to use a variety of genres, forms, and topics in written communication
- Provides substantial evidence that the student's skillful control of a variety of distinctive voices makes the portfolio richer, more interesting and more focused

- Provides substantial evidence that the student has attempted to create a portrait of him/herself as a learner by experimenting, attempting imaginative or unusual pieces, or approaching a topic or text in an innovative way (NSP Draft High School Rubric, June, 1994)

Criteria linked to the rubric were explicitly conveyed to students in the NSP handbook. With respect to range and versatility students were asked to show that they could:

- Write for different kinds of readers using different writing styles
- Write for a variety of purposes
- Write for a range of audiences
- Write in a range of styles and formats (NSP, Student Portfolio Handbook, High School English Language Arts, 1994)

There are definite advantages to a dimensional framework of the kind developed in this project. One is that it makes the evaluators' expectations and standards explicit. At the same time, however, it gives students and teachers some latitude in making decisions about how those standards will be met. In one class a student might decide to include a letter to a friend, an essay (to the teacher), and an editorial for the public. In another a student might decide to include a children's story, a movie review, and a character sketch.

An open-ended framework of this kind can bring other benefits, especially when it is developed in a process which engages stakeholders. In both the CLAS Portfolio Project and in the New Standards Project, a consensus building process was attempted which allowed stakeholders representing various constituencies to have a voice in identifying those elements of an English–language arts education that would be assessed. In addition, all of the portfolio projects described here involved a large number of teachers in the development process. The teachers piloted materials, reported their results, and collectively analyzed each other's portfolios. Not surprisingly, teachers who engage in the portfolio development process value the experience. For instance, participants in the portfolio pilot for the 1993 Golden State Examination in Science reported that "portfolios were the most powerful tool they had used to help them incorporate educational reform and the most relevant staff development opportunity they had experienced" (Martin 1994, 4).

Assessment-development-as-faculty-development can also lead teachers to make significant changes in their beliefs and classroom practices. Karen

Sheingold, Joan Heller, and Susan Paulukonis report, for instance, that 86 percent of the teachers who participated in a project to develop curriculum-embedded assessments noted changes in one or more of the following five categories of their practice:

> 1. Using new sources of evidence
> 2. Sharing responsibility for learning and assessment
> 3. Changing goals of instruction
> 4. Using new ways of evaluating evidence
> 5. Changing [their] general view of the relationship between assessment and instruction. (Sheingold et al. 1994, 15)

These changes came about as the result of the particular roles teachers were asked to play. Teachers in the project

> took on a genuine and complex responsibility, which left them in control of their own change, conducted practical inquiry in their classrooms through generating and testing assessment tasks . . . and were provided social support (discussions and other activities with colleagues and experts) to carry out and consider the results of their efforts in terms of student learning. (Sheingold et al. 1994, 29)

Participating in the assessment development process can be a powerful impetus for change; teachers increase their understanding of these new forms of assessment at the same time that they are empowered professionally.

It is worth noting that each of the projects described here put teachers in collaborative roles with assessment specialists to learn from each other and develop new knowledge. The faculty development experience provided in the assessment development process thus differs in an important way from the typical "training" model of faculty development. As Judith Warren Little reminds us, the training model, no matter how useful, perhaps, for preparing teachers for "textbook-centered or recitation-style teaching," and "no matter how well executed," will not enable us to realize the present reforms in subject matter standards, curriculum content, and pedagogy which call for fundamental changes in teacher-student interactions (Little 1993, 132-33). Rather, as Little proposes, reform requires:

> the kinds of structures and cultures, both organizational and occupational, compatible with the image of "teacher as intellectual" (Giroux 1988) rather than teacher as technician. And finally, it requires that teachers and others with whom they work enjoy the latitude to invent local solutions—to discover and develop practices that embody central values and principles, rather than to

implement, adopt, or demonstrate practices thought to be universally effective. (Little 1993, 133)

Current reform efforts call for teachers who are equipped to engage students in the pursuit of genuine questions and problems and to transform their classrooms into educationally rich communities of learners (Darling-Hammond and Snyder 1992), and for teachers who are prepared to make informed decisions about assessment—its purposes and content—just as they are expected to make informed decisions about teaching and learning. This vision of teachers acting as professionals in reform will not be moved forward by top-down tests, or for that matter, by top-down portfolio assessments which specify particular content to be covered and which attach sanctions for noncompliance. Professionalism in teaching calls instead for flexible systems which accommodate diversity in the ways individual teachers, schools, and districts provide evidence of their accountability to agreed upon standards. In addition, teachers will need time and support, as well as opportunities, to engage in frequent and open dialogues about effective ways to enhance instruction and learning through assessment. In sum, teachers will need an educational climate which encourages intellectual growth and professional development.

Student as Independent Learner versus Student as Reactor

In the bureaucracy of today's schools, with a few exceptions, students' roles have been ironically parallel to the roles played by teachers. Relatively powerless, students are most often the recipients of tests and curriculum prepared by others. They have little authority to determine what they will learn, or how they will be assessed, or on what. That authority rests instead with the experts of external agencies or in the classroom with the students' own teachers.

As John Mayher explains, teacher-controlled assessment goes hand in hand with teacher-centered instruction. In teacher-centered classrooms, he says, almost all writing is done "on teacher demand, on teacher-set topics, in teacher-determined forms" and it is assessed by the teacher who functions as "grader and judge" (Mayher 1990, 30). This "common sense" tradition is widespread. Arthur Applebee's recent national study, *Literature in the Secondary School*, indicates that most classrooms remain largely teacher-centered, although there is some concern with student-centered goals and motivation in relation to writing. Alternative, more student-centered approaches to English language arts curriculum, such as the personal growth model described by John Dixon in *Growth Through English* or the integrated language arts curriculum described by James Moffett, have not had much impact in America's schools.

Well-known exceptions to the teacher-centered approach, of course, can be found in the classrooms of teachers like Nancie Atwell and Linda Rief, who have created student-centered learning communities, where students have some freedom—and responsibility—to shape their education and where independent reading and writing are the core of the curriculum, "not the icing on the cake" (Atwell cited in Rief 1992, 7). In a similar vein, in the literature on portfolios there are frequent calls for students to assume more authority and responsibility for their education in areas in which they have previously had little voice. For instance, along with several researchers who hold similar views, teachers who use portfolios in their classrooms argue that students should themselves be involved in establishing guidelines for their portfolio (Rief 1990; Paulson, Paulson and Meyer 1991; Tierney et al. 1991).

Teachers who use portfolios have devised a number of ways to accommodate a degree of student ownership. In some classes teachers let students include, in "wild card" categories (Camp 1992), whatever pieces are most important to them, along with more specified entries. In other classes, portfolios are designed to showcase the students' best pieces; in others, as in the two large-scale projects described here, portfolio contents are defined via broad guidelines, so that students have room to make choices. These kinds of more open-ended portfolio designs give students a stake in the assessment process, a stake for the decisions they are empowered to make, not just for the consequences of failure.

It goes without saying, of course, that students don't make these decisions in isolation. In a portfolio culture, students make these decisions with guidance and support from their teachers (Yancey 1992c). In portfolio classes, as Mary Perry (this volume) suggests, teachers help students learn to set goals. They collaborate with students in the process. "Portfolios," as teacher Joan Reynolds says, "are purposeful collections of evidence that students have made progress toward goals that they and I have set" (Reynolds 1995).

Teachers also make the development of criteria a collaborative process. Ann Roussea asks her students to generate criteria for their writing that she can use when she evaluates them. She has learned that portfolios encourage each student "to take greater responsibility for his or her own growth as a writer," because each must "review patterns and determine ways in which he might improve." Students initially generate criteria individually. Then small group and full class discussions follow, and finally a vote to determine criteria for the class as a whole.

Linda Rief uses samples of writing with varying degrees of strengths and weaknesses to guide her students as they generate criteria for writing. She asks the students to read each piece, assign a holistic number (from 1 = ineffective, to 4 = most effective) and write down three reasons for the score. In small groups, students share their criteria for the most effective pieces and reach consensus. The small group discussions are then synthesized and condensed even further on a handout for the students (Rief 1992).

Similarly, in Kathryn Howard's classes in Pittsburgh, students produce wall charts containing lists of qualities the students perceive to be essential to the creation of a good piece of writing. During the year, as the students learn more about writing, the lists are revised. Howard believes these lists are important "because they are student-generated and because they provide a foundation for personal standards and criteria for good writing as well as an internalized and personalized writer's vocabulary" (Howard 1993, 91).

Developing criteria for portfolios, as opposed to standards for individual pieces of writing, is a goal in Jan Bergamini's classroom in Concord, California. Together, students and teacher generate lists of statements about what it means to be good readers and writers. In turn, the statements guide the students' portfolio selections. In this classroom, as in many other portfolio classrooms, assessment is a collaborative process.

It is worth noting that in each of these portfolio classroom scenarios, assessment is *negotiated* by teachers and students. This represents a rather radical change from the traditional classroom assessment scenario, in which the teacher makes all the decisions. In portfolio classrooms, the teacher does not have sole authority and responsibility for assessment; nor is the teacher merely a scorekeeper for right answers on tests. In a portfolio culture, teachers play a much more collaborative role. In turn, students play a much more active role in their own learning and assessment. Assessments are constructed jointly, integrated with instruction, and mediated by social interaction. In a portfolio culture, assessment has become an occasion for learning and an integral part of a collaborative teaching/learning process. This transformation of culture is, of course, the point of reform.

Conclusion

The roles of teachers and students in the bureaucracy of today's schools are often ironically similar. In all areas of schooling, teachers and students must cope with requirements. Teachers must cope with district curriculum, scope and sequence charts, word lists, schedules, and the like. Students in turn, must cope with workbooks, required reading, tests, teacher-designed topics, and prescribed forms and processes for writing. Requirements, although certainly necessary in the process of schooling, can impart a sameness to the educational enterprise.

Portfolios offer teachers a way to individualize instruction and make it more student-centered, to acknowledge that "the ability to find interesting problems is . . . as important as being able to answer someone else's questions," and that "individuality and invention" are as important as "mastering technique or knowledge" (Wolf 1987, 26).

Portfolios provide a means for both students and teachers to redefine their roles in assessment. When portfolios are not defined by prescriptive menus which dictate particular assignments, they leave room for students to play a more active and generative role in their own education. They allow students to gain some control over the assessment process, and they encourage students to gauge their own progress and development. They provide a useful complement to other assessment techniques available to the classroom teacher and a powerful alternative to "prepackaged," bureaucratic kinds of large-scale testing.

When teachers engage in portfolio practice, they are no longer cast simply in the "teacher-as-examiner" role, as Britton et al. (1975) describe it. Rather, in the process of portfolio construction, teachers act as coaches and counselors. And, in situations in which students and teachers make the examination of portfolios a collaborative venture, both teachers and students become researchers with a range of data that can reveal what students have accomplished and what might be done next (Murphy and Smith 1992).

However, the shift in stance from "examiner" to "co-researcher" can only occur in an educational climate in which teachers are personally and professionally empowered. Professionalism is undercut by prevailing, prescriptive conditions in schools which, as Calfee and Hiebert put it, "steer teachers toward the role of 'meter readers' " in assessment and instruction (Cafee and Hiebert 1987, 45). To change this state of affairs, portfolios need to be linked not to rewards and sanctions for noncompliance, but to policies which support the professional development of teachers.

Teachers need "adequate opportunity to learn (and investigate, experiment, consult, or evaluate) embedded in the routine organization" of their days (Giroux 1988, 133). Like students, they need opportunities to generate their own curriculum goals and assessment strategies and, as Garth Boomer says, "negotiate." That is, teachers need to be able to negotiate the specifics of curriculum within the constraints placed on the learning situation by central values and principles held by the community at large. Curriculum frameworks and assessment systems need to be flexible enough to allow room for diverse forms of expression, so that teachers and students, instead of simply complying with rigid requirements, "enjoy the latitude to invent local solutions" (Giroux 1988, 133) while honoring those principles and values.

The essence of educational reform is the enhancement of both student and teacher growth. Reformers look to assessment as a means to drive this reform. Yet externally mandated, prescriptive forms of assessment linked to policies that use test results to reward or impose sanctions are not likely to contribute to the professional development of teachers, nor to the development of students as independent learners and empowered citizens who are critically and civically engaged. Portfolios can move us forward, but they must be linked to policies which complement, not contradict, the goals of reform.

6

Establishing Sound Portfolio Practice

Reflections on Faculty Development

Cheryl Evans Ause
Gerilee Nicastro

OUR FORMAL INTRODUCTION TO PORTFOLIOS BEGAN DURING THE 1992 TO 1993 school year when we were invited to participate on a district portfolio training committee. The committee provided us with the opportunity to train and collaborate with other teachers and administrators who were interested in integrating portfolios into their classrooms or schools. In addition to receiving books and materials on portfolios, our participation on the committee enabled us to attend conferences both in and out of state. In return, our district leader asked only that we do our best to implement what we were learning in our own classes and, when possible, share that knowledge with other interested teachers at our various schools. In addition, some of us might be called on from time to time to present at district or state teacher in-service workshops.

The two of us had known each other professionally for a number of years, but it was through working together on the training committee that we realized just how closely aligned our teaching philosophies and practices were. Throughout the course of our discussions, we not only recognized the potential for extending portfolio use within our own departments but also saw the possibility for portfolio sharing between schools. Because Bonneville Junior High is the main feeder school to Cottonwood High, providing 80 to 90 percent of Cottonwood's sophomore population in any given year, the idea of exploring the potential uses for portfolios between schools seemed both plausible and full of possibility, especially since many of Geri's ninth grade English students ended up each year in Cheri's sophomore English classes.

Our intention in this chapter is to describe our experiences of experimenting with the application of portfolios in our own classrooms, training other teachers at our schools in portfolio practice, and extending the use of portfolios beyond the individual classroom and school. In formulating our thoughts for this piece, we found the discussion revolved around four main issues: What constitutes sound portfolio practice in the language arts classroom? In what ways can teachers work together to develop unified portfolio programs without infringing on the individual teacher's prerogatives? What necessary adaptations must be made as portfolios move between classes, teachers, or schools? And, finally, what roles do state or district mandates play in relation to grass roots portfolio practice?

Finding Our Separate Ways to Classroom Portfolios

Geri's interest in portfolio development began in 1990 when she read various articles on portfolio assessment and attended workshops focusing on ways to manage student-generated writing throughout the course of the school year. Previously, she kept student writing folders in her Bonneville Junior High classes in which she collected all pieces of student writing completed during the school year. Students informally viewed these folders in the spring and then took them home. A logical and practical extension of these folders led to Geri's trying to develop her use of portfolios with one or two classes each year. The portfolios extended the basic writing folder to include student selections of three to five pieces per semester, metacognitive activities, and peer, parent, and teacher reviews. This in turn led to further study of portfolio development and assessment as she gradually reached a level of comfort and flexibility, both philosophically and practically, as evidenced by her inclusion of portfolio work in each of her ninth grade English classes.

Meanwhile, at nearby Cottonwood High, Cheri's use of portfolios in the classroom had also been evolving. By the time she joined the district group, Cheri, too, had been collecting student writing in folders, one for each student, that she stored in a file cabinet in her classroom. The folders contained a wide variety of materials including freewrites, essays, and reading response writings and were excellent vehicles for displaying the range and depth of student writing that Donald Graves writes about in the introduction to *Portfolio Portraits* (Graves 1992).

At the end of each semester, Cheri would distribute the folders to the students, most of whom were surprised at how the collection had grown. As a culminating activity, Cheri had her students compose a folder evaluation, an activity she constructed by combining elements from various reflective writing assignments found in James Moffat's *Active Voice* (Moffat 1991). Although the students initially complained about the assignment, their enthusiasm grew as they perused the contents of their folders. By the time the students completed the assignment, which each then read to the rest of the class, they had discovered or rediscovered much that was good about their writing, themselves as writers, and the uses of writing.

Cheri was more than satisfied with the results. In fact, she was sure she was "doing portfolios." But as she learned more about portfolios through the training committee and reading, in particular Kathleen Yancey's compilation *Portfolios in the Writing Classroom: An Introduction* (Yancey 1992b), she understood she had been depriving her students of one crucial element of sound portfolio practice: ownership. Because she was the gatekeeper of their folders, students had little access, except through her, to their work and, in turn, limited opportunity to control their writing processes and products.

Each of us had been preparing for the work ahead on the portfolio committee in her own way. As experienced writing teachers who believed in using writing for learning and for self-expression, who taught the writing process as the foundation of effective writing, and who relied on peer response as a means of improving our students' writing as well as their sense of community, adding portfolios to our classroom mix was a logical next step. As a result of our training and research, we both restructured our use of writing folders during the 1992 to 1993 school year so that they incorporated the key portfolio elements of collection, selection, and self-reflection. We also turned the responsibility of keeping folders organized and up-to-date over to our students. Having made these necessary changes in our own classes, we were ready to extend our support to those teachers at our schools who showed interest in instituting portfolios in their classes.

Portfolio Development on the Department Level

In 1993, Geri began talking through this course of portfolio investigation and experimentation with members of the Bonneville English department, a few of whom subsequently initiated some type of writing portfolio development within their classrooms. One teacher incorporated portfolios within the context of poetry writing and study. Another used year-end selection and reflection to build portfolios from writing students had evaluated and reflected on over the course of the school year. Each type of portfolio included varying degrees of evidence of process writing, student selection, metacognition, and peer, parent, teacher, and self-evaluation.

These experiments sparked the interest of others within the department who began attending district in-service classes on portfolio development. Under Geri's leadership, her department agreed to incorporate some type of portfolio use within each classroom for the 1993 to 1994 school year. Over the course of that year, they met monthly to share, discuss, modify, and evaluate individual and grade-level portfolio proposals and practices. The four ninth grade teachers agreed to work closely to develop similar and complementary portfolio programs. Their intent was to assemble some form of a portfolio each term, building from term to term and culminating in two types of end-of-the-year portfolios.

The first type would be a personal portfolio which would involve student selection, self-reflection, and evaluation of various writing pieces chosen from the English class, learning logs, and reading responses, as well as some items selected from writing done across the curriculum or outside school. In particular, the ninth grade English team would work with the ninth grade geography teachers to develop cross-curricular writing projects.

The second portfolio would be built from the first and would extend beyond the classroom. This demonstration portfolio would be passed on to Cottonwood High School, which most of the ninth graders would be attending. It would include a letter of introduction and reflection (addressing each piece of writing included as evidence of writing development), one piece of writing focusing on some form of literary analysis, and two other selections. One of these pieces would show evidence of process writing. The purpose of these demonstration portfolios was twofold: to provide students a means of evaluating their own progress as writers throughout their ninth grade year and to give their tenth grade teachers a means of meeting incoming students and their writing abilities. There was no formal assessment for either type of portfolio. Students received full credit for completing their portfolios according to the general guidelines listed above.

At Cottonwood High School, events were proceeding along similar lines. The school received a substantial state education grant for the 1993 to 1994 school year, one feature of which proposed that all sophomore English classes would become portfolio classrooms. During the summer of 1993, the six sophomore English teachers met to develop a guiding philosophy for portfolio use for the coming year. In preparation for their retreat, the teachers read selected materials Cheri culled from the training committee materials and books, along with additional information taken from the Yancey portfolio collection and Linda Rief's *Seeking Diversity* (Rief 1992).

They agreed that portfolios would be an effective tool for increasing student proficiency in English. As such, the portfolios would include all types of writing from in and out of class, reading response logs from students' outside free choice reading (as seen in Rief 1992), peer responses to writing, student self-evaluations of writing, and self-reflections on learning. All six teachers agreed to maintain the general principles and guidelines, although each was free to tailor her approach and the specific portfolio contents to match her individual class aims and student needs. The group planned to meet regularly throughout the year to share their experiences and to assess program development.

Focusing on Developing Practice

The Cottonwood project teachers all followed a similar procedure for managing portfolios. Student folders were stored in the classroom in crates labeled by class, but in contrast to what Cheri had done in previous years, students had access to them at any time and were free to take all or part of the folders home, provided they had what they needed for work in class each day. Students were responsible for keeping their folders organized and up-to-date. Each folder contained a writing log on which students recorded items as they added them to the folder. Students still wrote periodic evaluations of their folders, but because they had access to their folders at all times, reviews were scheduled more frequently than in the past and for a wider variety of purposes. All teachers noticed immediate benefits to this system, including the fact that students were better organized and completed more work. The folders did not necessarily reduce the paper load for teachers, but it did change the way the teachers approached writing with their students. Teachers did not read more although their students did write more. The folders brought control to the high volume of writing generated in the typical English classroom. Self-evaluation and peer review provided feedback to student writers even when teachers did not see papers.

Periodically throughout the year, teachers asked students to compose reflections about the contents of their folders and their language arts progress in general. Depending on the purpose for the evaluation, the structure of the activity varied. For example, early in the quarter, the evaluation focused on the student. Many teachers used questions similar to Linda Rief's reading/writing survey as the basis for this first inventory (Rief 1992). This evaluation then was used as a baseline against which students could measure their progress throughout the year. At midterm the evaluation emphasis would shift to materials in the folders. Students reviewed their work-to-date, noting any changes and finding evidence of improvements and persisting or emerging problems.

At the end of the year, the focus turned to creating the final demonstration portfolio from the works collected throughout the year in the writing folder. Students wrote reflections on selected items from their folders in which they discussed the significance of each work and considered each in terms of achievement. Teachers read the reflections as they perused the portfolios. Teachers who were able to schedule the time conducted portfolio conferences one-on-one with students. These conversations created a sense of closure for both teachers and students. All teachers, regardless of whether they conducted final conferences or not, found that in talking to students about what they learned, they also discovered much about how students learn in their classes, including insight into how they might better serve their students in the future.

Teachers organized their portfolio selection criteria into categorical guidelines rather than listing specific items for inclusion or asking students to freewheel it and create their own portfolio structure. Categories would vary from teacher to teacher, but often would include categories such as the piece of writing the student worked the hardest on, the one the student was most proud of, and the one that taught the student something about writing. Other categories might ask for work that showed all phases of the writing process or that demonstrated exemplary samples of reading response logs or that illustrated progress toward language goals. Teachers also had students select three to five personal choices. These were works students felt revealed something unique about themselves as writers or people. Selections could include finished pieces as well as freewrites or unpolished drafts because the sophomore teachers felt it important to allow students to select from the entire pool of writing for their final portfolio selections in order to let them see that writing is dynamic and that it can be significant and worthwhile during any phase of the writing process.

Most often teachers assigned grades for the portfolios based on whether the student had completed the selection and reflection tasks. Others included a grade for conferencing. Often collection folders were graded based on how complete they were. More significantly, by the end of the year, grades seemed almost superfluous in light of the fact that students had in fact developed a sense of pride in their accomplishments and ownership over the materials that Robert Tierney's research also found. When students were asked at the end of the year what they planned to do with their folders, teachers were surprised by the answer. Most students said they were planning to save all or at least some of the materials they had accumulated. For some, that meant adding to an already ongoing collection they had been keeping since their early school days. For others the writings represented the beginning of a future collection.

Working Across the Curriculum

Meanwhile at Bonneville, Geri found another opportunity for portfolio development, this time outside the English department. During the 1994 to 1995 school year, she began to work with the ninth grade English and geography team at her school to develop cross-curricular term writing projects in conjunction with developing portfolios within the context of the English classes. These cross-curricular projects presented new ways to connect students to learning through portfolios, but they also gave rise to new problems. As the year progressed, she found that constraints arose due to the coordination of English/geography time lines for project completion which prevented her students from generating as much writing of their own choice as they had done in previous years, thus limiting the selections available for their portfolios. The English/geography projects became extensive writing and research projects in and of themselves, often taking most of the quarter to complete. Geri outlined revisions and refinements of the projects for the following year, although she recognized that the time commitment would no doubt remain. In addition, she planned to move from term to semester portfolios in order to allow students more time to experiment with their writing and build a larger base for portfolio selection.

On the other hand, the WAC (Writing Across the Curriculum)-centered portfolios at Bonneville became a composite of experiences that replaced what might have been separate sets of content knowledge. Writing and reflection within the portfolios helped both student and teachers understand and strengthen the connections between subject areas. The first term's poetry project afforded a means of exploring geographical concepts and terms—as well as the physical and cultural geography of various countries—

through metaphor, imagery, and other figurative language. Both students and teachers established connections between geography and English classes, as well as between geography and creative writing. Portfolios were filled with poetry that first term. This project provided a strong, positive beginning for further cross-curricular activities.

Clearly, teachers working as a team to develop portfolio practice within a department or school is one key to effective implementation, but perhaps even more important is the idea that teachers must arrive at the new practice voluntarily rather than by mandate (Yancey 1992b). By the end of the 1993 to 1994 school year, other teachers from Cottonwood's English department had become interested in what the sophomore teachers were doing. Seeing this interest as a chance to possibly expand portfolio usage departmentwide, the teachers asked their tenth grade students to select any three pieces done during the year to send to their next year's English teacher. An accompanying letter served two purposes: after introducing themselves to their prospective teachers, students reviewed their strengths and weaknesses in language arts as well as articulated their expectations for the upcoming year. Furthermore, the letters explained the significance of the three attached pieces of writing. Most teachers accepted these demonstration portfolios in the spirit in which they were sent, namely, as an opportunity to learn a little bit about their incoming students' abilities and needs as they entered their classes. It wasn't long before problems with this proposal began to emerge.

The first problem was possession of materials. When these selections and their accompanying letters left the students' hands in May 1994, they were placed in a central file in the English office where teachers could pick them up when they received their new class lists in the fall. Most teachers returned the portfolios to the proper owners in the fall. However, some portfolios were never picked up. As a result, these student folders remained in the English file for the greater part of the 1994 to 1995 school year where they did no one any good, especially those students who owned the materials. Short of giving up entirely, the sophomore team agreed there must be an alternative for the following year.

At the end of the 1994 to 1995 school year, the sophomores wrote letters to junior English teachers again, as had been done by other tenth graders the year before. They did not, however, select pieces of writing to pass along with the letters. Instead their teachers advised the students to keep track of their portfolios over the summer with the express purpose that their junior English teacher might ask them to bring in some writing from the year before. The sophomore teachers then added a new category to the final portfolio selection guide. They asked students to list three to five selections they would present to their next year's teachers if asked to do so in the fall and to explain their choices. The writings will leave the students' possession only at that time. While this solves the problems of rightful possession, it is not a perfect solution, of course. Some teachers will never ask students for their work; some students will not keep their portfolios. But at least the writing stays in the hands of the rightful owners while those teachers who are interested in expanding their opportunities for getting to know their students will still have the opportunity to do so.

The second problem highlighted by the situation at Cottonwood is teacher involvement. While other teachers expressed an interest in receiving the sophomore portfolios, enough failed to follow through with picking up the materials to make the sophomore group reconsider the efficacy of passing portfolios from grade to grade. Likewise, some teachers said they were curious about ways to use portfolios in their classes, but only two actually added some type of portfolio to their classrooms. In order for portfolio programs to work on a departmentwide or even broader base, teachers must be willing to use portfolios in their teaching. They must see that portfolios can work for them, their students, and their curriculum. Without that vision, no amount of coaxing or coercion will result in a successful transformation to a portfolio-based classroom.

Connecting Schools Through Portfolios

Our affiliation with the district committee and with each other has continued since those first meetings in 1992. Since that time, one of our primary considerations has been how to coordinate portfolio practice between our schools, in particular between the ninth and tenth grade teachers. Because Bonneville is Cottonwood's main feeder, we sought to establish continuity and a closer articulation between what happens to our students in the seventh, eighth, and ninth grades and what can reasonably be expected of them in grades ten, eleven, and twelve. We saw the potential for portfolios to bridge the gap between junior and senior high.

We found ourselves in the position of acting as liaisons for the teachers in our departments in creating a plan for passing portfolios from school to school. We also found that in spite of the failed efforts at passing folders from tenth to eleventh grade at Cottonwood, the sophomore teachers welcomed the idea of receiving portfolios from Bonneville students who would enter in the fall of 1995. The portfolios arrived at Cottonwood in June 1995. As mentioned earlier, the junior high portfolios included a letter of introduction, reflections on one work of literary analysis, and two personal selections. At this writing, the folders are waiting to be picked up from the Cottonwood English office by sophomore teachers as soon as they have received their final class rolls.

Benefits of Grassroots Development

Our experiences over the past few years have enabled us to see the benefits to both students and teachers of using portfolios in the classroom. The greatest advantage for students is the opportunity portfolios provide for reflecting on their learning process and progress. Another advantage is that portfolios help students develop good organizational skills. By keeping a writing log of all their folder entries and keeping their folders organized, students learn a systematic way to track assignments and work completed. Another unanticipated result teachers saw in their students was that the mere act of accumulating work in one place gave some previously reluctant students the impetus to produce more. The portfolios gave writing a place to be and a reason to exist beyond the teacher's assignment.

For teachers, the greatest benefit is flexibility in terms of teaching style and course content. This was a crucial element in introducing portfolios to our coworkers at Bonneville and Cottonwood. At both schools, the writing portfolio was an excellent vehicle for making connections, within, between, and across subject materials. Learning logs, reader response journals, research papers (including all preparatory materials), historical fiction, poetry, essays, freewrite lists, and quick writes all found a place in the writing portfolios.

Perhaps the most profound benefit we have observed at our schools has been the creation of new communities of teachers working together and supporting each other in the face of both our successes and setbacks. Sharing philosophies, developing practice, and establishing standards collaboratively with our coworkers has opened new communities of discussion within and between our schools. In doing so, we have redefined or at least reconsidered what it means to be a teacher within our various teaching environments. As a result, we have new-found respect for our coworkers, from whom we learn and find support. Coming together with others in this common project has shown us how to break through the artificial boundaries of subject matter, grade level, experience, and course content that William Condon writes so vigorously about in chapter thirteen of this volume.

As much as we have sought opportunities to collaborate with other teachers, we have reserved the right of teachers to create their own patterns for portfolio purpose and content. Moreover, because all of us encourage our students to develop both range and depth as readers, writers, and learners, we reject standardized, top-down, mandated portfolio programs, in spite of the fact that our own portfolio projects have been funded from state and district sources.

We are guided by the idea expressed by Catharine Lucas in the Introduction to *Portfolios in the Writing Classroom* that the most effective assessment of student ability takes place at the classroom level (Lucas 1992). We recognize that local and state school boards are interested in promoting the use of portfolios in any classroom. We applaud the efforts of schools and districts such as our own which support the development of portfolio programs at the grassroots level. However, we part ways with those states or districts which have turned to portfolios as a formal means of alternative assessment or those that deny teachers or principals any choice as to whether or how portfolios will be implemented and to what ends they will be used. Mandated portfolio assessment can lead to confusion and demoralization as in the case of Vermont (ASCD Update 1994).

In *Detecting Growth in Language*, James Moffat argues convincingly against the use of standardized tests as valid measures of learning. He writes: "But standards don't have to be set by *tests* and in fact *cannot* be set by tests, because standards are ideas of excellence that will always exceed what standardized instruments can afford to measure." In point of fact, he claims that standardized testing has led to learning standards being lowered rather than being raised for no other reason than they must "accommodate the masses." For Moffat, the answer to the assessment crises lies in "the three Ps—performances, portfolios, and projects" (Moffat 1991). We subscribe to Moffat's view. Through vehicles such as these we can see the complexity of our students' various learning environments. We also believe that the farther from the point of origin that learning is assessed, the more rigid and limiting the standards must be to assure accountability and reliability, a point implicit in Moffat as well. Likewise, district or statewide portfolio standards, because they define tasks that are achievable by the majority of those being assessed, might also lead to the mediocritization of achievement. Minimal standards open the door to minimal effort for many, if not for most, a situation antithetical to education in general and portfolio practice in particular.

Those of us at Bonneville and Cottonwood who have viewed firsthand the power of portfolios would no doubt resist any efforts by district or state officials to institutionalize portfolio practice in Utah should the occasion for such action ever arise. We prefer to continue exploring the possibilities portfolios offer with our students and in conjunction with other like-minded teachers. We prefer our current level of practice—changeable, dynamic, and engaging—to any generalized portfolio program that would be doable for most, but stimulating to none. We would like to reserve the right to let the portfolios speak for our students within the context of our classrooms. In a world of such static achievement indicators as grades and standardized tests, the portfolio stands out as a dynamic portrait of student interest and ability.

7

Of Large-Mouth Milk Jugs, Cosmic Trash Compactors, and Renewal Machines

Reflections on a Multi-task Portfolio Assessment

Charlotte W. O'Brien

THE EMPHASIS ON PERFORMANCE ASSESSMENT HAS ENCOURAGED EDUCATORS to seek ways to actively involve students in authentic activities which are challenging and interesting. As an English language arts consultant working to help classroom teachers bridge the gap between theory and practice, I know that performance assessment should also model and support good instruction. Without a doubt, writing portfolios in the classroom have this potential. Is it also possible for such potential to be supported through large-scale portfolio assessment? I believe that it is.

Portfolios provide a forum of understanding for both learners and teachers. This occurs for the learner, when, as Yancey observes, "The writer's pieces are not seen so much in isolation or relative to others' pieces, but rather relative to the writer's own development as represented in the portfolio" (Yancey 1992b, 106). It occurs for teachers when they no longer find themselves asking the question, "Now that I've got all these portfolios, what do I do with them?" In *A Fresh Look at Writing*, Graves explains, "The portfolio can serve as a medium for teaching and learning as well as for evaluation . . . External evaluations can be satisfied if the main emphasis is on the student as the improving/learning writer" (Graves 1994, 174). Murphy and Smith concur, "Portfolios can integrate assessment and good practice. When the two complement each other—good practice and assessment both requiring purposeful, contextualized tasks performed in authentic situations—they can serve the learner and the learning" (Murphy and Smith 1992, 59). I know that this can happen with writing portfolios in the classroom. I also believe that it can occur in a *multi-task portfolio* assessment such as the one I developed and piloted for possible use as part of a communication arts statewide assessment. This type of *event*, to use an assessment term, incorporates reading, writing, speaking, listening, viewing, and visually representing ideas and information. Students complete a series of tasks which lead them to compose a culminating piece of writing and to reflect about these tasks and about themselves as readers, writers and thinkers.

The use of portfolios in large-scale assessments, however, is a hotly debated issue. In fact, Lucas, in her powerful indictment of large-scale portfolio assessment, identifies the "co-option [of portfolios] by large-scale external testing programs" as one of the three major pitfalls that must be contended with if the portfolio movement is going to realize its potential. Certainly this danger must be considered. Yet I believe a carefully crafted large-scale portfolio assessment may be used hand-in-hand with portfolios in the classroom to support what Lucas describes as "evaluation in the service of learning" (Lucas 1992, 11).

The Multi-task Portfolio

Writing portfolios most often contain a variety of pieces composed and selected over a period of time. I view this as a *horizontal* approach. In contrast, the portfolios discussed in this chapter provide a window into each student's thinking and writing at a certain point in time. I see this as a *vertical* approach. According to Yancey, the defining features of the *horizontal* portfolio include collection, selection, reflection, diversity, evaluation, and communication. *Vertical* portfolios are much the same although they are more akin to "slice of life" vignettes. They, too, contain diverse collections of written responses. The choices, however, are made by students in how they respond to the tasks. They communicate their thoughts through writing and reflecting. Finally, readers evaluate the portfolios holistically using a rubric. (See the Appendix for the multi-task portfolio rubric.)

For five class periods, seventh and eighth graders performed seven tasks in response to a student-produced video and a collection of written materials. The resource booklet contained letters, short articles, an editorial, charts and graphs, a cartoon, a poem, and fun facts all reflecting some aspect of the theme, "Renewable Resources and Energy Efficiency." Students worked cooperatively in small groups, as well as individually, discussing the resources and sharing ideas with each other. As they processed information presented in a variety of formats, they were required to: 1) demonstrate understanding and processing of the content—"I understand"; 2) produce evidence which enabled the reader to understand the content—"I can help you understand"; and 3) write reflectively about the thinking and writing which occurred as they responded to the tasks and developed their written responses—"I can show you how I understand." Teachers served as facilitators, free to ask and answer appropriate questions but not to make suggestions or corrections concerning students' responses to the tasks.

Tasks and Responses

Tasks one to three actively involved students and stimulated their thinking about the many different problems and solutions associated with the topic under consideration. Students were free to discuss their ideas related to the theme, tasks, and resources, but they wrote individual responses. Tasks four to six encouraged students to use process-writing strategies as they developed a thoughtful response to the theme. Task seven gave them the opportunity to reflect about their work and about themselves as thinkers, readers and writers.

Task One: Writing A Summary

After discussing with several classmates the twelve-minute video which offered tips to save energy around the house, each student wrote a letter to a friend responding to the information presented in the video. Students liked the informality of the letter format, and their voices came through clearly. Even though they were critical of the video, its offbeat humor got them thinking about the topic in an enjoyable way.

Colleen's response:

> Maggie—
>
> We just watched a video in English. It was about saving energy. I guess it was OK but it wasn't my favorite. It was good, though, considering kids wrote it. Anyway, it showed how you can save energy in each room—the kitchen, living room, bathroom, bedroom, and basement. It told us to do things such as take shorter showers, fill the freezer with gallons of water, and get more energy

saving light bulbs. If I could change anything about it, I'd probably give it some better jokes and the actors be a tad less enthusiastic. Overall, it was educational and got the point across.

See you!
Colleen

Brad's Response:

Dan,

My group did not like the video much at all. We thought that it was weird and sort of for kids maybe under our age group such as 3rd or 4th graders. Even though I did not like the movie it kind of got a good point across about how and where to save energy in the home. The video didn't really teach me anything that I didn't know already. I guess that is why I didn't care for it too much. Well, how did you and the group you're in like it? That's all I've got to say, bye.

Your Friend,
Brad

Task Two: Identifying Important Ideas/Themes

In groups of four or five, students read and discussed assigned pages from the resource booklet which included information presented in a variety of formats (e.g., letter, editorial, chart, cartoon, etc.) to understand how these related to the theme of renewable resources and energy efficiency. Each student was responsible for reporting to a second group about the main ideas or themes in the resources her or his group reviewed; however, all students had the complete resource booklet to which they might refer at any time during the assessment.

Task Three: Drawing Conclusions

After forming new groups which included at least one representative from each of the groups in Task Two, students briefly summarized the gist of the resources reviewed in their previous groups and listened as others did the same. Then, noting that people draw many different conclusions when they gather information from various sources, students individually wrote down several conclusions concerning the resource material which made the most sense to them. Examples of seventh grade responses included the following:

- We have improved in reusing and recycling but we definitely need to do even better. We need to better use our renewable energy and improve our water quality. We need to recycle all recyclable things and get kids to become environmentally involved because the future is in their hands. If we don't, we will end mankind.

- I think that we waste too much trash. We don't recycle and reuse things enough. People are always writing articles, and drawing charts, graphs, and cartoons like the ones we've read. But a lot of people still don't reuse and recycle, and we need to think of another way to get people to reuse and recycle.
- We need to be concerned for the future, which meens [*sic*] reusing, conserving, and not pretending like "we" own the earth, for we "are nothing but a strand in the web of life."

(In the last example, the student is referring to a poem attributed to Chief Seattle which was included in the resource booklet. When she composed her piece for the culminating task, she chose to write a poem.)

Tasks Four to Seven: Generating Ideas, Organizing Ideas, Writing About a Problem or Issue, Reflecting About Your Thinking

These tasks replicate those usually included in process writing assessments—with the addition of the reflective section. Students talked with each other about ideas they might develop and about how they might plan their written responses to the theme presented in the resource booklet. In addition, they also looked back at any of the resources and previous tasks they thought might help. Marsha Sisson, who piloted the assessment, observed, "These [performance] assessments on the whole tend to be somewhat linear in nature. This multi-task activity isn't at all. Thanks. Students are going to their earlier tasks to find information. They are also rereading the resources."

The freedom to clarify and solidify thinking on a topic through interaction with others and with resources did not, as one might suppose, lead to copying ideas but to creativity. The following directions prompted students to write about a problem or issue in Task Six: "You have viewed, read and discussed a variety of materials which touched on the theme—renewable resources and energy efficiency. In the twenty-first century, we will have to make many important decisions related to this subject. In many cases, there are no easy answers. There is usually more than one side to the story. Now it is time for you to give your opinion about a problem, issue, solution, plan, or invention concerning renewable resources and energy efficiency." Students seemed more confident in their ability to complete the longer written piece; they knew they had something to say about the topic. Finally, they were able to share important insights about their thinking and writing processes.

Portfolio Examples

Six portfolios containing Tasks Four to Seven demonstrate more completely the progression of students' ideas and insights. After generating ideas through brainstorming and prewriting for Task Four, students wrote a focus statement at the top of the page. For Task Five they wrote down the main idea before making note of details or possibilities they might include.

Brenda's Portfolio

Task Four: Generating Ideas
Figure 1

I WILL WRITE MY PAPER ABOUT Solar Power as an Alternative to electricity.

water pollution
wasting electricity
recycling
{ Solar power
over use of electricity (skylights)

Task Five: Organizing Ideas
Figure 2

MAIN IDEA: We need to conserve electricity

QUESTIONS TO DECIDE	DETAILS OR POSSIBILITIES
AUDIENCE? FORMAT? BEGINNING?	It will be a letter to my best friend, alison Walz, so she will be my audience. The beginning will an example of how my family has started conserving electricity by keeping lights of or low.
ISSUE/PROBLEM? MAIN POINTS?	The issue or problem is that too many americans waste a lot of electricity. Some of the main points are that we need to conserve our electricity and a lot of people would save on their electricity bills as well as save the world.
DETAILS/EXAMPLES?	My parents started punishing us if we don't turn off lights when we're not around, and bought a dimmer switch to put on our dining room light. That skylights and windows let in alot of light and are cheaper too
CONCLUSION?	The conclusion will be that I will ask her to please conserve electricity the way that my family does, because even if we do just a little, it will still help our planet

For Task Six, Writing about a Problem or Issue, Brenda wrote a personal letter.

Dear Alice,

What's ⇑? My parents have become total energy efficiency freaks. At first, I thought they were just being mean, because they'd punish me for leaving the light in my bedroom on when I was some place else. Then I decided they were just being weird, because I'd walk into the kitchen and find my mom cooking with the only light coming from an open window. I just didn't understand—I've always been a person who hated dim rooms. When I brought these points up to my mom, she sat me down on the couch and gave me a little talk. Actually, it was a long talk. But what she basically said was that she and my dad both agreed that too many Americans waste a lot of electricity, and that they decided that doing even just their share would benefit the environment. And keeping the lights off would lower the electricity bill, anyway. They're even thinking of putting in a skylight in our living room. I hope they do. Skylights are neat.

I wrote this letter because now I want to conserve electricity, too. I'm never in trouble for leaving lights on anymore. And I want you to get your family to become as energy efficient as mine. Just tell your parents that we should all do our part. And if that doesn't work, point out that they'll save money. It'll work. And maybe, if you write a letter like this to someone else, it'll be even one more thing that'll help the earth.

—♡ ya,

Brenda

After drafting and revising their papers in Task Six, students answered the following questions about their thinking and writing for Task Seven:

1. What task did you like best and why?
2. What task was the most difficult and why?
3. How do you get ideas for writing about a topic?
4. What connections did you make between Task Six and the tasks that preceded it?
5. What do you think is important for your reader to know about you as a writer and thinker?

I have taken the liberty of consolidating Brenda's responses to these questions into a paragraph. Brenda explained:

> I liked writing the best, because I like doing creative things like that instead of evaluating things and summarizing things. I think Task Three was the hardest, because I am bad at coming up with conclusions to things, and evaluating them on my own. To get ideas I think about other things I've read about that topic, and other things I've heard, seen, or done about that topic. The tasks that preceded Task Six got me ready for writing. They gave me information to work with, and ideas to use. As a writer, I like to write what I want, not have a defined topic, or way of writing. As a thinker, often it's hard for me to get ideas, but most of the time, once I get one, I can't stop!

Earlier in Task Three (drawing conclusions), Brenda wrote, "we need to think of another way to get people to reuse and recycle." When she generated ideas in Task Four, she thought she would write about solar power as an alternative to electricity. In Task Five she did a good job planning her paper. It's interesting that she decided to use the letter format. The response to Task One was a letter, and several of the selections in the resource booklet were letters to the editor. Notice she said she gets her ideas from reading and from what she has heard, seen, or done. She listed only a few in Task Four, and they were all very broad, with the exception of the word *skylights* which was an afterthought. In the letter to Alice, Brenda does not copy what she has written from the chart, but she does incorporate those ideas into the body of the letter. According to Brenda, the hard part was coming up with an idea, but we can agree with her that once she found one, she had no problem writing about it.

Joey's Portfolio

Task Four: Generating Ideas
Figure 3

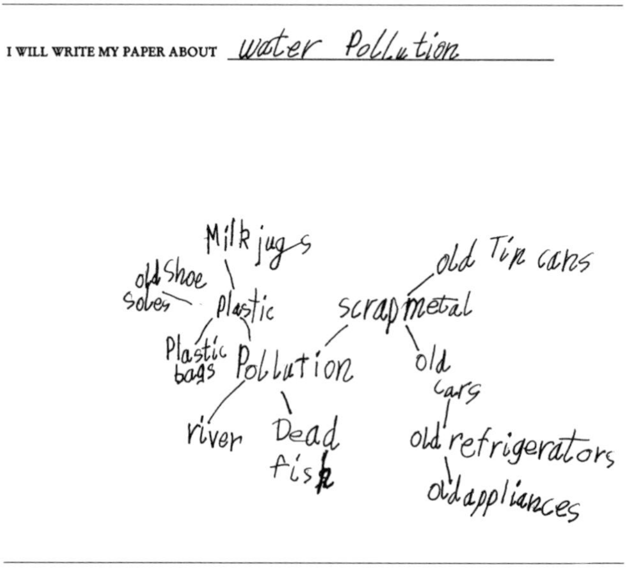

I WILL WRITE MY PAPER ABOUT water Pollution

Milk jugs
old Shoe soles
Plastic
Plastic bags
Pollution
river
Dead fish
scrap metal
old Tin cans
old cars
old refrigerators
old appliances

Task Five: Organizing Ideas
Figure 4

MAIN IDEA: We need to stop stream and lakepollution

QUESTIONS TO DECIDE	DETAILS OR POSSIBILITIES
AUDIENCE? FORMAT? BEGINNING?	teacher, classmates Poem
ISSUE/PROBLEM? MAIN POINTS?	Pollution fishing stream pollution
DETAILS/EXAMPLES?	catching milk jugs instead of fish, tires
CONCLUSION?	no fish just trash.

Joey wrote a poem for Task Six:

Large Mouth Milk Jugs

Going fishing,
Going fishing,
Gonna have some fun,
Burning in the sun.
Whearing my gas mask to breath
Our fresh clean air,
When we get home we'll have to
get the tar out of are underwear.

Polluting,
Polluting,
It was Incesticides,
I wish we could change,
Or ever rearrange.
The pain is great,
The stench is strong,
If we only relized whats going on.

Joey's case illustrates one of the problems encountered in performance assessments which are done over a period of days or weeks. Joey was absent for several days and did not have a chance to make revisions or complete the reflective task. We can tell from what he wrote that a lot of thinking was going on. Notice he does not mention large-mouth milk jugs in the body of the poem, but the picture of a pond where large-mouth bass used to be easily caught comes to mind immediately—except now it is polluted, and the only things the fishermen catch are large-mouth milk jugs and other trash. I wish we had Joey's reflective writing because now I see what an important piece that is in understanding his thinking processes.

Jake's Portfolio

Task Four: Generating Ideas
Figure 5

Task Five: Organizing Ideas
Figure 6

MAIN IDEA: WAter Supply

QUESTIONS TO DECIDE	DETAILS OR POSSIBILITIES
AUDIENCE? FORMAT? BEGINNING?	I Am writing to peoples house holds to watch diffront how much water they use A day.
ISSUE/PROBLEM? MAIN POINTS?	(P) To much water is being wasted In missouri (I) I'm tri to Stop it (m) WAter.
DETAILS/EXAMPLES?	We Are lossing millions Of gawEns of wAter A year.
CONCLUSION?	put A stop to wasting water And cAlling pluse writing to people to stop.

Jake wrote a letter to the editor for Task Six:

Figure 7

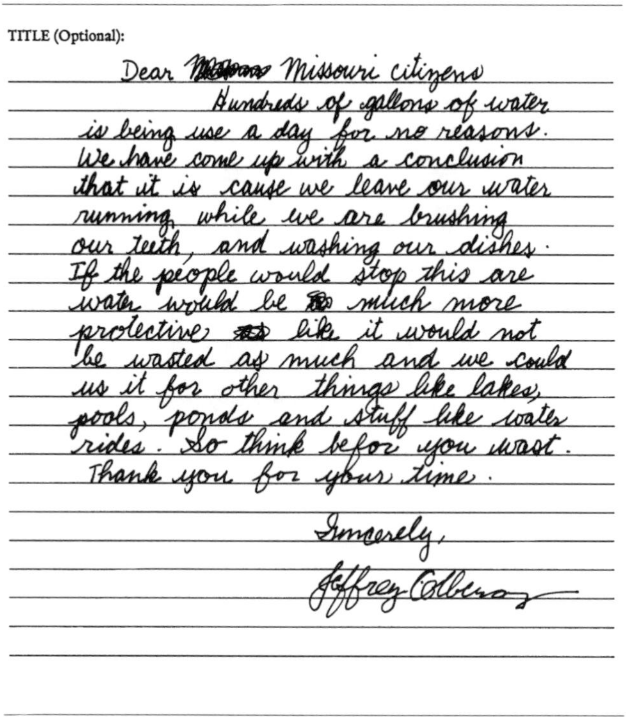

TITLE (Optional):

Dear Missouri citizens
Hundreds of gallons of water
is being use a day for no reasons.
We have come up with a conclusion
that it is cause we leave our water
running while we are brushing
our teeth, and washing our dishes.
If the people would stop this are
water would be much more
protective like it would not
be wasted as much and we could
us it for other things like lakes,
pools, ponds and stuff like water
rides. So think befor you wast.
Thank you for your time.

Sincerely,
Jeffrey Colberson

Jake picked up on the information contained in the video (which showed lots of ways to save water around the house). His letter is much more forceful than those contained in the resource booklet. He has given facts and examples, projected what might happen if people stopped wasting water, admonished Missouri citizens, and remembered to be polite. Jake explained about his thinking and writing: "The task I really liked was Task Two because I like reading educational stuff that I never knew before. Task Six was the hardest because I didn't know how to put my words into writing. I get ideas for my topic by reading diffront things. I really just read. When I read I don't only think I also study."

Jake has a reading/viewing strategy that works and his interest in "educational stuff" provided some of the details for his letter.

Dillon's Portfolio

Task Four: Generating Ideas
Figure 8

I WILL WRITE MY PAPER ABOUT how to get rid of all the garbage that is building up. You can send it to the ~~mantle~~ mantle in the earth where it will burn and no pollution will be given.

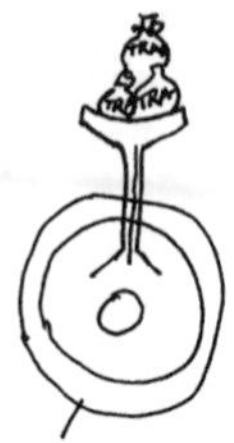

Earth Split Open

Task Five: Organizing Ideas
Figure 9

MAIN IDEA: How to get rid of trash that is building

QUESTIONS TO DECIDE	DETAILS OR POSSIBILITIES
AUDIENCE? FORMAT? BEGINNING?	The Resident will lissen. The format will be an editorial so I can get the point that I want to get across. The beginning will state the problem and what we should do about it.
ISSUE/PROBLEM? MAIN POINTS?	The trash is building up very fast and we're running out of places to put it and scientists aren't getting many ideas except to put it in space. People need to start worrying about it because soon its going to.
DETAILS/EXAMPLES?	Every year 50 million Tons of trash in the United States alone. Millions of Countries are cleaning except us.
CONCLUSION?	We need to start thingh about our world and where to put the trash.

For Task Six, Dillon wrote an expository paragraph:

> What to Do About Trash
>
> The United States is one of the most wasteful contries [*sic*] in the world. Trash builds up constantly and landfills are filling up just as fast as we throw it out in the ocean where we think it will sink to the bottom and it won't effect anyone. But really it does. The chemicals leak and pollute the oceans, trash starts to float to the shores where people swim. Our country really needs to start thinking about how we are going to deal with trash. My best idea was that we could build a channel through the Earth's crust and into the mantle. We could have all major trash fills be loaded up and dumped where they would be burned instantly. It is so hot at the mantle that if the trash let off pollution, the pollution would be burned also. So you see we really do need to start thinking about our world.

Dillon reflected:

> [On the task he liked best] Drawing because it is fun to think of really neat ways trash can be desposed [*sic*] of. [On the task he found most difficult] Identifying important ideas because we had to find so much information and write it down. [On getting ideas for writing] Usually I just stop and think about what's going on in the world today and that gives me ideas. [On connections] The tasks before it just organized and gathered information about a subject and then you tie it all together in Task Six. [On himself as a writer and thinker] I come up with very different ideas about things and my topics are strange.

Dillon stayed with the idea he came up with in the drawing and used most of what he wrote in the chart, but he did not indicate in Task Six that the intended audience for the editorial was the president of the United States. Maybe he dropped this idea altogether, or maybe that was still his intention—but he forgot to inform his readers. We can agree with him that his ideas are very different, but knowing that he stops and thinks about what is going on in the world today gives us confidence in him as a thinker. (Years later, when we are disposing of trash in the way Dillon suggested, remember. You first heard about it right here!)

Kara's Portfolio

Task Four: Generating Ideas
Figure 10

I WILL WRITE MY PAPER ABOUT Recycling

Task Five: Organizing Ideas
Figure 11

MAIN IDEA: We need to recycle if we're going to save the planet

QUESTIONS TO DECIDE	DETAILS OR POSSIBILITIES
AUDIENCE? FORMAT? BEGINNING?	Mrs. Sisson / People who want to read this I don't know yet! Article ? ← Format
ISSUE/PROBLEM? MAIN POINTS?	We need to recycle more OFTEN!! If we don't recycle, we'll run out of resources, and have to spend our money on research for finding new power methods (of production)
DETAILS/EXAMPLES?	If everyone would take time to recycle, the world would be cleaner, and we'd be a lot better off. Everyone needs to do their share, because we're all in this together.
CONCLUSION?	If we don't recycle, we're like a ship in the middle of the desert there's not much we can do.

Kara decided to write a short article for Task Six:

Why Recycle?

"Why recycle?" That's what lots of people ask. "Why should I recycle if everyone else does? Isn't that enough?" Those, too are popular. What many people don't realize is that we're running out of our natural resources. Things like oil, coal, and other resources are running out. We won't have them around forever. Someday, when we run out, we won't have much of a choice.

We'll have to find another energy source.

It's not just about energy, though. Plastic is made from oil. Recycling plastic will save some oil, as well as some space in a landfill. What many people don't realize is the simple facts: recycling is easy, inexpensive, and good for the earth. What could be better?

What about paper? Every Sunday, thousands (no, this is not an exaggeration) of trees are used to make America's Sunday newspapers. If people would recycle paper, less trees would have to be used.

Aluminum cans? No problem! Take them to the store. You'll get five to ten cents for each one. The same can be done with glass bottles.

In short, recycling is a great thing. So, before you go to the store, put your old milk jugs, cardboard, paper bags, aluminum cans, glass bottles, and cracked Tupperware into the car, and do something nice for Mother Nature.

When Kara reflected about herself as a thinker and writer, she wrote:

> I liked Task Four best because I love clustering. I get so many ideas out, it's lots of fun. Task Five was the hardest for me. I'm not an organized thinker. When I write, I like to just let the pen go, so my words flow out onto paper. I don't write as well when I'm constantly referring to a chart. When I clustered, I noticed I kept getting ideas about recycling. I figured I had a lot of ideas, enough so I wouldn't get Writer's Block, so I decided it was the right topic for me. Tasks One to Five sort of build up until you've been assigned a paper, so it's not such a shock. It makes you aware, and you have more ideas that way. I don't like organized writing. To me, there's nothing worse. I like to let my ideas flow, not harden in my head.

Although Kara ended up with a well-organized paper, it was a struggle for her. Many students (and teachers) who go through the motions of clustering just make an outline in circles. For Kara, however, clustering is a tool that really works. She likes to go with the flow that clustering enables her to generate. Consequently, Task Five was a hindrance rather than a help to her; yet it did make her mindful that she needed to work to organize her paper. She explains that the preliminary tasks got her thinking about the topic, so writing the paper was not such a shock. Consider that for a minute. Did you ever think that a writing assignment out of the blue is like someone throwing a bucket of cold water in your face? That's the feeling a lot of students experience, especially when they have little confidence in themselves as writers. Kara, however, is not one of these. She has plenty of ideas, and even though she resists categorizing them in a linear fashion, I really don't think they have "hardened" in her head.

Barak's Portfolio

Task Four: Generating Ideas
Figure 12

I WILL WRITE MY PAPER ABOUT Using things even when they get old, and not throw them away.

Paper about:

Ideas

1.) recycling—as a whole
2.) landfills
3.) Styrofoam
4.) Plastic
5.) electric cars
6.) solar power and energy
7.) catilitic converters
8.) geothermal power plants
9.) nuclear power
10.) mass transportation
11.) things made out of trash
12.) Packaging of items
13.) The recycling process
14.) Using things even when theyget old, and not throw them away
15.) Replanting trees

Task Five: Organizing Ideas
Figure 13

MAIN IDEA: Use things even when they get old

QUESTIONS TO DECIDE	DETAILS OR POSSIBILITIES
AUDIENCE? FORMAT? BEGINNING?	classmates, teacher, Charlotte O'brien persuavive essay. Question?
ISSUE/PROBLEM? MAIN POINTS?	Use things till they wear out 1. Save old thing 2. use till worn out 3. Do not throw away use for something else
DETAILS/EXAMPLES?	the machine will change old run-down things into new fresh shiny things.
CONCLUSION?	we shold all do our part to save. the environment. Using things again and again certanly helps!

For Task Six, Barak wrote a fictionalized account of an invention which will save the world:

The Renewal Machine

Before the Renewal Machine we were a wasteful, trash-filled society. And we still would have been if not for this marvelous invention of Professor E. Pluribus Unum. The Renewal Machine works as simple as it sounds. You simply put an old rundown item into the machine, push the button and—zap—its [*sic*] just like brand new! Oh, by the way, since new machines can be made from one (1) Renewal Machine, they're free! All right then here's an example. Ordinary scrapaper [*sic*]. You find scrapaper around the house all the time. Now, instead of throwing it in the trash as you would have before, put the paper in the machine, push the button and look! You've got brand new paper! Even more than you had in the beginning. Now, let's look at a harder example. Take a computer for instance. An old, broken, out-of-date computer. Again, put it in the machine, push the button, and—zap—a brand new, working, top-of-the-line computer! Impressed? There is also another feature. The Renewal Machine shrinks or enlarges to the size of the item, so that it does not take up much

> space. This system is great, although it does have one side effect. To most earth-loving people this effect is great, but for earth-hating energy wasting people, its their worst nightmare. As a person uses the machine, he or she gets kinder, more energy efficient, and his or her drive to save the planet increases to the point where a person no longer needs the machine. Then he or she may pass on the Renewal Machine to a new person so that it may work its magic on them. The cycle will go on and on until no one will ever waste again. This machine will not only save our planet but bring peace to all countries of the world. There will be no hunger because the Renewal Machine can also turn something into nothing. An example: Take the scraps from your meal, put them in the machine and then, five minutes later you literally have a meal that could feed the entire country. And there will be no homelessness because a homeless person can turn his cardboard box into a three story mansion. As Professor E. Pluribus Unum once said, "The Renewal Machine is limited only by the imagination."

Barak explained that he liked Task Four best because it is easy for him to think of ideas. He writes:

> Although this was my favorite, I pretty much enjoyed all 'tasks.' But I do not think 'task' was a good word for the items since they were so fun! I thought Task Six was the most difficult because it was where all the tasks became important. Most of the time, I get ideas off the top of my head. But sometimes I get ideas while I read, watch TV, or just from being outside. Lots of times I get ideas from listening to music. Without all the other tasks it would have been very difficult to do Task Six. I get ideas out of nowhere. When I think something is very good, most people think they're strange or impossible. Well, to me anything is possible and anything can be good. That is the reason I am so creative and think the way I do.

When we look back at Barak's Task Four, we see the number and variety of his ideas. At this point there is no clue that he will come up with the renewal machine. In Task Five he stays with his main idea—to use things when they get old—but doesn't really progress much on paper until he starts to think about details or examples he wants to include. This is where he has his brainstorm: "The machine will change old rundown things into new fresh shiny things." His idea for a conclusion sounds pretty run-of-the-mill in Task Five; however, notice how it plays out in his paper: "As a person uses the machine, he or she gets kinder, more energy efficient, and his or her drive to save the planet increases to the point where a person no longer needs the machine." Now Barak is really cooking! This wonderful machine will solve all the problems of the world. Barak knows that his strength is his creativity and feels confident that he can take a "strange or impossible" idea and turn it into something good!

Conclusion

By taking advantage of the social nature of language-learning, the assessment supported a risk-free environment in which all students were able to obtain some measure of success. Interest remained high throughout the assessment. Students developed a strong sense of ownership, and a number of them wanted to include their multi-task portfolios as part of their class portfolios. In addition, their teachers were surprised at the variety and creativity displayed in the written responses to the tasks.

Not only does the multi-task portfolio provide excellent examples of why reflection about writing and thinking are so important to consider—for both student and teacher—it also enables teachers who have not had time to incorporate portfolios into their curriculum to participate in portfolio evaluation and analysis. Hopefully, this experience will serve to inspire these teachers to make portfolios an integral part of the writing curriculum in their classrooms.

Teachers whose students participated in a later pilot of the multi-task portfolio met together to develop an appropriate rubric (see Appendix) and then used the rubric to score the portfolios; however, they did not score the work of their own students. At the end of the scoring session, they left with their students' portfolios and were able to return these the next day. Teachers commented that their involvement in this project was one of the best professional development opportunities they had ever had.

As research and practice continue to inform us about writing and writing instruction, we must develop assessment models which encompass these findings. Camp explains that writers use different approaches and strategies to accomplish the same task; that they switch among processes and strategies depending upon their perceptions and plans for addressing the task; that they learn in process from each other; and that it is important for them to become aware of how they go about writing and how they think about it. Through assessments such as the one I have described, students enthusiastically take responsibility for their own learning; teachers see themselves as co-conspirators rather than omniscient purveyors of knowledge. Both class portfolios and large-scale multi-task portfolio assessments provide fertile ground for supporting a learner-centered curriculum as well as for increasing our understanding of how students learn. The multi-task portfolios described here, developed as part of a statewide communications arts assessment, demonstrate how portfolio pedagogy can encourage large-scale assessments which are compatible with instructional goals. In the development of performance assessments that support theory and practice, we are, as Professor E. Pluribus Unum would say, "limited only by our imagination."

Appendix

Missouri Multi-task Portfolio Rubric

(4) An *Outstanding Portfolio* contains evidence of

- superior understanding of resources as demonstrated in task responses
- strong connections between ideas and tasks
- fresh and/or insightful conclusions
- strong control of language, vocabulary, and sentence structure
- creative approach and individual perspective
- writer's message clearly unimpeded by errors in conventions and mechanics
- reflective statements that clarify task responses and explain strategies/processes

(3) An *On-Track Portfolio* contains evidence of

- clear understanding of resources demonstrated in task responses
- obvious connections between ideas and tasks
- logical conclusions
- clear control of language, vocabulary, and sentence structure
- some creativity of approach and individual perspective
- writer's message unimpeded by errors in conventions and mechanics
- reflective statements that are relevant but may not be specific

(2) An *Emerging Portfolio* contains evidence of

- basic understanding of resources in task responses
- limited connections between ideas and tasks
- facts restated in attempt to draw own conclusions
- limited control of language, vocabulary, and sentence structure
- little creativity of approach and/or individual perspective
- writer's message that may be inhibited by frequent errors in conventions or mechanics
- reflective statements that are minimal and general

(1) An *Underdeveloped Portfolio* contains evidence of

- little or no understanding of resources and/or tasks
- little or no attempt at connecting ideas and/or tasks
- facts copied or restated rather than drawing own conclusions
- lack of control of language, vocabulary, and/or sentence structure
- lack of creativity of approach and individual perspective
- writer's message that may be impaired by frequent errors in mechanics and structure
- reflective statements that are minimal and/or irrelevant

(A *Nonscorable Portfolio* does not contain enough completed tasks to score. To be scored a portfolio must contain at least four tasks, including Tasks Five and Six.)

8

Portfolio For Doctoral Candidacy

A Veritable Alternative

Janice M. Heiges

THE INCREASING USE OF PORTFOLIOS FOR EVALUATION AND ASSESSMENT embraces all levels of education today, including the relatively unexplored territory of considering portfolios as equivalent to doctoral candidacy exams in English. Current literature continues to expand the portfolio dialogue (Belanoff and Elbow 1991; Elbow and Belanoff 1991; Yancey 1992a, 1992b; Graves 1992; Gallehr 1993), including an entire conference on portfolios at Miami University of Ohio in October 1992, where the issue of graduate candidacy portfolios was initially raised, and the 1994 series of NCTE (National Council of Teachers of English) portfolio conferences, where in a panel discussion I reported on the accomplishment of attaining candidacy through a portfolio.

As a doctoral candidate in composition at George Mason University in a program granting a D.A. in Community College Education, I began considering the use of a graduate portfolio in lieu of a doctoral candidacy exam in June 1992 after reading "Portfolios and the M.A. in English" (Hain 1991). After nearly a two-year quest, I have succeeded in becoming a doctoral candidate by presenting a portfolio of selections encompassing my graduate course work instead of writing a traditional nine-hour exam based on three questions about my content area. The journey, however, required not only much research and self-examination on my part, but also considerable justification to various faculty and committees that a portfolio could be a valid equivalent for a candidacy exam.

Background

The Hain article planted a seed which didn't begin to germinate until August 1992 when I agreed to participate in a portfolio evaluation program at Northern Virginia Community College (NOVA) where my developmental English classes were to be part of a five-campus assessment project. Up to this time my only experience with portfolios was in a graduate seminar where I submitted a final portfolio of selected writings including a reflective letter. Plunging into the thick of portfolio administration with scant portfolio experience or knowledge, I followed the rules established by a previous two-year pilot study at NOVA. As with any new concept, we constantly learn by experience—reshape our views, redirect our energy, reexamine our goals, and retask as necessary.

In September 1992 I proposed the idea of a portfolio as an alternate comprehensive examination for candidacy to the director of my graduate program, and he agreed to explore the idea as a pilot project. Shortly after, I attended the Miami University portfolio conference which provided me with much needed exposure to the breadth of portfolio use as well as to the inherent problems still requiring pedagogical research and analysis. One of the last sessions at the conference was a panel discussion on portfolios and graduate education. Ten questions were posed by Peter Elbow, Pat Belanoff, and other panelists on how portfolios might be used in the regular graduate curriculum sequence in lieu of or in conjunction with comprehensive exams and the problems that may be encountered. Among other questions about institutional barriers to portfolios, graduate faculty and student attitudes, and types of portfolios was a major concern about portfolios at the graduate level leading to students developing similar, lesser, or greater competency in their field of study and the question of how a department would arrive at a better sense of graduate students' knowledge bases in a discipline by means of a portfolio. The audience consisted of many doctoral candidates who expressed interest in the portfolio as an alternative to a candidacy exam; consequently, this meeting served as the opening dialogue, at least for me, for what could become a viable alternative method of graduate evaluation.

At that conference a few institutions were mentioned as having experimented with portfolios for graduate candidacy: a Michigan university and SUNY Stony Brook, both of which had their own versions of a graduate portfolio. Questions were raised by the conference panel as to how a written exam would certify proficiency, if portfolios would provide enough coverage to consider competency, and whether portfolios would change the goals of a department. Some felt that a nine-hour comprehensive written exam, for example, is an artificial determinator of learning experiences over many years of course work because the conditions of an exam are unlike how one usually works in the field, and that a less traditional graduate program could more easily incorporate the portfolio idea. Elbow, who was in an exploratory mode about this topic, suggested that graduate students interested in pursuing doctoral candidacy portfolios should propose to their institutions a portfolio concept that would demonstrate writing and reading depth, not only as graduate students but also as professionals.

Already three and one-half years into my doctoral program, I was more determined after attending this panel discussion to pursue the idea of substituting a portfolio for the traditional candidacy exam which I would be taking the following year. Since my D.A. program is teaching-based with flexible requirements at a university where portfolios are widely used as evaluative instruments in most undergraduate composition classes, I began to envision the efficacy of a portfolio for my particular situation particularly because of the reflective aspect of portfolios. Many years have lapsed between my M.A. degree and my doctoral program during which time I was employed first as a writer and editor and later as a college English instructor. Moreover, my doctoral course work has been particularly strenuous because of the need to catch up with years of composition theory that was evolving during my absence from teaching. Thus I have brought to my D.A. program a wealth of professional experience that, added to my expanding knowledge from course work, provides a rich tapestry for reflection. I envisioned the opportunity in a portfolio to make pedagogical connections between my real life experience and composition theory in order to become a better teacher-researcher.

Upon returning from the October conference, I began to press my case for permission to institute a portfolio for the candidacy exam. Several memos of clarification about my intent were requested by various faculty and committees. (See Appendix for two of the key memos.) With each writing I had to rethink my goals for this project to better explain my position. One of the biggest hurdles to overcome was the perception by some faculty that a portfolio would be an easier way to obtain candidacy than the traditional exam method. Nevertheless, I perceived such a portfolio project to be considerably more work than a written exam because, instead of specific study on a few issues, I would be engaging in major review and reflection not only on my graduate education but on my evolving teaching philosophy over many years as well.

Development of the Portfolio Project

The doctoral program in which I am enrolled at George Mason University was established in 1988 to enable "existing community college faculty to become more effective community college teachers and to educate prospective community college teachers." The individualized program allows students to take courses from any appropriate department in the university in developing a program of study which meets their educational needs, and students develop educational contracts which formalize their programs of study. Furthermore, the candidacy exam requirement is called a "comprehensive experience" which students will complete "to test the student's mastery of the knowledge area and the teaching core curriculum in the same way that comprehensive examinations test knowledge acquired in conventional programs." This directive was the opening I needed to explore the idea of a graduate portfolio as a viable alternative to the "comprehensive experience."

Early in September 1992 I spoke to the incoming director of the community college education program about the idea of creating a portfolio for my candidacy exam. Having no prior knowledge of portfolios, the director asked for a memo about their use. He replied in mid-September that my proposal for an alternative comprehensive examination was "interesting and well-written" but "quite different" from the traditional written comprehensive exams which are "proven methods" of gauging comprehensiveness. He was, nevertheless, open to pilot projects and would be agreeable if the English department accepted this mode of examination on a trial basis. However, he indicated he was still "struggling" with the idea of how the revision of a previously submitted paper would help a committee judge my comprehensive knowledge of community colleges or a particular field of study. Therefore he requested more specific information about my idea and about portfolios in general. (See Appendix.)

At that time I was not anxious to expend a great deal of effort on a portfolio with the potential risk of its being rejected or of my being required to take written comprehensives as well. I contemplated whether portfolios were still too experimental an idea to function in a doctoral program. My advisers, however, were in favor of the concept but emphasized that the portfolio should not only present a collection of my work but also a "rethinking" of it which would ideally use the same kinds of primary sources generally encountered in comprehensive examinations. They envisioned a "synthesis paper" in which I would use primary sources along with my own writing and teaching experience. They also felt a portfolio candidacy was appropriate in my case since my dissertation was to focus on portfolio evaluation as well. First I needed to attain approval from the English Graduate Curriculum Committee since my idea constituted a departure from established policy.

A week later I attended the Miami University conference which gave me ammunition with which to convince the English Graduate Curriculum Committee and the Community College Education Director of the validity of my proposal. I submitted justification for a portfolio to the English Graduate Curriculum Committee, using material from the conference to bolster my request. My major premises for this proposal were as follows:

1. Portfolios are an established form of evaluation/assessment nationwide.
2. Portfolio programs have been used in other universities to replace doctoral candidacy exams.
3. D.A. programs nationwide tend to be more flexible about requirements than Ph.D. programs, and the GMU program specifically allows a comprehensive experience.
4. Portfolios could competently evaluate the learning of a Community College Education candidate whose mission is to teach large numbers of students in a community college.
5. Portfolios would allow a more thorough review of a Community College Education candidate's preparation to teach because of the inclusive review of course work engendered by the reflective paper, a focal point of many portfolios.

Since research has shown the value of portfolio assessment in creating strong writers and thinkers who come to grips with their strengths and weaknesses especially by means of the reflective paper, the innovative nature of the Community College Education program made it the ideal situation to offer the portfolio for advancement to candidacy.

In mid-October the chairman of my doctoral committee, who was asked to defend my proposal before the English Graduate Curriculum Committee, requested some talking points in order to present my case. The most persistent question voiced about a graduate portfolio was whether the portfolio was desired as an easy way out of taking a lengthy written exam. On the contrary, I felt preparing a portfolio would perhaps be even more rigorous because I would be reviewing more than just some specific areas to be tested but also my entire graduate program and relating it to my teaching career. Therefore to assuage this notion, I prepared the following information:

Portfolio assessment is *not*

- merely a rehashing of old papers
- an untested idea
- a personal whim to be different
- an easy way out of taking a written exam

Portfolio assessment *is*

- an opportunity to write a lengthy reflective paper that will show the depth of a student's ability to apply theory and methodology to current teaching practices
- a way to review several years of course work with a focus on a particular program as it relates to the field at large
- the opportunity to rethink and revise the work in some courses that may not have been fully assimilated at the time they were taken
- a recognition that because graduate study is an ongoing process, a written test on two or three areas doesn't necessarily pull the entire experience together
- an opportunity to test the validity of a methodology used in the community college classroom
- an idea that has been successfully implemented at some universities and which is in the planning stages at others
- an occasion to set up some criteria for portfolios to be an alternative for other disciplines in the Community College Education program
- an innovative idea that is in keeping with the innovative nature of the Community College Education program, which itself is the first of its kind
- the apogee of a graduate student's program of study prior to the dissertation
- the focus of current research showing that portfolios of student work are part of new criteria to "more closely track the learning process" (Winkler, Karen J. 1992. Researchers Leave Labs, Flock to Schools for a New Look at How Students Learn, *The Chronicle of Higher Education* , 14 Oct. 92:A6).

Other questions proposed for consideration were the following:

1. Have you ever written a text that you changed at a later time based upon new views or insights gained as a result of your expanding knowledge?
2. Are the texts you submit to a publisher ever returned for revising or rethinking?
3. Are your publishable texts ever critiqued by peers or editors?
4. Have you ever considered the intellectual impact that can accrue from "reflecting" on previous scholarly research?

By this time, the two months of memo writing on this topic began to refine and solidify my views on the portfolio process and persuaded me further that this should be a possible option for the Community College Education program. In addition I was anticipating the prospect of doing a pilot study because I was convinced by further research that the portfolio had become a viable entity in the field of evaluation.

In late October, the English Graduate Curriculum Committee agreed to my proposal as a pilot case with the following stipulations for the format of the portfolio:

1. I would submit in the portfolio three revised area papers in English and one from education.
2. I would submit a "reflection" paper which focused particularly on the place of my papers within the larger field.
3. Upon submission of these papers and their acceptance by my portfolio committee (composed of two doctoral advisers from English and one from the Community College Education faculty), I would take an oral examination to be administered by my committee and open to the public (as is generally the case with doctoral qualifying exams). This exam would give my committee and others the opportunity to respond to my papers and ascertain the "comprehensiveness" of my understanding of the field. It would also give me a chance to expand upon issues in my reflection paper.

Despite this encouraging breakthrough, the director of the Community College Education Center requested further justification of the validity of the portfolio. By now it was late November with Christmas break nearing, and I became anxious to proceed with the portfolio, if it were to be approved.

In January 1993 the director notified me to submit a portfolio contract, which I did on February 4. (See Figure 1.)

Figure 1
Contract for Pilot Study

Portfolio-Based Alternative for Advancement to Candidacy

1. Three revised area papers in English and one in Education
   Engl 801: New Developments in English
   Engl 615: Proseminar in Composition Instruction
   Engl 610: Proseminar in Teaching Literature
   EDCC 801: The Community College
   The English papers would be read by the candidate's English advisers, Dr. Henry and Dr. Thaiss, and the Education paper would be read by an adviser in the CCED office.
2. Reflection paper: this paper would focus on the place of the candidate's papers within the larger field. This paper would be read by all three readers of the area papers.
3. Oral Defense: because this is a pilot study, upon completion of reviewing the papers, the three readers will meet with the candidate to respond orally to the papers and to assess the use of a portfolio as a viable alternative to the standard written comprehensive exam. This group would then submit to the CCED office a recommendation for future use of the portfolio alternative for advancement to candidacy.

Janice M. Heiges
Doctoral Candidate

Dr. Gustavo A. Mellander
Director, Center for Community College Education

The contract was based on the guidelines of the English Graduate Committee. A few weeks later I received a signed copy of my contract, meaning I could proceed with the portfolio. By then it was late March, six months after my initial request to launch a portfolio for advancement to candidacy. Although at times during this process I became impatient, in retrospect I believe it was a healthy period for a pilot project that needed discussing and refining by committees who were initially unfamiliar with the idea. Also my continual need to justify the portfolio candidacy only solidified my view that it was a viable activity.

Portfolio Project

At the outset of confirmation to begin a graduate portfolio, I soon realized that my adventure with the portfolio was just beginning. With the approval of my adviser, I selected the three English seminar papers I thought would be most useful for content analysis rather than selecting what I considered to be my best-written papers. In fact, one of these was perhaps one of the worst papers I had written as a graduate student. We decided rather than actually rewriting the papers I should review them in light of reader comments and my own evaluative analysis. Because the guidelines of my contract were very general, I wrestled with the type of format to shape the written discussion. After struggling with these problems for several weeks, I met with my doctoral chairman in early July, at which time we decided that instead of rewriting any of the papers, I would write a preface for each seminar paper setting up the parameters for the initial assignment and then prepare an addendum to each one describing and analyzing the changes in my thinking and research since writing each paper.

Through this reflective process, I saw connective threads that paired the papers written early in my graduate study as well as the two written later. The two papers written several years earlier, when my knowledge of composition theory was minimal, required me to review my thinking on the topics and my entire methodology of conducting research. The other two papers, written in my last two seminar classes, reflected my metamorphosis from a neophyte researcher to one more versed in analytical techniques. Therefore, I ended up writing two prefaces, one for each set of papers indicating the connections between them. Then, to further orient the reader, I included a page before each paper with the following information: course description, objectives, texts, and assignment.

Each addendum contained reflection and synthesis of my emerging knowledge in the field of composition studies. They also revealed that my criteria for inclusion of papers favored types of courses over content of papers because the Curriculum Committee required one paper from an education course and three from English. For example, in my first addendum I write: "Reviewing this piece of writing—my very first doctoral

Figure 2
Table of Contents

seminar paper in 1989—makes me grin at my naiveté. It is a most sincere and dogmatic piece full of lusty justification for my views. But it represents my fledgling viewpoint of theory (or lack of) as I embarked on a program of graduate study." I continue to examine my rationale for the paper with a discussion of the paper's deficiencies in light of my expanding awareness of theory-based research. Next I address written comments on the pages made by the initial reader in order to answer questions or explicate problem areas. Finally I review ways I would change the content such as with the following passage: "Today on reviewing my paper, I see where I made attempts to interact with Britton's theory (see pages three, nine, and ten), but I was really using Britton as an introduction to my viewpoint without much analysis throughout the paper. Now I would integrate Britton's theory into my discussion beginning on page two where I address the freshman English curriculum." At this point I reanalyze these parts of the paper and offer my new insights. The second addendum of each pair also contains comparative references to the first paper, thereby eliciting continuity in the discussion of each pair of papers.

The Table of Contents (Figure 2) illustrates the format that emerged from trying various ways to best present the portfolio material. At the time I was perplexed by the lack of specific guidelines to shape the portfolio, but upon current reflection of the process, I feel portfolios need to assume their own shape because of discrepancies in doctoral programs. The temptation to standardize portfolios is risky since portfolios should be content-specific.

Now I believe the general guidelines in my contract actually allowed me more reflection as I struggled with how to contain the portfolio.

After the July discussion, it took me four months to complete the portfolio. The bulk of that time was spent on the reflection paper, which encompassed over ten years of professional writing and editing, and over twelve years of teaching college composition with minimal pedagogical skills, since my M.A. was completed in the late 1960s when composition theory was just evolving. The idea of reflection embedded in many portfolio constructs would provide me opportunity for metatextual reflection, a rare opportunity in the crunch of graduate education, especially if one is employed full-time while working on a degree part-time, as I have been. My final portfolio became a document of over 120 pages which I submitted in triplicate to my three-member committee in November.

Portfolio Defense

On December 17, 1993 I met with my three-member committee for the oral discussion as outlined in my contract. It was a friendly meeting lasting perhaps one and one-half hours during which the committee was particularly interested in my views of the portfolio project now that it was completed. We discussed its application for other graduate students and its usefulness as a comprehensive evaluation tool. I suggested that it would be difficult to set up too many formal guidelines for a graduate portfolio given the wide variety of graduate student circumstances. For example, a portfolio from a graduate student without much professional experience but with more initial theoretical knowledge might be very different, especially if a portfolio contract were to be part of a graduate program at the outset. This type of portfolio might include more revision drafts as a means to show the development of a student's thinking at the time of writing a paper, whereas my portfolio was a backward glance at finished products to decipher new insights. Moreover, a portfolio was an appropriate alternative to candidacy because of the nature of this D.A. program which states that students may "propose alternatives to take-home or in-class examinations." These alternatives should be designed so that they "demonstrate 1) the student's ability to synthesize, evaluate, and communicate the underlying assumptions affecting research and practice in his or her knowledge area and 2) the student's mastery of the material covered in the core teaching curriculum."

The committee appeared satisfied that the portfolio had adequately tested my knowledge within the larger field of composition as it pertains to community college teaching. The twenty-three–page reflective letter seemed to be the adhesive that bonded the entire document into a unified whole, demonstrating my ability to "synthesize, evaluate, and communicate" my expanding knowledge of research and practice in the field of composition.

Conclusions and Recommendations

Although portfolios represent an evaluation instrument geared to a particular need and situation, several factors should be considered in establishing a graduate portfolio for candidacy:

- determine what the portfolio will be replacing and if it will accomplish the goals of its replacement;
- require a written justification by each student to determine knowledge of portfolio concepts;
- require students to have experience working with portfolios and to read a short bibliography;
- establish parameters for the reflective paper to include specific sections pertaining to individual programs;
- and establish a time frame for completing the portfolio.

The trade-offs of doing a portfolio over a traditional candidacy exam are perhaps more unique in my situation because this was a pilot study. Some of the problems I encountered included:

- confusion over purpose of substituting a portfolio for a traditional exam;
- need to "sell" the idea to some decision-makers;
- length of time to initiate the final contract;
- lack of specific guidelines to shape the portfolio;
- and lack of time limit to complete the portfolio.

From my experience with a portfolio as a candidacy instrument, I highly recommend that other doctoral students consider this option but caution that it may not be the ideal venue for every student. A primary question to consider is what outcomes are desired. No one portfolio will work for all institutions or all graduate students because portfolios are program-specific. Furthermore the outcomes may be different if a student initially establishes a portfolio along with a graduate program of study. A major consideration should be the format of the portfolio. Should papers be rewritten rather than reexamined as mine were? In retrospect I would recommend my type of portfolio for the more mature student because the portfolio focuses reflection on the overall graduate experience rather than on individual papers.

Institutions should be supportive of graduate portfolios for candidacy, but graduate students must fully understand their motives and be sufficiently knowledgeable about the ramifications of portfolio use. This portfolio project exemplifies that traditional written comprehensive exams are not the only way to measure fitness for doctoral candidacy. In my case, I believe I learned more by "rethinking" my entire graduate and professional experience while reflecting on my teaching methodology as it pertains to the profession than I would have by answering three written questions about three segments of my graduate program. Although my quest for doctoral candidacy was a lengthy and often tenuous experience, it was a worthwhile effort. Hopefully I have broken ground for others to follow.

Appendix

Correspondence with Graduate Curriculum Committee

To: Dr. Eileen Sypher/Graduate Curriculum Committee
From: Janice Heiges, doctoral candidate
Re: Justification for using a portfolio for advancement to candidacy
Date: October 6, 1992

Regarding our phone conversation yesterday, I am happy to enclose more information about the validity of using a portfolio as an alternative for admission to candidacy in the doctoral program for Community College Education (CCED).

Over the past weekend I attended a federally funded conference (Fund for the Improvement of Postsecondary Education) sponsored by Miami University of Ohio devoted entirely to the topic of portfolio assessment. The three-day conference (which included over 100 papers in 12 sessions, six workshops, and two keynote speakers) covered all aspects of portfolio use and was attended by over 400 participants from at least 35 states.

Fresh from a 1 1/2 hour roundtable discussion of about 75 participants on the use of portfolios in graduate education including such eminent scholars as Peter Elbow (U.MA), Richard Larsen (Lehman), Pat Belanoff (SUNY, Stony Brook), and Chris Anson (U.MN), I am spurred on to pursue the portfolio as an alternative to the comprehensive exam for candidacy in the CCED program. The session provided specific proposals as well as far-ranging suggestions in defense of extended portfolio use in composition and rhetoric programs or any English program at the graduate level. My justification for advocating a replacement of the written candidacy exam with a portfolio is based on the following premises:

1. Portfolios are now an established form of evaluation/assessment nationwide.
2. Portfolio programs are established in other universities to replace doctoral candidacy exams.
3. D.A. programs nationwide tend to be more flexible about requirements than PhD programs.
4. Portfolios better evaluate the learning of a CCED candidate whose mission is to teach large numbers of students in a community college.
5. Portfolios allow a better review of a CCED candidate's preparation to teach because of the comprehensive review of course work engendered by the reflective paper which is a focal point of the portfolio.

This conference was particularly impressive because of the magnitude of portfolio ideas already developed and prospering in so many high schools, colleges and universities nationwide. Portfolios are now past the trial stage and into full blown use. Established by Peter Elbow and Pat Belanoff at Stony Brook in the early

80s, this innovative assessment tool is now considered one of the most viable forms of assessment in composition and rhetoric classes. The wealth of ideas shared at this meeting demonstrates that the portfolio concept is no longer just a new fad but has become an entrenched format with far-reaching implications yet to be discovered.

Several universities have already established innovative portfolio programs in lieu of a written exam for advancement to candidacy and others are in the experimental stage. Two programs already in place are the following:

Michigan State U: A candidate's doctoral committee decides what form the admission to candidacy takes and doctoral students may elect to do a portfolio in which a student selects three papers and works with the committee until those papers are of publishable quality. In this way the advisers are also mentors to teach the student what is involved in preparing a document for publication, something not usually taught in graduate classes. In addition the student must write a lengthy reflective paper reviewing what has been learned through the course work and how this knowledge will be utilized in teaching.

SUNY Stony Brook: Doctoral candidates are admitted to candidacy through a three-hour oral exam based on a portfolio of three documents submitted by the student: a syllabus for a class, one seminar paper, and one paper of the student's choice. The doctoral committee spends an hour with the student on each of these three documents.

Miami University of Ohio and University of Minnesota are discussing the use of portfolios as an option for the advancement exam with the idea that the candidate would compile a selection of seminar papers with a longer reflective piece that would indicate how the graduate studies relate to the candidate's teaching. There are more programs in the planning stage but these were specifically discussed at the conference.

Peter Elbow expressed the idea of cutting back on the candidacy exam in favor of a candidate creating a piece or two of publishable quality under the supervision of a faculty member. Many of the panelists agreed that the conditions of a lengthy written exam do not necessarily measure one's teaching ability and are entirely unlike how faculty in the field write with much peer review and collaborative editing.

Since research has proven the value of portfolio assessment over a written exam in creating strong writers and thinkers who come to grips with their strengths and weaknesses especially by means of the reflective paper, I submit that the innovative nature of the CCED program makes it the ideal situation to offer the portfolio for advancement to candidacy. Moreover, I suggest the portfolio concept could be worked into the initial contract under which students develop their CCED program.

The faculty at the portfolio meeting plan to take portfolio assessment as a means of advancement to candidacy to the MLA meeting as well as to NCTE and 4 Cs. They urged graduate students to petition their universities to begin effecting portfolios as an alternative to the traditional written exam for admission to candidacy. Faculty in the audience who had recently been allowed to use the portfolio for admission to candidacy praised its value as a practical yet intellectually stimulating alternative which allowed them to assess their particular programs of study and reflect on their learning in ways not fostered by a written exam.

Thank you for considering my proposal. My doctoral committee, Jim Henry and Chris Thaiss, fully support me in this endeavor, especially since my doctoral project is on the use of a portfolio system of assessment for developmental writers at my community college, which is encouraging all composition faculty to implement portfolios in the classroom.

I would be happy to meet with you to answer any further questions. You may reach me at 893-0015.

October 23, 1992

Janice Heiges
1002 Salt Meadow Ln.
McLean, VA 22101

Dear Janice:

The Graduate Curriculum Committee of the Department of English met yesterday to discuss your request for a pilot portfolio-based alternative to the written comprehensive exam for admission to candidacy in the doctoral program for Community College Education (CCED). The committee feels that parts of your proposal are very strong but is also concerned that you meet the requirement of "comprehensiveness." Accordingly, we propose:

1. That you submit the portfolio of three revised area papers in English and one from Education. (This is part of your original proposal.)
2. That you submit a "reflection" paper which focuses particularly on the place of your papers within the larger field. (Note: This is a change from your proposal which seems to emphasize more, or at least as much, the place of your papers in your own intellectual growth. This paper would rather focus on the papers' location within the field.)
3. That upon submission of these papers and their acceptance by your committee, you take an oral examination. This examination would be administered by your committee and open to one public (as is generally the case with doctoral qualifying exams). The exam would give your committee and others the opportunity to respond to your papers and ascertain the "comprehensiveness" of your understanding of the field. It would also give you a chance to expand upon issues in your reflection paper. (Note: This is different from

your proposal. We are here following SUNY Stony Brook's model of the use of the portfolio in graduate assessment.)

We feel that these changes will both enhance your own work yet ensure that the examination process fulfills the "comprehensiveness" criterion so central to this stage of your career. Your advisor, Professor Henry, attended the meeting and will be happy to answer any questions, as will I. Your examination process will be a pilot; that is, should students in the future wish to use this form, the committee will need to decide whether to continue it.

Sincerely,

Eileen Sypher
Director
English Graduate Studies

cc: James Henry, Christopher Thaiss, Don Boileau, Deborah Kaplan, Gustavo Mellander, Hans Bergmann

II

Pedagogy

9

Behind the Scenes

Portfolios in a Classroom Learning Community

Mary Ann Smith

I STARTED MY TEACHING CAREER TWENTY-FOUR YEARS AGO BY FURNISHING A large corner of my classroom with a couch and a rug made of carpet remnants. There my eighth graders lounged, upright or prone, while I fed them books and blank pages for their writing. The arrangement did little justice to the student-centered curriculum of James Moffett and B.J. Wagner which was, at the time, in serious contention with the one-lecture-fits-all approach, supported by desks in a row. If anything, couches and carpets were proof that ambiance is overrated.

On the other hand, students spend thirteen or more years in classrooms. The design of those classrooms—beyond carpeting, recliners, or desks—definitely matters. Design matters if learning is to be more than just a furnishing. It matters if special practices, like portfolio assessment exist, not as the "right" curriculum or the privileged pedagogy of the year, but as a tool in the service of student learning.

In this chapter, we will look specifically at classroom designs that make portfolios a means to learning, rather than an end—designs that extend, rather than freeze portfolio practices, and therefore, help students stretch themselves. In fact, any look at portfolios—what they are and how they work—simply must take into account their residences. Are there living arrangements that accommodate portfolios better than others?

At the outset, it should be noted that portfolios are not necessarily the most efficient path to learning—especially not compared to methods that treat students as inhalers of knowledge. When students simply breathe deeply of the wisdom that fills the room and then exhale on command, they move in a direct line from point to point. Whether or not the inhale/exhale method makes use of their past experiences, curiosities, or special talents, however, is of no consequence.

On the other hand, in classrooms that honor students as participants in their own learning, the learning is no longer one-way or exclusive of individual commitments. In fact, individuals are expected to care, to keep tabs on, and take responsibility for their progress because they are asked to do the following:

- actively build knowledge, not just consume it;
- read and write everyday with their peers and their teacher;
- and think about and evaluate their own work.

Classrooms that ask students to be centrally involved in their own learning answer to a number of names: constructivist classrooms, learning communities, or interactive environments. They are the kind of classrooms that nourish portfolios, earning them yet another name: portfolio classrooms.

What do these classrooms look like?

Knowledge Building in Portfolio Classrooms

When students treat their learning as a personal endeavor that demands their significant contributions, they are less likely to watch from the sidelines. They are key players in writing, thinking, researching, experimenting, and debating.

Jan's Classroom

Jan Bergamini, a California high school teacher, asks her students to be authors of their own learning. When the students arrive in September, they receive two folders. The first is their writing folder. All of their writing goes into this folder, every scrap and draft. In Jan's class, the second folder is the portfolio. Every so often students choose a piece from their writing folders and put it in their portfolios. Jan asks them to write about why they picked that paper and what they intended when they wrote it. She may also ask them to write about how they wrote it, what special problems it posed, and what they learned about writing. In May, the students submit their portfolios to the English department. They write a letter of introduction to the portfolio, justifying each choice and talking about themselves as writers, their strengths and weaknesses. In other words, the students have the main responsibility for preparing and presenting their work for evaluation. They may revise their work as often as they want to get it ready. Jan works with them all year on the writing and on the specific things the other teachers will be looking for when they read the portfolios.

The next year the portfolios follow their owners to their new classes, where once again they fill them with the writings they choose as most representative of their work. By June of their senior year, these students have more than a diploma or a string of grades. They have a whole portfolio of their writing accomplishments and of what they learned. They leave as authors with a collection of their best writings (Murphy and Smith 1991, 11–12).

It is worth noting that in Jan's portfolio classroom, there are established procedures and containers and deadlines. But significantly, the classroom culture demands much more than simple adherence to the rules. Rather, it demands students to be thoughtful: to take themselves seriously. Their choices count. Their revisions matter. Their work stands for something—for their accomplishments and aspirations, for their progress, for their ability to select and assess markers of excellence.

In other words, portfolio classrooms invite students into the thick of thinking, into living their literacy rather than just rehearsing it. "To get beyond Thinking Appreciation," Dan Kirby and Carol Kuykendall explain, "students must be actively involved in purposeful tasks that engage mind, eye, and hand in sustained effort toward some goal that matters today as well as tomorrow. Furthermore, those tasks must be rooted in a context that is both engaging and meaningful—a context that holds intellectual work together so that students can make sense of it" (Kirby and Kuykendall 1991, 37).

Joni's Classroom

Joni Chancer, a California elementary teacher, provides another example of a classroom in which students actively build knowledge. After months and months of mini-lessons and writing workshops and writing conferences and book clubs—when the children's writing folders are bulging—she demonstrates what comes next in the process of constructing portfolios of their learning:

> With my fourth and fifth grade students, the purpose of the first portfolio commonly focuses on showing several things: best work; a range of work; revisions and process pieces; first drafts, second drafts, final drafts and published books; and often the pieces the student cared about the most. I want my writers and readers to be impressed with themselves, to say, "Wow! When I show you this body of work, there will be no doubt that I am a writer and a reader!" And so we brainstorm together what kinds of selections they might make in putting together the portfolios.
>
> Frequently, I share my own portfolio with the students and I talk about the reasons behind my selections. I read them my own letter of introduction to the contents I have chosen. Sometimes I show them copies I have made of student portfolios from previous years. I am very careful to share several varied portfolios that clearly demonstrate a range of possibilities. Looking at and hearing aloud the introductory letters written by other students is critical. Students need to hear from other students. It makes a powerful statement about ownership . . . The children quickly come to see that there is no single "right way" to put together a portfolio. (Chancer 1993, 41-42)

In this portfolio classroom, Joni uses her own experiences with portfolios as a resource for students. She also discusses the work of former students, making writing and thinking and ultimately, portfolios, a matter of collaboration as well as personal responsibility, of open field running as well as defined expectations, of analyzing choices as well as simply making them.

Joni exemplifies, too, the importance of teachers in portfolio classrooms—of their potential as role models and as companions in learning, in being open to different possibilities. This potential, according to Geof Hewitt, has a direct effect on students:

> If a teacher is timid, afraid to experiment, the students are unlikely to take risks. The same principle applies to portfolios. If the teacher dictates an official portfolio format, then tells the students which pieces of their writing to include, the students are likely to sit back and let the teacher manage their portfolios. Most teachers I know don't have that kind of time. (Hewitt 1995, 65)

Rather than manage, teachers in a portfolio classroom design, in the best sense of the word. They set the tone, the openness to learning—through modeling, through immersing students in reading and writing, and through working with their own literacy.

Jane's Cassroom

Jane Juska, a California high school teacher, issues a written invitation to her seniors to actively build their knowledge. In it, she asks students to think about their learning as a continuum, rather than as a series of discrete, isolated assignments:

> Portfolios due at the end of the semester. No grades till quarter time and those only a report of progress, then no grades again till semester. Semester grade based on the quality of work included in the portfolio. Why, you are asking. Why can't we do like always: hand in papers and get comments back and grades and then we'll know how we're doing and we won't have to worry and wonder if we're passing and what're we supposed to tell our parents, huh? Why can't this class be like my seventh grade English class which was my favorite . . .
>
> Now, calm down. You and I will work our ways through different kinds of writing, different kinds of literature. You will give me drafts of your writing, the record of which I will keep in my grade book, and I will comment on the drafts with an eye to helping you revise. You'll be writing comparison/contrast papers, definition papers, argumentative papers, personal experience/reflective papers, stories, poems—and you'll be rewriting them to get some or all of them ready for the portfolio. You will be learning and relearning throughout the semester, and in the end you will put together a demonstration of your proficiencies in writing and in understanding and appreciating literature. That demonstration we will call a portfolio. You will be proud of it. (Juska 1993, 63-64)

Notably, Jane reassures her students about their upcoming portfolio classroom. "You and I," she says, designating that learning is not confined to the ranks of students. "Learning and relearning," she says, defying the idea that learning is for once and for all. No real grades until semester, she says, goading the group into thinking beyond a single unit of curriculum. She might also say, "No worksheets. No underlining the subject once and the predicate twice." Clearly, she has rejected notions that learning can be charted, mastered, and recited on demand. Rather, learning can be a way of proceeding.

In other words, Jane intends to carry students beyond the value of "doneness" (that moment when students gratefully abandon their work into the hands of the teacher for some kind of evaluation). This portfolio classroom recognizes a life beyond the lunchbell, the end of the quarter, or any other school-designated period of learning, as well as a reward greater than grades.

Relying on grades to motivate students, Catharine Lucas points out, has limits when it comes to inspiring more than superficial efforts:

> Beyond the extrinsic motivation of test scores and grades must lie some intrinsic reward, some freedom to feel curiosity, if a student—or any other performer—is to muster the long-range commitment that makes deep and lasting learning

> possible, and with it the kind of deepening perception, steady concentration, critical thinking, and creative imagination that we hope our students will aspire to. (Lucas 1992, 3)

Portfolios, whether or not they are graded, can upgrade the notion that learning is an event or an assignment. In a classroom like Jane's, one event can trespass on another in the interest of extending learning.

Mary Kay's Classroom

Mary Kay Deen negotiates with her Mississippi second graders about what it means to build knowledge. They are hesitant, she discovers, and they need her encouragement:

> We agreed on three purposes for developing the portfolios: to help the students see their growth and development as writers over a period of time; to help the students develop self-confidence by celebrating their accomplishments as writers; and to help the teacher see the students' growth as writers.
>
> Our first struggle with change came when we began talking about the selection process. I realized how little power my children assumed they had, for they did not even consider that they could make their portfolio selections. However, with more discussion about writers and the choices and decisions they make in the process of writing, the children realized that writers know their own work better than anyone else. Writers know which piece is their best, their most important, and their favorite. Since the children were the writers who were developing portfolios, of course they should select the pieces! As a security net, I asked their permission to make a selection. They granted my request, and they also gave their parents an opportunity to choose a piece for their portfolio. (Deen 1993, 52)

Children learn all too early, as Mary Kay illustrates, that they are unworthy of having opinions, ideas, choices. Portfolio classrooms depend on the alternative: that children will learn, with the support of teachers like Mary Kay, that their knowledge is viable and valued and at the very least, a solid starting place for discovering and claiming even more knowledge.

Donald Graves shares Mary Kay's concern that children not be denied the opportunity, and therefore the ability to make informed portfolio selections:

> Students need to learn to evaluate their own work. When I first began to teach writing thirty-five years ago, I allowed my students just one day of writing a week, corrected the daylights out of what they wrote, and knew I was the only one with enough sense to judge their work. They wrote for me, and I was proud of my standards. They feared my red pen; I called their fear respect. Worse, I

> called their fear learning. Not once did I ask them to evaluate their own work. Consequently, they developed little skill in reading their own work. (Graves 1992, 85)

Graves suggests that with the teacher's guidance, young students practice making choices from their writing folders and labeling those choices with words such as "like," "hard," "surprise," "promise," "keep going," and "burn." Some papers may merit several labels and these multi-dimensional papers may look attractive to students as choices for their portfolio. The point is that students are learning about different ways to value their writing (Graves 1992, 93-94).

In Mary Kay's classroom, second graders grow steadily as portfolio decision-makers. Young Amy notes that she is good at "making the beginning, middle, and ending of my story . . . I can all so do revision very well." She especially appreciates the "sloppy copy" draft as a place where "I can jot down everything that flashes throw in my head." At the end of the year, her teacher says that Amy is "a little girl who knew the joy of learning" (Deen 1993, 57-58).

These stories teach us some of what it means to build knowledge in portfolio classrooms. Not everything they describe is neat or comfortable or even the same from class to class which, of course, makes us believe them. Portfolio classrooms are not like tract houses. One blueprint will not do for everyone. But at the same time, the teachers using portfolios share some common assumptions. For example:

- Portfolios are basically selections of student work for a purpose or purposes. The purposes can vary tremendously. In Jan's classroom, for example, portfolios exist to show growth over time and to give students the deed to their own learning. In Jane's class, they provide a respite from weekly grading and a reason to collaborate, revise, and move from one kind of writing to another.
- Portfolios contribute to learning best when they are under-invented. That is to say, if portfolios ask students to represent their own thinking, then students can no longer rely on the kind of "hand-me-down" requirements that put boundaries around their thinking. In Mary Kay's classroom, little eight-year-olds are treated as responsible and capable. Rather than being confined to what the teacher knows or requires, they qualify as members in good standing in a community of learners.

- Portfolios are, in fact, a tangible symbol of the construction of knowledge. Portfolios are actually built, piece by piece. In the process, they are nailed together and pried open and examined and nailed back together numerous times as students make and justify their portfolio decisions.

Reading and Writing in Portfolio Classrooms

In portfolio classrooms, teachers and students work together as readers and writers, researchers and learners, partners and mirrors for each other. Two different classroom stories—a high school and a primary school—illustrate this kind of culture.

Jan's ESL Classroom

I spent a year visiting Jan Bergamini's second period English class at Mount Diablo High School in Concord, California. All the students in this class were second language learners with two or three years of English under their belts. They came from Vietnam, Mexico, and Central and South America.

In Jan's class, they continued to learn English by being readers, writers and speakers of the language. The class in no way resembled what I remember from my high school experience with trying to learn a second language—an experience that can be described as "accuracy first, genuine communication second." As I remember, we were all terribly self-conscious when it was our turn to write or talk. Our fondest wish was to become somehow invisible.

Jan's students started out with the same wish, I'm sure. They were shy, reluctant to expose their awkwardness with the language, uneasy voyagers on a precarious sea. Immediately, Jan asked them to keep learning logs, to record sentences or passages from their reading and respond in some honest way: "I don't understand," they might write, or "this reminds me of . . ." or "this makes me feel . . ." From the learning logs, students began to talk to each other, to share papers, to take parts in plays, to ask questions. Most important, they paid attention to each other. In fact, the focus changed from frightened individuals who were turned inward, protecting themselves from any embarrassment, to an inclusive community of readers and writers who were turned outward, learning together and often from each other. The students began insisting that even finished projects be shared. The desks were constantly in motion, it seemed, forming small circles and then large circles and then no circles—just a swap meet, with papers passing from student to student.

Jan worked backwards. She had her students read novels before they read short stories. She had them write to real people who lived outside the classroom before they wrote to her. So they became real readers and writers without having to pass through the ordeal of school reading and writing.

For example, Jan found a young reader medal novel called *Children of the River*. It is about a seventeen-year-old Cambodian girl named Sundara who comes to the U.S. alone, without her immediate family, to live with her aunt and uncle. She speaks no English and has no experience with American customs. In the course of the story, she attracts the attention of an American boy named Jonathan, who is equally ignorant of Cambodian customs, but who has his sights set on Sundara. Jan's students, especially the girls, read fervently. Here were their very own fantasies of adolescent love mixed together with their very own experiences as immigrants. Jan invited the students, once they finished reading and talking about their reading, to write to the author. Jan would write with them.

They gobbled up the invitation. Read what one student wrote, in part, to author Linda Crew:

> Dear Ms Crew
>
> Hi! My name is Tien. I am sixteen years old and I am in 11th grade. I came from Vietnam, but I am Chinese. My grandparents were born in China. They went to Vietnam because of the war, so my parents and I were born in Vietnam.
>
> Now, let me tell you about my experience as an immigrant in the United States. In 1989 I arrived in America. I was about twelve years old and I was in the seventh grade. I remember the first day I step my foot to the new school. My fear of starting a new school did not subside. I feared not being able to fit in, not knowing my way around the new school in America, and not getting used to the different teachers who have different techniques of teaching. While I was looking for my first period class the bell started ringing and all the students came rushing past me. There were no familiar faces. Most of the students were white, black, Mexican and others, but not Vietnamese or Chinese.
>
> By the time I found my class the tardy bell rang and I was late. When I walked into the room everyone was starting at me and I didn't comfortable at all. For the whole day I was sitting in the classed not knowing or understanding what the teachers were saying. I felt like I was stupid. The students even treated me like I am stupid too. Sometimes they make fun at me. This fear kept following me through the whole year and I was not able to concentrate in my classes, because I did not understand anything.

The first year in America and in school could be the worst year of my life. I hated to be an immigrant to a different country and to be a new student in a different school. I was so sad, but I still go to school everyday, because I want to learn English well to understand what they say and I want to show them that I am not stupid at all. Now, my English is not well yet, but at least I can understand what the teachers are saying.

The things that I liked this book is I told us the situations of the immigrants in this country and how hard for us to survive. Your novel is so similar to my life as an immigrant. And now I would like to ask you some questions. Do you really know Sundara? Can you please tell us what happen after she went out with Jonathan? Did they get marry?

Sincerely,
Tien

Let me comment on Tien's letter in this way. I came to Jan's class to learn more about second language acquisition. Yes, I was also curious about how portfolios worked in this kind of classroom, and I was also just plain curious. Tien asked me early on why I was visiting. "To learn from you," I said. "Well, you should have come last year when we still behaved," she said.

Indeed, they did behave—like extraordinary human beings and like readers and writers—behavior that makes portfolios possible. Try to imagine portfolios that would represent less than who you are, less than your achievements as a reader and writer—a portfolio of worksheets, for example. To bother with a portfolio is to bother with what makes a portfolio: a classroom culture that creates a common currency of reading and writing, a culture that encourages turning outward for genuine communication, and a culture that messes up the desks in the name of creating a community of learners and risk takers.

Lois's First Grade Classroom

Lois Brandts gives us a picture of what readers and writers look like in a first grade portfolio classroom, beginning with a description of the comings and goings of her young students:

> . . . this first grade consisted of twenty-eight children, five of whom were bilingual. Eight of the children were sent to the reading specialist for a daily half hour of instruction, two went out for speech and language instruction twice a week, five saw the English Second Language teacher three times each week, and two saw the school counselor on a regular basis . . .
>
> Overall, the class was wildly exuberant and often volatile. The yard duty personnel and other teachers frequently had to intervene in confrontations. Several of the boys worked at the art of rug-rolling, practicing it with determined

> persistence. During nondirected instructional time the noise level often became unacceptable, prompting a substitute teacher to leave me a note asking if I had changed the class rules from "Speak in a soft voice," to "Yell whenever you get the chance."
>
> Not visible on first appearance was how the culture of the classroom had evolved to bring the children to an understanding of themselves as participants in their own learning. From the first day of school, I incorporated community building activities and daily writing time. In September I sent each child a personalized letter at home welcoming them to school, and I invited each child and parent to join the community of first grade readers and writers. I also invited them to bring a favorite book for me to read during the first few getting-acquainted days. (Brandts 1993, 108-109)

What do we have here? A community that invites parents to be partners with their children in the process of becoming readers and writers. Lois asked the parents to write to her about their children, using an approach she learned from Lucy Calkins: "I want to fall in love with your child," she told the parents in her note to them. "You have had several years to get to know one another intimately but I only have a few months to be with your child. Tell me all the wonderful things about your child. You can brag to your heart's content." Lois also asked the parents to stop in and browse through their child's writing folder and to sign up for a home visit. It was this kind of contact that helped Lois to know her students more personally, to know what they might read and write about.

The children participated eagerly in the class writing workshop; so eagerly that one of them complained, after Lois had been absent, "We didn't like it when you were gone. We didn't do writing workshop *once*!" In the process of their workshop, they made portfolio selections three times during the year and dictated their reflections. Their final selections in their showcase portfolios, and their final reflections, went home with them, along with a letter from Lois asking each member of the family to thoughtfully read the portfolio and write a letter to the child about it.

And so the parents became readers and writers in concert with their children. One parent wrote:

> Dear Alisha,
>
> I just read your work from your writing portfolio. I really enjoyed your stories!
>
> Your spelling has really improved since the first day of first grade. So has your handwriting.
>
> I found out more about you by reading your stories and I always like finding out more about you!

> I look forward to reading more of your stories in the future. Keep up the good work. You are a great author.
>
> I love you, Mom
>
> P.S. I like the story about Cally's babies and about Jessie and Lacey. (Brandts 1993, 115)

What Lois and her students and their parents teach us is that the power of portfolios lies behind the scenes: in the rug-rolling, the choosing of topics, the exchange of letters between home and school, the writing conferences between teacher and student, in short, in the community of readers and writers. Everyone can be a learner and a decision-maker in this classroom culture.

Notably, there are some absences from Lois' classroom. Absent are any kind of anti-thinking devices: packaged or standardized portfolios, generic writing assignments, formulaic representations of the writing or reading process, as if these could be superimposed on every child in every literacy situation. No, this classroom is living proof we do not need to purchase decisions. The price is too high. We would be denying ourselves and our students the fundamental value of being educated: the opportunity to think and solve problems and look critically at what we do. And in the case of portfolios, they would eventually starve to death in a classroom where thinking is out of favor.

Are there, then, essential features of a classroom in which portfolios thrive? According to Linda Rief, yes:

> First, students must be immersed in reading, writing, speaking, and listening. Second, they need to be given time in large blocks. Third, they need to be allowed choice as to what they are writing and reading—for their reasons, their purposes. Fourth, they must receive positive response to their ideas. (Rief 1992, 145)

Reflection in Portfolio Classrooms

In the case of portfolio classrooms, reflection means inviting students to analyze and evaluate their own learning.

In Jan Bergamini's class of second language learners, the students set goals for themselves, goals that they could later use as criteria for evaluating the work in their portfolios. Notice that their goals may be somewhat different than those of native speakers:

- Jose from El Salvador is not proud of his portfolio because it lacks long words, a goal for him. "In the real world," he says, "You use long words. I should start to, right?"
- Yen from Vietnam writes that her goals for the year were to "write an accomplish paragraph and I have to pass my writing test but this year I have done just one part of my goals." She sets her goal for the next year "to pass the writing test that I have fail on this year," and she also takes note of her other needs as a writer: "I sometime confused about vocabulary and about match sentence and verb."
- Tien, whom we have met before, laments that she, too, has not perfectly accomplished her goals: "By this time in my life I feel my writing is not good enough, because the way I write is not terse, I have to make a very long sentence to make people understand me, but there is one thing that I like about my writing is my detail, because I give a lot of example to make people understand. The goals that I working on are to make my writing to be terse and my grammer to be correct, I think I am getting better on this, better than last few years, but I want to be more better. Base on my writing I think people will know that my English is not well enough."

From goals like these, the students make selections for their portfolios throughout the year, reflecting as they go on what they are learning and what helps them learn. By the end of the year, they are ready to make final choices and to present them to the entire English department at Mount Diablo High School. Here is the way one student evaluates her portfolio.

Miyuki is Asian and Latin. Her English, as you will see, is exceptional. She told me once when we were walking together on a field trip to the Berkeley campus that her next goal is to learn Japanese. She was asked to introduce her portfolio by addressing:

- what you like about your writing,
- what your goals were this year and how well you accomplished these goals,
- how someone would describe you based on your writing,
- and what helps you to do your best writing and how your next year's teacher can help you.

Miyuki writes:

Dear English Teacher:

My name is Miyuki and I'm sixteen years old now. I came to the United States in December '91 and this was my first year at Mt. Diablo High.

In this portfolio I have five different pieces of writing that I've made throughout my junior year, especially the second semester.

About my writing I like everything. I like how I can develop a complete essay from a little idea or just the fact that I can write in English and others can understand what I'm trying to say.

My goals in this class are similar to everyone else that is learning English. I want to perfect my writing in spelling, punctuation marks, and the construction of stronger paragraphs and sentences. I've been reaching the beginning of my goals little by little with the passing of time, but I think I still need to get to the finish line.

By looking at my writing someone, I believe, would describe me as a responsible person who needs inspiration and encouragement to write strong, complete pieces of writing.

To do my best writing it helps me to have time to think about the issue and write a rough draft.

Sincerely,
Miyuki

Then for each piece of writing, Miyuki writes a separate introduction. For example:

The next piece was an assignment we did about courage. We were reading the book called "The Old Man and the Sea" and as you may know Santiago, the main character challenges the sea and goes beyond human boundaries of strength. He manages to survive because of his courage.

The purpose was to express what we knew as courage, or what courage meant to us at that time, using Santiago's example. You can look for expanded ideas, more details and stronger paragraphs.

I wasn't satisfied with the writing because it didn't show a well developed essay. It was only three paragraphs long and it didn't have strong content.

Notice that she provides a context—in this case, an assignment arising from her reading of a particular novel and the purpose of that assignment. She tells us what she was trying to accomplish and how the writing could be improved.

Most important, however, Miyuki has to make something of her writing and learning. It is not enough to simply produce and pick out pieces of writing, to slap together a table of contents and to check off requirements. In a portfolio classroom, the student is as responsible as the teacher for being a thoughtful observer and critic of her work. In effect, the student reconstructs her efforts, rethinking the decisions and processes that went into the writing, and interpreting the results. In turn, these interpretations inform the teacher and often, other students as well. Learning becomes a collective enterprise, a pooling of experiences, information, and research, without the kind of limits that occur when only one person in the classroom—the teacher—is sanctioned to know something. To put it another way, no one is exempt from commitment, from thinking, from sizing-up learning.

Patience may be the watch word, however, as Rob Tierney warns us:

> Don't expect a rapid return. It may take time to develop the necessary trust with your students and time before students become connoisseurs of their efforts, improvement, and process and effective self-monitors of their progress and future goals. We have found that students' evaluations initially may seem rather glib and limited. Over time, however, they do develop in scope and depth. Their involvement in the process may be what counts more than their diagnostic skill (Tierney 1991, 109-110).

As teachers, we need to be patient with ourselves as well. Few of us were ever the beneficiaries of a school or classroom that encouraged and taught choice, selection, and reflection. On the bright side, we may be free of preconceptions; we can be genuine partners-in-learning with our students.

Creating Learning Communities

Assessment, including portfolios, has often been called the tail that wags the dog. According to conventional wisdom, if we mandate another test, we will improve teaching and learning.

This is not so, and never has been. Simply hurling portfolios into classrooms will not magically transform teaching and learning anymore than rearranging the chairs will guarantee collaboration among learners. In any case, a classroom learning community, which is at the very heart of the assessment matter, cannot be mandated. To build such community, most of us need models and firsthand experiences.

Professional organizations like the National Writing Project, in their summer institutes and school year programs, engage teachers in the construction of knowledge so that the abstract concept "learning community" becomes more concrete and personal. Rather than skimming the surface of a discipline ("covering curriculum"), these programs invite teachers to dive deeply into their disciplines, to write themselves, to conduct classroom research, and to demonstrate and debate practices that support student success in writing.

Any teacher who is experimenting with a new classroom culture deserves to work with other colleagues, or at the very least, with one trusted friend. Just as students can break out of isolation in a learning community, teachers can cast-off the school-imposed isolation that too often prevents them from taking on the role of learners. By collaborating with other professionals—whether in planning together, watching each other teach, developing class projects, or reading each other's portfolios—they can create learning models for their own classrooms.

Another approach to developing a classroom of thinkers and learners may be for the teacher to wear as many hats as possible:

- the *we're-in-this-together hat* that prompts teachers to collaborate with colleagues and with students to construct an inclusive environment where each person has a valued role and an acknowledged responsibility for advancing as writers and thinkers;
- the *participant/observer hat* that allows a teacher to teach and learn at the same time, to ask questions that are equally desirable for students to ask: what are we learning? what helps us learn? what do we need to learn next?
- the *disposable hat* that gives teachers, and therefore students, permission to experiment with new ideas and structures, to pile the counters with boxes and muddle through a system for picking up or passing out folders of writing. To establish a shaky truce with change, knowing that it will feel like a third arm for a while. To wave a white flag and start over when it is time to regroup, with the same determination but perhaps, a new set of conditions, informed by experience.

Clearly, none of us is going to create a hospitable home for portfolios by simply reading a book or following a checklist. On the other hand, if teachers' learning takes place in the classroom, along with the students', the character of everyone's learning changes. It becomes "authentic"—a word that refers to authoring. When every classroom resident is involved in authoring—in planning, reading, writing, researching, collaborating, decision-making, and evaluating, chances are that learning will be both an individual and a communal enterprise, a collective construction of wisdom.

Questions about Portfolio Classrooms

How can we prevent portfolio classrooms and their advocates from fossilizing and proselytizing? Portfolio classrooms could be an endangered species if they become "the answer." As with other "good ideas" in education, they could move predictably through a cycle that begins with thoughtful exploration, but soon gathers hard and fast converts, only to be used to separate teachers (traditional vs. progressive, cutting edge vs. sliding slope). In the final stage of the cycle, portfolio classrooms could be "dummied down," reduced to easy steps that barely resemble the original idea.

How can we keep portfolio classrooms alive and dynamic? Claude Goldenberg gives sound advice when he asks teachers not to throw out all their old strategies when new ones come along. Portfolio classrooms, with their constructivist notions are "seductive." But they are not a reason to ban teaching techniques like giving explanations and providing information:

> Even Vygotsky advocated direct teaching. There is abundant evidence that when done well, explicit teaching aids learning . . . We should expect professional teachers to have at their disposal a wide range of skills and knowledge and be able to use specific strategies and techniques for well-defined purposes. Principles suggested by constructivist conceptions hold considerable promise; some argue they can revolutionize schools. But it would be unwarranted to give up instructional tools of demonstrated utility. The challenge is to achieve a productive balance and to use techniques and approaches strategically, not monolithically. Otherwise we risk constructivism's deconstruction. (Goldenberg 1995, 3)

How can we keep the focus on portfolio classrooms rather than on portfolio furnishings like folders? According to Dennie Palmer Wolf, Eunice Ann Greer, and Joanna Lieberman, if portfolios are to be "worth their manila," teachers and administrators may need to reorder their priorities:

> In the years of working together, we have learned that you cannot collect, honor, and discuss student portfolios for very long without saying, "Why, oh why, didn't we realize that you need to rethink teaching, curriculum, and learning before you rush about collecting and scoring their results?" (Wolf et al. 1995, 4)

How do we extend portfolio cultures beyond individual classrooms and into whole schools? Are there models of schoolwide learning communities? Central Park East Secondary School in East Harlem is one model. Its teachers and students unify every school and classroom endeavor around five "Habits of Mind." These habits include weighing evidence; taking into account different viewpoints; making connections between ideas, people, circumstances, and time periods; predicting or imagining various possibilities or alternatives; and assessing value to people and individuals. These goals are "neither academic nor vocational." They are inclusive of academies and families and streets. They guide teaching, learning, and assessment. In short, they are "intellectual habits" that do not stop at the door of any single classroom, but rather, apply to life in school and out (Darling-Hammond and Ancess 1994, 7-8).

As powerful as the Habits of Mind seem to be, it is the process of creating them that is even more powerful. When professionals sit down together to decide what they want for their students, when they work together in exactly the same manner they want their students to work, they are establishing a learning community throughout their school. The model here is not the finished product. To superimpose it on some other school would not have the same effect as developing it. How we extend a portfolio culture is a question of how to enable teachers to design that culture.

How can we keep portfolio practices focused on real learning? How can we protect the initiative and investigative attitude they seem to foster? Real learning demands a "let's see what happens" attitude. If we can resist nailing down a single answer for teaching or a single way of defining portfolios, we may be able to resist narrowing our options or defending a particular practice. Instead, we will give our students and ourselves the permission and power to candidly reflect on our work and to revise as often as necessary. We will increase our capacities, both individual and collective, to learn from our experiences, to be resourceful in creating new options, and to be courageous enough to decide on our own bright futures.

10

Using Portfolios to Assess and Nurture Early Literacy from a Developmental Perspective

Sandra J. Stone

PORTFOLIOS FOR YOUNG CHILDREN SHOULD BE A POWERFUL INSTRUMENT for assessing and nurturing early literacy development for both the child and the teacher. However, if a teacher does not understand the developmental process of children's early literacy, the instrument remains monodimensional and flat, rather than interactive and dynamic (Stone 1995).

When something is *interactive*, there is a link between key elements so each affects the other; when it is *dynamic*, it possesses a power or force that produces change. Within an early literacy portfolio, the elements of interaction for the teacher and child are the knowledge of early literacy development, the evaluation of the development through reflection, and the child's early literacy development as documented in the portfolio. To be dynamic, the interaction between these key elements should produce change—for both the child and the teacher. For the child, the portfolio is a tool that encourages her to reflect on her current stage of development in light of her previous stage of development and to begin the process of moving to the next stage. She first becomes aware of and then actively engages in her own learning. She continually changes in her understanding of her own literacy development and begins setting goals. The teacher also uses the portfolio as a tool to reflect on the child's current and past stages of development and to inform her practice, making changes in her instructional strategies in order to help nurture the child's development to the next stage. As Gomez notes, "portfolios give teachers a rich opportunity to reconsider their teaching practice by making tight connections between instruction and assessment (Gomez 1991, 627–28).

In order for a teacher to harness the power of an early literacy portfolio, she must have a solid understanding of early literacy development. Only then can the portfolio become an interactive and dynamic tool which can promote a child's literacy growth. Thus, the knowledge of early literacy development becomes the context for documenting, interpreting and nurturing a child's literacy development within the portfolio framework. Without this context, an early literacy portfolio may succumb to simply being a collection of children's work. The following discussion provides one way of understanding early literacy development context for situating portfolios.

The Developmental Process of Literacy—The Foundation of an Effective Early Literacy Portfolio

New Zealand's Marie Clay first used the term "emergent literacy" to describe the development of young children's literacy (Clay 1966). Based on her research, Clay demonstrates that literacy is a developmental process with the child being an active participant in his or her own literacy development (Clay 1966, 1972, and 1975). Goodman suggests that children "discover and invent literacy as they actively participate in a literate society" (Goodman 1984, 102). If teachers are aware of the process, the discovery, and the invention, they are empowered to document this development in a portfolio and support literacy development through appropriate instructional strategies.

If teachers are unaware of the processes of emerging literacy for young children, they place themselves in the unwitting position of not being able to recognize a child's emerging literacy and, thus, cannot effectively celebrate, value, protect, and nurture the process. In order for the portfolio to be effective, the teacher must know where the child is in his or her developmental process within the context of known literacy developmental patterns and as documented by the child's work in the portfolio. Knowledge of early literacy development informs the teacher of what to look for in each child's development. Only then is the teacher able to assess and interpret the child's current literacy. This knowledge helps the teacher support the child's next developmental step through appropriate instructional strategies. Knowledge of literacy development and its process is thus the foundational piece of early literacy portfolio assessment. This knowledge will help teachers effectively use portfolios to 1) document student progress and growth; 2) support and guide instruction; and 3) communicate each student's successful growth to both the child and parent. For young children this type of formative portfolio assessment, which helps children develop, will be most beneficial.

The Process of Early Literacy Development

Early literacy portfolio data collection, evaluation, and interpretation must reflect knowledge of the process of early literacy development. For example, in the process of written language development, the young child enters the writing process as an inventor, first drawing, then scribbling or making letter-like graphemes. Figure 1 illustrates the context of known early literacy developmental patterns based on research of young children's writing (Sulzby 1988; Gentry 1981; Sulzby et al. 1988; Clay 1975).

The child, in this developmental process, writes strings of random letters, moves next to writing random and initial consonants, and then begins using letters for initial and final consonants. Next, vowels appear in her writing. Finally, the child is able to write multiple related sentences and many words with correct spelling.

When conferencing with a young child on a writing piece for her portfolio, the teacher may use the Stages of Writing Development chart (figure 1) as well as the Writing Development Checklist (figure 2). Both guide the teacher in discerning and then interpreting the developmental nature of the child's writing. Knowledge of this context is crucial to using the portfolio as a tool in supporting early literacy development.

However, this knowledge must also be embedded in the attributes of the process of this development, which will significantly impact portfolio data collection and evaluation. The process of early literacy development takes time, of course, and should be placed within a meaningfully and functionally literate environment for the child.

In the process of learning to write, the teacher gives the child time to develop. For example, Krista conferenced with her teacher about her daily writing journal. Krista, age five, wrote *Dwxps*. Orally, she read, "I have a funny cat." The teacher asked Krista, "Are you using letters? Do you have a capital at the beginning? Do you have a period at the end?" Krista smiled and answered, "Yes" to each question as she evaluated her own work. The

Figure 1

STAGES OF WRITING DEVELOPMENT CHART

Example	Stage
1. [house drawing] (This is my house.)	Pictures
2. [scribble] (This is my house.)	Scribble (Approximation)
3. ACMAOWA (This is my house.)	Random Letters
4. IVADAAO (I have a dog.)	Random and Initial
5. ILMB (I like my bike.)	Initial Consonants
6. I lk mi Bk. (I like my bike.)	Initial and Final Sounds
7. I lik to pla with my cat. (I like to play with my cat.)	Vowel Sounds Appear
8. My favorit dinosor is the stegosorus. (My favorite dinosaur is the stegosaurus.)	All Syllables Represented
9. Today I am going to the stor with my mothr. I am going to by a present for my brothrs brthday. He is thre yers old.	Multiple, Related Sentences and Many Words with Correct Spelling

Stone, S. J. (1996). *Creating the multiage classroom.* Glenview, IL: GoodYear Books/ScottForesman. Used by Permission.

teacher realized from her knowledge of literacy development that Krista was in the random letters (letters not associated with sounds) stage, so she helped Krista listen for consonants in the sentence she was orally communicating, nurturing her to the next stage of development. The next day Krista wrote a similar piece using random letters. In fact, she wrote using random letters for several months before she moved to the next stage of using random and initial consonants. Every day the teacher conferenced with Krista, nurturing her to the next stage of development by helping her hear the consonants

Figure 2

WRITING DEVELOPMENT CHECKLIST

Name ______________________ Date ______________________

STAGE ONE	SEP	OCT	NOV	DEC	JAN	FEB	MAR	APR	MAY
Pre-letter writing/pictures									
Approximation (scribble)									
Random use of letters									
Uses random and initial letters									
Random use of sight words									
Copies letters/words									
STAGE TWO	SEP	OCT	NOV	DEC	JAN	FEB	MAR	APR	MAY
Transfers thoughts to paper									
Uses initial consonants									
Uses initial and ending consonants									
Uses sight words									
Begins to form letters correctly									
Reads back accurately at conference									
Writes from left to right									
STAGE THREE	SEP	OCT	NOV	DEC	JAN	FEB	MAR	APR	MAY
Writes a complete sentence									
Beginning to use periods									
Leaves space									
Beginning to use vowels									
Beginning to use capital & lower case letters									
Beginning to represent all syllables									
STAGE FOUR	SEP	OCT	NOV	DEC	JAN	FEB	MAR	APR	MAY
Writes multiple sentences									
Uses vowels									
Represents all syllables									
More correct spellings than word approximations									
Sequences ideas									
Uses periods									
STAGE FIVE	SEP	OCT	NOV	DEC	JAN	FEB	MAR	APR	MAY
Can carry a story									
Uses punctuation (periods, commas, question marks, exclamation marks, quotation marks)									
Edits own writing (i.e., spelling, content)									
Uses a variety of genres (factual, imaginative, poetry, personal narrative, etc.)									
Organizes writing webs									
Writes with paragraphs									

Stone, S. J. (1996). *Creating the multiage classroom.* Glenview, IL: GoodYear Books/ScottForesman. Used by Permission.

in her oral language. The teacher used the Stages of Writing Development and the Writing Development Checklist to guide her in conferencing with Krista. The teacher and Krista chose samples of both stages of development from Krista's daily writing journal to include in Krista's portfolio in order to document her writing progress. The teacher also included the personal anecdotal records she recorded daily regarding her observations of Krista's writing and the conferencing strategies she used with Krista.

It is important to note that if the teacher were not aware that it takes time for a child to develop to the next stage, she may have pushed Krista beyond her understanding and personal construction of how writing goes. Understanding that children take time to develop written literacy is an important component of conferencing with young children.

Early literacy development is also embodied in a positive attitude, with the teacher excited about each emerging step a child takes. During every portfolio conference, the teacher praises Krista for writing with letters, using a capital and a period, and her efforts to listen for the sounds in her oral language and match the sounds to letters. Each of Krista's stages of emergent literacy is celebrated. Together, they place selections of her writing in her portfolio with each stage recognized as having value and importance, reflecting Krista's personal construction of the writing process.

Another attribute of the process is providing a meaningful and functional writing environment. Understanding this aspect directs the teacher to provide meaningful and functional writing experiences for the children. For example, Krista wrote about her world in her journal, she wrote notes to friends at the Mail Box center, and she wrote books at the Writing Center. Because Krista wrote for real reasons, her writings meant more and eventually found their way into her portfolio.

A literacy portfolio also reflects the teacher's understanding of the stages of reading development. Reading is defined as the "*process* of deriving meaning from the printed page or written words" (Wolfgang and Sanders 1981, 116).The concept of emergent literacy suggests that a child does not learn to read suddenly, but that becoming literate is a process that begins at birth. Sulzby, in studying the emergent reading behaviors of children ages two to six, classified steps to the process of becoming a reader (Sulzby, 1986). Her developmental schema included 1) attending to pictures but not forming stories; 2) attending to pictures and forming oral stories; 3) attending to a mix of pictures, reading and storytelling; 4) attending to pictures but forming written stories; and 5) attending to print. When conferencing with a young child on reading for her literacy portfolio, the teacher uses the Stages of Reading Development chart (figure 3) as well as the Reading Development Checklist (figure 4). Again, both guide the teacher in looking at the developmental nature of the child's reading.

The underlying point in learning to read, as in learning to write, is that it is a process which takes time. For example, one day Gabriela asked her teacher if she could read her a picture book which had several paragraphs on each page. Telling the story through the pictures, Gabriela sounded as if she

Figure 3

STAGES OF READING DEVELOPMENT

Example	Stage
1. *Goldilocks and the Three Bears* "Bears . . . There's the girl . . . look at the beds . . ."	Attends to pictures; Does not tell story. (Labels or comments on pictures)
2. *Goldilocks and the Three Bears* "Once upon a time, three bears lived in a forest. One day . . ."	Attends to pictures; Tells story. (Sounds like child is reading the story)
3. A *Zoo* "A tiger lives in the zoo. A bear lives in the zoo." A tiger lives in the zoo. / A bear lives in the zoo.	Attends to pictures; Memorizes simple patterned text; Knows print contains meaning. (May finger point matching words to memorized text, but no reading)
4. A *Zoo* T "A tiger lives in the zoo." A Tiger lives in the **zoo.**	Attends to pictures and <u>some</u> text. (Uses picture clues, memorized text, beginning sounds and sight words to access "story")
5. A *Zoo* "A tiger lives in the zoo." A Tiger lives **in the zoo.**	Reads simple, patterned text. (Relies on picture clues, familiar story, beginning sounds, and sight words to access "text")
6. *Goldilocks and the Three Bears* "One day a <u>lost</u> girl <u>went</u> in the <u>f-f- fast</u>." One day a <u>little</u> girl <u>wandered</u> <u>into</u> the <u>forest.</u>	Reads text with inconsistent strategy use (meaning, syntax, phonics).
7. *Goldilocks and the Three Bears* "One day a <u>lost</u> . . . a little girl wandered in the <u>f- for- forest</u>." One day a little girl wandered into the forest.	Reads text independently; Uses all strategies effectively (meaning, syntax, phonics); Self-corrects.

Stone, S. J. (1996). *Creating the multiage classroom.* Glenview, IL: GoodYear Books/ScottForesman. Used by Permission.

were actually reading the book. The teacher, recognizing this developmental stage of reading (attends to pictures; tells a story), recorded Gabriela's stage of reading development in her anecdotal records. The anecdotal records along with Gabriela's Reading Log were added to her literacy portfolio. During small group reading, the teacher built on Gabriela's stage of development by using strategies that helped her begin moving to the next stage of attending to print, a move that took Gabriela almost four months.

Figure 4

READING DEVELOPMENT CHECKLIST

Name ______________________ Date______________________

STAGE ONE	SEP	OCT	NOV	DEC	JAN	FEB	MAR	APR	MAY
Front/back of book									
Top/bottom of page									
Attends to pictures: Labels/comments									
Attends to pictures: Tells story									
Print contains meaning									
Differentiates letters/words									
Concept of word/space									
Identifies some environmental print									
One-to-one matching (voice to print)									
Knows where to begin									
Left-to-right/Return sweep									
Memorizes text									
STAGE TWO	SEP	OCT	NOV	DEC	JAN	FEB	MAR	APR	MAY
Attends to some print									
Identifies some letters									
Identifies sight words									
Uses picture clues									
Uses familiar story									
Uses beginning consonants									
Uses beginning and end consonants									
Uses some strategies (mean., syn., phon.)									
Expects reading to make sense									
Expects reading to sound right									
Uses knowledge of letter/sound relationships									
Takes risks without fear of making errors									
STAGE THREE	SEP	OCT	NOV	DEC	JAN	FEB	MAR	APR	MAY
Reads using all strategies (mean., syn., phon.)									
Uses decoding to confirm or disconfirm other strategies									
Self-corrects									
Rereads for meaning									
Reads on to gain meaning									
Retells story (set., char., theme, plot, res.)									
STAGE FOUR	SEP	OCT	NOV	DEC	JAN	FEB	MAR	APR	MAY
Reads with fluency (expression, rate)									
Silently reads new text independently									
Integrates all strategies (mean., syn., phon.)									
Reads different ways for different purposes									
Comprehends text (literal, inferential, critical)									

Stone, S. J. (1996). *Creating the multiage classroom.* Glenview, IL: GoodYear Books/ScottForesman. Used by Permission.

The teacher's knowledge that it takes time for a child to understand what it means to read significantly influenced how she conferenced with the child. She patiently gave Gabriela time to develop and used the portfolio contents to help her identify appropriate instructional strategies that would support Gabriela's shift to the next stage. Also included in the portfolio were running records (Clay 1985) that documented Gabriela's emerging use of the cueing system and independent reading strategies. She also included Gabriela's progress in retelling stories to document her comprehension skills.

Every portfolio conference was permeated with an attitude of celebration. The teacher encouraged Gabriela by focusing in on the good things Gabriela was doing. She said, "Gabriela, you are using picture clues to read the word," or "You self-corrected that word. Good job!" She also asked Gabriela questions to encourage Gabriela's own reflection on her reading strategies. "Gabriela, you read the word 'open' here. Does that make sense? Does that look right?" The teacher used what she knew about Gabriela's reading process as documented in her portfolio to inform the teacher's own instructional strategies and in conferencing with Gabriela. The portfolio also documented the child's successful growth in her personal construction of the reading process over time.

Effective Portfolio Assessment of Early Literacy

We have briefly looked at the developmental processes of writing and reading and how this knowledge interacts with portfolio assessment in the classroom. Why is this knowledge crucial to effective portfolio assessment?

Without this knowledge, the early literacy portfolio becomes simply a collection of work. The child is the producer of the work; the teacher is the collector. Without the knowledge of the developmental processes of reading and writing, the portfolio becomes an artifact rather than an interactive, dynamic tool used to support early literacy development.

Let's look again at the three main components of this type of portfolio: 1) documenting student progress/growth; 2) supporting and guiding instruction; and 3) communicating to both the child and parents each child's successful growth.

First, an effective literacy development portfolio *documents growth.* It is the knowledge of the developmental process of literacy that gives the teacher a yardstick to measure growth. From the Stages of Writing and the Writing Development Checklist, the teacher knows what to look for as the child constructs her knowledge of the process. The teacher can celebrate the beginning stages of the child: 1) drawing to represent the world, 2) beginning to use letters, 3) using letters for sounds, and 4) writing multiple sentences with many correct spellings. The examples in Figure 5 show how a child's writing in his literacy portfolio document the growth the child has made in the process of becoming a writer.

Figure 5

In reading, the teacher recognizes the beginning stages of reading development by using the Stages of Reading Development and the Reading Development Checklist. When a child begins to attend to pictures of a favorite book and tells her own stories, the teacher can document this behavior as emerging literacy. When a child begins to read back her scribbles, the teacher knows the child is beginning the process of learning that print contains meaning. The teacher records when the child uses memorized text and reads with inconsistent strategies at the instructional level as indicated by a running record. The examples in Figure 6 from a child's portfolio document the child's growth in the reading process.

Figure 6

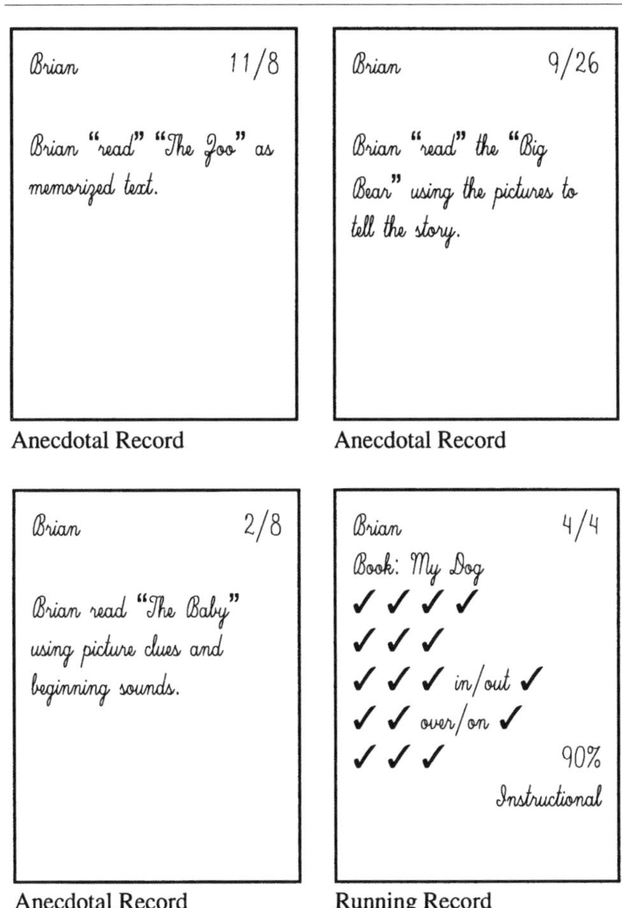

As the teacher conducts portfolio conferences with each child about her growth, the child is able to see the progress she has made, thus encouraging the her to continue to grow. The standard is growth on a developmental scale, remembering that each child is an individual developing at her own pace. No one is labeled below or above grade level.

Without the knowledge of the developmental processes of reading and writing, the teacher is unable to celebrate the growth steps because she does not know what to look for. The uninformed teacher may actually impair the growth of the child, because she does not know the next step in development (Gomez et al. 1991). It is the knowledge of the process of literacy development that gives the teacher reason for celebration, as well as direction in appropriate instructional strategies.

Second, an effective portfolio also *supports and guides instruction.* Knowing the developmental processes of reading and writing directs the teacher to the next growth step she needs to support for the child. For example, if a teacher conducts a portfolio conference with Conrad and discovers he is in the beginning stages of using letters for sounds, the teacher then uses this knowledge from the portfolio to interact with her instruction. As the teacher works with Conrad, she will support him with opportunities to use letters for sounds. As Conrad shows progress in sound-symbol relationships for initial consonants, the teacher will then support him in developing the sound-symbol relationship for vowels. The teacher knows the next developing stage (figures 1 and 2) and is able to intelligently nurture the next step in Conrad's development. Without this knowledge, the teacher is not able to effectively use portfolio assessment to support and guide her instruction.

Lastly, the portfolio *communicates to both children and parents each child's successful growth.* A teacher's knowledge about the process of literacy development enhances conferencing with both children and parents about the contents in the portfolio. The teacher, as well as the child, selects work to represent the growth the child has made. Parents find that the portfolio based on developmental processes gives them more information about their child and an understanding of their child's own literacy development.

For example, in Maria's portfolio, items were chosen to reflect her development throughout the year. Maria began the year at the preletter writing stage. She could draw simple pictures. Within a few months, Maria began to write letters and then strings of letters. By midyear, Maria was using letters as substitutes for sounds. By the end of the year, she was writing simple sentences. The teacher and Maria placed evidence of each stage of development in Maria's portfolio and checked the selections on the developmental checklist. The teacher, Maria, and Maria's parents could celebrate her growth during the year.

Children who are not involved in documenting their own literacy development through portfolios are often denied the opportunity to see for themselves that they are growing and developing in their literacy abilities. Fortunately, Maria had the opportunity through her portfolio to see her progress and celebrate her own success, leading her to see herself as a competent, successful learner.

Knowledge of developmental literacy also helps the teacher effectively interpret literacy growth to the child and parents. To a parent, Charles's scribbles may hold no meaning or value. The parent may only view Charles as one who cannot write letters yet, seeing only what Charles *cannot* do. But the teacher can help the parent see what Charles *can* do. She can help the parent understand that a scribble is an important part of the developmental process of Charles's literacy growth. Charles knows that writing on paper is a way to communicate. The scribble is a positive indication of his emerging understanding of literacy. Only within the context of the developmental process does the child's scribble find merit, and does the child see that what he knows is valuable. The parents also see their child's work as positive stages in his development.

Interactive, Dynamic Tool

The portfolio also provides the tool for children to interact with the knowledge of what they can do and also reflect, as thoughtful evaluators of their own work, on what they will do next on the developmental continuum. As Donald Graves suggests, "The portfolio movement promises one of the best opportunities for students to learn how to examine their own work and participate in the entire literacy/learning process" (Graves and Sunstein 1992, 4).

For the teacher, the early literacy portfolio is a tool to celebrate children's current literacy development which interacts with instruction, so the teacher is able to effectively guide and support future literacy development. The teacher reflects on the child's learning and her own instructional strategies. The teacher reflects on what each piece in the portfolio says about the child's current development, what the next step should be, and what the teacher can do instructionally to support the child's next developmental step. Reflection on the portfolio contents not only guides instruction, but it helps the teacher and child decide on additional contents for the portfolio and set goals together.

What the teacher knows about the developmental process of reading, each child's development, and the evaluation of the development interacts to create a portfolio that is truly dynamic, producing positive change in both the teacher and child. As a dynamic tool, the portfolio supports the assessment of the processes of early literacy development and helps teachers to make changes in instruction in order to meet the needs of the learner, thus becoming a formative assessment that helps children develop.

11

Portfolios and Flow

Thomas Philion

Nurturing Student Engagement

LIKE MANY LITERACY EDUCATORS, I AM AN ADVOCATE AND USER OF portfolios. I use portfolios in all the classes that I teach: an undergraduate English course on young adult literature, a methods course for prospective secondary English educators, and a graduate seminar on English education. My approach to portfolios is slightly different in each of these classes. In my undergraduate literature course, students choose two writing projects to develop and then share with me the evolution of their work in the form of a final portfolio. In my methods course, students work collaboratively using computers to produce an electronic portfolio that represents their collective knowledge, interest, and ability with regard to the teaching of English. In my graduate seminar, students write a fifteen- to twenty-page research paper that they then submit to me in a final portfolio that contains the various materials they accumulated in undertaking their project. Within these different approaches, there are similarities. In all of my courses, students share writing with one another and revise their writing using the feedback they receive from peers and from me; this process of feedback and revision is always documented in the final portfolio. Additionally, all portfolios contain an introduction and a reflective conclusion. In their reflective conclusions, students comment on their experiences as writers, assess their achievements, and speculate as to their future goals and activities.

In developing a rationale for my portfolio pedagogy, I have drawn primarily from recent scholarship in composition theory and practice. Persuaded by composition teachers and researchers that students need time, ownership, and constructive feedback in order to improve their writing (Calkins 1983; Knoblauch and Brannon 1984; Atwell 1987; Goswami and Stillman 1987), I have used portfolios to nurture student engagement in writing practice, revision, and self-evaluation. Believing with these same teachers and researchers that it is important to evaluate holistically the quality of my students' writing and to examine my own teaching, I have used portfolios to obtain insight into my students' writing processes and to reflect upon the nature of my writing assignments and teaching practices. As do Steve Zemelman, Harvey Daniels, and Arthur Hyde, I have conceived portfolios as an excellent means of achieving "best practice" in writing instruction (Zemelman et al. 1993).

Flow

Recently, however, the work of the educational psychologist Mihaly Csikszentmihalyi has begun to inform my thinking. In his various books, Csikszentmihalyi develops the notion of "flow," or a subjective state in which a person is "completely involved in something to the point of *losing track of time and of being unaware of fatigue and of everything else but the activity itself*" (Csikszentmihalyi 1993, 14—italics added). Csikszentmihalyi's research suggests that there is a strong relationship between learning and flow; when people are involved in an activity so deeply that they lose all awareness of time and fatigue, they report higher levels of enjoyment, concentration, and psychic complexity than in other situations (Csikszentmihalyi 1993, 15-16). Consequently, Csikszentmihalyi argues that educators ought to foster the conditions that nurture flow in classroom environments. Clear goals, immediate and unambiguous feedback, and a balance between opportunities for action and abilities to act all contribute significantly, explains Csikszentmihalyi, to the achievement of flow (Csikszentmihalyi 1993, 14). Csikszentmihalyi emphasizes that fostering such conditions is not easy. Teachers must be passionate about learning, attentive to the conditions that enhance the experience of intrinsic rewards, and attentive to the shifting needs of students (Csikszentmihalyi 1993, 190-193). He also suggests that individual personality, social environment, and family life will constrain any teacher's effort to engage students in flow in school (Csikszentmihalyi 1993, 6-8).

Optimal Learning and a Critical Lens

Csikszentmihalyi's notion of flow seems to me important for teachers using portfolios in two different ways. On the one hand, Csikszentmihalyi's ideas about the conditions that produce optimal learning provide an additional theoretical justification for teaching with portfolios in literacy classrooms. Features of portfolio pedagogy that I perceive as significant—giving students opportunities to select topics and forms for writing, providing repeated opportunities for peer and teacher feedback, and inviting students to evaluate their work—all potentially coincide with or nurture the conditions that Csikszentmihalyi claims are crucial to the achievement of flow. Giving students choice in their writing enhances the likelihood that they perceive clear goals and a balance between their abilities and their opportunities for action. Providing repeated opportunities for peer and teacher feedback diminishes the likelihood of miscommunication about goals and expectations. Inviting students to evaluate their work also can clarify goals and can provide teachers with an important opportunity to attend to the shifting needs of students. While I am not so naive as to believe that a portfolio pedagogy can guarantee the creation of the sort of intensely focused learning environment that Csikszentmihalyi envisions, I do believe that a carefully and flexibly enacted portfolio pedagogy can contribute in important ways to meaningful and inspired student learning.

Csikszentmihalyi's notion of flow also can provide portfolio teachers with a valuable critical lens through which to reflect upon their teaching. As I just indicated, attempts to involve students meaningfully in writing through portfolios do not always meet with success. Recently, for example, one of my students completely ignored my feedback on her essay and submitted it unrevised, and with only a cursory reflective conclusion, in her final portfolio. Another student declined to submit any portfolio at all. In these and similar instances, Csikszentmihalyi's notion of flow helps me to interrogate my teaching. Were these students confused by the complexity of my portfolio pedagogy? Was there an imbalance between their abilities and the opportunities for writing and revision that I organized in my classroom? Did I miss an opportunity or somehow fail in my effort to clarify my goals and expectations? Did factors of which I was unaware impinge upon my students' ability to succeed in my course? Did additional factors constrain my own ability to create a nurturing classroom environment? While these questions do not always yield firm answers, they do help me to consider the complicated nature of the context in which I teach. They help me to examine *how* I enact my portfolio pedagogy, and perhaps even to plan new ways of situating myself in relation to my students.

For me, this is the real value of Csikszentmihalyi's work. From within the conventional conceptual framework of portfolio pedagogy (i.e., composition studies), it sometimes is easy to forget the complexity of what is involved in making any pedagogical method function meaningfully in a classroom setting. An awareness of the conditions that nurture active learning can help portfolio advocates to see beyond the exigencies of pedagogical method. With a knowledge of these conditions, literacy educators can ask critical questions: Are the goals of my portfolio pedagogy understood by my students? Do my goals intersect in a meaningful way with my students' assumptions and interests? Do I engage my students in repeated conversation about our shared goals and methods? Is there a balance between abilities and opportunities for action in my classroom environment?

These assumptions—that portfolios facilitate the creation of an optimal learning environment, and that flow theory and research can provide portfolio pedagogues with a critical lens upon their teaching—were confirmed by a paper I heard at the NCTE-sponsored conference "Portfolios, Reflection, and Teacher Research." Lauren Sewell, then a graduate student at the University of Louisville, pointed out that the professional literature on portfolios rarely speaks to the difficulties inherent in teaching with portfolios. Sewell suggested that this lack of critical perspective could very well undermine efforts to advance portfolio pedagogies. By way of example, Sewell told a story about an orientation for beginning teaching assistants in the composition program at her university. During this orientation, Sewell and other members of a portfolio reading group enthusiastically shared insights about portfolios that they had gleaned from their reading and teaching. However, after the orientation was over, Sewell and her colleagues discovered that many of the orientation participants had characterized their session as "preaching" and "indoctrination" in written evaluations. This feedback, Sewell explained, had awakened her to the shortcomings of a professional discourse that celebrates portfolios without acknowledging problems. Sewell concluded her talk by challenging her audience to devise better ways of introducing portfolios to beginning and/or skeptical literacy educators.

Sewell's presentation produced a series of reflections that eventually led me to the insights regarding portfolios and flow that I outlined above.

Immediately, I thought about Csikszentmihalyi's notion of flow and how the conditions that nurture it must have been missing in Sewell and her colleagues' session on portfolios. I speculated as to the reasons for this—did the participants in this session share the same goals as Sewell and her colleagues? Did the orientation organizers devote time before the orientation to obtaining feedback on the proposed goals, content, and methods of the various orientation sessions? In the session on portfolios, were the participants able to perceive an intersection between their abilities and what they were being advised to do as literacy educators? From my position in the rear of the conference room, it seemed to me that these types of questions could help Sewell to develop a critical perspective in relation to the apparent miscommunication that took place in her and her colleagues' session on portfolios.

Having made this connection between Csikszentmihalyi's ideas and Sewell's narrative about a problematic orientation to portfolios, I began to think about what seemed to me the obvious contrast between the presentation that I had just heard and the session on portfolios that Sewell had described in her talk. In contrast to the session that she had described, Sewell's conference presentation was an exemplary model of how to talk about portfolios when addressing other literacy educators. Sewell's talk had was extremely clear in terms of its goals, and Sewell invited feedback from her audience. Her use of storytelling techniques and her explicit focus on the difficulties involved in working with portfolios created a context where I could perceive an intersection between my abilities and what Sewell was inviting me to consider. I began to think that perhaps Csikszentmihalyi's ideas could help literacy educators not only to reflect on good ways of speaking to one another in professional contexts, but also to interrogate and explain the nature of their portfolio pedagogies.

Fostering an Intense Involvement in Learning

The insight that I obtained at that moment has remained with me to this day. A portfolio ought not to be conceived as solely a tool or a series of strategies that literacy educators employ in order to nurture and evaluate student writing. A portfolio also should be thought of as a creative means of fostering a classroom environment in which an intense involvement in learning can occur. An awareness of the conditions that nurture flow can help literacy educators be sensitive to the multiple ways in which their portfolio pedagogy might serve this end. Additionally, this awareness can enable the interrogation of those situations where portfolio pedagogy does not work, or does not work as well as one would like. Problems with portfolio pedagogy never lie in the idea of a portfolio itself; instead, they lie in the complex relations between our students, our classroom environment, and our enactment of our portfolio pedagogy. It is this point that Csikszentmihalyi's work makes most clear, and that I hope readers of this essay take with them into their future teaching.

12

Producing Purposeful Portfolios

Mary Perry

Recognizing a Need for Portfolios

EVERY BELIEF I HAD EVER HELD ABOUT EDUCATION WAS CHALLENGED during the summer of 1991 as I learned about project-based instruction with a group of approximately twenty-five other educators in a month-long session sponsored by the school district where I worked. We studied and debated the educational implications of documents prepared by local businesses showing math, reading, and writing skills needed for employees to be successful in various occupations. Another document with a business focus, *What Work Requires of School*, from the Secretary's Commission on Achieving Necessary Skills confirmed the need for major changes in education. We also looked at the work of educators. Daily, we revisited Dewey with a chapter by chapter discussion of *Experience and Education*. And we looked to more contemporary work, studying "The Foxfire Approach: Perspectives and Core Practices," as well as the works of Dennie Palmer Wolf and Lauren Resnick.

I returned to a high school English classroom in the fall, determined to use projects and portfolios with my students. They enthusiastically began work on projects, and I was thrilled with the high quality of work they produced. I had no doubt that their portfolios would reflect their best efforts, and I planned to use portfolios as a culminating task during the last grading period of the year.

First Effort

The first time I asked high school students to put together portfolios of their work, I suggested they review their writing folders and consider work they had done in other classes as well as their interests outside of school. And I required four items: a resume, a letter explaining their portfolio entries, and at least two pieces of writing.

Yes, they could include video tapes. Yes, they could include science experiments. Yes, they could include drawings. While most of the questions centered on what to put in the portfolio, some students asked what we were doing this for and who was going to see it. "Well," I said, "you know." I knew I was in big trouble with the group the moment I said "you know."

"You might want to use it to try to get into college, or you might want to use it to get a job." And when I could tell that these reasons were not particularly appealing to my ninth graders in the last several weeks of the school year, I quickly added the lamest reason of all, suggesting, "You might want to show it to next year's teacher," which held no water since we all knew that I would be their tenth grade English teacher the following year.

It was a miracle that rebellion didn't follow, and the fact that it didn't was indicative of the classroom climate. The students remained polite, but totally disengaged in their work. As the deadline drew nearer, they still seemed relatively unconcerned.

While my students were working on their portfolios, I, too, worked on assembling a portfolio showing my professional work. Producing a portfolio of my work was one of the professional goals I had established for myself that year, and I planned to present my portfolio to my supervisor as part of the annual evaluation of my performance. I shared my progress with my students and asked their permission to include a class project in my portfolio. They asked why I wanted to include their work, but readily gave me permission when I explained that their hard work reflected the work and commitment I'd given to the class.

But even though I was modeling both the task and the process, in a class that had gone better than any I had ever taught before, it wasn't enough. Most of the students waited until the last possible moment, threw work from their writing folders into their portfolios without even considering further revisions, added their resumes, and then drafted cover letters that were included in first draft form. These they presented to me.

Knowing the quality of work these students had produced during the year, I was disappointed with the results. These students had spent most of the year studying the SCANS (Secretary's Commission on Achieving Necessary Skills) competencies from the U.S. Department of Labor, comparing the competencies with our district's ninth grade language arts curriculum and writing a proposal suggesting that the curriculum be changed to reflect the SCANS competencies. Most of the students included this document as one of their portfolio entries, but they put little effort into their other selections. The portfolios simply did not live up to my expectations, but how could they since I had never even clearly identified my expectations? Knowing the problem was greater than end of the year burnout, I reminded myself that this had been a learning experience for all of us, and I was determined to help the students do a better job the following year. There was no failure attached to the portfolios, and I rested easier knowing high stakes for the students had not been attached to our initial portfolio experience.

Time to Reflect

Just a few days after the school year ended, a group of teachers who had worked and planned together the previous summer reconvened to discuss our year using project-based instruction. Some spoke of their problems with portfolios; others planned to use portfolios the following year; I confessed nothing. But when we devoted a day to discussing portfolios, I realized the major errors in my efforts with my students.

Had I not gone through the process of putting together a professional portfolio, my students' problems might still have eluded me. But, as we discussed portfolio contents and purposes and audiences, I realized I was able to successfully put together my portfolio because I had a clear sense of both the purpose and the audience for my work while my students knew neither. Knowing the purpose and the audience allowed me to gather appropriate contents. So, I reasoned, if my students had both a clear sense of purpose and audience, they too would be able to assemble better portfolios. And, I knew the purpose needed to be relevant to the students. These students had been willing to work on the curriculum document through numerous revisions because they knew the work was important. It wasn't just school work; it had a real purpose and audience outside the school building. But, I couldn't imagine a singular portfolio purpose that would meet the needs of all of my students.

Year Two

"You're gonna have to put together a portfolio," one young man who had been in my class the previous year told a newcomer on the second day of school. He looked at me for confirmation, "Right, Ms. Perry?"

"That's right," I said. "We are all going to put together portfolios, and we're going to do a better job this year." Everyone anticipated portfolio work. Without my prompting, students who had a portfolio shared their experiences with others. Each time portfolios were mentioned, I pointed out my expectations for improvement the second time around.

Near the end of the first semester, I asked students to begin three lists on the wall in the room. The lists (see Appendix A) were labeled Possible Portfolio Purposes, Possible Portfolio Audiences, and Possible Portfolio Contents. Students added to the lists as new ideas struck them, but I said very little about the lists.

By the time we placed the lists on the wall, I was making plans to move out of the area at the end of the school year. Again I shared my portfolio with students showing them how I changed the contents as I interviewed for different positions. I put certain items in for an interview with a testing company. I rearranged the contents before meeting with school district personnel. And, I told my students, potential employers were visibly impressed with my efforts. My portfolio gave me an edge over others applying for the same positions I was interested in, and this was an edge over the competition that I wanted them to have.

We picked a date at the beginning of the last grading period, and each student came to class and declared his or her portfolio purpose. Clearly the purpose of the portfolio determined the audience. Most decided to use their portfolios in order to get jobs; the audience for these students' portfolios would be potential employers. Another large number chose to design portfolios in order to gain entrance to or a scholarship for college; the audience for these students' portfolios would be admissions officers or scholarship committee members. One student came to class and said, "You know I'm going to college. Before I go, I'll put together a portfolio for that. But I need a job this summer, so I'm going to work on a portfolio that will help with that now." The students were beginning to recognize portfolios could be tools to help them reach their goals.

Students then began to work with other students who shared the same purpose and audience. Only after the students determined the specific purpose and audience for their portfolio effort could they successfully consider contents.

The plan was for each group to figure out whom they could interview in order to get an idea about contents for their portfolios. Each group was charged to design interview questions, and each student was to conduct an interview. Group members were then to review the data collected from the interviews and to design a rubric to be used in order to score the portfolios. Each group would have a rubric, and each group member could then assemble a portfolio to meet the specifications set forth in the scoring guide.

The students who were trying to get jobs—and there were two groups of these students—conducted interviews (see Appendices B and C) with people in area businesses who often hired high school students. These groups had few problems, but the students who were putting together portfolios to get into college had a very different experience. They contacted admissions officers (see Appendix D) at different colleges and universities and had trouble getting any helpful information whatsoever. Admissions officers told them they just needed to submit a completed application for admission, a copy of test scores, a high school transcript, and at least two letters of recommendation. The students realized they were being told what every student who wants to enroll was told, and they were frustrated.

We held a group conference, and I pointed out that if the admissions officers could quickly and easily describe appropriate portfolio contents, it would be because many students were submitting portfolios. Thus, they would have no edge over their competition. I reassured them that it was truly a plus that help was not so readily available. We renegotiated deadlines for their interviews, and they tried again with much the same results. However, one young man came in one morning saying he'd had no luck getting any helpful information from the school he called. "So," he said, "I walked two doors down and asked a prof who teaches science what he'd like to see in a student's portfolio. He said he'd like to see some of a kid's good work from high school." This group designed their rubric to include the items typically requested by the admissions office as well as school work other students might not include. They then bombarded the counselors' office with requests for transcripts and test scores. The students decided to use the scores from the state test taken earlier in the school year as a place holder until they took the SAT as eleventh or twelfth graders.

I asked the students to consider not only contents, but also the quality of contents as they designed their rubrics, so I was concerned when they equated quality of contents with whether or not the entries were typed or written (see Appendices E and F), but rather than lecturing or holding a conference, I waited and watched. Again I was concerned as some groups designed rubrics that made it very easy for someone to just skate by with a passing score, but I watched and waited. Students took ownership of their portfolios, and no one tried to take an easy way out.

One rubric (see Appendix G) contained a point value breakdown for contents and the quality of contents. I liked the specificity of this rubric; however, I talked to the group members and expressed my reluctance to use this rubric when I realized that a student could get twelve points for well-organized in the high category but fifteen points for semi-organized in the average area. They explained to me that there should be no confusion since each group member would declare whether her portfolio (all members of this particular group were girls) should be scored on the high scale or on the average scale.

Once the students had the rubrics, they began to select the contents for their portfolios. Unlike the year before, revision took place, and the students in all the groups had many impressive entries to include in their portfolios. Most students included self-assessments of their work. Some of the students included a chapter they had written for an educational book. In this chapter the students discussed their work putting together the curriculum document the previous year, and by the time the students were assembling their portfolios, the chapter had been accepted for inclusion in the book. Several students had done presentations at professional educational meetings. These students had conference proposals and conference programs to display in their portfolios. One student wrote about the portfolio experience itself as a portfolio entry:

Problems With Presenting The Portfolio

1. . . . the college I called . . . did not know about portfolios. Ex. They said "That they were confused about what portfolios were used for."
2. (The college) didn't put me in touch with the right people. Ex.They kept transferring me to different departments, neither of them knew what I was talking about.
3. One mistake I made was that I probably didn't give enough information or fully explain what a portfolio is.
4. Another mistake I might have made was not asking for the right department.

In conclusion, I think that there was a lack of communication on my part and theirs. The next time I contact a college or any important building or business, I will be fully prepared.

I was very pleased with this entry because it showed a change in attitude over the course of the two years we had spent together. Initially reluctant to accept responsibility for anything that did not go well, students came to realize the value in taking risks and learning from mistakes.

At some point during this work, all of us agreed that the score on each portfolio would be used as the student's grade for the last six weeks' grading period. We planned for each portfolio to be scored three times: once by the owner, once by a peer selected by the portfolio owner, and once by me. However, the group that put together portfolios for college was understandably behind schedule, and most of those portfolios were scored only twice, by the owner and by me. But it didn't matter; scoring conflicts were nonexistent. I scored the portfolios the same way the students scored them. Portfolios with three scores had three matching scores.

Another Group's Efforts

Since my work with the high school students, I have helped students in an alternative middle school setting put together end-of-year portfolios. The purpose of these portfolios was to demonstrate readiness for the next grade, a most meaningful purpose since many of these students left the regular academic setting with numerical averages that would have meant certain failure without an alternative form of assessment.

These students selected the contents of their portfolios to show they were competent in the areas of language arts, math, science, and social studies. In addition, they included self-assessments where they discussed their progress toward meeting the individual goals they had set when they entered the alternative program. One student included an office referral she had received earlier in the year for disruptive behavior and placed beside it a discussion of her current behavior. This juxtaposition was a most effective strategy for her purpose and audience. And all of the students gained positive recognition for their efforts when the portfolios were displayed at a fine arts fair and reviewed by the principal.

Implications and Conclusion

Most importantly, the purpose and audience of any portfolio must be explicit. Moreover, the purpose must be meaningful to the students. All students do not have to assemble portfolios for the same purposes and audiences, but all must have explicit rubrics for scoring. Teachers should model the portfolio process, sharing their portfolio efforts with their students. Models of student portfolios are helpful as well, but these should, however, only provide a place to start, so each portfolio can be an expression of its owner.

Portfolios are flexible, adaptable instruments; to be useful, they must change constantly. A portfolio that is several years old is like an old photograph. It might be pretty, but it doesn't give a clear picture of the owner's current strengths. Certainly, it is appropriate to include entries from years past in a portfolio, but the portfolio should be revisited and revised regularly. Not only should revisions take place for new purposes or audiences, but also they should take place for self-reflection.

Another significant factor is the classroom climate. Much is written about risk-free environments in schools, and certainly this type of environment is necessary for the creation of successful portfolios. If I had been overly critical of my students' first portfolios or had placed high stakes on their initial efforts, the students would not have generated enthusiasm for another try. And students will only be able to be active participants in the portfolio process if their involvement in all phases of their work at school, from planning projects to negotiating deadlines to assessing their efforts and the results of their efforts, is routine.

My guiding principle then is to ask students to do work, and that includes assembling their portfolios, only if it will truly benefit them and/or the community. And the students are active participants in deciding what they should do. Once this principle began to guide my efforts with students, the quality of their work increased dramatically. The evidence to support including students in all phases of classroom decision-making is overwhelming when I consider the differences between portfolios from the same students, who one year assembled them to meet the course requirements and the next year assembled them based on their own needs.

When a student works hard to produce a portfolio that meets the student's needs, there is a sense of accomplishment, pride, and ownership. "Yes, Ms. Perry, you may borrow my portfolio to show at the conference," one student graciously said. "But you'll have to carry it on the plane. I trust you, but you can't let it out of your sight."

Appendix A

Student Lists of Portfolio Possiblities

Possible Portfolio Purposes
- to be evaluated for a grade
- to show off abilities
- to get a job
- to get into college or get a scholarship

Possible Portfolio Audiences
- self
- friends
- parents
- teachers
- possible employers
- college admissions officers
- scholarship committee members

Possible Portfolio Contents
- stories
- poems
- plays
- self-assessments
- reports
- experiment results
- video tapes
- audio tapes
- photographs
- controversial issue papers

Appendix B

Purpose of Portfolio: To Help Obtain Employment

contacting________________________________
person interviewed________________________________
title________________________________
phone number________________________________
address________________________________

1. What would you like to see in the portfolio of a student who is a potential employee?
2. What do you look for in a potential employee?
3. Does the appearance of a potential employee matter to you?

Appendix C

Purpose of the Portfolio: To Help Obtain Employment

contacting____
person interviewed________________________________
title____
phone number____________________________________
address____

1. What would you like to see in the portfolio of a student who is a potential employee?
2. What kind of writings would you like to see in a portfolio?
3. What would impress you most about a potential employee?
4. What do you expect when hiring somebody?
5. What typing qualifications are required to be hired as a secretary?

Appendix D

Purpose Of Portfolio: To Help Obtain Entrance And/Or Scholarship To College

contacting____
person interviewed_________________________________
title____
phone number_____________________________________
address____

1. What would you like to see in an incoming student's portfolio?
2. Is a portfolio required upon entrance?
3. Would the presence of a portfolio affect the entrance of a person in college?
4. Do most of your students have a portfolio when entering your college?
5. What happens when a student does not show a portfolio?

Appendix E
Portfolio Scoring Guide

Portfolio Purpose: to obtain entrance and/or a scholarship to college

HIGH 91--100		AVERAGE 80--90		LOW 0--79	
contents	**quality of contents**	**contents**	**quality of contents**	**contents**	**quality of contents**
resume	typed	resume	typed	resume	typed
table of contents	typed	table of contents	typed		
transcripts	printed	transcripts	printed	transcripts	printed
test scores	printed	test scores	printed	test scores	printed
recommendations	written	recommendations	written		
previous school work (5 samples)	written	previous school work (2 samples)	written		

Appendix F
Portfolio Scoring Guide

Portfolio Purpose: to help obtain employment

HIGH 91--100		AVERAGE 80--90		LOW 0--79	
contents	**quality of contents**	**contents**	**quality of contents**	**contents**	**quality of contents**
resume		resume			
cover sheet	all typed	cover sheet	all hand-	cover sheet	all hand-
table of contents	and edited	table of contents	written	table of contents	written
past employment records			or typed		or typed
references		references			
transcripts					
self-assessment		self-assessment		self-assessment	
writing sample		writing sample			

Appendix G
Portfolio Scoring Guide

Portfolio Purpose: to help obtain employment

HIGH: 100

contents:	**70 points**
resume (1 or 2 pages)	10 points
cover letter	10 points
one or two letters of reference	10 points
anything else (at least 4 entries) that shows responsibility, reliability and dedication (for example: writings, books, videos presentations, class projects)	10 points each, 40 points total

quality of contents	**30 points**
contents typed and edited	13 points
well-organized	12 points
on time	5 points

Grades may be flexible

AVERAGE: 85

contents:	**50 points**
resume (1 or 2 pages)	10 points
cover letter	10 points
anything else (at least 2 entries) that shows responsibility, reliability and dedication (for example: writings, books, videos, presentations, class projects)	15 points each, 30 points total

quality of contents	**35 points**
contents typed or handwritten few mistakes allowed	15 points
semi-organized	15 points
if on time accepted 2 or 3 days late	5 points

LOW: a poor average

13

Building Bridges, Closing Gaps

Using Portfolios to Reconstruct the Academic Community

William Condon

Context is everything: What a surgeon does, under any other circumstances, is assault with a deadly weapon.
Jesse Jackson

ONE OF THE FIRST LESSONS WE LEARN WHEN DEALING WITH ANY KIND of assessment is that context is indeed everything. If we fail to understand the context for the assessment, then we cannot know the questions the assessment is to answer; we cannot collect appropriate samples, define appropriate criteria, set appropriate objectives, nor know whether we have achieved them. In short, without a full understanding of context, we leave ourselves open to just the kind of disaster Jesse Jackson mentions: instead of accomplishing a skilled act that does good, we end up hacking the "patient" apart, leaving it worse off than before we began.[1] Of course, the more the context resists understanding, the greater the danger of violating the first principle every surgeon swears to uphold: first, do no harm.

Our context—our educational setting—alas, does resist understanding, primarily because it already resembles the outcome of a bad surgical procedure. Education has been sliced and diced, cut up into pieces by level and discipline to the point that learners and teachers alike pay more attention to the differences between those classes and levels than to the similarities. For a variety of sound educational and logistical reasons, we have divided the educational process into segments. In doing so, however, we have also created gaps—spaces between the segments—gaps that often obscure the many necessary connections (common goals, basic intellectual tools, etc.) that unify the whole enterprise of becoming educated. Wielded effectively in an appropriate context, assessment can be the scalpel that provides a means for alleviating the discomfort and "disease" these gaps occasion.

Fragments and Gaps

The principal obstacle educational assessment faces at all levels, but especially in higher education, is the way the context has become fragmented. We have something called preschool, which is separate from elementary school, which in turn is separate from middle school, which is separate from high school. And whereas in the past the high school got its name because it was located on the top floor of a building that contained all the grades from kindergarten to twelfth, today each stage occupies a different building, often in different parts of town. At each stage, in many districts, there is a commencement, a graduation ceremony that encourages students to think that when they arrive at their new building, they are making a new beginning. Faculty, too, are caught up in specializations that emphasize the differences between what teachers do at their different levels and in their different locations, rather than the continuity in their common endeavor. An educator with a degree in Elementary Education does not teach in the high school, nor does an educator with certification in Physics teach second graders. In the elementary years, teachers at a single grade level are encouraged to think of themselves as separate from each other, as members of a small group whose purposes are different from those of other small groups, rather than members of a large group engaged in a common enterprise—educating young people. In addition, the higher the grade, the greater the teacher's specialization, so that by the high school level, teachers are almost always separated into departments by subject area. At every stage, the structure emphasizes difference, not commonality.

The largest gap of all occurs as young people leave high school and enter college, where most often they not only change buildings but also towns. Of course, physical location is not all that separates their high school years from their college ones. Colleges make use of an admissions process that widens the gulf, that encourages teachers and students alike to perceive these two stages as differing more widely than any of the prior stages did from each other. Basically, the admissions process employs assessment to accomplish this end. Prospective students take tests and submit scores and transcripts to validate their applications, to prove themselves worthy of entry. And, upon entry—most often at an orientation session that occurs several weeks before actual enrollment—students are further tested in order to determine at what levels they can begin different parts of their studies. The simple fact that colleges rely on local assessments in making these decisions, rather than on students' earlier performances, reinforces the notion that somehow students arrive on campus *tabula rasa*; that their earlier experiences and performances are meaningless in this new setting, where they must prove themselves anew.

Once in college, students will eventually choose a major concentration, and that choice will determine in which building or even on which campus they will spend the bulk of their time, in which library they will study, and sometimes in which dormitory they will live. Just as their professors isolate themselves, and are isolated by various institutional barriers from their colleagues in other departments, even other colleges, so students tend to take on identities and form peer groups along disciplinary lines. Simply, they associate with others with whom they have the most in common, and one of the most powerful common interests in a higher education setting is the field of one's concentration.

Admittedly, these separations have occurred for sound reasons. Early childhood education, as an endeavor, differs substantially from the kind of education adolescents need, which in turn wildly differs from what college-age students are ready to do. Breaking education down by subject matter makes perfect sense too, for as Gerald Graff points out, since at least the time of the Industrial Revolution, knowledge has advanced to the point that only the most foolish or the most arrogant would profess expertise over a wide range of subjects. Thus, from the middle school years onward, teachers increasingly specialize because they teach at a more advanced level. From these years, this fact of educational life only grows more apparent, and teachers specialize more and more narrowly, yet no one can reasonably argue at this point in the history of education that we ought to erase these boundaries, that we ought or even that we could go back to the days when generalist teachers taught all things to all learners.

Building Bridges

What we must do, however, is recognize and overcome the obstacles we have placed in the way of education even as we have separated it into logical segments. In effect, our boundaries are more than mere borders; they are gaps, often great yawning chasms, that separate stages and subjects more widely than they need to do—and much more widely than they ought to do. In a keynote address at Miami University's Composition in the Twenty-first Century Conference, James Berlin characterized this fragmentation as a kind of Fordism, arguing that education, in the process of attempting to run itself like a business, adopts attributes of business that are incongruous with education. In making his argument, Berlin focused on the Fordist economics of education, but he might just as well have focused on the metaphor of the assembly line (Berlin 1994), one of three metaphors Michael Williamson employs in exploring the problems educators create by pursuing efficiency in the educational enterprise, instead of attending, first, to the actual needs of all the stakeholders in our schooling system (Williamson 1994, 170-171). In a very real sense, we move students from station to station along the line, and each station is staffed by a specialist, by someone who supposedly knows just what part to add and just how to add it. This assembly-line mentality is perhaps the most dominant underlying assumption shaping modern education, and as efficient, pragmatic, and even unavoidable as it may be, it nevertheless places significant obstacles in the way of education. Perhaps most significant for present purposes are the problems posed by the fact that each station on this intellectual assembly line seems to exist independent of the others. (Here Graff's arguments about the post–Industrial Revolution era's separation of knowledge from expression—from language—vividly illustrate the problems.) We teach writing in writing classes, chemistry in chemistry classes, sociology in sociology classes, etc. We locate these classes in different departments and different buildings, and for the most part, college curricula, echoing this physical separation, leave students to discover the connections among all these institutionally disparate components of a typical degree program, just as they have to discover how to find their way from one class to the next.

However, what learners need to do typically spans these boundaries, or needs to. They write in their science and social science classes; they use statistics in their science and social science classes (and, increasingly, in humanities classes as well); they *reason* across the curriculum, applying interpretive skills learned in, say, literature classes to bodies of information acquired in a psychology or a history class. Most important of all, they bring—potentially—the sum of all their past education and experience to each new semester, each new class.

This contradiction—fragmentation in the curriculum and unity in the individual learner—creates a tension that resonates with what Mary Louise Pratt has called a "contact zone." Pratt uses the term to describe the difference between how the educator needs to perceive students and their responses to assignments and the existing range of possible and actual student responses. She characterizes the contact zone as a place "where cultures meet, clash, and grapple with each other, often in contexts of highly asymmetrical relations of power" (Pratt 1991, 34). Carl Lovett and Art Young, writing about an experience in which they tried to introduce portfolio-based assessment to the Finance faculty in Clemson University's School of Business, demonstrate that the concept of contact zones extends usefully into the arena of writing across the curriculum. Lovett and Young played the role of teacher-proselytizer, bringing the good news of portfolio assessment to their "students," all professors of Finance. In this case, the deliverers of a service were essentially ambushed by the recipients, as a well-designed portfolio-based system for evaluating Finance students' written products from several courses could not survive the faculty's unanticipated—and unfounded—objections on the grounds of academic freedom. In each case—Pratt's and Lovett and Young's—those who were in charge of delivering a service, to adopt the Fordist analogy Berlin critiques, had institutionally valid needs that conflicted directly with the needs experienced by the consumers of that service. Looking at the structure of education, and in particular higher education, we can easily see that Pratt's definition of the contact zone extends to the level of the curriculum itself, where the culture of the teacher, who needs the comfort and isolation produced by fragmenting the body of knowledge students set about to acquire, meets, clashes, and grapples with the culture of the learner, whose needs for continuity and coherence are frustrated by the way the academy has deconstructed itself into disparate programs, concentrations, departments, and colleges.

Students face two almost unbridgeable gaps in their attempts to achieve a college degree. The first, described above, occurs as they enter college. The second, somewhat more subtle gap is the one that separates their curriculum into individual, discrete classes, thereby obscuring not only the many ways in which the knowledge learned in one class relates to that from another, but also the ways in which intellectual tools—writing, critical thinking, textual analysis, quantitative reasoning, logic, and so forth—develop throughout the entire experience, the entire curriculum. Somehow we need to bridge those gaps, to find ways of encouraging students to discover the connections, to use the tools more broadly. We need to use assessment as one tool for accomplishing these means. Let me explain how, using the two most apparent gaps to illustrate both existing and potential bridges.

Bridge One: Portfolios at Entry to College

First, and perhaps most straightforward, we can use portfolio-based writing assessment to bridge the gap between high school and college writing. The University of Michigan's experience developing a portfolio-based assessment for five thousand entering students each year has demonstrated that, at any level, a carefully designed and executed portfolio assessment reaps benefits that extend far beyond the immediate purpose of placing students into courses that most closely meet their needs as writers.[2] In fact, we discovered early on that placement was the simplest and least interesting outcome of portfolio-based assessment. Even at this early stage—two years of piloting and three years in which all entering students have been required to submit a portfolio—the events surrounding our placement process extend backward into the high schools that send us students and forward into first year writing courses and even to the upper division writing-intensive courses that are the heart of our university's Writing Across the Curriculum (WAC) program.

Requiring incoming students to submit a writing portfolio has already begun to affect curriculum at the secondary level, as the example of the University of Michigan's placement procedure demonstrates. Since 1978, the University of Michigan has based placement into the first year writing curriculum on a direct test of writing (Morris 1983, 266). Until 1993 that sample was a fifty-minute impromptu argument, written on the first day of orientation. At the time it was instituted, that direct test represented an innovative step forward (Fader1986, 79-80). Among other benefits, the test delivered the message that students' placements into appropriate writing courses would depend on *writing*, not on indirect measures such as multiple-choice tests. High schools, in response, began requiring students to write more. However, as the years passed, writing instruction in the high schools became more and more focused on helping students succeed on our test and on other similar tests (e.g., the timed samples on the AP English test). Teachers repeatedly told us, in interviews we conducted to evaluate the assessment, that they had their students practice for our test by writing timed essays modeled on the prompts we used in our assessment.

Thus, students were not receiving more or better preparation for college writing; instead, they were receiving more and better preparation for our test. Roberta Camp has discussed the obvious drawbacks of structuring curriculum around a writing task that does not reflect a functional context for writing (Camp 1993a, 54-55 and 66-67). In our case, we came to realize that, while our assessment had had one positive effect—more writing practice in high schools—it also had the effect of producing only the most limited (and limiting) kind of practice.

In part, we instituted a writing portfolio to induce the schools to teach both the kinds of writing that would prepare students for college writing and to induce schools to teach writing in ways that would be more likely to result in stronger, more effective writing on the part of students. Thus, we require three samples from work students have already done:

- one piece that responds critically or analytically to something the student has read;
- one piece from a class other than English;
- one piece that the student identifies as her/his best, favorite, or most representative.

In addition, we ask students for a two- to five-page reflective essay that informs our readers about the background for the pieces the student has selected and that explains any substitutions the student has made for any of the required pieces. We ask what the assignment was, why the student selected these particular pieces, what the student likes about each piece, the process used in writing each piece, and what the student feels he or she has learned from writing each piece. Beyond those particulars, we encourage students to tell us about their development as writers, to give us more information about their experiences as writers than the three pieces alone can do, and to give us any other information which they feel will help us understand the portfolio. We encourage students to reflect thoroughly and thoughtfully about their writing and about themselves as writers.

This model, on its simplest level, requires that students have samples of writing; therefore, schools that want their students to perform well on our assessment must provide opportunities to write. They must incorporate writing into their curricula in areas other than English. They will have to teach students enough about writing for students to produce impressive samples and to respond to the challenges presented by the reflective piece. While the specific long-term effects of the new requirement are not yet clear, preliminary results indicate that the portfolio is having the desired effects. Interviews with teachers from across the state indicate that they are aware of our requirement. In response to it they are making an effort to increase the amount of writing students do and to give students more chances to revise their writing. Administrators in the schools we visit reveal that they have set up various means of assisting students in assembling portfolios. State officials have contacted us, welcoming the portfolio as an agent for positive change in Michigan's schools. We find, even at this early stage, that the requirement is having a marked effect on writing in the secondary schools and that the portfolio encourages what we would call institutional good practice,[3] both in the kinds of writing assignments and the kinds of pedagogical approaches the portfolio requirement is inspiring.

As we bridge the gap between high school and college, we also find that teachers in our first year composition classes suddenly have access to a much wider range of information about their students' strengths and needs, learning histories, and wide-ranging competencies. We know, in great detail, the range of tasks our newest students have been asked to perform, and we know how successful those performances have been. Some of the information we gathered during our reading process confirmed what we felt we already knew: most assignments in the portfolios asked for summary, rather than analysis, for report rather than argumentation.[4] In other cases, the information surprised and delighted us: 82 percent of students were able to produce a piece of writing from a class other than English. We had asked for such a piece, at the suggestion of many secondary English teachers, in order to promote writing across the curriculum in secondary schools, so the fact that more than four-fifths of our first year class could include such a piece in their portfolios meant that we had, at least in this regard, underestimated the kind of preparation our students receive at the secondary level.

Teachers in first year composition classes can take into account what they learn from these portfolios in making decisions about course curricula, instructional methods and materials, assignments, etc. Individual teachers who read their students' entry portfolios gain a great deal of useful information about where to begin by knowing, for the first time, where their students have been. And students, able for the first time to receive consideration for work they produced in high school, not only feel that the university is making a fair judgment about their writing ability, but they also report that the transition from high school writing to college-level writing is far less forbidding and difficult than they had feared it would be. Students in my own Writing Practicum—a course for the weakest of entering student writers—testified that the ability to sit down with me and discuss their portfolios was a uniformly positive experience. They were able to show me what they can do, and they were able to listen to and discuss my feedback about their portfolios. As a result, their natural resentment toward being placed into this lower level course eased, and they were able to understand specifically how their writing abilities either did not match or fell short of the competencies that university level writing would demand of them. The students were also able to begin our relationship by supplying me with a high level of knowledge about them and their history as writers, information that helped me approach each of them as an individual learner, rather than as a member of a group. As a result, my plans for the semester developed along even more individualized lines than they usually do.

The information we gather in the entry-level portfolio assessment also feeds into programmatic change. For example, this year, for the first time, the faculty who are responsible for the nine different courses—located in eight different departments or programs—that can satisfy the first year writing requirement are sitting down together to share knowledge about what happens in those courses. In several focus groups, in committee meetings, and in other venues, these faculty are using information from the assessment as the basis for some sort of consensus that will allow the English Composition Board, in turn, to place students into appropriate courses and know that those placements have what we have come to call "systemic validity." We will be more certain that the assumptions we use to place a student are accurate with regard to the curriculum actually administered in courses at that level. Similarly, as our research progresses, groups of faculty from the humanities, social sciences, and natural sciences will gather to read selected portfolios in an activity that serves at least two important functions. First, the portfolios allow us to communicate to the faculty at large a detailed portrait of students' writing at the time of their arrival on campus. Second, as these faculty members from across the College of Literature, Science, and the Arts discuss these portfolios, they will tell us, the assessors, what they value in students' writing. This two-way sharing of information will inform the ways existing courses are taught, and it will also inform the effort, just getting under way, to revise the college's writing program. Thus, we can see that bridging the gap between one level and another changes the very process of education at each level, raising interesting questions about what might happen if we push portfolio-based assessment into the arena of writing across the curriculum.

Many institutions today are attempting to find ways of accommodating the often contradictory needs and competing cultures of both teachers and learners. Portfolio assessment can help build bridges of coherence and continuity, for teachers and for learners, because portfolio-based assessments allow us to be more aware of the contexts within which the assessment and the learning are taking place. In fact, this kind of assessment embodies its context. A portfolio is at once a means and an end, a product that incorporates a process, and it is so for each party in the learning experience. The teacher designs the portfolio so that when she reads it, she can tell whether a student has learned what he needs to know, and how well. A well-designed portfolio is a collection of performances that embody the course's goals and objectives, so the process of constructing and perfecting the portfolio grants a large measure of control over outcomes to the learner, at the same time as it allows the learner to participate directly in achieving the objectives of the course. With Liz Hamp-Lyons, I have argued elsewhere that this sharing of objectives and the responsibility for achieving them, together with the information the teacher gains from reading and judging those performances, results in a kind of continual improvement in curriculum, since at each iteration of the course the teacher has more information about the effectiveness of assignments, sequencing, teaching materials and methods, and so forth (Hamp-Lyons and Condon 1993, 177). Thus, on the level of the individual course, portfolio assessment affects each participant and each aspect of the course primarily because the portfolio participates so completely in the multiple contexts for teaching and learning which the course presents.

This ability to serve multiple purposes is a primary advantage in portfolio assessment. The contents of Pat Belanoff and Marcia Dickson's volume, *Portfolios: Process and Product,* demonstrate that from the beginning portfolios have served in contexts as disparate as basic writing courses, Writing Across the Curriculum (WAC) courses, efforts to evaluate undergraduate curricula, barrier assessment at exit from college, proficiency testing at college admission and between sequenced first year writing courses, and a host of other contexts. Research in assessment theory and practice is beginning to recognize the value of serving multiple contexts and of an assessment instrument that, as Pamela Moss has pointed out, can provide not only reliable judgments in cases involving "consequential decisions about individuals or programs" (Moss 1994a, 11), but also the kind of systemic validity that promotes "potent and value-laden models of the purposes and processes of school, of the appropriate roles for teachers, students, and other stakeholders in the discourse of teaching and learning, and of the means through which educational reform is best fostered" (Moss 1994b, 124; see also Bryk and Hermanson 1993, 453-467). In all these cases, portfolio assessment serves as a highly flexible tool since a portfolio yields information about student performance *and* information about the student's opportunities to perform. Knowledge about context is crucial to the ability to make reliable decisions in cases where the stakes are high, and the extensive knowledge about individual students' learning contexts presents the opportunity to examine curriculum and practice, even systemwide educational efficiency and efficacy.

Bridge Two: Portfolios and Writing Across the Curriculum

As colleges and universities recognize and attempt to bridge the gaps in academic curricula, they set up multidisciplinary or interdisciplinary programs in order to address the learners' inherent need to put things together, to find the coherence in their courses of study. Perhaps the most extensive effort to create this needed continuity and coherence is writing across the curriculum. If we look at the underlying assumptions of WAC, we can see its potential for bridging some of the gaps, for allowing both learners and teachers to see some of the common elements in what they do from class to class, semester to semester. As Barbara Walvoord and Lucille McCarthy state them, these assumptions clearly span single courses and even single courses of study. WAC assumes that we cannot separate writing from thinking, reading, investigating, or oral communication. These faculties—what we might call the infrastructure of higher education, perhaps of education in general—are so closely allied that treating them as if we could teach them separately is simply wrong. WAC also recognizes that people discover what they think by writing about it, that thinking and writing are recursive and complementary processes. Next WAC assumes that writing and speaking about a topic are powerful means for learning about it. Additionally, writing ability develops over time and across opportunities to write. It does not develop all at once, in only one class. Moreover, since each discipline has its own ways to pose questions, seek answers, and communicate results (in other words, to make knowledge), learners need help as they develop into members of a particular discipline's discourse community. Finally, we teachers serve as the mentors for students seeking entry into those discourse communities, so our oral and written interactions with the learners in our charge are crucial to the learning process (Walvoord and McCarthy 1990, 19-22). WAC helps bridge the gaps in our academic community because its assumptions transcend our most common institutional structures—programs, departments, schools and colleges—thus undercutting the assumptions on which those structures are founded. WAC begins to disassemble the academic assembly line, since WAC operates on the assumption that the stations on that line really cannot be separate and distinct from one another.

Portfolio-based writing assessment extends WAC's assumptions, even allows them to be realized in concrete form. If we compare what WAC's assumptions mean in terms of how we teach, and if we compare those results with what happens when teachers use portfolios, then we can see that WAC and portfolio-based assessment make natural partners. For example, as Walvoord and McCarthy point out, WAC demands a shift from content-centered to assignment-centered instruction (Walvoord and McCarthy 1990, 21-22). Rather than focusing on what a course will cover, teachers focus on what learners can do, on how and to what extent learners demonstrate what they know at a given point in time. Since, in part, a portfolio is a collection of the products of learning, portfolio-based assessment reinforces this aspect of WAC, making the conversion from content to assignment easier by giving the teacher the means to accomplish two significant ends: first, to keep track, as the items for the portfolio evolve, of the students' learning as it progresses; and second, by manipulating the portfolio's contents, to maintain an accurate yet flexible outline of the learning opportunities the course presents. In addition, the WAC course's focus on writing and on creating a way for learners to join the teachers' discourse communities demands that learners have frequent opportunities to receive feedback and to revise their written work. In this way, learners move from outsiders to insiders, from observers of a discipline to participants in it. Finally, WAC assumes that active learning is better than passive learning; that students will learn more and faster if they are actively engaged in the knowledge-producing methodologies of a discipline. One of the most powerful benefits of portfolio-based writing assessment is that delayed grading creates more time for active learning to occur and for students to become successful in their learning. Thus, portfolio-based assessment reinforces the major components in Writing Across the Curriculum courses.

We can also see how portfolio-based assessment adds to the context developed in a well-designed WAC program, extending and augmenting the benefits of the bridging structure WAC provides. First, the increased emphasis on performance assessment goes beyond merely reinforcing WAC's emphasis on assignment-based courses. Converting a course from content-centered to assignment-centered merely creates a context within which performance assessment can take place. Carrying out the conversion to portfolio-based evaluation completes the task by transferring the responsibility for learning onto the learner. Given the fact that performance will be the basis for evaluation and that learners have many opportunities to incorporate their learning into revisions of their writing, using performance assessment allows learners to work as hard as they will and progress as quickly as they are able. In addition, placing the emphasis directly on learners' performances creates an environment in which the learner's goals and objectives are congruent with those of the teacher and the curriculum: all three agents in the process combine to pursue the same set of goals and objectives.

Another way in which portfolio-based assessment extends and magnifies the bridging effects of WAC programs lies in the effects of delayed grading.[5] When students' products are graded as they are presented during a term, the effects are not, on the whole, conducive to learning.[6] Granted, this method provides students with information about their eventual grades; however, this benefit is canceled by the degree to which this process emphasizes the grade as a goal, rather than as the description of a learner's performance. Delaying grading decreases the temptation, on the teacher's part as well as the learner's, to see grades as ends in themselves. Thus, learners feel freer to take risks, since they have a cushion—the risk may not pay off, but there will be more chances to raise the level of that performance since the learner can revise it before the moment when the teacher assigns a grade. In this way, delayed grading helps create "teachable moments," when teacher and learners can work together over a problem or set of problems, with a high degree of investment for both. Learners are fully engaged because the feedback they receive can help them improve the performance before they have to submit it for a grade; the teacher is fully engaged in part because the learners are so responsive and in part because the energy she invests in responding to her students' work can go directly into promoting learning, rather than into justifying a grade. Finally, and in part as a result of this change in the timing, delayed grading alters the teacher-learner relationship for the better. Traditionally, teachers are the watchers at the gate; in one sense, the teacher is the enemy, the one who controls the learners' fate and who is therefore to be kept at a distance, never fully trusted. Every time a teacher grades and hands back an assignment, she emphasizes that relationship. Delaying grading, then, helps recast the teacher-learner relationship so that the teacher is more of a partner in the learning, with the learner taking the major share of the responsibility. Since grades are delayed, they no longer act as a constant reminder of the teacher's disproportionate power so communicating and building trust becomes easier.

On the whole, then, portfolio-based assessment takes the assumptions and the goals of WAC an important step further. WAC changes the emphasis from what the course covers to what the students can do in order to demonstrate that they have acquired a specific body of knowledge. Portfolio-based assessment—indeed, performance assessment in general—takes advantage of that transformation in order to alter the way a course is conducted, changing the whole process in ways that promote greater learning by giving learners the means of assuming responsibility for their learning, by giving teachers the means of becoming genuine mentors for learners, and by creating a time period within which learning can progress. The combination of performance assessment and delayed grading potentially furnishes each learner with the means to succeed, both in the sense that she achieves the goals and objectives of the course and in the sense that she earns a favorable grade. Combining WAC and portfolio-based assessment, even within the confines of a single course, provides a bridge from one learning experience to another, a means both for tying the experiences together and for creating a document that encourages learners to reflect on the ways those experiences reinforce or build upon each other.

The ultimate expression of this sort of learning mechanism would be a truly cross-curricular portfolio, one that comprises work a student has produced in a variety of courses over an extended period of time. Such a portfolio would provide an unprecedented record of learning, of course, and as such it would be an extremely useful tool for assessing both the student's skills and the ability of the curriculum to accomplish the goals it was designed to meet. More important, though, the act of assembling a cross-curricular portfolio, reflecting on it, and discussing it with fellow students and with a teacher would provide a rich capstone experience for any college student. As well it would provide a mechanism faculty might use to ensure that graduates leave with both a firm knowledge of their strengths and needs as writers and a means of demonstrating their abilities to prospective employers and to any graduate and professional programs a student might seek to enter. Extending portfolio-based assessment beyond the context of a single course would also extend the bridge, providing learners with the occasion to discover some of WAC's most important lessons: that learning is continuous, that writing is itself a learning process, that communications abilities improve over time and with practice, and that no one act of learning is ever fully isolated from any other act of learning.

The cross-curricular portfolio at Eckerd College in St. Petersburg, Florida, accomplishes these goals and more. In "Portfolios Across the Curriculum," Susan Harrison identifies the benefits that accrue to teachers as a result of "a portfolio-based writing competency graduation requirement" (Harrison 1995, 39). The transition from timed writing sample to portfolio engaged the faculty in discussions that led to their agreement that all faculty share responsibility for students' writing (Harrison 1995, 39). Common sense tells us that the presence of such a requirement acts as a powerful motivator for faculty to assign more writing by making writing an integral part of the learning opportunities each course presents. The portfolio also, as Harrison points out, "engage[d] faculty in a collaborative development of an assessment tool" that emerged from frank discussions of common and disparate theories of learning and pedagogies, discussions that continue as faculty take their turns as portfolio evaluators (Harrison 1995, 41). As these discussions progressed, faculty standards for writing and for other aspects of students' performance rose, as did the level of awareness among all faculty for the kinds of thinking and writing that occur at various stages of Eckerd's curriculum (Harrison 1995, 43-44). Finally, the effects on students have been equally encouraging. The portfolio indeed helps students to see writing as a transaction between the writer and various audiences and to understand that one's writing improves with frequent opportunities to write for a variety of purposes and audiences (Harrison 1995, 44-45). In short, students are more engaged with their writing—wherever they write—now that they see a purpose beyond the next deadline for a paper or beyond the grade on a term paper. Eckerd's experience suggests that a carefully instituted portfolio-based cross-curricular assessment of writing does indeed bridge the gaps, both by bringing faculty from different departments together in order to pursue a common purpose and by providing students with an incentive to *think* about their progress as writers across the artificial boundaries of course and term. A cross-curricular portfolio, as an agent of writing across the curriculum, alleviates many of the negative effects of a fragmented curriculum, providing learners with the means to make the connections they need to make among the seemingly discrete, disparate learning experiences that the typical college curriculum presents.

Conclusions

From all the examples cited above, we can see that in any of its instantiations, a well-designed portfolio-based writing assessment bridges gaps. It brings teachers closer together with learners. It brings together administrators who, though working in different departments and programs, share common interests, goals, and functions. Even in its narrowest context, that of the single class, portfolios bring manifold benefits. As the context for assessment expands beyond the single class to encompass the writing program, its benefits expand accordingly, as even the earliest such programs demonstrated (Belanoff and Elbow 1991). Extending portfolios across an entire curriculum, then, brings a commensurate expansion of benefits, not least of which would be a surer accomplishing of the several vital ends of writing across the curriculum. Ultimately, combining WAC with portfolio-based assessment could provide the kind of consistency, coherence, and continuity that our learners need and deserve in their educational experience. At the same time as it would involve teachers in rich and exciting conversations about the one enterprise we all have in common, teaching. And the more fully we extend the partnership between WAC and portfolio-based writing assessment, the greater the potential to benefit the educational process as a whole, from both the learners' and the teachers' perspectives. As we collect WAC portfolios from multiple classes, what will we learn, and how might it affect what and how we teach? We may find that addressing the learner's need for continuity will help learners solve some of the problems that stem from the fragmentation of our academies and, at the same time, help teachers solve their own deeply entrenched and seemingly intractable problems with curriculum.

Extending portfolio assessment across institutional lines so that students bring their writing performances with them as they move from one level to the next—elementary to middle school, middle school to high school, and especially from high school to college—helps bridge the largest gaps in our schooling system. Those portfolios allow teachers to know more surely what experiences their new students have had, what learning opportunities the students have pursued, and how well the students have performed in that work. This kind of portfolio allows teachers to design curricula based on actual knowledge of learners' performances and to develop materials that address learners' actual needs. Learners, in turn, benefit from the ability to bring their accomplishments with them from one level to the next. Our experience with entry-level portfolios at Michigan indicates that students appreciate the effort we put into reading their portfolios, and they have a high degree of confidence in the results, even when the placement is lower than they had expected. The portfolio raises students' comfort level as they enter our first year curriculum: students testify that the experience of putting the portfolio together provides an opportunity for self-assessment, for taking stock; and the knowledge that Michigan has treated them seriously as individual writers helps ease the stresses of coming into such a large, complex, and often intimidating institution.

Context, as I noted at the beginning of this essay, is everything. Portfolios, more than any other means of assessing learning, incorporate, even embody the contexts that produce the work. Because portfolios reveal the kinds of challenge students have met in their curricula—because portfolios necessarily depend upon the contexts in which the work was prepared—portfolios bridge the gaps between one subject area and another, between one level and another, in ways that benefit both learner and teacher. These varied benefits, more than the ability to make more accurate assessments of students' learning, give us the most compelling reason to move forward with portfolio-based writing assessment at all levels and in all areas of our system of education.

Notes

1. Many writers have advanced this argument for the interrelation of, for example, instruction and assessment. Edward M. White offers a comprehensive look at this relationship in his *Teaching, Assigning, and Assessing Writing.*
2. This remarkable program is the child of Emily Decker's brain and the fruit of her hard labor as the ECB's Associate Director for Assessment. Without her knowledge and leadership, the project would never have become reality. The assessment is described in greater detail in an article she and several members of her team are developing for *Assessing Writing.*
3. Cp. A Preliminary Study of the Feasibility and Utility for National Policy of Instructional "Good Practice" Indicators in Undergraduate Education. U.S. Department of Education; Office of Educational Research and Improvement. NCES 94-437. August, 1994.
4. In fact, on June 8, 1994, after we had read approximately 3500 portfolios, the latest report from the National Assessment of Educational Progress (NAEP) confirmed just this fact: high school graduates can summarize well, since assignments in high school most often ask for some sort of summary or report; however, graduates are often much less adept at analysis or argument since they were not often asked to perform those tasks during their school years.
5. Of course, eliminating graded writing courses altogether is preferable to merely delaying the moment at which a teacher must assign a grade, but a long time will pass before such a move can occur in a program that affects as many academic departments

and disciplines as WAC does. Thus, this discussion assumes that learners will receive grades for their work in courses, and that teachers have a fair amount of freedom to determine their own methods for grading.

6. The remarks in this section stem from my own experience with the portfolio-based exit assessment from the ECB's Writing Practicum which was instituted in 1988. However, that experience parallels almost exactly what Irwin Weiser describes in the basic writing program at Purdue. I was delighted to discover Weiser's cogent account, since it suggests that the benefits we both describe are generalizable to many other classroom contexts.

14

Portfolios in Law School

Creating a Community of Writers

Susan R. Dailey

IN MY WRITING WORKSHOPS WITH FIRST YEAR LAW STUDENTS, I OFTEN GIVE them a completely inscrutable piece of writing and ask them to comment on it. The single paragraph of approximately 200 words is full of legal jargon, unnecessarily long sentences, Latin phrases, and pretentious diction. I always hope to hear the blunt response, "This person needs to write in plain English." Instead, the students approach the text warily, making timid jabs at its obscurity. "It could be organized better," one student suggests. "It needs a topic sentence," another adds cautiously. They seem to be so accustomed to reading prose they don't understand that this paragraph in part represents to them what it means to "write like a lawyer."

This story illustrates the problem faced by those of us who teach writing at law schools. Students who will one day depend heavily on their writing to serve their clients and advance their careers seem to lack the confidence to exert control over their writing or recognize the power that language can wield. It is hardly surprising that helping students become "confident and comfortable with legal discourse and composition" is such an important but elusive goal to many legal writing teachers (Rideout and Ramsfield 1994, 39).

Calling for a "revised view of legal writing," Christopher Rideout and Jill Ramsfield recommend the model of an interactive classroom in which students take responsibility for their own learning and the professor ceases to be "the lone voice lecturing at the front of the classroom" (Rideout and

Ramsfield 1994, 66). Portfolios are certainly compatible with this model "because of the messages they send, the authority they assign, the ways they motivate students, and the insights they challenge students to perceive and articulate" (Yancey 1992a, 105). Portfolios have only recently been introduced into the legal writing classroom, but in many ways they are particularly well suited to meeting the needs of students who are learning to write within a new discourse community.

Writing in the Context of Law School

The contribution portfolios can make to legal writing pedagogy can best be understood in the context of student writing experiences in law school. Collaborative writing, for example, is a customary practice within the legal profession, but it is rarely encouraged in law school (Kunz et al. 1993, 6-7). Students thus miss the opportunity, commonplace in other writing contexts, "to compose with their colleagues, to collaborate in workshops and in peer groups, to learn methods of planning and invention, [and] to share writing with others . . ." (Yancey 1992a, 105). This is one of several factors that contribute to the student perception of isolation, conveyed rather vividly when I asked my students what kind of feedback they found least helpful when revising their writing. Their answer had been firm and unanimous, "No feedback at all."

Although most law schools have a two-semester writing course in the first year, upper level writing requirements vary from one institution to another. Our school, however, is typical. Students are required to write one paper each semester during their second and third years. Three of the papers are short (ten pages or less), and one is a substantial piece of scholarship. The other writing students do for their courses is in the context of their exams. For most courses, the grade is based solely on the final exam, and to ensure anonymity in the grading process, students identify themselves by number on their examination booklets. Once the grades are posted, of course, students may ask to review the exams with their professors, but the exams themselves are not routinely returned, and most students do not take advantage of the opportunity for feedback.

Outside of the classroom law students have many chances to write in various professional contexts: internships, clinics, law journals, and law-related extracurricular activities. Many students write for summer jobs or work at law firms during the day and attend school at night. But in busy law offices there is little time to worry about quality of instruction when work is being done under the pressure of a deadline. Supervisors often rewrite student work completely, and often the response to a piece of student writing is silence. As a result, many novice legal writers work in isolation and never develop a clear sense of the needs of their audience.

Portfolios at University of Texas

At University of Texas School of Law, Terri LeClercq has addressed a number of these concerns in a course that combines practical employment issues with sound pedagogical theory. During the semester, students write client letters and other "real world" documents and then revise their writing based on comments from their peers. Students select their best work for a portfolio to submit during employment interviews. The portfolios appeal to prospective employers because they contain written work in a variety of legal genres. The students are confident of the writing they submit because it has undergone extensive revision for multiple audiences (LeClercq 1993, 3).

LeClercq found that this practical application of portfolio use motivates students to sign up for the course, which is always oversubscribed, and work hard while they are in it. The portfolios also encourage students to focus on the writing process and learn how to revise. "Students rewrite (not merely edit) each paper," LeClercq reports. "That forces them to assimilate all comments and create what they consider a perfected document. Students also more frequently attend office conferences to discuss the editing comments because they are in the process of responding on the next version" (LeClercq 1993, 3).

Portfolios and the Advanced Legal Writing Seminar

In designing my own advanced legal writing course, a Law and Humanities seminar, I wanted to help students develop a fuller understanding of contexts for their writing and challenge them to discover the power and vitality of language. Achieving these goals would require that students expand both their reading and writing strategies. As Fajans and Falk have noted, law students "too often scan judicial opinions for issue, holding, and reasoning and call that 'reading,' or produce a paraphrase of the text and call that 'writing' " (Fajans and Falk 1993, 163). Literary texts, I hoped, would encourage students to read more carefully and pay closer attention to language and rhetorical structures. As they explored the multiple meanings of the literary texts, they would be engaged in an activity shared by lawyers and literary critics alike (James Boyd White 1985, 415). I hoped the result would be "strong, original, self-aware writers" who would one day be "skillful counselors and more effective advocates" (Fajans and Falk 1993,168).

Portfolios were central to my vision of the course for a number of reasons. They would complement the process-oriented design of the course because students would have ample opportunity to revise written work before selecting pieces for portfolio evaluation at the end of the semester. This was especially important because students would be writing a substantial piece of legal scholarship for the first time, and consequently would need support as they selected topics and moved through the unfamiliar territory of an interdisciplinary field. I wanted them to explore freely, understand the recursive nature of the composing process, and take some risks with their writing. To accomplish all this, the students would need to become less focused on the grading of individual assignments and from the beginning, view the course as an exploration of the process of scholarly reading and writing.

Portfolio assessment would also contribute to the type of dynamic classroom environment I wanted to encourage. I theorized that many writing problems were rooted in the students' failure to develop a strong sense of audience. Peer review of written work is rarely a part of law school curriculum, and when it is, such as in our first year writing program, instructors are often disappointed with the results. For example, in an assignment that asked students to respond to a classmate's paper in the role of a senior partner or fellow associate at a law firm, students' comments were frequently superficial or surprisingly mean-spirited. Comments were typically directed to the instructor rather than the writer. "Nice use of parallelism," one student editor wrote next to a sentence that bore no visible signs of a parallel structure.

I hoped to eliminate this type of feedback by encouraging students to respond in the role they knew best: law students who were engaged in a common struggle to write a good paper, think through complex legal issues, and meet impossible writing deadlines. I knew that these students had much to offer each other if they had the opportunity. The portfolios would provide an authentic context for the peer reviews because students would be encouraged to help each other achieve their best work to submit at the end of the semester.

The basic structure of the course reflected a concern for the writing process. Students would write short papers at the beginning of the semester as they explored possible topics for the seminar paper. Later, they would focus on the task of revision and spend class time discussing their papers and offering each other suggestions for revision. At this point in the semester, students would be writing peer reviews and multiple drafts of their seminar papers. I provided them with an extensive bibliography under five general subject headings related to issues in law and humanities: "Justice and Revenge," "Law and Equity," "Narratives of the Disenfranchised," "Women, Law, and Society," and "The Ethics of Persuasion" (Terre E.Foster 1993; James Boyd White 1985; Fajans and Falk 1993; and Gemmette 1989). Students were to explore the bibliography and develop their own topics, but I expected that by limiting them to five subject areas there would be enough of an overlap in topics that they would be able to provide each other with informed feedback. At the end of the semester, students would select the revised work to submit in their portfolios for grading. Each portfolio would contain two short papers on literary texts, one peer review, and the final draft of a seminar paper.

Such was the theory behind my course design. It seemed sound, but I was uncertain. In my six years as a law school writing specialist I had seen a number of clashes between pedagogical theory and the practical realities of legal education. Students who work full time, take classes at night, and do most of their studying on weekends tend to keep a watchful eye on the bottom line. They want to write well, but they are typically impatient with the learning process. Early drafts are often written too hastily and the students have a healthy skepticism about any assignment for which there is no perceptible purpose. Would they take the time to respond helpfully to each other? Would they understand the mutual benefit to be derived from reviewing a classmate's paper? I was uncertain if portfolios would work in a law school class that was not, like Terri LeClercq's, specifically structured for creating an attractive work product for a future employer.

Applications

For the first five weeks of the semester, the students wrote short pieces of expressive writing in which they analyzed some feature of literary texts we had not yet discussed in class. These assignments gave students an opportunity to explore possible topics for their seminar papers while developing confidence in their own voices. Students reported they were happy to be writing papers that did not require them to "obsess." Before they selected two of these assignments to be rewritten for their portfolios they would receive verbal feedback from their peers and a written response from me.

The assignments also challenged them to read the texts carefully and analyze rhetorical features. I had chosen complex literary texts, including *Hamlet*, Sophocles' *Philoctetes*, and Toni Morrison's *Beloved*, so that students would be forced to grapple with the language. Or so I thought. Unfortunately, students seemed to be skimming literary texts the same way they skimmed their reading for other classes. I was learning that "[h]elping law students to get beyond purely denotative, case-briefing notions of reading is . . . no easy thing. In an age of reading comprehension tests, students are trained to read only for facts, for information" (Fajans and Falk 1993, 164). Their writing showed that they had some good ideas but needed to understand the nuances of language better if they were to write good papers.

After an uncertain beginning, however, many of the goals of the class were slowly being realized. Using the bibliography, students had come up with topics that seemed to run the gamut of Western Civilization, from an exploration of the revenge society of Aeschylus' *Oresteia* to a discussion of the role of women in the legal system in *To Kill a Mockingbird*. Although the topics were interesting and creative, many of the first drafts were less impressive. The interdisciplinary topics required that students do a certain amount of original thinking, but the way these ideas developed varied greatly. Nevertheless, although some of the students had done a good job of exploring an issue in a creative way, others simply used the draft as an opportunity to summarize some of the articles in the bibliography. Another rather significant problem was that a few of the papers showed that the writers had significant problems with editing and proofreading their work.

By midsemester, when I began reading the peer reviews, my concerns about the course began to disappear. While one or two students continued to see me as the primary audience for the peer critique, in most cases there was an authentic dialogue between the two writers. They commiserated about common problems, expressed enthusiasm for each other's projects, and invariably provided feedback on topics and issues I had missed.

The students' developing sense of autonomy was particularly evident in their use of my carefully constructed bibliography. One student found Corbett's *Classical Rhetoric For the Modern Student* "boring as hell," but recommended it to a classmate who was struggling to find a way to describe a writer's use of rhetorical techniques. Other students in class discussion and written critiques recommended appropriate readings that were not on the bibliography. They suggested readings from other classes or mentioned their own research.

In many respects the first drafts of the seminar papers tested any budding sense of community that was developing. In addition to the usual problems involved in treading the fine line between rigorous but tactful editing, the papers often revealed different political viewpoints. Class discussion occasionally grew heated, but in their written comments, students found ways to express their views fairly and open-mindedly. The students who had submitted poorly edited first drafts got a very clear message about the impression this created on their readers, but the editors were also diplomatic.

The value of allowing students to select their own topics became apparent in class discussion. A number of students had chosen subjects that tied into a special interest or area of expertise outside of the classroom. A doctor, for example, chose a topic that allowed her to explore medical issues in law and literature. Several of the women in the class chose topics in feminist jurisprudence, and a student who worked for the state government chose a topic that allowed him to analyze the persuasive power of speeches. Their sense of ownership over their topics seemed to give them confidence in responding to editorial suggestions for revision.

This sense of confidence was particularly evident in their conferences with me. Students were very attentive when we discussed editing issues or matters of writing style. On the substance of their papers, however, they were more likely to trust their own instincts. The students were also taking responsibility for their own learning in other ways. In their conferences students revealed that they were reading papers they had not been assigned to review. They looked for how others had handled common problems and frequently mentioned a paper they particularly admired. In short, they were doing the "extra" work they didn't believe they would ever do.

At the end of the semester I judged the success of the course in part by the work submitted in the portfolios. The papers were thoughtful and well-written. Students had struggled with fine-tuning their work, creating interesting introductions and conclusions, tying the disparate parts of their papers together more effectively, and carefully editing and proofreading. More importantly, however, students had shown that they could benefit from the experience of working on their writing together.

Reflections

Toward the end of the semester I would often look at the businesslike faces of the adults in my class and wonder what they really thought of this course that was different in so many respects from their other classes. I was pleased with the classroom dynamic and the written work but wanted some confirmation of what they had learned about the writing process. Without a metacognitive component to the course, all I could know for sure was that the students had been able to write well in one advanced writing class. Because I did not want the students to think of these reflections as part of their assessment, I asked that they submit them anonymously.

In their reflections, students evaluated their own work and mentioned their writing goals, their reactions to peer reviews, and their opinions about reading and writing assignments. Although I had never discussed the theory behind the design of the course, students were able to see the reasons for most of the work they did. They used the opportunity, in fact, to comment on almost every aspect of the course, from the relaxed atmosphere of the classroom to the "structured approach" of writing the seminar paper.

Some of the more interesting comments concerned the peer reviews. Although many students mentioned that the peer reviews were one of the key factors contributing to the improvement in their writing, one student said the "objectivity" of the peer reviews was one of their greatest assets. This comment reflects a view I had often heard in my capacity of writing specialist as I helped students revise their papers for other professors. Students often suspect that professors' comments are guided entirely by subjective standards and individual style. Accustomed to the rigorous objectivity of anonymous grading in their exams, law students may be more likely to view writing assessment as stemming from the individual idiosyncrasies of the reader. Such rationalization is less likely to occur when three or four readers make similar comments.

Conclusion

Reflecting on ways to help law students develop confidence in their writing, Rideout and Ramsfield state that such confidence "must be based on good training throughout their law school careers, and that training must look beyond legal writing problems to solutions" (Rideout and Ramsfield 1994, 39). Portfolios can play a number of roles in promoting pedagogical solutions to the distinctive problems legal writers face.

Writing portfolios changed the dynamic of the Law and Humanities writing class by creating an authentic context in which students could read and critique early drafts of each other's work. Adult students are particularly sensitive to exercises that seem to have no purpose. The portfolios shaped the course, created a purpose for the peer critiques, and forced the students to reflect on their writing process. Portfolios gave students the confidence to take some risks and see the class as an opportunity for ongoing improvement.

Writing teachers in law schools confront a number of rather specialized problems. We have a short period of time to acquaint students with the reasoning and language conventions of a new discourse community. Nevertheless, law students, like all writers, need guidance, confidence, and a clear sense of the needs of their audience. They also need to feel a sense of ownership over their work, and know the steps, recursive or otherwise, of producing a good piece of writing. Portfolios can be an important part of that learning process.

III

Teaching and Professional Development

15

Portfolios as a Way to Encourage Reflective Practice Among Preservice English Teachers

Robert P. Yagelski[1]

ONE OF THE TENETS TO HAVE EMERGED IN THE BURGEONING LITERATURE ON portfolios is the importance of self-evaluation. Linda Rief writes that portfolios offer "possibilities in diversity, depth, growth, and self-evaluation" (Rief 1990, 26). She asserts that when her seventh grade students used portfolios, "[t]hey thoughtfully and honestly evaluated their own learning with far more detail and introspection than I thought possible" (Rief 1990, 26). Others have made similar claims for portfolio use in their writing classrooms (see Belanoff and Dickson 1991; Yancey 1992b). Dennie Wolf writes that "portfolios can promote a climate of reflection" (Wolf 1989, 37). This potential of the portfolio to promote self-evaluation among student writers also makes it a powerful vehicle for critical reflection in the training of preservice English teachers. Used in this way, portfolios can help teacher educators address one of the most challenging tasks they face: training new teachers to be what Donald Schon has called "reflective practitioners" (Schon 1987).

In this chapter, we examine some of the difficulties that teacher educators face in preparing preservice English teachers for critical, reflective practice, and we describe a portfolio system we developed as part of an effort to address those difficulties. Our goal was to find ways to make critical reflection routine among our preservice teachers; the portfolio system we describe here provided a means to that end in the way it enabled us to integrate theory, observation, and practice and encouraged our students to engage in ongoing self-assessment. In the course of our discussion, we argue that the use of portfolios, if carefully designed for specific contexts of use, can become a crucial element in the effective preparation of English teachers to meet the difficult challenges of the secondary school language arts classroom in the 1990s and beyond.

Preparing Reflective Teachers

The difficulties of preparing student teachers to become effective educators are by now well documented (Blanton et al. 1993; Feiman-Nemser and Buchmann 1985; Goodman 1985; Richardson-Koehler 1988; Zeichner 1990). For us, chief among those difficulties is the apparent tension between the need to prepare student teachers for the day-to-day pressures and practicalities of classroom instruction and our desire to encourage among student teachers what Schon calls "reflection-in-action," the ability to think critically about what they are doing as they face unfamiliar or difficult situations in their practice as teachers (Schon 1987, 26). Understandably, many of the preservice teachers we work with are anxious about their ability to handle the many practical tasks facing classroom teachers: developing and carrying out effective lesson plans; dealing with student behavior in the classroom; accommodating school and state curriculum guidelines; handling mundane but pressing daily responsibilities like attendance and discipline; and managing the paper load. For our English preservice teachers, these anxieties are exacerbated by their belief that they must become expert grammarians if they are to be successful teachers—a belief that is reinforced by many inservice teachers and by the important place of formal grammar instruction in the English curricula of many of the middle schools and high schools in which our students work. As a result, we feel a need to acquaint our preservice teachers with the traditional content and methods of instruction that they will likely be expected to know when they leave our program and to prepare them to handle the many practical tasks that often characterize the work of secondary school English teachers.

At the same time, we are also committed to the broader, ongoing project of improving practice in English classrooms. We believe, as Marilyn Cochran-Smith puts it, that "[p]rospective teachers need to know from the start that they are part of a larger struggle and that they have a responsibility to reform, not just replicate, standard school practice" (Cochran-Smith 1991, 280). Furthermore, we share the concern of many teacher educators that field experiences, which are a standard part of most teacher preparation programs, can reinforce problematic classroom practices and lead to unthinking acceptance of those practices, that, as Salzillo and Van Fleet put it in their review of teacher education field experiences, "student teaching [can] become simply an exercise in adapting new personnel into old patterns" (Salzillo and Van Fleet 1977, 28; see also Feinman-Nemser and Buchmann 1985; Goodman 1985; Zeichner 1990). In many cases, anxious preservice teachers placed in classrooms for field experiences may focus on the obvious responsibilities of daily classroom teaching, such as managing student behavior, taking attendance, covering required content, grading, and so on, and abandon important theoretical perspectives they may have gained in their university courses. In one study of student teaching, for example, researchers reported that student teachers rejected much of the content of their university courses in as little as two weeks after they began student teaching (Richardson-Koehler 1988). In such instances, early field experiences could, as Jesse Goodman phrases it, "stifle students' potential for reflective inquiry and experimental action, while encouraging mindless imitation" (Goodman 1985, 46). Goodman's study of the effects of an early field experience revealed that the majority of the preservice teachers in his study "learned that teaching was primarily the transmission of utilitarian skills to children and the efficient management of curriculum and pupils" (Goodman 1985, 46).

Yet it is during student teaching and related early field experiences that preservice teachers are most likely to have opportunities for the kind of careful, critical reflection on their own teaching that can result in effective classroom practice and in their participation in efforts to improve current practice. In order to avoid the kinds of problems Goodman describes, field experiences must be constructed in a way that makes ongoing critical reflection as routine for preservice teachers as the practical, everyday responsibilities of the secondary English classroom. In our view, such field experiences should engage student teachers in "authentic" classroom practice over an extended time period but also protect student teachers in some sense from many of the day-to-day pressures of classroom management and "curriculum delivery." Furthermore, field experiences should provide regular, structured opportunities for reflection on that classroom experience in a way that fosters examination, not only of classroom practice itself, but also of the assumptions that inform that practice. As John Mayher writes, "Questioning such assumptions requires both reexamining and reinterpreting the meaning of our own learning experiences in and out of school by looking at them through new theoretical lenses" (Mayher 1990, 1). Our goal, then, is to develop in our preservice teachers a critical awareness of what they do as English teachers that becomes a lens through which they view their teaching, their colleagues' teaching, and curriculum and schools in general.

In order to accomplish this goal, Joy Seybold, the English department head at Jefferson High School in Lafayette, Indiana, and I worked together with two other members of Joy's department, Bonnie Fusiek and Lana Snellgrove, to redesign a university English methods course required of all secondary English education majors. That course became the centerpiece of our efforts to prepare preservice English teachers for reflective practice, and portfolios were the critical element in making the course a practicum for reflective practice. Drawing on the experience of the Jefferson High English department in designing and implementing a portfolio system for grades nine through twelve, we emphasized the potential of a portfolio to provide opportunities for ongoing self-reflection that becomes a routine part of the process of completing the portfolio. Just as students in English classes must regularly evaluate their own writing as they compile portfolios, our preservice teachers, we hoped, would evaluate their own work—and that of the experienced English teachers they observed—in secondary English classrooms as they completed portfolios for the methods course. Moreover, in the same way that writing portfolios can provide a detailed picture of a student's written work over time, we wanted to use portfolios to encourage our preservice teachers to reconsider and assess their work in high school classrooms over the course of a semester. Although we believe the portfolio system we eventually designed enabled us to accomplish these goals, the task was not an easy one and reveals the complexities of designing and implementing effective portfolio systems.

Beginnings: The Methods Mentor Program

Our early efforts to address the problems described above focused on expanding the field experiences for preservice English teachers at Purdue University. Before we began our project, English education students at Purdue had only one formal early field experience prior to their student teaching semester. That field experience was generally limited to observation and often involved little or no hands-on classroom work; students thus had few opportunities to engage in active learning in their field experiences. Many students were unhappy with this situation since they believed they needed more time in classrooms in order to prepare them adequately for full-time teaching. Many teachers agreed. At Jefferson High School, located a few miles from the Purdue University campus, teachers' concerns about the preparation of preservice teachers led many of them to agree to participate in our project when we proposed incorporating a field experience into the existing English methods course at Purdue.

Initially, this project, which we called the Methods Mentor Program, involved developing a limited field experience component for the methods course. Students would be paired with "mentor" teachers at Jefferson High School and would work with those teachers over a two-week period to design, develop, and teach several lessons in a high school English class. The students would then write a detailed report in which they would describe and reflect on their experiences in the high school classrooms. We conducted the program in this manner for three semesters.

Although in many ways our program seemed beneficial, a number of problems emerged. First, the field experience was simply too limited for the methods students to gain the perspective they needed to begin to reflect critically on teaching English in a high school setting. Second, the limited nature of the experience encouraged students to focus on the practical pressures, especially the need to learn to deal with student behavior, and to ignore the broader issues of curriculum and theory we wished to highlight. Finally, other than the written reports the students produced after their field experience, nothing about the program itself promoted the kind of critical reflection we had hoped to encourage among our students.

As a result, we spent several weeks during the summer of 1993 radically redesigning the methods course for the upcoming fall semester. A faculty retirement in the English education program at Purdue left a vacancy that provided an opportunity for the methods course to be team-taught by Joy, Bonnie, Lana, and me. We thus reconceived the course as a collaborative effort between the university and the high school. Next, we expanded the field experience component so that it became the focus of the students' work in the course: instead of two weeks, students would spend ten weeks working in a classroom at the high school. Then, we paired students with classroom teachers at the high school so that each student teacher worked closely with a mentor teacher during those ten weeks. And finally, we divided the students (usually twenty each semester) into smaller discussion groups of five or six students; these groups, led by one of the course instructors, met weekly to discuss assigned readings and related assignments and to reflect on their classroom experiences. In essence, we restructured the course so that it became an extended on-site practicum at the high school.

The most important change we made in the course involved portfolios. In redesigning the course, the stickiest problem we faced concerned assessment: If we sent students off to work independently with classroom teachers, how would we assess their growth and learning? The crucial issue was to develop an assessment method that might document learning but also encourage critical reflection on the part of our students. The portfolio enabled us to do so.

The Reflective Portfolio

Although the portfolio we designed was intended to be the vehicle for the kind of critical reflection we hoped to encourage in our new version of the methods course in the fall of 1993, the flaws in the design of that portfolio quickly became apparent. We asked students to collect a series of documents, most of which we specified, that they had produced during the course of the semester. Although some of these documents (such as lesson plans and self-evaluations of their teaching) were related to the students' classroom experiences and resulted from their independent efforts and self-reflection, most were simply course assignments that the students had completed at various points in the semester (e.g., sample unit or lesson plans and responses to assigned readings). Unwittingly, in trying to make the portfolio a comprehensive portrait of the students' work in high school classrooms over the semester, we had squelched the opportunity for careful reflection and ended up with what amounted to collections of documents; moreover, what reflection did occur was largely summative in the sense that students were evaluating their work for the portfolio *after* the fact and not in an ongoing fashion.

Our dissatisfaction—and the students'—with the portfolios led us to reexamine our approach. At the end of the fall 1993 semester, we discussed the problems we had experienced with the portfolios and considered adjustments. In doing so, we identified three key features that should characterize the portfolios:

1. the portfolio should encourage ongoing reflection and not simply document the students' work;
2. the portfolio should grow out of and reflect a range of experiences and competencies related to teaching and learning;

3. the portfolio should include a variety of student-selected materials related to those experiences and competencies.

In short, the portfolio would be not simply a means to *assess* growth and reflection but a vehicle for that growth and reflection.

We identified four areas of teaching secondary school English in which competency and experience were, we believed, essential for our students as they prepared for student teaching and beyond:

1. design and development of effective lessons and curriculum;
2. observation and critique of classroom practice;
3. assessment of adolescent students' reading and writing;
4. teaching performance.

These four areas represented key objectives we set for our students as they trained to become effective classroom teachers. At the same time, as we note above, we were not interested in simply helping students learn, for instance, to design good lesson plans. We also wanted them to understand the complex connections between classroom activities and the assumptions about language and learning that drive those activities; we wanted them to be able to identify those connections, to understand their assumptions and the implications of those assumptions, and to develop lesson plans accordingly. In short, we wanted to encourage our student teachers to be critically reflective in these four crucial areas of their practice.

With these goals in mind, we restructured the course portfolio for spring semester 1994 as an ongoing, semester-long activity—one that required students not only to document competency in these four areas but also demonstrate their own efforts to think critically about what they were doing and to examine carefully why and how they engaged in the various activities described in their portfolios. During the first few weeks of the semester, before the students began working in the high school classrooms, we set forth the guidelines for the portfolios (see Appendix). From that point, their work in the course, and particularly in the high school classrooms to which they were assigned, was shaped by these guidelines. In effect, each student was being asked to construct a critical portrait of her or his learning and growth as a teacher during the semester; that portrait would emerge in the documents each student selected for the portfolio and in how those documents were presented and evaluated by the student.

The Reflective Portfolio in Practice

The reflective portfolios shaped the students' work in the methods course in two important ways. First, the portfolio assignment encouraged the students to evaluate and reflect on their work in the course *as they engaged in it*. Since they were responsible for documenting their learning and growth in the four areas listed above *over time*, they could not wait until the end of the semester to think about these four areas. Instead, they had to structure their work in ways that would enable them to engage in, for example, assessment of student writing or reading; moreover, they had to find ways to demonstrate that they had engaged in such work and had also reflected on their learning in that area. As a result, the students made decisions throughout the semester about what their classroom experiences should include and how to document those experiences. These decisions represented perhaps the most important reflection they engaged in during the semester.

This sort of reflection was illustrated in a conversation that occurred approximately halfway through the semester on the electronic bulletin board that we established for the class.[2] In this instance, Abbie[3] comments on her first experience in teaching a lesson to the high school class in which she was working:

> Initially, I was a bit frustrated, but I soon realized that I had to remain poised and confident in my abilities. Usually I am easygoing, a real "softy", but today I proved that, although I may be little, I can be quite firm. The student evaluations that I got were very good. I plan to include them in my final portfolio, for they seemed to show that I had good rapport with my students. Of course some students judge your teaching abilities on the basis of your physical qualities. One student wrote, "She had my attention because she was pretty." Others thought I could have done a better job by "handing out cokes." Though these comments lacked instructional value, they were OK, for they too indirectly say that I am approachable, OK to joke with. As my teacher remarked, "It's OK Sometimes you have to use other things to gain attention." Teaching is just not a transmission of knowledge. It is energy, personality, appearance, credibility, rapport, communication skills, confidence, patience, delivery, organization, planning, creativity, and spontaneity, all in one person. It is a skill, an art, and a talent.

Here Abbie is reflecting on her experience in the high school classroom and drawing conclusions from that experience about what it means to be a teacher. Although it's quite possible that she might have made such a comment even if she was not required to document the experience for her portfolio, it's likely that the portfolio encouraged this kind of reflection on her experience. As she thought about how to document her experience for her portfolio, Abbie had to reflect on the experience itself and what it might have revealed to her about her own teaching and teaching in general. In addition, she had to think about such issues *during* the experience, since she knew that the portfolio required her to document and reflect on her learning in a way that precluded waiting until the end of the semester. In other words, it would have been impractical (and perhaps impossible) for Abbie to return to the high school classroom several weeks later at the end of the semester and ask for student evaluations. Instead, she had to gather and think about student evaluations as she was in the midst of the experience; she also had to decide what these evaluations revealed about her teaching and about teaching in general. In the end, she did include the student evaluations in her portfolio among the other materials she selected to document her teaching performance and growth during the semester. Her decisions about what to include in her portfolio thus reflect her thinking about what that experience meant. But as her comment suggests, she was already thinking carefully about what the students had said long before the semester was over and while she was still working with those students in the classroom. In this way, the portfolio encouraged ongoing reflection as preservice teachers like Abbie engaged in various experiences related to the course requirements.

The portfolios also encouraged a kind of critical reflection that went beyond the examination of a classroom experience described in this example. Whereas Abbie was encouraged to examine her experience in a way that might enable her to document what she learned about classroom teaching, we also saw evidence that students were beginning to develop an understanding of what it means to be *critically reflective*. For example, as the deadline for the portfolio approached near the end of the semester, several students discussed on the electronic bulletin board the ways in which the portfolio assignment required them to reexamine their work. Again Abbie commented, but this time she focuses on the portfolio itself:

> This final task is the kind that students need, for it demands creativity, organization, originality, reflection, and revision. There are no "right" answers and no amount of "cramming" will help get it together. Furthermore, the portfolio doesn't isolate learning into a restricted time frame. Instead, it is the culmination of weeks of observation, critique, teaching, assessment, and

> reflection. The value of the portfolio rests on one's ability to synthesize and apply, to fit the weekly "pieces" of knowledge we gain into a complete puzzle. Isn't this exactly what Wiggins encourages in education?

In her comment Abbie relates the activity of completing her portfolio to the use of portfolios in high school English classrooms. In addition, she refers to an article on assessment that we had asked the students to read (Wiggins 1993b), drawing from that article an important theoretical perspective that she then applies to her own practice. In other words, the act of compiling the portfolio encouraged her to make connections between new theoretical concepts she was learning and her own experience as a student and preservice teacher.

A few days later, Abbie remarked:

> With a portfolio project, it is impossible to just get by without it showing in your final product. I've been working on my portfolio, so this has become abundantly clear. It just demands so much from the student, and in order to develop a well-organized, coherent, reflective representation of hard work, mental growth, and engaging thought, the student has to be fully engaged and aware of the material.

Such comments are all the more meaningful because they were unsolicited and occurred in a forum in which we as course instructors participated but which we did not moderate or control in the way we might manage an in-class discussion. As a result, the students often spoke more freely on the electronic bulletin board than they might have in a face-to-face group discussion (see Riedl 1989).

The variety of materials the students included in their portfolios was remarkable and indicated, we believe, the kind of careful reexamination of their experiences we hoped to encourage. These materials included:

- lesson plans, assignment prompts, quizzes, exams, etc. that they had developed
- copies of student essays to which they had responded or which they had graded
- evaluations of their classroom performance from teachers, from high school students, and from their peers in the methods course
- evaluations of other teachers' classroom performances
- evaluations of their peers' classroom performances
- notes made of various classes they observed

- handouts, overheads, and other materials they developed for use in the classes in which they worked
- reflections on the assigned course readings as they related to one of the four areas they were to document in the portfolio
- a videotape of a lesson taught by the student teacher

In most cases, these materials were accompanied by a statement or self-evaluation by the student describing and explaining the documents. These statements amounted to written descriptions of the kind of reflection students engaged in as they selected and gathered the documents for their portfolios. For example, in reexamining for her portfolio the lesson she taught from a rhetorical perspective set forth in some of the assigned course readings, Abbie concluded that the assignment, in which she asked students to write letters to a newspaper editor, "had one major flaw":

> Though I concentrated on making this a realistic task, it ultimately became another writing assignment for the teacher to grade. Now, I can think of a more realistic approach. Perhaps the disturbing problem of grammar would have been eliminated if the context were real. Obviously, it is impossible to completely disregard academic focus. However, by encouraging students to actually send their letters to the newspaper for publication, assessment could have taken place amidst a practical task.

Here, Abbie assesses her experience in teaching her lesson from a perspective provided by the course readings, a perspective that enables her to draw conclusions about what happened and why. In other words, as she tries to document her experience for her portfolio, she attempts to evaluate her own practice, using theoretical ideas provided by the course readings, and then considers how to adjust her practice accordingly.

Using Portfolios to Encourage Reflection: Implications

Our experience with portfolios in a university English methods course adds another bit of evidence to the growing literature that suggests that portfolios can indeed promote critical reflection. But the process of designing, developing, and implementing a portfolio system—in any course—is a decidedly complex one that requires teachers to adapt the portfolio to the specific contexts within which they teach. Portfolios in and of themselves will neither solve the problems of assessment that confront teachers nor promote the kind of self-evaluation or reflection teachers often hope to encourage among their students. Such goals must be integral to the portfolio process and must inform the design and development of that system within a specific classroom context. To do so requires adjustments that may significantly influence pedagogy. For instance, one case study of a teacher who implemented portfolios in her classroom reveals the ways in which her teaching "was clearly changed by using portfolios with her students" (Gomez et al. 1991, 627). In addition, the teacher "found that instruction is not a one-size-fits-all proposition," and that she needed to make significant changes in the organization of her classroom and the ways in which she monitored her students' work (Gomez et al. 1991, 627). We also needed to make such adjustments, and as we changed our portfolio system, we also changed the course in which we used it, as we note above. In short, the portfolios were integral to the structure of the course; one would not, we believe, be effective without the other. Although such an assertion is not new to those who use portfolios, we found this notion of the integral relationship between the portfolio and the course context to be perhaps the most important implication of our experience.

A second and related implication is that such uses of portfolios as we employed in our methods course can result in, as Gomez, Graue, and Bloch point out, "a new role for teachers and students, requiring collaboration in a way that honors learners as makers of knowledge" (Gomez et al. 1991, 627). Encouraging our students to engage in reflective practice led us all—instructors and students alike—to adopt new roles and new perspectives on the work we were doing and on how to accomplish that work. As course instructors we ultimately had to become mentors at the same time that we retained responsibility for evaluating the students' performance—something not always comfortable for us.[4] In addition, in evaluating the portfolios at the end of the course, we found it necessary to adapt to new criteria that grew out of the ways in which students had constructed their portfolios. For example, we allowed the students great flexibility in deciding what kinds of documents to include in their portfolios, and we had to be careful about comparing one portfolio to another because of the variety of documents the students chose to include. In this sense, we could assess the portfolios using neither a norm-referenced nor a criterion-referenced approach; rather, we needed to develop some hybrid approach that grew out of our objectives for our students and the flexibility we allowed them in completing their portfolios. For the students the task was something like what Grant Wiggins describes as an "ill-structured and authentic task . . . though the methods and the criteria are quite clear to all students in the course, there are no pat routines, procedures, or recipes for solving the problem" (Wiggins 1993b, 205). As a result, not only did students have to think in new and perhaps unfamiliar ways to solve the "problem" of putting together their portfolios, but our assessment methods needed to be flexible as well.

In order to address these complexities, we found we needed to engage in an assessment session similar to the kind of rating session Edward White describes in his discussion of large-scale holistic assessment (White 1993, 163-167). White asserts that readers of essays in large-scale holistic scoring need to become "an assenting community that feels a sense of ownership of the standards and the process" of the scoring (White 1993, 164). Similarly, we found a need to read through several portfolios, sort them in a general way, compare our initial evaluations, then begin to identify shared criteria. Once we did so, all four course instructors read and evaluated each portfolio, then compared evaluations before agreeing on a final grade. Such an approach took a great deal of time, but it was necessary in order to achieve reliability in our assessments of the students' work.

Initially, the process was uncomfortable, since we sometimes felt that the criteria that were emerging through our discussions of the portfolios had not necessarily been made explicit to students at the outset of the course. For example, as we read through and discussed the students' portfolios, it became clear that having a variety of perspectives on their classroom performance was crucial in helping us "see" and understand what they did as they taught their lessons. Although we had suggested early in the semester that students might gather a variety of evaluations of their teaching (from their mentor teacher, their peers, the students they taught), we did not "require" it; we wanted to open up rather than limit possibilities for documenting teaching performance, so we remained general in our guidelines. Yet as we tried to assess the portfolios, we realized that the most effective portfolios had this variety of perspectives and documents. This variety of perspective thus became an important criterion in our assessment of the students' portfolios. Eventually, we formalized these criteria to some extent and made them explicit to students in subsequent semesters at the outset of the course. In this way, our criteria for evaluating these portfolios have emerged from our own views about what the portfolios should be like, from our shared (and sometimes negotiated) standards for student performance, and from our evaluations of previous student portfolios.

For the students, a different problem emerged as they engaged in thinking about and completing their portfolios. They felt a tension between the role of professional educator—which in many ways our portfolio system encouraged them to adopt—and their official status as students. Although such a problem is typical of student teachers (see Richardson-Koehler 1988), in this case the tensions created problems that we had not foreseen and which we needed to respond to during the semester. Some students were frustrated by the lack of *specific* requirements for the portfolios. They saw the flexibility as a liability, one that made it difficult for them to determine what they needed to do to achieve a good grade. In retrospect, we realize that this tension grew out of their desire to do well in the course and perhaps their unfamiliarity with adopting the perspective of a professional educator. At the time, we pressed them to think like teachers and not like students, to see their work as part of their professional development and not as a set of requirements they needed to fulfill in order to complete their programs. Despite our efforts to encourage such a stance, some students felt uneasy, some resisted openly, and a few believed we were being unfair.

Although such uneasiness and resistance represented a minority view among the students (at least as reflected in their anonymous final course evaluations), it raises concerns about the pressures we can inadvertently place on students in using a portfolio system. We believe the same kinds of uneasiness can occur among students in a portfolio-based writing class, as some researchers have found (Gomez et al. 1991). Although our students, as preprofessional educators, were in a position that differed in significant ways from students in, say, a freshman composition course, students in any kind of course often feel the same pressure to achieve a high grade. That pressure can emerge as an obstacle in courses structured around portfolios. As Burnham writes of the demands a portfolio can place on students, "It asks students to strive for excellence and long-term development rather than settling for the immediate gratification available through traditional grading" (Burnham 1986, 136). Teachers thus need to be aware of such pressures and adapt their portfolio systems accordingly.

One final implication of our work had to do with the kind of collaboration we saw our students engaging in as they put their portfolios together. A few weeks before the deadline for the portfolios, one student, Don, posted the following message to the electronic course bulletin board:

> Since we are getting down to the wire, I'd like to talk about peer tutoring as it pertains to our portfolios. Help! I would like to get together and read some of

> each others stuff some time before the portfolios are due. I know we are all busy, but I think it's important to get feedback on this. Jake and I met last Friday evening to discuss what we are putting into our portfolios and to discuss our impressions of the whole 422 experience. I found this experience very useful although somewhat unfocused. Anyone wanting to share work, post a note about it.

We learned that a number of students had, with no prompting from us, begun to gather together to do just what Don proposed: consult with each other and assist each other in compiling their portfolios. In retrospect, we realize that the entire course was structured in a way that encouraged collaboration among the students, and the portfolio was integral to that structure. And although we were never present at any of these student gatherings (we were, in fact, never invited), we suspect that the kind of collaborative efforts in which the students engaged encouraged the very kind of reflection we hoped the course would encourage. Our belief is that portfolios can foster such collaboration in a way that enhances the critical reflection students might engage in as they compile their portfolios—in a writing class, a methods class, or any other sort of class.

Conclusion

At the end of the 1993 to 1994 academic year, we assessed the adjustments we had made to the course and the course portfolio. Our own view, which was supported by virtually all of the students in their anonymous course evaluations, was that we had taken a big step toward achieving the goal we had set for ourselves at the outset: to design a field-based course that fostered our students' development as reflective teachers. We also concluded the portfolio we had designed was integral to achieving that goal. Although circumstances in our respective institutions have made it impossible to continue the team-teaching arrangement we enjoyed during 1993 to 1994, the methods course remains structured around the reflective portfolio we developed during that year. That portfolio, we believe, enabled us to assess our students' work much more accurately and fully than we might otherwise have been able to do. But the greatest benefit we saw has been in the critical reflection that the act of constructing the portfolios seems to have encouraged among our preservice teachers. It is impossible to say whether the portfolio will have lasting effects in encouraging our students to become lifelong reflective practitioners of the kind Donald Schon writes so compellingly about, but we see the portfolio—and the course into which it is built—as an important step in their training as thoughtful teachers. We hope a comment one student wrote anonymously on a final course evaluation speaks for most of our students:

> More than anything, this course has showed me the importance of thoughtful reflection. I appreciated the opportunity to think for myself and make my own decisions with regard to teaching decisions and the construction of the portfolio. The final portfolio was one of the most valuable academic tasks that I have done. It provided helpful guidance, but it also allowed us to be individuals. There were no right or wrong answers, so to speak, and you could not study for this test of learning. Instead, the portfolio demonstrated each individual's mental growth during the semester. The portfolio taught me more about myself and my abilities than any test could ever do.

Notes

1. This chapter was prepared with invaluable help from Bonnie Fusiek, Joy Seybold, and Lana Snellgrove of Jefferson High School in Lafayette, Indiana, who helped develop the course and the portfolio system described below. The "we" in this article refers to me, Bonnie, Joy, and Lana.
2. The electronic bulletin board we set up was a Usenet newsgroup established for the course to allow students to engage in asynchronous "discussions" at their leisure about their work in the course. Students could log into the newsgroup at any time to read comments posted by their classmates or to post their own comments. These online discussions usually focused on issues we discussed in class, the students' experiences at the high school, and sometimes events elsewhere that related to the educational issues we were discussing (such as the development of a new standardized test in Indiana).
3. Pseudonyms are used in place of the students' real names throughout this article.
4. Burnham discusses the same kind of tension in working with new teaching assistants for a first year college composition course.

Appendix

Guidelines for Course Portfolio

The portfolio is the major project for this course. It is intended to reflect your efforts and learning in the class and to provide you with the opportunity to document demonstrated competencies in the teaching of English which you have developed over the course of the semester. Although you should construct a portfolio that best reflects your work in this course, you should adhere to the following guidelines as you put together your portfolio.

Contents. In essence, the portfolio will contain materials that document each student's learn and competency in five key areas in the teaching of English: (1) designing, developing, and planning lessons; (2) assessment; (3) observation and critique of instruction; (4) teaching performance; and (5) understanding diversity. The specific contents of the portfolios will vary from student to student, and you should choose materials that best exemplify and document your work in the four areas discussed below. At the same time, several specific requirements for each of these five areas should be met. These are described below.

1. *Designing, Developing, and Planning Lessons.* This section of your portfolio may include a variety of materials, such as lesson plans and materials you developed and used at Jefferson, assignments you might have given, notes you made as you designed lessons, etc. It must include one complete unit plan. This unit plan, which should cover at least a two-week period, should include the following components:
    a) a day-by-day outline of the unit;
    b) at least five complete lesson plans that best reflect the activities, design, and objectives of the unit;
    c) a rationale of approximately five pages which discusses the objectives of the unit and how the specific activities and assignments meet those objectives.

    Ideally, the unit plan will grow out of the lessons you developed and taught in the class you were assigned to at Jefferson, but it need not. You may decide to develop a different unit or you may rethink the lessons you taught at Jefferson. Each section of the unit plan should be clearly labeled and you should indicate the appropriate grade level and time of year for implementing your unit plan.
2. *Assessment.* This section of the portfolio should document efforts you have made during the semester to develop understanding and competency in assessing students' reading, writing, speaking, etc. in English classes. Some possibilities:
    - develop and assess a specific writing or reading assignment in the lessons you teach at Jefferson and include appropriate copies in your portfolio;

- assist your mentor teacher in assessing students' essays or exams; include copies of these materials along with a discussion and critique of what you did in assessing the students' work;
- include copies of tests or quizzes you gave to students and discuss these;
- observe and participate in the use of portfolios in Jefferson English classes, describing and critiquing your participation for your portfolio.

The documents you include in this section should show clearly what you did and what you learned about assessment. You should also attempt to draw on the assigned readings in your discussion/critique of your assessment work.

3. *Observation and Critique of Instruction.* In this section you should document efforts you have made to learn from other teachers by observing and critically reflecting on their teaching. Some possibilities: include notes and descriptions of your mentor teacher's lessons; observe other teachers and write a critique of their classroom performance; observe and critique one of your classmates as she or he teaches a lesson.

   The purpose of this section of your portfolio is to demonstrate that you have learned how to observe and assess what occurs in a classroom from a teacher's perspective.

4. *Teaching Performance.* This section should document your actual classroom teaching. It should show clearly what you did as you taught lessons, how you performed as a teacher, and what you learned from your teaching experiences. Documents might include some or all of the following:
   - a written evaluation of your teaching by your mentor teacher;
   - a written evaluation of your teaching by one or more of your classmates;
   - written evaluations of your teaching by your students;
   - notes made by your teacher during your lessons;
   - notes you made on your own classroom performance.

   This section should not only demonstrate preparation and actual classroom performance, but it should also show evidence of careful reflection on your teaching: what happened and why; what went well and why; what did not go well and why; what you might have done better.

5. *Understanding Diversity.* This section of your portfolio should document your efforts to understand and accommodate diversity in the secondary school classroom, particularly with respect to teaching the language arts. Obviously, your efforts to understand and accommodate diversity in the classroom should always inform your teaching, but this section of your portfolio should highlight those efforts. Some possible documents to include:
   - a discussion of your experiences with students of varied ethnic, racial, socioeconomic, religious, or cultural backgrounds in the classroom in which you worked;
   - your ESL assignment essay or a revision of that essay;

- copies lesson plans or assignments you developed that specifically address issues of diversity;
- a discussion and critique of those lessons or assignments.

In addition to the documents you include in each of the five sections described above, two other documents are required in your portfolio:

1. *An Introductory Overview.* This document should serve as a kind of table of contents and guide to your portfolio; it should let a reader know what the contents of your portfolio are and how they are arranged. It is also an introductory statement by you that should set the tone for your portfolio.
2. *A Self-Evaluation.* This document should be a careful, critical reflection on your portfolio and the work and learning it represents. It should include specific reference to each of the four areas of competency described above, and it should reflect your learning and growth as a teacher during the semester. Please note that this is a key part of your portfolio.

In all, then, your portfolio will contain five sections and two separate documents. You will decide which specific documents to include in each of the five sections, but you should do so according to the guidelines described here.

Format. The format of your portfolio is up to you and should reflect to some extent your sense of your work in the course. But keep in mind that the format and organization of your portfolio will influence how a reader evaluates that portfolio and thus affects your grade. Above all, you should strive to make your portfolio understandable and readable so that it best reflects your work in this course. Be sure to type all documents you write for the portfolio. (Class notes, student work, etc., of course, need not be typed.) Also be sure to label each document clearly and organize the portfolio so that it is easy for a reader to read and make sense of.

Grading. As the syllabus indicates, the portfolio is worth 50% of your grade for the course. The grade for the portfolio will be determined on the basis of the completeness of the portfolio, the relevance of the documents, the organization of the portfolio, and the depth of thought and self-reflection demonstrated in the portfolio.

A Final Note. Although this portfolio is primarily designed to shape your work for this course and provide the instructor with a vehicle for evaluating that work, it is also intended as the first step in developing a professional portfolio, which may help you have a worthwhile student teaching experience and a successful search for a full-time teaching position after you graduate. As a result, it makes sense to put together a good portfolio that you can use as you move through your undergraduate program and into a professional position.

16

Teacher Portfolios

Lessons in Resistance, Readiness, and Reflection

Kathleen Blake Yancey

I HAVE TAUGHT ENGLISH "METHODS" COURSES FOR OVER A DECADE NOW: the courses that are intended to help students learn enough about the teaching of English so they can walk into a middle or high school classroom populated with *live* students and not panic at the sight. As a former public school teacher who herself took such a course, I know both what that course did for me and—as important—what it didn't. What my English methods course equipped me to do was to teach suburban white students, mostly males, preparing to attend Harvard. This preparation proved only minimally useful, of course, when, two years later, I found myself teaching eighth graders in Clear Spring, Maryland, a community whose members hadn't heard of Harvard and whose members weren't impressed when they did. In brief, for the teaching I actually found myself doing, I wasn't—how shall we put this?—very well *prepared.*

To be fair, I'm not sure that we can prepare students to teach in all contexts. I understand this. On the other hand, precisely because of my own experience, I believe that we can help students to think about a diversity of contexts and a diversity of students, and I was delighted when, in 1987, I was asked if I'd like to teach the class where I might try. I went about preparing to teach this course as I prepare for most: choosing texts and creating assignments, but with an eye toward what I thought might specifically work for these students-who-were-becoming-teachers. In particular, I made two choices that I considered crucial: I selected professional readings rather than textbooks (for example, Golub's 1988 collection on collaborative learning), and I asked the students to compose a paper entitled "My Ideal Classroom." The readings were intended to introduce students to the kind of texts that they would use as classroom teachers, in part to help them learn to navigate those texts *before* they were classroom teachers.

The paper on the ideal classroom was intended to help students think about themselves as teachers in a specific context, to idealize that context so that they would create their own picture of what was possible, a picture that would guide them as they began to teach and that would serve as a touchstone as they continued teaching. Both choices thus worked toward helping students think about how classroom practice might work, but also they worked toward helping them effect a kind of transition from university preparation to classroom practice.

A Gap: Theory and Practice

In theory, loosely defined, I still think these choices sound useful. Lord knows, I was well-intentioned enough. But you can see what's coming: the students didn't see the course as I did. Quite the contrary. Regardless of where I taught the course, at Purdue from 1987 to 1990 or at the University of North Carolina in Charlotte from 1991 to 1994, the students for whom it was so carefully designed pretty much universally found it unsatisfactory: confusing, disorienting, too advanced, too much, and decidedly not helpful. During this time, of course, I experienced various reactions. Disappointed, I tinkered with some of the text selections. Sympathetic, I changed the authorship of the curriculum unit from single to collaborative, if students chose, so that they could work in teams to create the unit. Annoyed, I moved to include more kinds of assessments and to provide them more often. In brief, although I tried to be responsive to the complaints, they continued. As Pogo might say, I had met resistance and met it hard. As of the fall of 1994, I was reluctantly concluding that, again as Pogo might say, I was the problem, and that I should simply give up teaching this course. I wasn't quite bitterly disappointed.

In the spring of 1994, I encountered my colleague Bob Yagelski at a conference; we talked particularly about the methods course, and I discovered that his experience matched mine: resistance. In early summer, I talked to Beth Burch, then at Alabama; her experience matched ours. In late summer, I talked to Sarah Robbins at Kennesaw State; her story in the methods course was also plotted through resistance. I began to understand that I was not alone. What we all had seemed to experience, at least partially, was what Ann Gere and her colleagues talked about recently in *College English*: a sense on the students' part that what they needed to know was how to teach decoding skills *correctly*, how to be an authoritative and knowledgeable teacher who told her students what to do, and how to manage the classroom efficiently. We, on the other hand, seemed to want our prospective colleagues to work in a collaborative way to *discover* ways of communicating with their students.

I decided to give the course one last try: I redesigned it. In so doing, I made five major decisions:

First, I changed the books we used. Rather than use Golub's text on collaborative learning and Anson's on response to writing, I chose a basic English-teacher-education text, the Gere et al. *Language and Reflection*, (1995) a text that is designed for methods students. I allowed ample time to work with it: eight weeks of the sixteen-week term. I also chose two others, however: John Mayher's *Uncommon Sense* (1990), to give the students just a bit of theory and an introduction to a professional text; and my own edited volume on portfolios (Yancey 1992b), so that they could see teachers redesigning their curriculum and conducting teacher-research.

Second, I reduced the amount of reading and the number of assignments. Previously, we had read five texts; now we were down to three. I dropped the Ideal Classroom paper. I made the curriculum unit collaborative. I kept the midterm, but allowed students to rewrite unsatisfactory answers to it (for learning and for credit) when they included it in their portfolio.

Third, I put the students on a closed listserv discussion group and asked them every other week to respond to a prompt I had posted there. The prompts asked students to do different kinds of tasks: to summarize and respond to a reading; to critique a recommended practice; to choose a quote from the reading that seemed particularly valuable and talk about why; to find something that a colleague had said and react to that. I also invited a former student teacher of mine, Scott Diehl, to participate on the list. Scott has taught in various contexts, from alternative schools to the local high school in State College, Pennsylvania, so he understands diverse environments and students, and as someone who had his own struggles with me as his university supervisor, understands how the students might (still) feel.

Fourth, I changed the portfolio model. Previously, I used a model based on the American Association of Higher Education's (AAHE) model. It includes four components: preparation of teaching, teaching, assessment of student work, and professional development. I expected the students would follow this pattern and produce something they might take to a job interview: I expected *professional.* Now I designed a new, more student-centered model with three component parts: concepts, application of concepts, and development. In this portfolio, the expectation was that I would see the teacher they thought they might want to become, and that to do that they might arrange the exhibits anyway they liked, and that they might develop a theme for the portfolio. I expected *thoughtful and/but tentative and analytical.*

Fifth, I emphasized reflection, seeing it not so much as something that came at the end of the portfolio process, as is so often the case (Conway 1994), but as something that threaded throughout the course, in multiple forms and for multiple intents. I asked students to write me biweekly *reflective letters* in which they commented on anything that seemed germane; I asked them to write *goal statements* at the beginning of the class and to revisit those goals periodically; I asked them to write what I called *Learning Summaries*, in which they commented on their learning and how it was progressing; I asked them throughout the term to choose portfolio exhibits and write one page *rationales* for those exhibits; and I asked students to write a culminating *reflective essay* for their teacher portfolio.

The Students' Portfolios

Laura's Portfolio

I want to use Laura's portfolio to demonstrate how well these changes worked, just so you know (that I know too) the master narrative here. And even so, this claim is disingenuous: a strong student, Laura will do well regardless of context. I understand this; it's only fair that you should too.

Like all the portfolios from this class, Laura's is not a writing portfolio but a teaching portfolio, and as such, it is a different genre of portfolio. While writing is certainly the primary medium, teaching is the focus of the portfolio, a teaching that for the purposes of the portfolio and the course we have analyzed into three component parts: *knowledge*, *application of knowledge*, and *development as a prospective teacher*. Students may use these categories to organize their exhibits, or they may develop another pattern or schema. Laura has created her own of six parts. Entitled "To Be a Teacher," the portfolio includes:

I. Beginnings and Realizations
II. Progressions

III.Collaborative Efforts
IV.Applications of Knowledge
V. Realizations
VI.Reflection

Laura's portfolio isn't terribly fat; this is the third portfolio she's created, and she understands the value of selection. She includes diverse materials, however: reflective letters; some rationales for portfolio exhibits she chose throughout the term; her midterm; an abstract of the curriculum unit; a paper on a field experience independent study she took concurrently with this class; some emails, including one to the Purdue Online Writing Lab; and her reflective essay. Her midterm shows knowledge, her curriculum unit shows application, and her letters and emails show development. Her portfolio will earn a good grade, that's clear.

What's as important, to me as to Laura, is the articulation of the learning underlying the knowledge, the application, the development—and *the person best suited to articulate this is Laura. Better than anyone, she knows about her own learning*. This seems so obvious, but it is perhaps the most unacknowledged idea in learning I have ever encountered. One of Laura's exhibits is telling in this way: a portfolio rationale for her first exhibit, it documents *what she learned.*

> After searching desperately for something to include in my portfolio, I've finally found something! I've decided to use the first sneaker-net activity done in the class: . . . [which asked students to tell why English should be taught]. I want to include this piece because it reveals that I have good intentions about *wanting* to teach English, although it proves that I'm really off-base in determining *why* it should be taught.

That Laura was *desperate* tells me at least as much about my request as it does about Laura. Even for Laura, who had composed other portfolios, this task—choosing a single exhibit according to her own criteria and then showing how it met those—was strange and risky. Still, Laura brings to the task two qualities that go into good teaching: first, she is able to *assess her own readiness* accurately and unflinchingly; and second, she *understands the process* by which we develop readiness, as we also see later in that same rationale:

> My response in the sneaker-net activity seems to be an early sketch of things I want to accomplish as an English teacher. Although the reasoning seems logical,

> my argument is flawed. My reasons for wanting to teach English assume that all students will become enamored of the "wonderful world" of English when I "reveal" it to them. In a sense, I'm assuming that all students will magically fall in love with literature the same way I did. Now, my previous reasons for wanting to teach English almost seem unrealistic and illogical.
>
> I believe that "assumption" is the greatest mistake new teachers make. I realize (not even halfway through the semester), that it is crucial to recognize individual differences in students and their individual preferences for English, as well. For this reason, I want to include the activity as the *first* piece in my portfolio. I feel that it is extremely important to show progress in the portfolio—moving from the illogical to the logical.

It may be, of course, that Laura's progress will not move altogether from illogical to logical, but she does see both process and progress. She also locates herself as a member of a larger class, the class not of students but of *new teachers*, and she makes this identification, as she says, prior to the completion of the term. Her theorizing about new teachers takes place without our even discussing the idea of theorizing. Although a student, Laura is practicing as a teacher: locating herself among teachers, discerning patterns, and theorizing about those patterns.

A second exhibit in Laura's portfolio is a multivocal paper focused on her field experience; it alternates between 1) descriptive discourse chunks that describe what happened as she attempted to help Courtney, a tenth grader, write well enough to pass the state writing test and 2) reflective chunks that attempt to *make sense of* the experience. What did Laura learn? Among other things that teaching

> is a great learning experience. It enables you to learn so much about yourself although those aren't the things you *want* to learn . . . Somehow in my adult stupidity, I forgot that she [Courtney] had feelings—that she actually wrote something she liked—and that I was tearing her creation apart every time we met for a tutoring session. Giving her the opportunity to own her own work enabled her to feel more comfortable changing it with suggestions *instead of orders.*

Laura concludes the paper by asking for a course called "Real Life," where she would learn

> how to be quick on my feet, how to catch curve balls, how to survive in a classroom with kids who could care less about you, how to plan (no, I really haven't mastered that yet), how to follow the most boring state curriculum imaginable without losing the attention of the students, how to still feel confident at the end of the day, and how not to give up.

(After twenty years of teaching, I'm still looking for this course.)

Finally, I come to Laura's reflective essay. At three pages and large font, it is spare rather than saturated. What I learn from it:

- that at the beginning of the term, Laura was "preoccupied with trying to fit the mold of the standard teacher to be";
- that trying to do what you are "*supposed*" to do isn't always the right thing to do and that teaching "is *not* easy, *not* painless, and *not* without the occasional discouraging moment";
- that the "Uncommon Sense methods of instruction" made sense when they were put to use in a real classroom;
- that Laura finally got to *use* what she was learning and that this was the first time this had occurred to her in her college experience;
- and that she feels ready to student teach.

What I also learn has to do with the relationship between what I have come to think of as two curricula: the *delivered* curriculum and the *experienced* curriculum. The delivered curriculum here is my curriculum of English 4170: philosophies of teaching English as represented in the Gere text (for example, artifact, expressive, developmental/cognitive, and social constructionist); ways to teach reading and writing; the role of formative and summative assessment in teaching and learning; and what uncommon sense is and how it works. I look for documentation that the students have learned this curriculum when I evaluate the portfolio. I look for evidence of concepts acquired, applications created, and development managed. The task here is to see if the students "got" the curriculum I "delivered;" the irony here is (of course) unmistakable. *I* might very well be the reason they haven't "got" it, but we show this gap with *their* grade.

At the same time, as I read Laura's portfolio, I am very aware that she is experiencing her own curriculum, based on who she is, on what kind of teacher she wants to be, on what she perceives her needs to be, and on what she experiences throughout the semester *in my class* and *out of it*. In Laura's case, "out of it" is the key to "in it": the field experience brings into play *real application* with *real students*, one of whom has a very real and altogether unpleasant timed state writing test to pass. Accordingly, Laura's experienced curriculum is a good match with the delivered curriculum. What does this mean? I think what I've discovered here is that there are always these two curricula[1]: the delivered (the teachers', the institutions') and the experienced (the student's version of that delivered curriculum), and that when courses work well, they provide a point of intersection between the two.[2] In Laura's case, because she took the independent study, she found that point of intersection both accessible and large. What can we do, I think, to increase the likelihood that such an intersection is always available? is always large? How can we know when it's not, and what can we do about it so as to change it?

Kenny's Portfolio

Kenny's portfolio is fat—or hefty, at least. He's also divided his into sections, his modeled on a child's learning to walk. Thus we find:

I. Introduction
II. Baby Steps
III.Searching
IV.Somewhere Between Searching and Applying
V. Applying
VI.Beginning to Walk on My Own

Kenny's portfolio is comprised of eighteen exhibits, some of them like Laura's—the midterm, an abstract of the curriculum unit, emails—and some of them unique to Kenny. For instance, he includes an interview with Lisa Philips, a special education teacher, to show one of the most important things he learned: that teaching calls for a special kind of commitment.

> As someone interested in teaching, I believed there must be nothing to it. Get up each morning, teach some kids, and then go home for dinner with the family, but I was shown during my "Baby Step" entries that there is a certain commitment that you must be willing to make to become an effective instructor. I am using an interview from another class that helped to open my eyes to what a committed, caring teacher can be.

Again, I think, the student learns by explicitly connecting what happens outside my class with what goes on inside. The portfolio, as constructed here, not only asks for that connection, it requires it. Put another way, the portfolio asks that the student bring together the "component parts" of experience, put them into dialogue and dialectic with each other, and make sense of them through the rhetorical situation of the portfolio.

By far the largest exhibit in Kenny's portfolio is his Why Should English Be Taught paper, and the set of drafts and notes and peer responses and transmittal forms—companion pieces that contextualize the formal papers—that accompany it. He's framed his paper as a speech "given at a high school PTA meeting" in his home town, the place where he wants to teach. It's taken him four drafts and thirty-some pages to get to the final draft; by his own account, this collection taught him about the nature of writing and about himself as a writer. Asked to talk about the paper as terrific, Kenny says,

> I feel this is a terrific paper because I took the time to edit and redraft several times which is not something that I usually do when writing. Along with personal editing, I sought help from outside sources and tried to answer their questions and listen to their advice. The fact that I was not willing to "go it alone" should help to make this a terrific paper.

I see the same theme of writer development reiterated in Kenny's reflective introduction to the portfolio: "The email assignment from March 8 is a testimony to my conversion from a single-draft writer to the multiple-draft writer that I need to be." For Kenny, *the methods course was a writing course.* This wasn't quite my intent, I think, although it's true that English teachers need to be writers and readers. This was what Kenny needed from the course, however; this was a part of his experienced curriculum.

Kenny also includes what I have called a Learning Summary, (which I take to be) an opportunity for students to think about what they are discovering in class; to think about that in relationship to their earlier expectations for the course (which itself presents one way to think about development); given this relationship, to think about what should come next for them as individual students; and to consider what strategies will help the students reach those newer destinations. We conduct this reflection through four questions, each one asked only after its predecessor is completed:

1. What have you learned so far in this class?
2. Is this what you expected to learn?
3. What else do you need to learn?
4. How will you go about learning it?

Kenny believes that he has learned a lot, and he sees how the class members as a community have fostered that learning.

> In this class I have learned that writing, the ability to write, and written comprehension are essential elements in the English classroom. Methods of instruction (i.e., language as development, language as social construct, etc.) are

> concepts that I have become more familiar with in this class. These are things that I never really gave much thought to in the past, but I now realize how important they are in determining your own teaching method. The fact that teaching is not one or the other but is a meshing of ideas from them all is also something that I have learned so far in this class. I have also been introduced to the difficulties of grading. Finally, I have learned that the ideals and views of the prospective English teachers in this class are somewhat similar as well as different.

Kenny is learning the delivered curriculum—the concepts and the beginning application evident here—even as he is implicitly disappointed in it. He had apparently hoped for a simpler, more direct answer to the question of how to teach English: "I thought that the focus of the class might be more centered around the 'standard' methods of teaching English. I also thought (or perhaps, hoped) that we would be shown a 'right' way to teach English." Still, Kenny sees what he needs to learn: "how to mesh the methods that we are discussing to best fit my personality and abilities." I think what I am watching here may be a loss of innocence that—necessarily?—accompanies good teacher preparation. I hadn't thought of teacher preparation in this way before, but then again, I hadn't really asked the students for their perceptions in this way. If we don't ask, we (teachers) won't learn. As important, what we ask matters: it can't just be, did you (student) get what I (teacher) am supposed to deliver? It has to be more and other than that: it has to be, what are you (student) learning (in this class)? And at the same time, I think, as I read Kenny's portfolio, what I am also watching is a growth in authority: now that Kenny understands what is possible, he can make choices that suit his *personality* and *abilities*. In the portfolio reflection, he notes how important the Learning Summary was: "This entry shows that I recognized what I needed to improve and that I had to make an effort if I wanted to improve."

Kenny's portfolio introduction narrates his story of the class. In it he highlights why he chooses to use the metaphor of a child learning to walk as a way of talking about what he's learned: "I decided to use walking as a metaphor for my portfolio because it seems to me that once you find yourself walking as a child, you then become ultimately responsible for the ways that you get to where you are going." Where Kenny is going is to work with others, and bringing those others—his prospective students—into this equation was also part of what he learned. He includes an email, for instance, that "shows a willingness to forget my needs and wants so that I may concentrate on the student." He includes the curriculum unit and abstract and the worksheets used to create both because they exemplify "how a unit can be taught with regards to the student's world and not only what Norton's *Anthology* can spew forth." He is beginning to see himself as a *teacher of students*.

> I also placed an email assignment from April 4 and the sneaker-net responses to the quote I chose from *Uncommon Sense*. In both I see the teacher I want to be. In my email discussion I came to the realization that I could not do to my students what was done to me because, honestly, I have forgotten much due to poor presentation. Then, through Tim's response on sneaker-net I was shocked to find him looking for new and better applications like myself. To close out "Applying" I have placed my edit and redrafts of the essay. I had taken advice from this class and applied it in a process that was tedious and against my grain, but I knew that I had to take measures to improve just as I will be asked to do each time Johnny does not "get it" in class discussions.

I see Kenny synthesizing what he has learned: he sees the recursive processes of writing that felt so uncomfortable and foreign as the *same recursive processes* he will need in the classroom. An impressive connection; it's not one that I've made *until he shows it to me*. More generally, I think I discern the pattern of Kenny's development: he moves from student-who-has-naive-constructs-of-teacher, to a more reality-based-prospective-teacher construct—focused on what kind of teacher he will be given his own assessment of his personality—to prospective-teacher-of-students.This development too can be recursive.

Kim's Portfolio

Kim's portfolio, like Laura's, is slender, but I am not surprised: most of Kim's work this term has tended to the slender. Like Kenny's portfolio, Kim's is themed: "From Heart to Mind to Hand." I read her portfolio reflection, but its brevity does not bode well:

> In February, I wrote what I wanted my portfolio to show, ". . . the evolution of myself as a writer and future teacher." My portfolio definitely does this. How? As you flip through the pages of my work, you see evidence of my improved abilities, as well as a change in my attitude. What I mean is, my first works show me as a student that needs revision and a more concrete opinion of myself as a writer, a learner, and a teacher of English.
>
> After reflecting upon my own work, along with the system of opinions I have collected in this class, I can conclude several things:
>
> 1) I, as a student, *need* revision

> 2) I, as a student, am living proof that writing to learn must precede writing to perform
> 3) I, as a teacher, will integrate and put great value on this process of writing
>
> My portfolio shows my work move into the direction of writing to perform. Although there is not one piece of writing in the entire portfolio that could not use another revision, there are some that I would not change at all. I am speaking mainly of the in-class writings that show my views on a particular subject as they come straight from my head . . . some of these views changed over the course of the semester, and this can be seen throughout my portfolio, but they always moved in the same direction. This is evidence that I, as well as my work, changed . . . changed for the better, I think.
>
> From Heart, to Mind, to Hand. I feel that, as a teacher, I can help students follow a similar path, where performance will come in time, just as mine has, and still is.

Reluctantly (*is this it?*), I see the portfolio reflection as telling me another story, the story of a real mismatch between the delivered curriculum and the experienced curriculum. Like Kenny, Kim finds in the methods course a writing course that she thinks she needs; that, I think, is all to the good. But unlike Kenny, Kim does not move beyond that need of hers as a student, does not see that other students—her prospective students—might experience the same need, does not express any relationship between the processes of her learning and her prospective teaching, does not even predicate students except in the most generic sense. Kim, I think, shows me the identity of student well. Where is the identity of prospective teacher?

I go to the first writing Kim provides, an introduction to her composed on the first day of class. She tells me that she is just "getting started on my English concentration," and that her second concentration, in science, is nearly completed; presumably she is prepared to teach science, and presumably she has thought in terms of science students and their needs. She loves to read, she says, mentioning the Bible, Shakespeare and Hurston as texts. Her main goal in class: "to become more computer literate and be able to use it as a tool and helping aid." Should I have seen something wrong here, right from the start?

I go to a portfolio rationale; here Kim explains that she will include in her portfolio the paper "Why English Should Be Taught," commenting that:

> What I wrote was fairly simple, but crude. My ideas were somewhat shallow. . . .
>
> There are a couple of reasons why I chose this essay. First, because I am a work in progress, it shows the evolution of my thoughts . . . that is to say,

> through our class discussions and through the readings, my thoughts on the subject of English changed. I think they matured a little and even expanded. My essay shows this progress. Also, it is an example of me, as a student, writing to learn, which must come before writing to perform. This is definitely seen in this first essay due to all the editing errors, and the poor flow of the paper.

Interesting: the paper is focused on why English should be taught, is thus quite clearly content-specific, is thus asking her to *take on the role of teacher*. Yet Kim's perspective on it is single-minded: on it as her student text. More disconcerting, it's not a strong reflective analysis, relying as it does on floating signifiers like *editing* and *flow*. Also interesting: at the top of the rationale in the right hand corner, I had earlier penned in response to it:

OK—this is great for you as student; what about you as teacher?

No comment; no addition; no change.

I look to Kim's Learning Summary. In the first section, focused on "What Have I Learned," Kim seems to have learned (my) delivered curriculum.

> From the text, I have learned about several approaches to teaching English, such as the developmental and Language as Artifact approaches. In class, through group work, I learned how those approaches might be applied in the actual classroom. On a broader level, I have learned that there is much more to teaching English than just reading and writing, such as being able to fairly grade the student's work. I have always thought, and especially now, that attaching a mere letter grade to a student's work is not always a fair assessment of his or her capabilities. English can take on so many broad topics and can be so subjective at times that it becomes necessary to give room for creativity. Then the question becomes how creative is too creative? These are the things I am learning a lot about in this class.

On the one hand, this *sounds* like someone who is working within the parameters of the delivered curriculum, especially when Kim talks about specific approaches to teaching and the issues that inform grading. On the other hand, when Kim says *especially now*, my guess is that her concern with grading is motivated more by student than teacher identity: she had expressed considerable dismay about the C she earned on her essay.

In the second question of the Learning Summary, she says, yes, what she is learning is what she expected to learn. As to what she needs to learn now: "This is a hard one. I'm pretty comfortable working with literature as far as reading it from different perspectives and then analyzing it. Ah, I've got it. I need to know more about grading written papers. This is what I would love to avoid because I have a hard time writing a good paper, myself." Again, Kim as student.

And what strategies will Kim employ to learn about grading? "Well, I'm still a student, so I plan on learning it from my instructor." The delivered curriculum—how to become a teacher—has somehow almost disappeared completely; it has been rewritten for Kim by her need to learn to write, as expressed in the experienced curriculum.

The problem here, I think as I review this portfolio, is complex. Most obvious and first, portfolios will not work magic: if a student is not ready, the portfolio cannot change that. I'm not even certain that it can accelerate readiness. Second, my assessment is that Kim is not ready to think of herself as a prospective teacher, which is what she has pretty consistently told me all along. Third, she expresses a kind of resistance to the idea of being a prospective teacher: *I am a student*, she says, not a prospective teacher. Fourth, now that I think I see this pattern—a student who cannot, is not ready to, add the identity of the teacher to that of the student, who does not see them as two sides of the same coin, really—what do I do about it? More generally, what does this pattern suggest? If we were to frame the course as a journey from student-to-teacher, would we see typical patterns of development in the course? If so, are these patterns typically more like Laura's, that is, moving from wanting to be the "standard good teacher" to redefining the good teacher? Or are the patterns more like Kenny's, whose view of teaching was increasingly complicated and situated over time? Are there multiple typical patterns? And are there likewise characteristic patterns for students who, like Kim, aren't ready for the delivered curriculum?

Kim's portfolio has probably taught me more than it has taught her. In showcasing her experienced curriculum, it has shown me how far short of the delivered curriculum we have both fallen. It has helped me understand more theoretically what is involved in *becoming a teacher* and the *accretion of identities* that it requires. And it has helped me understand more pedagogically the developmental patterns I might look for the next time I teach this course.

What I've Learned: My Own Reflection

This chapter resembles a portfolio: I've chosen a collection of materials from the course and from the students with which I can tell my story of the course, and I've tried to do so in a way that honors their intents, and in a reflective way that shows how I've interpreted these selections and what

I've learned from them. It's important, however, that we remember that this story is mine. Even though I've included the voices of the students, I've appropriated them to show my theme, not theirs. Constructed from the same materials, their stories about this course—Laura's and Kenny's and Kim's—might be very different indeed.

But still, I have learned here, and I'd like to talk a little about what it is that I think I've learned and about how that learning happened. What I am supposed to say—we all know this—is that the portfolio made it happen. To a certain extent, that's a legitimate claim. The portfolio is a key part of the redesign of the course, and more than any other component of the course, it motivated the reflection that became the way of being of the course. And it is a doubled experience since it is through combining my reflection with the reflections of the students that I have come to understand the key concepts here:

- delivered curriculum
- experienced curriculum
- intersection of the two curricula as the most productive site for learning
- student-to-teacher identity issues

The key concepts, however, aren't all that I've learned. In thinking about them and how I've learned about them, I understand what helped produce them: flexible, valid portfolios that are vehicles for reflective ways of understanding our intellectual work. More specifically, let me offer some corollary observations.

Portfolio design is a central issue in any program, and certainly in teacher education programs. What we choose to allow in our model of portfolio will not only affect the students (although that's true, of course), but it will also shape in crucial ways what we see and thus how we understand our own curriculum. I said earlier that the portfolio as I have constructed it accomplishes certain goals. Both Sandra Murphy and Susan Callahan have made this point elsewhere: the portfolio in and of itself accomplishes only what the teacher or an institution makes possible in terms of the kinds of freedom permitted to students. In my case, I was particularly interested in the reflective aspect of the portfolio, and I was also interested in the connections that students made between what we were doing in the methods class and other experiences—both academic and otherwise—that *they saw as related.* Issuing this invitation to include whatever they perceived to be relevant—from a curriculum unit completed for another class to a paper for an independent study to an interview with a practicing teacher—proved especially valuable, both for the ways that students could construct themselves and accordingly for what it allowed me to see. Simply put, such an invitation asks them to construct a whole from the fragmentation we call education.

Portfolio design (or construction), which we see in the constraints we place on the portfolio, may seem like a minor point, but I don't think so. Originally, I had constructed the teacher portfolio for the methods students as a professional vehicle, thinking that such a design would help students most. It did not. And even when I used this professional model of portfolio, I intuited at least some of the limits of (my own) narrow construction of portfolio. In the fall of 1992, for instance, I gave a talk at the annual convention of the National Council of Teachers of English (NCTE) on this teacher portfolio, arguing that if we thought of it as a professional text, we would lose the chance to learn from the portfolio what it can teach us: that the only way that it can teach us is by not being too rigid, too fixed, too (in this case) professional in its construction; that allowing freedom in it provided one way for students' voices to be heard, and that to learn about and from the portfolio, we probably needed such freedom and such voices. Even so, it took student resistance to *make me ready* to give up the professional portfolio, ready to understand that this move in portfolio design wasn't an abandonment but an enhancement. Like Laura, I too was trapped by my sense of what I was *supposed* to do.

In sum, I think I have learned from this reflection on this methods portfolio, and I think I was able to do so because I've designed the portfolio as inclusive of student experience—as much oriented to experienced curriculum as to delivered curriculum. And I have then understood this distinction between curricula in the bargain. One of the key changes here involved exactly that: moving to a portfolio that was in character more student-oriented than professionally-oriented.

Just as the *validity* of the portfolio model is, in part, a function of its relationship to the curriculum, such validity is also enhanced by its power to teach the teacher. One of the more recent understandings in assessment has to do with validity, the concept that what you measure in fact is what you intend to measure. Portfolios are so popular in part because they seem to be more valid measures of what it is that we are trying to get at. Researchers like Roberta Camp and Pamela Moss have taken validity one step further, arguing that when we consider how valid a measure is, we have to take a look at the effect of the measure on the students. If the effect of the measure on the students' learning is harmful or disconnected, they say, then the validity of the measure is *decreased.* Since portfolios, as discussed here, are intimately connected with a student's learning, their validity is enhanced. There is a corollary to this idea of effect as a factor in assessment, however, that I'd like to suggest. I agree: the connection from assessment to learning needs to be made, and it needs to be felicitous. But it is also true that when an assessment functions well, *it teaches the evaluator as much as the student.* That is what this portfolio did for me, and thus it is a more valid instrument; I understand not only how my students performed, but *why.*

Community is a subtle theme threaded here as well. Kenny mentions that he learned from the practicing teacher and from his colleague in class. Laura mentions that she learned from Courtney, the student, how to teach. Kim doesn't mention people from whom she is learning: what might this signify?

Students seeking to become teachers don't shift *identities*: they begin to develop a new one, the teacher identity. I've used a language here suggesting that the trip to teacher is from student, but I think that this is decidedly not what I think. This is Kenny's trip as he describes it, yes. But I don't think this was Laura's trip, nor do I think trip is quite the metaphor. I don't think there is a shift, which is what the metaphor trip seems to be about; rather, I think the methods course is to help students develop an additional identity, that of teacher, and to keep the identity of student, in fact to see that a teacher is, first and foremost, a student. It's *both/and.*

I've subtitled this chapter "Lessons in Resistance, Readiness and Reflection," trying to suggest this text provides lessons for all of us who are students. And I take that to be all of us. Originally, student resistance helped me develop a readiness to change. That readiness increased when, through talking with others who teach this course, I understood that my experience wasn't unique but almost prototypical: I too relied on community. In terms of the portfolio, my readiness to change increased as well when I gave the talk on portfolios at NCTE. In contrasting a classroom writing portfolio with my earlier version of the teacher portfolio, I saw for myself how the freedom of the one helped us see things that the fixed character of the other would preclude. And then because of continuing resistance, I changed the course, threading the reflection of portfolio throughout—in Goal Statements, in Learning Summaries, in Transmittal Forms, in Portfolio Rationales, and finally in reflective essays. And as Laura's and Kenny's portfolios suggest, I met with less resistance with the redesigned course. It's not totally gone, of course, as Kim makes clear, but at least I can theorize now about what it might represent: a stage in a developmental model. And even for students who complete this developmental model, resistance can be an important part of it as another student in this class, Scotti, tells me in her last reflective letter:

> I think you are the type of person who can appreciate honesty, so here goes . . . This class has been the most demanding class that I have ever taken at the university. At the first of the semester (and at several points during the semester), I truthfully thought that I hated this class. And I don't mean that I simply disliked it; I mean that I HATED it! I would bitch and moan about all the stuff that we had to do in here, but somehow I managed to come to class and to do everything that I was supposed to do. . . .
>
> Something about this class that really made it difficult was that it made me *think*. It made me think in ways that I have never thought before. No longer was someone holding my hand and saying, "OK, one day when you are a real teacher, what are you going to do?"
>
> Instead, you have been there demanding, "OK, you *are* a teacher, so what are you going to do?" I must admit to you that this SCARED me to death! I was terrified of you and of this class for probably half the semester because I had to think for myself, and that was something that I had not done in a long time. The coolest part about this, though, is that once I got comfortable thinking for myself, it started spilling over into my other classes as well.

Given my current understanding of resistance, and its relationship to readiness and to reflection, I've shifted focus: what, I'm asking, are the sources of this kind of resistance? How do they play out in various developmental models? When is it productive, and when not? What do I mean by productive?

These are the lessons in resistance, readiness, and reflection that, I think, are worth coming to know.[3]

Notes

1. In fact, I think there are three curricula. As Jennie Nelson's recent *CCC* article suggests (Nelson 1995), students bring with them what she calls their lived curriculum, their understandings of how school works and knowledge is demonstrated. So a complete theory would need to show how these three intersect; I take this to be beyond the scope of this paper. But we do see evidence of the lived curriculum even in Laura's short excerpts: her notion of the "standard teacher to be" seems to be one she brought with her as a product of years of schooling, as is her idea that students would love literature as did she; this curriculum is then in dialectic with the delivered curriculum and the experienced curriculum of the course. Bringing them together in some coherent way may be what it is that we ask of students in any course.

2. We might more accurately call the delivered curricula the articulated or the designed curricula since the point of a portfolio, like any assessment, is to ascertain whether or not the curriculum has in fact been *delivered.* I like keeping the term delivered, however, because of the irony it suggests.
3. Thanks to Bud Weiser, Bob Yagelski, and Sarah Robbins for their help in understanding resistance.

17

Finding Out What's in Their Heads

Using Teaching Portfolios to Assess English Education Students—and Programs

C. Beth Burch

THE PORTFOLIO HAS TYPICALLY BEEN VIEWED EITHER AS A PEDAGOGICAL strategy or an assessment tool. As a pedagogical strategy, the portfolio grounds the notion of the student's personal process and provides a framework for the display of both process and product. As an authentic assessment tool, the portfolio assesses students' multiple abilities under the ideal of mastery learning; in this capacity it has been used to place students in academic programs, to determine whether they were ready to leave those programs and/or levels, and incidentally to award them grades or at least indications of progress. The portfolio can also, as Irwin Weiser has noted, have specific advantages for preparing writing teachers, particularly inexperienced instructors treading the murky waters of evaluating student writing for the first time (Weiser 1994, 224-225). But portfolios also have other important uses: they can reveal, in the aggregate, the state of an academic program; they can provide valuable insights into what students know and how they construct that knowledge; they can provide institutional barometers, if you will, that suggest programmatic highs and lows, strengths and weaknesses. It is chiefly in this institutional context that I undertook a kind of class ethnography, with portfolios and metaportfolio writing at the center of my investigation. I used written artifacts to describe the group's "customary ways of life" in my course (Zaharlich 1991, 207); I wanted to know what my students, soon-to-be teachers, were learning, what they knew about English, and how they were conceptualizing the discipline.[1]

Teaching portfolios had been an integral part of my Teaching Secondary English "methods" class for four years. Operating on the supposition that novice teachers would benefit from a portfolio assignment requiring them to create, collect, and select materials—and then to reflect seriously upon what they had selected and why—I had had an "open" teaching portfolio assignment in place for these years. This means that I required that methods students submit three original teaching units for the portfolio, but that the remainder of the portfolio was open—simply up to them. The context of the entire course was consciously conducive to and supportive of portfolio pedagogy; it included collaboration on projects, reflection (usually in writing), and self-assessment. As a class the students and I collaborated to develop the scoring rubric for the portfolios. We decided that the required units would be 40 percent of the portfolio grade and that the optional material would account for the other 60 percent. We agreed on certain criteria for evaluating the portfolios; we articulated desirable qualities for the portfolio including organization, originality and creativity, variety, pedagogical soundness, practicality, and evidence of effort. But when we couldn't reach consensus on weighting the criteria, I left that task up to each student. The result was a rubric allowing adjustments for individual strengths and weaknesses (see Fig. 1, Portfolio rubric).

One spring, instead of merely assessing the teaching portfolios from the methods class, I determined to study them via a kind of particularized ethnography. My study focused primarily on the documents comprising the portfolios but also included reflective pieces introducing portfolios, portfolio tables of contents, and individual reflective pieces written during the portfolio process but not included in the actual portfolios. I surmised that each student's portfolio would reveal idiosyncratic strengths and weaknesses; I hoped that each portfolio would provide a glimpse into the developing teaching personality and that each would show something of its creator's sense of the discipline in the portfolio content and structure. I hoped that, considered all together, the portfolios would give me a sense of what my preservice students as a whole knew about English and how they conceptualized the discipline.

What I learned was fascinating and sobering: it has given me pause, led me to reflect on the nature of the entire English education program, and finally drawn me to the conviction that we shortchange our students. We frequently do not give them the preparation and experience in English

Figure 1
Portfolio Rubric

Portfolio Evaluation
CSE 379 Teaching Secondary English
Dr. C. Beth Burch

Name: __________
Date: __________ Circle one: Language Arts? English?

Required Material (40 points)

__ Table of contents (5 points)
__ Overview reflective letter, memo, or essay (15 points)
__ Unit on composition and language, including one original activity/plan (10 points)
__ Unit on literature, including one original activity/plan (10 points)

__ **Total points for required material (40 possible) and comments about required material (see also the individual units and the reflective piece):**

Optional Material (60 points)

Please write in the parentheses below the number of *possible* points you want for each category, with a minimum of 5 points and a maximum of 15 points per category. If you want each category weighted equally, write in 10 points for each, but *make sure* your total possible points add up to 60!

__ Organization and accessibility of items ( ) points
__ Originality and creativity of material ( ) points
__ Variety of material chosen ( ) points
__ Pedagogical soundness of teaching material ( ) points
__ Effort apparent in compiling portfolio ( ) points

__ **Total points for optional material (60). See the back of this page, the table of contents, and throughout the portfolio for comments on the optional material.**

__ **Required Points + __ Optional Points = __ Score for Portfolio**

---

course work that they need to be confident and capable teachers. Our novice English teachers are too often inadequately prepared to teach writing and language, especially, and their understanding of literature is frequently limited to a very traditional canon and to a literary-historical approach to texts. In this paper I will explain the specific findings that led me to this conviction by first describing the research population, my methods students; then explaining what I learned about them via an ethnographic investigation into their portfolios; and finally suggesting implications for teacher preparation in English.

Research Subjects: Facts and Impressions

The class whose portfolios were the subject of this study was in all ways very typical of the undergraduate methods courses at this state university of approximately 17,000 students, a Southern university with a liberal arts tradition and a terrific football team. As in all my methods classes, most of the nineteen students were female; 85 percent of this particular class were women. All but one student were twenty-five years old or younger. Eleven percent of this class were graduate students—that is, graduate students with undergraduate degrees taking the undergraduate methods course to make up a "deficiency" in their undergraduate backgrounds before going on to graduate course work in education. Over half of the students in this particular class were very close to the end of their course work and thus near the beginning of their internships: 53 percent of them would begin internships the following semester; 26 percent would intern in two semesters; and 11 percent were taking the methods course inordinately early (contrary to my advice) and would intern in three semesters. One student in the class had already been in the classroom, but as a social studies teacher, not as an English teacher; this student (the only one older than twenty-five) was returning to the university specifically for certification in English. One student would later drop out of the program and not attempt the internship; one student would begin but not complete the internship; and the remainder (89 percent) would complete internships, graduate, and become certified to teach. Of this class, 68 percent were English majors and 32 percent were language arts majors. This distinction reflects two paths to English certification at this university. Students may elect either to have two teaching majors or certification areas of approximately thirty hours each (the most common combination of which is English and history), or they may choose a comprehensive language arts major which includes, in addition to a core of literature and language courses, classes in speech and theater. This option requires about forty-eight course hours (see fig. 2, Teaching Fields).

Figure 2
Teaching Fields

Teaching Field (Comprehensive): Language Arts	**48**
EH 101 and EH 102, or EH 2103 English Composition	6
One of the following two sequences of courses: Sequence 1 EH 205 English Literature EH 206 English Literature EH 340 Major American Writers I EH 341 Major American Writers II Sequence 2 EH 209 American Literature EH 210 American Literature Two courses from the following: EH 366 Shakespeare EH 374 Major English Writers 1660–1780 EH 383 Major Romantic Writers EH 387 The English Novel	12
EH 320 Introduction to Linguistics *or* EH 423 History of the English Language	3
Approved writing elective	3
Approved linguistics or writing elective	3
Approved 300-level or higher literature or American Studies courses	3
SC 101 Introduction to Speech Communication	3
TH 142 Beginning Acting I	3
Approved speech communication electives 6	
JN 416 School Publications *or* JN 417 Teaching of Journalism	3
Teaching Field: English	30
EH 101 and EH 102, or EH 103 English Composition	
EH 205 English Literature	3
EH 206 English Literature	3
EH 320 Introduction to Linguistics *or* EH 423 History of the English Language	3
EH 340 Major American Writers I	3
EH 341 Major American Writers II	3
EH 366 Shakespeare	3
Approved 300-level or higher writing course	3
Approved English or American studies elective (EH 200 is recommended)	3

Students opting for the English major were openly concerned that language arts majors would have an advantage in the construction of portfolios because they would have had more English-related courses from which to draw material. This turned out to be quite a false fear.

My day-to-day observations and impressions of this class yield nothing unusual about them; the students were as usual, from a mix of rural and suburban backgrounds and socioeconomic groups. They were typically eager to get in the classroom and very fond of talking about how they imagined teaching should be done. They had many questions about my experience in the secondary classroom. They had varying prospects for employment; at one extreme, some already had the "promise" of a job where they had gone to high school, and at the other extreme, others hadn't the vaguest notion of where they might want to teach. Also, some students were quite adamant about not teaching at, for example, the middle school level, but others hadn't the slightest notion of what grades they would like to teach. All the methods students worried about classroom management and about knowing enough to teach English; all were intrigued by teacher lore. There was a common fear, often expressed in class discussions, of being inadequate for the demands of secondary teaching; yet there was also a concomitant eagerness to engage the adolescents who would materialize in their classes. There was also a frequently articulated desire to teach better than they had been taught, to improve the profession, and to change the way that high school students felt about English. These, then, were my methods students.

Method of Research

The semester of this study all portfolios were submitted as usual—on time with portfolio evaluation sheets, each reflecting what the student believed to be his or her strengths filled out for each portfolio. I scored portfolios also as usual, logging them in and out, writing notes to accompany the evaluation forms. But I also kept the portfolios longer than usual so that I could photocopy all the tables of contents, letters, and completed evaluation forms and so that I could prepare detailed descriptions of each item in each portfolio. My method was to note each item by name or general description, to indicate how many pages it constituted, and to determine if possible the source of the item. Items were recorded in the exact order of their arrangement by the student. I considered an item to be a unit of material, regardless of page length; thus a sample examination of four pages comprised one item.

This description turned out to be a very lengthy process indeed; handwritten lists of items and descriptions routinely ran to approximately twenty unlined pages per portfolio. After item lists and descriptions were prepared for each portfolio, I analyzed each student's list to determine how the portfolio was organized (of course the table of contents told me this, but the item list was much fuller than the table of contents, which listed only file folders or subcategories), what its unusual features were, and what the chief sources of its materials seemed to be. I then correlated the evaluation sheet, tables of contents, portfolio grade, and course grade with the portfolio description. Finally I traced each student's internship record through the clinical experiences office, added that information to each record, and began searching for patterns.

Contents of Portfolios: A Quantification and Description

The amount of material in the portfolios varied greatly, from the smallest portfolio of 99 items to the largest of 466 items. The overall mean number of items was 214; English majors had a mean number of 237 items, compared to language arts majors' mean number of 192 items. Thus the English majors' fears that the language arts majors would have a natural advantage proved groundless; English majors averaged 45 more items per portfolio than did language arts majors.

My initial sense of the portfolios was that their major contents mirrored, rather predictably, the way I had structured the methods course: divided into chunks about language, composition/rhetoric, and literature. I found material about literature, about writing or composition, and about pedagogical concerns in all the portfolios. In 95 percent of the portfolios I found material about teaching grammar. In an understandably smaller percentage of portfolios I found material about teaching journalism (37 percent) and speech (32 percent) (remember that only 32 percent of the students had been required to take courses in these areas because they were becoming certified in language arts as opposed to English and a second area major.)

More specifically, material about literature and literary study dominated all the portfolios. The literary material referred primarily to canonical English and American literature before the modern era; it consisted mostly of notes from literature classes. All portfolios had material on Shakespeare, for example, but only 15 percent of them included any information or material on modern poetry. Fifty-two percent of the portfolios contained material that could be considered multicultural literature, but all of these also included handouts on multicultural literature that I had provided in class. Also, most students conceptualized *multicultural literature* one-dimensionally, as Afro-American literature, probably because they had taken a course in Afro-American literature. Some students did create innovative literary categories; Fredricka[2] had a section on fairy tales and frontier literature; Shannon added a separate adolescent literature category. Among the disappointing finds were these: fifty-two pages of "canned" exercises and tests on *To Kill A Mockingbird* in one portfolio and in another two whole and complete volumes (anthologies) of American literature for Christians, the contents of which were not only expurgated, but carefully chosen to preclude anything explicitly challenging Christian beliefs and indeed presented in such a way as to reinforce them.

What I found in students' material about teaching writing was hardly more cheering. The material conformed nearly absolutely to modal distinctions (narrative paragraphs, etc.) and consisted primarily of writing assignments to be given to students plus information on invention strategies (my class handouts again). Many students included papers they had written in various English courses and other students' workshop copies of poems and stories (*creative* writing is emphasized more than *expository* writing in the English department at this university). What was striking was what was not, for the most part, there: professional articles about rhetoric or teaching writing; notes from writing classes or theories of rhetoric classes; information on evaluating and assessing students' writing, including grading schema, heuristics, even checklists; material on planning for writing or revising, editing, and publishing—all topics which we had addressed in class but not topics on which I had provided handouts. Clearly what James Berlin has called *current traditional rhetoric* was the conceptual model for my methods students; their sections on composition emphasized products, were rooted in the traditional modes, and provided only the rarest indications of formal knowledge of rhetoric (Berlin 1987, 36-43).

Studying the portfolio sections on grammar revealed similar inadequacies. The height of complex grammatical thinking was the eight parts of speech (and one student had a file on the parts of speech, yet omitted verbs!) and kinds of sentences (simple, compound, complex, compound/complex). No one had a file on sentence combining. No one had a file on building periodic or loose sentences. No one mentioned participles or even clauses except in the context of labeling kinds of sentences. No one included any materials demonstrating how grammar could function in the service of rhetoric and be integrated with writing and reading assignments. No one had a file on dialects or history of the language. No one had a linguistics file—although all students in both programs are required to take at least one linguistics course. But 73 percent of them had publishers' worksheets—from a total of twelve different publishers. The record was Melissa's 109 pages of grammar worksheets.

The portfolio files that were pedagogically related were somewhat more encouraging. Although most of these files contained some notes and handouts clearly identifiable from other education courses in such areas as special education, educational psychology, tests and measurements, and general methods, several students included material obviously collected independently: magazine and newspaper articles about schools and education; homiletic and inspirational material and poems about teaching. Sixty-eight percent of the portfolios contained something originally from *English Journal*—so we may assume that students are acquainted with this important professional resource.

Other findings: all the material about teaching speech and journalism came exclusively and clearly from speech and journalism courses. Several students did put unusual files in their portfolios: Ellen included a "Life Skills" folder; Mary had one on "Professional Ethics"; Jane had publishers' catalogs, sheet music, and information about grants; Amy included a file on "Middle Schools"; and Jolene had one file entitled "Just My Style," every item in which came, ironically, from me. I was amazed that many students included whole textbooks (Fran had eleven; Jolene and Tim, four). Fran also put in thirty-six empty folders (to indicate what she eventually hoped to add to her teaching portfolio) as well as a copy of the biographical introductions to every single author whose work was anthologized in a high school literature textbook. Bill padded his portfolio with 257 pages of unedited class notes and 125 pages of workshop writing (not all his).

Students drew from a variety of identifiable sources to compile their portfolios. All portfolios contained material from English and education classes: notes, papers written, examinations completed. All portfolios also contained material that I had made available to students in the methods class. This material constituted a sizable percentage of the mass of the portfolios—a mean of 20 percent of the total portfolio contents came from me, suggesting perhaps that students believed that I wanted to see my teaching imprint in their materials or that they simply appreciated the practical material. Other sources for portfolio materials were fellow students (the course structure encouraged extensive collaboration) and practicing secondary teachers. Frequently, my methods students acquired material from the education curriculum library and from my former methods students, many of whom were doing internships or teaching in the area. Determining the exact sources of material (other than from my class) was impossible, but the reflective letters indicated that students had drawn their material from these sources.

Organization of Portfolios

Although a portfolio organization was never suggested to the methods students and sample portfolios from previous classes were deliberately not made available, my methods students' teaching portfolios were remarkably similarly arranged and organized, or not arranged and disorganized, depending on one's perspective. Seventy-nine percent of the portfolios had a distinctive and perceptible overall organization. Of these *organized* portfolios, 80 percent were topically arranged along the topics of (in order of frequency) literature, writing/composition, teaching, grammar, language, drama, classroom management, journals, and speech. Thirteen percent of the portfolios combined topical with alphabetical arrangement. Seven percent of the portfolios were exclusively alphabetically arranged. Beyond major categories of organization, though, hardly any portfolios were further organized at all. Indeed, within the large chunks inside portfolios existed a startling degree of disarray; only one student of the nineteen (the graduate student with an undergraduate degree and an English emphasis for graduate study) had used an apparent system for arranging files within the major headings, even though the class had agreed that *organization and accessibility* would be a criterion for evaluation. Fran, for instance, arranged the literature section so that the file "Emily Dickinson" preceded "Beowulf" and "Plato" was adjacent to the "Romantics." Walter's poetry folders followed this perplexing arrangement, with these exact labels: "Burns," "William Carlos Williams," "Poe," "Gwendolyn Brooks," "Shakespeare," "Wordsworth," "Narrative Poetry," "Lyric Poetry," "Dramatic Poetry." Jill separated "Adolescent Literature" from her literature section and inexplicably placed it between folders labeled "Language Skills and Your Future" and "Journals." There were also some refreshingly interesting organizing strategies: Jennifer color-coded all the files within sections—blue for literature, green for composition. Jill cross-referenced many files. Christy used Post-it notes to call my attention to selected aspects of her portfolio. Several students included empty folders: Fran, thirty-six; Jill, seven; and Jolene, three.

Implications of Findings

My findings include observations about the students' constructs of the discipline and some conclusions about the students themselves. Three motifs about the students themselves emerged through this study, mainly through their self-assessments and reflections. The teaching portfolios revealed that preservice teachers believe their portfolios to be *personal and practical.* Bill believed that "a lot of what [he] would teach would come from [his] head." "I hope," he wrote, "that this reflects some of what's in there." Sandra wrote that she tried to "anticipate what [she] would run into" in the classroom. And Jenn wrote in her reflective letter, "Since I don't know what level I will teach, I have tried to include material in my portfolio which is applicable for grades seven to twelve." Students also reiterated the sense of *process* involved with the portfolio although they had not seemed aware of process (in reading or writing) for their students-to-be. "This is a fluid process," wrote Jill. And Bill echoed, "This portfolio is a work in progress." Sharon claimed that her portfolio "was not finished." "Even at the 'turning in' point," she wrote in frustration, "I have to restrain myself from rearranging folders and adding new things." Here is the clear awareness of new teachers' personal need for what Kathleen Yancey has called the "time to develop" (Yancey 1994b, 210).

On a darker note, however, students' constructs of the discipline appeared unsound, incomplete, and extraordinarily lopsided, with the emphasis strongly on literature, especially canonical British literature and American fiction. This imbalance reflects, I believe, the preponderance of literary courses in students' preparation as well as the structure of the English department at this particular university, a department clearly oriented toward literary studies and creative writing. This portfolio imbalance may also indicate students' primary interests; many teachers may agree that their interest in the discipline originated in their love of literature and reading. Students' constructs of the discipline were also marked by lacunae: noticeably missing from the portfolios were references to linguistics or language study, especially an even remotely sophisticated view of grammar; references to literary criticism or any informally articulated strategies of interpretation; and materials suggesting contemporary literature or any literatures other than English or American, particularly contemporary literature. What was not there, chiefly, was evidence of metalinguistic ability. The portfolios suggest that students do not possess many tools for talking and writing about texts. Without the means of sophisticated reflection, teachers and teachers-to-be are handicapped in their abilities to evaluate and create materials. Minus the metalinguistic tools of literary criticism, grammatical terminology, and linguistic understandings, preservice teachers (and in-service teachers too) can do little but succumb to current teacher-proof curricula, textbooks, and "quick-fix" teaching strategies, thus perpetuating the status quo and maintaining the influence of those (frequently outside) forces that determine curriculum and that structure schools.

These deficiencies in preservice teachers' knowledge were—and are—alarming, especially because so many of these preservice teachers were so close in time to independent teaching; immediately after the semester in which the portfolios were assembled, 52 percent of these students were performing internships in secondary classrooms. And one semester after that, they graduated and were certified to teach independent of supervision. No teacher-educator will argue that content knowledge is not among the most important components of the knowledge base for preservice teachers—and most will agree that content knowledge is at the top of the list of what teachers should "know." It has been so during the history of English education. Within the past thirty-five years, though, content knowledge, specifically metalinguistic ability, has been reiterated as necessary for successful teaching. In a chapter on English education in the *Handbook of Research on Teacher Education*, Roy O'Donnell summarizes the 1961 report on *The National Interest and the Teaching of English;* he includes an NCTE-sponsored statement from the Standing Committee on Preparation and Certification specifying that in addition to fundamental knowledge of language and literature, English teachers should have "an informed command of the arts of language—rhetoric and logic" as well as "the insight to use critical approaches in order to discover their literary and human values" (O'Donnell 1990, 707). The 1986 *Guidelines for the Preparation of Teachers* from this same standing committee called for the integration of language arts and argued that among many other necessary requirements, teachers need to know about "composition and analysis of language"—just what appeared missing from students' teaching portfolios and thus from their constructs of the discipline (O'Donnell 1990, 712). In a 1987 article in *Harvard Educational Review*, Lee Shulman argues for a more learned view toward teacher education and for a considerably increased liberal arts influence in the preparation of teachers. Shulman goes so far as to make specific what an English teacher should know:

> . . . English and American prose and poetry, written and spoken language use and comprehension, and grammar. In addition, he or she should be familiar

> with the critical literature that applies to particular novels or epics that are under discussion in class. Moreover, the teacher should understand alternative theories of interpretation and criticism, and how these might relate to the issues of curriculum and of teaching. (Shulman 1987, 9)

Shulman retells Grossman's story of Colleen, a new teacher, teaching two very different lessons with two very different outcomes. When Colleen taught literature, an area in which she was informed, competent, and interested, the lesson was effective and "highly interactive" (Shulman 1987, 18). When Colleen taught a grammar lesson, her performance was "highly didactic, teacher-directed" and by Colleen's admission "uncertain." Colleen had virtually no grammar instruction although she had two university degrees in English; and because of her inadequate knowledge of grammar, she had to devote the energy that might have gone into teaching the material into mastering the material. Clearly, teachers must know their subjects thoroughly and feel confident in these subjects before they can feel free to address students' learning needs and consequently their teaching styles; flexible and interactive teaching techniques are not available to Colleen, Shulman argues, when she does not understand the topic to be taught (Shulman 1987, 18). Sandra Hollingsworth also points out that "understanding subject specific content and pedagogy [is] a *necessary* but not sufficient condition for learning to teach" (Hollingsworth 1989, 177, italics added). An understanding of the subject to be taught is not all that teachers must master, certainly, but that is a necessary precondition for successful teaching. My methods students' teaching portfolios—even the *A* portfolios—revealed an understanding of English that was so incomplete as to make the teaching of English often unnecessarily difficult and thus to limit reform of practice. One may argue that this content learning may be done on the job—and that no professionals are at first totally prepared for independent practice. But learning one's subject and learning to teach simultaneously can be inordinately difficult. Neophytes in other professions frequently have more than four years of undergraduate preparation and a period of paid internship besides. Many teachers do not. The exception is the beginning teacher with a master's degree; indeed, one of the best portfolios was completed by the graduate student with an undergraduate degree in English, but one graduate student example is not sufficient evidence from which to generalize. This student was furthermore at the beginning of course work and would go on not only to take more courses in English but an additional course in graduate English methods besides. Teachers also have a high early attrition rate of 15 percent for the first year (Huling-Austin 1986, 2-5).

We cannot attribute burnout solely to inadequate preparation in the content area, but we can say inadequate preparation in the content area may contribute to the professional frustration of novice teachers.

It is also possible that teacher-educators and preservice teachers belong to cultures that are more distinctive and separate than any of us would like to believe. Preservice teachers are typically not sufficiently immersed either in the culture of school or the culture of English graduate studies to recognize what might be missing from their preparation to teach. And their aims are, after all, distinctly personal: to acquire the credentials for entrance to the profession and to be prepared to succeed personally in managing students and the material to be taught. Teacher-educators, who have teaching experience in secondary schools as well as extensive experience in the culture of graduate studies in English, generally want not only to prepare their students to succeed in the classroom but to sow the seeds of institutional reform. These goals are less tied to personal performance and more related to political aims than are those of preservice teachers. Thus the two cultures have different knowledge bases, different experiences, different perspectives, and different purposes.

What's a teacher-educator to do? How can we insure that English education graduates are better prepared? First, we need more time to prepare English teachers, more time to create more overlap between the cultures of preservice teacher and teacher-educator, and more time to include additional course work and experience, especially in composition and grammar. Accomplishing this goal will be politically risky, for it entails either adding on degree time (a five year program, at minimum) or reconfiguring existing degree programs and removing some courses somewhere to make room for additional content courses in English. Increased cooperation between departments of English and colleges of education will also help prepare more English-knowledgeable teachers. Many students in undergraduate English courses are education majors and vice versa; surely the two entities can find more ways to cooperate in the spirit of mutual interest. Finally, more specific attention to authentic assessment of our preservice teachers may yield valuable information about what they know and so may guide us toward developing better teacher education programs. Open teaching portfolios may be particularly potent reflections of how disciplinary content knowledge is constructed, and we should continue to use portfolios to assess programs as well as the progress of individual students.

Notes

1. Renee Clift's award-winning study of a novice teacher asks this question, among others: "Is it possible that teacher-educators have the same questions about their students' learning that Lesley [the subject of Clift's study] had about her students?" (Clift 1991, 369). The answer to Clift's question is *yes,* for that is exactly why I undertook this study.
2. All students' names have been altered to maintain anonymity.

18

A Different Understanding

Pearl R. Paulson
F. Leon Paulson

A TEACHER JOINED SEVERAL FRIENDS WAITING FOR CLASS TO BEGIN. ON HER way over from school to campus she had squeezed in some grocery shopping. "There I was, halfway down my list, when I realized that my portfolio was on the car seat. I left my cart in the middle of the aisle and ran out to the parking lot. What a relief! I had remembered to lock the doors." She seemed surprised by the intensity of her concern for her portfolio. The others were amused but empathetic. After all, they, too, were making portfolios, and their journals revealed similar levels of investment:[1]

> It seemed I never left my portfolio far behind; it was always with me. I found myself thinking about it as I drifted off to sleep, as I drove to school, and as I was talking to my son.

Another confessed:

> I love my portfolio, and I'm glad I have it. . . . It is an emotional time because of the reflections—you DO put yourself into it. You really do celebrate yourself while learning—and that's sweet.

As their instructors, we were pleased with their reactions. We had similar feelings as we constructed our own portfolios. One of our goals in teaching this portfolio class was for the teachers to discover that portfolios are a personal learning environment, not an assessment add-on. And sure enough, one of the teachers made this final entry in her journal:

> You have asked us to reflect upon the value of making portfolios as a requirement of this class. I would say that the actual making of the portfolio is essential. . . . Without applying what we are learning, we lose a valuable opportunity to create it in a way that is meaningful for ourselves. As with anything it is the application that is relevant. I don't know who said the following but I have always found it to be true:
>
> I hear—I forget
> I see—I remember
> I do—I understand.
>
> Without [having made our own portfolios] whole sections of understanding would be lost.

Our course strategy was to create conditions in which the teachers would discover that each decision about a portfolio has both instructional and assessment implications. At the same time, we wanted them to see how what they believed about learning, instruction, and assessment would influence the way they did portfolios with their own students. We had them keep journals so that they would have a place to record their reflections, particularly on the instructional and assessment implications of each procedural decision.

This chapter is the teachers' story of what happened. The first section describes the class; the last section presents our notions about what transpired. However, the central part of the story is told in the teachers' own voices, extracted from pages of their class journals.

The Setting

Our account is based on the self-reflections of twenty-three teachers. Twelve were in a portfolio class offered through Lewis and Clark College, and eleven were in a similar class offered through Portland State University. The Lewis and Clark class was part of a master's program, the Portland State class was part of the school's general graduate offerings. Collectively, class members taught the entire range from kindergarten through high school, and their specialties included math, science, drama, business, and language arts. About half were pursuing master's degrees. Teaching experience ranged from a few months to over twenty years.

Our curriculum presented portfolios as a means of looking at process as well as product, and especially as an opportunity to engage students in assessing themselves from their own and others' perspectives. Our goals were for teachers to prepare themselves to:

- get started, i.e., know how to establish portfolio activities in their own classrooms,
- facilitate self-direction, i.e., help students to organize their own portfolios, and
- use portfolios to tell a story, i.e., have students' portfolios portray their own learning.

The class was built on our Cognitive Model for Assessing Portfolios (CMAP) (Paulson and Paulson 1990; Paulson, Paulson, and Frazier, in press), which is also a graphic description of portfolio development. The CMAP framework, which was influenced by Guba and Lincoln (1989) as well as by Stake (1967), depicts evaluation as responsive to many stakeholders. As each stakeholder copes with constructions posed by others, individual constructions alter by virtue of becoming better informed and more sophisticated.

We used a variety of instructional approaches. We did a small amount of lecturing (for example, contrasting constructivism and epistemology in respect to the temporal versus fixed nature of knowledge and multiple perspectives versus one, thereby opening discussion to the implications of these philosophies for assessment), but mostly we engaged students in discussion. Approximately two-thirds of the time was devoted to presenting and discussing articles, sample portfolios (or slides of actual portfolios), and videos on portfolio assessment. Assigned readings (especially, Frazier and Paulson 1992; Short and Kauffman 1992; F.L. Paulson and P.R. Paulson 1991; Valencia and Calfee 1991; and Tierney et al. 1991) exposed teachers to differing views of portfolio assessment. Videos, both commercially produced (ASCD 1992; Van Buren ISD, undated) and some we made ourselves, demonstrated how different teachers used different strategies to stimulate self-reflection, support students' self-assessment, and prepare parents and other stakeholders to review portfolios. For example, we showed a video of how one kindergarten teacher preorganized folders so that children could easily compare similar pieces, talk about their differences, and choose ones to show parents. Another demonstrated how a second grade teacher (Paulson and Paulson 1992) gave students a scaffold of five questions (e.g., What did you use?) to help them write short paragraphs describing their math selections. We showed how a fifth grade teacher engaged her students and their parents in weekly assessment and goal-setting conversations at home, preparing both parties for student-led portfolio conferences. In another videotape seventh graders wrote and presented a play at the beginning of "Portfolio Night." It was the students' way of helping the parents view the portfolios from their children's perspectives.

We also used a variety of support materials collected from many teachers across the country. We showed rubrics developed by cooperative groups of fourth graders that they used to rate their own and each other's work and rubrics developed by fifth graders to judge their own writing. We distributed a variety of worksheets purported to stimulate reflection, choosing to do so because so many districts use them. (The teachers' reflections on these appear later.)

We also used simulations to encourage teachers to examine procedures from a number of perspectives. For example, we assigned Linda Vavrus's "Put Portfolios to the Test" (1990) and Linda Rief's "Find the Value in Evaluation" (1990). The teachers in our class simulated a district committee deciding whether portfolios would be introduced in the manner of Vavrus or Rief, and the "committee members" variously argued from the perspectives of students, teachers, parents, and board members. On first reading, the two authors appear to have similar philosophies. However, in preparing for the simulation, the teachers discovered that the two authors hold quite different views about the role of the teacher in a portfolio program.

The remaining class time was spent in small groups sharing portfolios and giving each other feedback. This afforded regular opportunities to share learning and receive the benefit of the others' perspectives.

The teachers worked on their portfolios between classes with minimal direction from us. We asked them to set the purpose for their portfolios, establish the criteria for selecting the contents, make their selections, and organize their portfolio any way that made sense. We let our students struggle through the difficult decisions, recommending only that each time they made a selection they should explain its significance and how it fit in with their overall purpose. Our goal was for each student to create a portfolio that was a personal, integrated story, not just a collection of pieces, or worse, compliance with a formula.

At the end of the term we asked each to present his or her portfolio to the rest of the class. This proved to be a particularly worthwhile activity. We assigned it as a catalyst for relating the portfolio's separate pieces of self-knowledge into one integrated, personal story. The presentation gave the teachers further reason to fully understand and communicate their choices of purpose, selection, organization, and insight.

One of the most important class requirements was the keeping of journals. We told the teachers that reflection was an essential part of portfolio development, and their portfolios would provide many occasions for reflection. We suggested that they make entries in their journals at each decision point, explaining why they chose a particular purpose and audience for their portfolios, how they went about selecting exhibits as well as the meaning of individual selections, and how they organized these into a portfolio. Equally important, they should take time to reflect whenever they changed an earlier decision. We collected the teachers' most recent journal pages weekly, acknowledging but not making judgments, sometimes asking them to clarify a point, and occasionally suggesting they talk with a classmate who was struggling with a similar issue. We learned that journal writing between classes engendered much more reflection on the part of students than the quick-writes and oral discussion we had relied on in other classes.

At the last class we collected copies of the teachers' journals (as pre-announced) in order to review them in their entirety. What follows is a synthesis of the self-reflections in the journals—a story of what happens when teachers make their own portfolios.

Purposes of Portfolios

The earliest journal entries were about how each class member decided what kind of portfolio to put together. In addition to asking them to brainstorm types of portfolios, we had shown them many examples including portfolios by young adults for job hunting or college application, artists' portfolios, portfolios by children celebrating the transition from writing pictures to writing words, and portfolios that reveal "who am I." The teachers in our classes could make a portfolio for any purpose they chose.

Not surprisingly, some participants found the lack of structure difficult ("just tell us what you want"); others seemed appreciative. At the second class session, when each teacher announced the purpose of his or her portfolio, it became clear that they had seized the opportunity for individualism. Here are samples:

> . . . showcase my qualifications as an educator more completely than a resume or job application alone.

> . . . an overall view of what we accomplish in our class during the year. This could serve as an introduction to a new year and new group of students, or as a memory-filled review as the year draws to a close.
> . . . an opportunity to evaluate my own teaching [and] to assimilate, document, and celebrate the changes that I have made in my classroom teaching strategies and curriculum.
> . . . a portfolio on how to run a portfolio approach in my classroom.
> . . . to provide personal information about me as a person, wife, mother, friend, and teacher [and] to leave an organized collection of personal memorabilia to my daughters.

Not only were the teachers introducing each other to even more kinds of portfolios than we had presented, they discovered the interdependence of purpose and intended audience, the most important being the portfolio's owner.

Owner as Autobiographer

The teachers' experience was that of an author recounting a personal story:

> It took a great deal of soul-searching [deciding] what was important in my life. As I put these things together, I have felt every emotion that a person could feel. I feel anger from indecision, joy and sorrow from past memories, and elation when I finally made a perfect choice.

Another explicitly identified the connection between portfolios and storytelling:

> Judging from my personal commitment to this project, it is easy to see why and how portfolios are such powerful self-evaluation tools and storytellers.

We have maintained (Paulson and Paulson 1991) that portfolios are stories and that the students, as owners of the portfolios, deserve the decision-making rights of authorship; their teachers take the roles of publisher, editor, and agent, alerting the authors to the perspectives of their readers, supporting them in their efforts to communicate with their audience, and opening up alternatives rather than closing them off. In the next series of quotations four teachers concur that the right of decision-making is as important for their students as it is for themselves:

> It was a very personal experience and I wouldn't have been comfortable with someone else dictating the pieces that I needed to include. The choice was mine and my students deserve that same opportunity.
>
> I certainly see the importance of each child selecting the material to be included in his/her portfolio. Who can be a better judge as to the most meaningful items to select? No one else could have chosen the most meaningful items for me.
>
> Surely a child can see the growth made over a period of time as I have seen the growth and changes that I have made.
>
> I can see how having children make a portfolio will help them to feel successful because I have felt that way doing mine. I have learned how important it is to feel ownership in what you are doing, especially if it is a reflection of yourself.

Reflection and Integration

Portfolios are holistic and integrative in nature, allowing their owners to build relationships between learning and construct schema of themselves as learners, not just accumulate knowledge.

> One of the most beneficial pieces of developing an individual portfolio for me was writing a reflection for each of my portfolio pieces. I began seeing a common thread to my work and/or my individual portfolio selections.

Portfolios press their owners not just to understand what they have already learned and have yet to learn, but to come to know themselves as learners.

> It was extremely helpful . . . reflecting on independent progress and making goals for future growth. I certainly know what an impact it had on me. I learned a lot about who I am and what is important to me as a learner and as a teacher.

Self-reflection, in the last two quotations, occurred as a natural adjunct to selecting and explaining exhibits. Many other occasions for self-reflection reside within the portfolio process. However, before discussing the variety of natural contexts for reflection, we will describe the teachers' experience with external prompts, forms and worksheets intended to elicit self-reflection.

The Use of Prompts and Worksheets

We ourselves do not use forms and worksheets in conjunction with portfolios. However, the teachers were almost certain to come across ready-made "reflection sheets" since they are in such wide distribution. We decided they should make independent judgments about their value but not until they had used them in connection with their own portfolios. Accordingly we gave out packets of checklists, rating scales, and questionnaires, asking them to use a variety and reflect on the experience in their journals.

One example of a checklist invites the owner to mark one of seven generic reasons for choosing an exhibit (e.g., "It shows I have great ideas"). Another checklist of more than twenty words (e.g., "good," "hopeless," "careless," and "wonderful") allows the portfolio owner to select ten that describe his or her feelings about the portfolio as a body of work. One example of a rating scale includes semantic opposites such as "heavy/light" and "skilled/awkward" with a thermometer between so that the portfolio owner can gauge his or her response to the portfolio process. An example of an open-ended question is, "If you had to make changes, what would you change and why?" (in this case, with two lines provided for an answer). Alternatively, an open-ended prompt (in this case, followed by several lines) reads, "Things I have learned about myself from my portfolio are . . ."

After using several of these, some of the teachers reported that the forms made the task look easier, others suggested that checklists might serve as a quick way to get an overall impression, and a number wondered if open-ended questions might support reflection on the part of beginners. However, the teachers' personal reactions to the forms were largely ones of dissatisfaction, and even resistance:

> I tried finding a form that would apply to the item I was including in my portfolio. I felt no ownership toward the form and no real involvement.
>
> I did not feel that I was able to reflect back over the entire [learning] process, instead I became focused with what the question was on top of the box to be filled in. . . . I kept thinking that I was trying to please the creator of the forms, rather than reflecting upon my learning!!!!
>
> It was as if someone else had set up the criteria for me and I didn't really need to get too involved in the process. So a little stubborn part of me decided I wasn't going to fill out a form. Perhaps there are students out there who have the same rebellious thoughts!

By way of contrast we also asked teachers to write their reflections on blank sheets of paper. A teacher compared the two experiences:

> As I began writing my personal reflections, I was amazed at how much I had to say. Thoughts came pouring to the surface. Many times I cried as I typed. I realized that checklists would never work for me, not if the exhibit was truly a meaningful one.

These teachers, already deeply engaged with their own portfolios, reported that the very forms purported to stimulate introspection and self-assessment actually restricted both the quantity and quality of their self-reflection. In contrast, blank pieces of paper permitted them to freely express what was on their minds. The limitations of the forms, as perceived by the teachers, stem from their external source, the fact that they are not an inherent part of the portfolio's creation, and they do not invite unlimited expression of unique experience. In short, the forms usurped ownership. If the teachers give their own students forms at all, they will be selective in their use. Most said they believed that they could conduct their portfolio programs in a way that would support reflection in natural ways and make forms unnecessary.

Natural Contexts for Reflection

> Throughout the process, I was making mental reflections about the purpose of the portfolio, items to be included, and issues surrounding both the purpose and selections.

Portfolio development offers multiple contexts for reflection. These include setting the purpose, selecting content, organizing that content, and preparing the portfolio for others' review (Paulson and Paulson, in press). The complexity of the decision seems only to enhance the quality of the reflection, but even seemingly mundane problems prove worthy of introspection:

> The next problem to solve was that of the container since many of my exhibits were not flat two-dimensional. I wanted the container to be large enough to allow further growth. I felt the container should be an integral part of my portfolio adding to the meaning held inside.

Many of the reflective statements in the teachers' journals seem to have been written while they were organizing and reorganizing the contents of their portfolios. The "work" of doing a portfolio may have more to do with organizing selections than choosing them in the first place. For some of the teachers, the task of organizing their portfolios was a turning point in recognizing the value of self-directed learning:

> I was somewhat dubious concerning the notion that students should make all decisions regarding their portfolios. When we reached class sessions four and five I became a total convert. I had begun to make some organizational decisions about my own portfolio. I became immersed in the process and began to understand personally the notion of ownership.

A few teachers described how they started the organization task by identifying issues and then grouping things that pertained to those issues. For most, organization evolved by virtue of repeated attempts. Relationships between exhibits became apparent during successive approximations:

> The information gathering process was relatively quick and easy—until I sat down to organize the mass of "stuff" that I had collected. The organizing was one of the most difficult steps in assembling my portfolio. I must have redone the order of my contents six times!

Despite their own frustration with the process, the teachers did not think their students, in turn, should be spared the challenge.

> I found myself reorganizing the contents again(!) [making] new connections to other learnings. I think students need also to feel this sense of freedom to experiment until they reach the right combination and order of contents to tell their story exactly the way they want.

One teacher discovered that organization came more easily once she reexamined her original purpose, clarified it for herself, and weeded out whatever portfolio contents no longer pertained:

> The difficulty of organizing my portfolio was in creating a cohesive story where all the pieces fit together. At first I was planning to tell a life story in chronological order, but after trying, I realized I was choosing events for the wrong reason. I was choosing events that told my life in an orderly way, rather than choosing events because of their meaning to me then and now. I decided to try organizing my portfolio another way. I concentrated on events that stood out in my mind because of their special meaning to me. I was much more comfortable with this format.

Another borrowed a strategy from her language arts curriculum:

> I decided to make a web of items to be included in the portfolio. This was a way to help me organize my thoughts and the material.

As teachers discovered more and more connections between the things contained in their portfolios, themes shifted or whole new themes emerged.

> Learning is experienced because there is a pulling together of facts and a new level of consciousness is realized. You become aware of the total picture of what you're presenting. You integrate parts with a whole—or into a whole. You often see yourself in some new way—that's you and how you feel about something.

> The secret seems to be to have a framework within which to collect appropriate data, and to be flexible enough to change.

One teacher had little success with finding connections, themes or organization, right up until the last class session. He struggled late into the night trying to pull everything together so that he could present his portfolio to us the following day. Here is how he described the experience.

> Putting together the portfolio was kind of like building a house without any real blueprints. I put it together one way, saw a better way, took it apart, tried, didn't like that, went back to the first way, got frustrated, watched *Northern Exposure*, thought of another way, and was too confused to be able to worry about it much more, so I compromised with myself and left it that way for now.
>
> I then wrote an introductory letter, and guess what I found? That's right! My missing blueprints. The only trouble was, I found that they were still incomplete and I had to fill in a lot of blanks as I went along. There are seven copies of my introductory letter in the recycle bin at this instant.

Writing the introductory letter helped this teacher organize, and organizing helped him discover what thinking was still required.

For all of our students, the physical act of organizing seemed very tied up with the cognitive task of constructing schema. The relationships between exhibits in their portfolios changed each time they moved exhibits. Conversely, each time they conceptualized the portfolio a new way, they scrambled to reorganize the contents. When they started with the pieces, a new whole took shape, and when they started with a new whole, the pieces reordered themselves. Organization and integration went hand in hand.

Audience Influence and Personal Risk

Several teachers described how constraints they place on themselves affect the portfolio as a learning environment. For example, one recounted how limiting portfolios to "best work" curtailed understanding.

> I completed a portfolio for another class but did so with the philosophy of only exhibiting my best work. A larger, more comprehensive model will show more of my thought processes and perhaps be more useful in developing future ideas. I would like to [show] not just my successes but maybe things that either only partially worked or didn't work at all.

Who would see their portfolios also affected what the teachers chose to include and what they chose to say about those choices. One who planned to use her portfolio when job-hunting wrote:

> I knew a prospective employer would not be interested in reading lengthy reflections. I had to "tell my story" in a direct manner. I could only reflect on the qualities that would make me a qualified applicant. But this was restrictive because it didn't give me the opportunity to focus on my weaknesses.

Another teacher described a different kind of audience impact:

> I felt a bit confined because I knew someone would be looking at it. Instead of being relaxed about what went inside I wanted only those things that would be meaningful for others as well as myself. We are always striving to do what will please others even though it might have to be fudged to feel successful.

The teachers recognized their need to tailor a portfolio for a specific audience (or multiple audiences) was a matter of how similar or dissimilar their perspectives were. They also discovered that the need to tailor a portfolio was influenced by how much personal risk could result were they to bare their own perspectives.

Reflections, even more than selections, tend to be personal. The teachers became acutely aware of this as the day approached for them to show their portfolios to their peers. A teacher who developed a family history for her children found this solution:

> I have selected some items that have a true meaning for me and I have written a few reflections. Some are very personal and I am not sure that I really want

> to share them with the class. As I was writing the reflections I realized that what I intended to put in the portfolio for my daughters to read was not really intended for other people to read. Since I felt unwilling to share many of my very personal thoughts with people other than my children, I have created two different versions—one for the class, and one for my daughters.

Another teacher handled the situation differently:

> As I prepared to share my portfolio with you and the class, I nearly became paralyzed. There was no way I could let all of you read my reflections. They were too personal and private. But since I talked so much [in my portfolio] about my struggles to develop self-confidence, I decided that this was just one more opportunity for personal growth. Therefore I included all my reflections intact. I know you are kindhearted souls who will read these reflections in a friendly way.

Apparently their self-consciousness in our class led to empathy for their students. Environments that nurture risk-taking became an important topic to the teachers:

> If I want my second grade children to share their portfolios in much the same way we will be doing, I had better "set the tone" and make sure that there is an attitude of acceptance in my classroom. How willing are the emergent readers or writers going to be to share their portfolios if there is a feeling that someone is going to "put them down" or make fun of their work? I have always worked very hard to create [a safe] atmosphere in my classroom but our last class made me cognizant that children must have the assurance that they can be risk-takers without being threatened.

One of the drawbacks of the course design was that the teachers made final presentations of their portfolios after we had had our last look at their journals. We know from their final entries that they approached the day with trepidation. The constructivist literature recognizes the power of the environment to press for adaptation; multiple selves behave in consonance with the rules of various subcultures. However, the results need not be restrictive since our personal constructions are not only revised but also enhanced when we are cognizant of the perspectives of others. Our observations that day were that each and every portfolio received an enthusiastic reception, and that their owners appeared without exception to thoroughly enjoy sharing them.

Summary Remarks

We believe that as the teachers developed their portfolios they came to share beliefs about learning and assessment not unlike our own. They learned that constructivist philosophy, which many were already applying to classroom instruction, could also apply to classroom assessment.

In many ways a portfolio is analogous to the concept webs or cognitive maps that graphically portray our comprehension of a topic. Portfolios are physical manifestations of covert cognitive constructions. If students are assisted overmuch with the physical construction, we do not know if there are parallel gaps in their understanding. For example, if we tell the students what kinds of things to select, we do not know if they grasp the parameters or scope of their subject; if we tell them what criteria to employ in making their selections, we cannot be certain of their value systems; if we tell them how to organize the work in their portfolio, we do not know if they themselves recognize relationships between the pieces. As teachers in our class struggled to put together their portfolios, we watched each come to a better understanding of whatever subject he or she had chosen as a portfolio focus. More important to us, their journals bore testimony that each had come to a better understanding of their portfolio's role in that learning.

Portfolio programs that entrust decision-making rights to students are often dismissed as "anything goes." The portfolios that grew out of this project were anything but that. As teachers in our course developed their own portfolios, they not only bore in mind the announced purpose of the activity, they acquainted themselves with highly regarded portfolio programs based on contrasting philosophies, chose their own course of action only after experimentation with different approaches, and drew on the perspectives of other stakeholders when making their own assessments. Consistent with our CMAP philosophy, throughout the class we did not present one way to "do" portfolios, but rather exposed the class members to many approaches, let them experiment with these in the context of their own portfolios, and let them construct their own approach to "doing" portfolios.

Similarly, we would not expect these teachers to take an "anything goes" philosophy to their classrooms. From their journal entries we anticipate they will expose their students to many perspectives, let their students think through complex issues (e.g., objectives and standards) in a self-assessment context, and encourage them to revise their standards commensurate with their growing sophistication in understanding the issues. In sum, our intention was not to prepare the teachers to direct portfolio projects, but rather, to prepare the teachers to support student-directed portfolios, each portfolio a personal construction of a student's learning.

Can students be entrusted with self-direction? Adults are used to making decisions for children, either to develop conformity across portfolios or to simplify the task for young learners. Committees of teachers and administrators decide "what *our* portfolios should look like." Too often, though, honest attempts at assistance close off natural contexts for reflection and inhibit rather than support learning. Impatient in our preconceived notions of a "good" portfolio, we cut short our students' opportunity to gather information, experiment, construct, assess, and revise, repeating that cycle again and again. In imposing our adult constructions we limit students' opportunities to create worthy constructions of their own.

The teachers quoted in this chapter came to appreciate, first, how intimidating self-direction can be, and then how freeing. At the end they found themselves committed to letting their students make decisions not only about what goes into the portfolios but also how they will be organized, presented, and used. By constructing portfolios for themselves, they constructed a personal concept of "portfolio" and its place in learning and assessment. According to one teacher:

> I have a totally different understanding of the procedure as I have gone through the experience.

Notes

1. Some words and phrases have been deleted from the teachers' reflections for the sake of brevity.

19

Revising Our Practices

How Portfolios Help Teachers Learn

Irwin Weiser

I REGULARLY TEACH A PRACTICUM FOR NEW TEACHERS OF WRITING, MOST of whom are first year graduate students and teaching assistants with little or no prior teaching experience of any kind. For these new teachers, many of whom were undergraduates only a few months earlier and are often only a few years older than their students, a major concern is their authority in the classroom. They are worried about whether they know enough to teach, whether their students will accept them as teachers, whether they will be able to handle any problems which might occur, and whether they will be able to make appropriate decisions in the classroom or in dealing with individual students. They are worried, that is, about all the things experienced teachers continue to worry about, but they have no base of experience which assures them that most of the time they will teach and interact with students successfully and responsibly. A central worry for these new teachers, students themselves and quite close to the undergraduate experience, is evaluating their students fairly. They understand that grades matter—that they help determine if a person will get into graduate or professional school, or get a good job, or in some cases simply stay in school—and they understand the anxiety and self-doubt low grades can cause even good students. They want to learn to assign grades fairly and appropriately and to be able to explain why they have assigned a particular grade should a student question them. And, like all good teachers, they want to establish a learning environment in their classes which encourages and motivates students, particularly those with less ability, rather than reinforcing students' often negative views of themselves as poor writers. Many wish to do even more; they want to decenter the authority in the classroom, to redefine—to the extent institutional constraints allow—their role and the roles of students.

In recent years, I have encouraged the new teachers I work with to use portfolios in their writing classes as a way to address several of the concerns I have just identified. It is my experience[1] that portfolios allow new teachers of writing to develop both confidence and skill, not simply as evaluators, but as classroom teachers, by temporarily relieving their anxiety about grading and allowing them to focus on learning to teach. In this chapter, I want to describe how we use portfolios in English 502, a graduate practicum in the teaching of composition, then discuss how portfolios contribute to the development of the new teachers who take this course.

English 502 is a one-credit course which graduate teaching assistants must enroll in during their first year of teaching at Purdue. Each semester, the students meet weekly with their instructor or mentor. Because English 502 carries only one credit per semester, because it is a practicum, and because the primary interest of most of the students is how to teach the composition classes they are assigned, the focus of these weekly meetings is on the syllabus, the text, the writing assignments, and practical matters of planning classes, working with students, and evaluating writing. There is plenty to consider, discuss, and learn in these sessions, and portfolios have helped open a space for that learning to take place.

I explain our use of portfolios in the context of the process-based pedagogy of our course.[2] During the week prior to the first semester when the practicum meets for a series of intensive sessions to learn about the goals and teaching philosophy of the course, we discuss the rationale, new to many first-time composition teachers, behind teaching writing as a process. We write about and discuss our own writing practices and processes, talk about the kinds of generalizations we can make and researchers in cognitive processes have made about how people write, and examine how each writing assignment will be approached as a series of overlapping processes of planning, drafting, revising, and editing. Through these discussions, it becomes clear that writing courses are unlike many other courses at the university. Whereas in some science or math or social science courses there is a fairly discrete content to be studied and which students can often be tested on in similarly discrete chunks, students' learning in writing courses can best be evaluated at the end of the course after they have had as much time as the calendar allows to practice, get feedback, and improve.

We expect, in fact, that students who are working at their writing, who are spending time planning, writing and getting responses to drafts, and revising and editing, will be better writers at the end of the semester than they were at the beginning; and thus we assume that the most accurate and fair measure of what they have learned is one based on their writing at the end. Our approach then, is to assign five papers over the course of a sixteen-week semester, all of which are responded to by the instructor at least once during the course of the term, and to require students to submit a portfolio containing new revisions of a specified number of these papers near the end of the course. As is typical of portfolio-based courses, the early versions of papers are not graded; nor are the revised papers in the portfolios graded individually. The portfolio receives a single grade which makes up the largest part of the student's course grade though additional assignments, participation, attendance, and so on influence the final grade the student earns.

How does this use of portfolios benefit new teachers? How does it contribute to their learning? Most obviously, new teachers benefit by not feeling the pressures of assigning grades as they are learning what it means to teach and evaluate writing. They are relieved from wondering if the grade they assign the first paper is too low and potentially discouraging and unfair to the student or too high and thus either sending an inaccurate message to the student or beginning a spiral of grade inflation as the student's work improves. Without the pressure to get the grade right, instructors (and of course this is a benefit shared by the students) are able to focus their attention, both in our practicum and in their comments, on the writing itself. Instead of trying to decide if we can agree on the *grade* a paper should get, we can discuss what the paper accomplishes, what its weaknesses are, how it might be improved, and most importantly, how all of this can be most clearly, helpfully, and positively conveyed to the student. What occurs is a form of learning parallel to that we hope the students are experiencing: instructors are gaining experience, through practice, at reading and responding to student writing, and they, like their students, are doing so without the specter of a grade peering over their shoulders.

If portfolios only helped new instructors become more experienced, confident readers of and responders to student writing, I would say they're worthwhile. But I think there are other ways instructors can learn by using portfolios. In particular, I want to discuss how working with portfolios brings into sharp focus our definitions of the writing process and successful writing. And in doing so, I want to acknowledge the contributions of Kathleen Yancey to this discussion since our email exchanges and conversations about this issue have been influential and helpful to me.

Portfolios allow us to consider the writing process in a broader context than the familiar planning, drafting, revising, editing concept of process does. While revision is an inherent part of portfolio approaches, the decision to use portfolios as the means of evaluating students' writing ability and development extends the process to include additional decision-making conditions: the *collection* of writing, *reflection* about that writing, the *selection* of pieces to be further revised for the final evaluation, the *revision* of those pieces, and finally, their *evaluation.* Each of these, often overlapping practices, contributes to both students' and teachers' extended understanding of what it means to write.

Collection is perhaps the most obvious element of portfolio use. The portfolio is, by definition, a collection of some or all of the writing students have done during the course. The very act of collection implies that what is valued in the writing course is not the individual written product, but instead development and improvement. For teachers, especially new teachers, as well as for students, such valuing may require a change in thinking about the purpose of the writing course—its major goal is not to teach students a particular set of skills or forms, each evidenced in a separate paper, but instead is concerned with continuing improvement, evaluated formally only because terms have ends. Teachers and students alike learn to view each piece as part of an ongoing process, and each piece can be considered as contributing to the student's development, not as a discrete marker of it.

Reflection can be considered in a variety of ways. On the one hand, reflection is an inherent part of revision. Whether students revise as a result of their own reflection about a version of a paper, or because of comments they have received from a peer or an instructor, the recognition that particular revisions can improve a paper requires reflection about that version and other possible versions it might become. Such reflection takes into account all of the matters we typically consider in revision: appropriateness for the rhetorical situation, clarity, organization, development, and style. In addition, reflection which leads to revision requires writers to consider the advice they receive about a piece—do they wish to accept the advice, do they agree with it, are they sufficiently invested in the piece to continue to work on it, and so on. Leaving such decisions up to the writer is a part of the decentering of authority many instructors want to bring about. A second form of reflection, one more exclusively the province of portfolio use, is the reflection which occurs when students write letters or statements which accompany the portfolio they submit for evaluation. In these writings, students typically are asked to reflect upon the work they have done in the course, to look back on and analyze their strengths and weaknesses and their progress, to articulate what they think the portfolio says about themselves as developing writers, to explain why they have chosen to include the pieces they have and what they think they have accomplished in revising them. Here reflection begins to overlap and interact with selection, another part of the portfolio writing process which I will turn to shortly. Like the decisions students make about how and what to revise, the reflective statements shift to students some of the responsibility and authority for their work, particularly in this case how that work may be perceived by those who grade it.

Instructors, in deciding how they will use portfolios in their classes, must consider how much of the authority for selection they will keep and how much they will give to students. In many portfolio systems, students are required to include papers representing a variety of discourse genres or assignment types[3] while in others, students are told the portfolio must contain a specific number of revised pieces, but they are to choose which pieces best represent their accomplishments during the course. Our practicum offers new instructors the opportunity to consider when one approach to selection may be preferable to another. In courses which focus on one or a very limited number of discourse types (for example, a course on the personal essay or review writing or autobiographical writing or argument), it makes sense for students to be responsible for selecting the pieces they revise for the portfolio, while in a course which introduces very specific genres (for instance, an introductory creative writing course in which students are asked to write both poetry and fiction or a course with some major projects and other less demanding work), the instructor will probably want to provide more specific guidelines for the contents of the portfolio.

Implied in each of these discussions is revision, though revision is so inherent a part of our conceptions of writing, of process, and of portfolios that it's easy to forget that new instructors may have little or no understanding of how to teach and encourage revision; that some may never have been required to revise, and, in fact, one could call an unrevised, unselected, unreflected-upon collection of writing, a portfolio. I would like to be able to say new teachers who use portfolios learn more about revision than they would if they graded each piece of writing when students submitted it, but I do not think that is necessarily the case. The principles of revision I introduce to teachers, and they in turn teach their students, are no different now than they were before we used portfolios. But what is different, I think, is the attitude toward revision portfolios encourage. When instructors allow students to revise papers which have already been graded, the focus becomes the grade, not the quality of the paper itself. For instructors, this means writing comments which not only attempt to be comprehensive, but which also justify the grade the paper has received. Yet extensive, comprehensive comments are likely to confuse and overwhelm students. If, on the other hand, instructors choose to concentrate their comments on the most significant problems of a particular paper and to offer suggestions for specific kinds of revisions, students may complain if their revised grade is not significantly higher since, they point out, they've done what the teacher told them to do. Portfolios allow the attention of instructors and students to remain on the quality and improvement of writing. Instructors can tell students their comments will focus on concepts they have emphasized in class or on revisions which will make the largest improvements in the writing, and by the end of the course, students will have accumulated a repertoire of writing abilities they can call upon when they revise their work for their portfolios.

Finally, portfolios can contribute to teachers' understanding of the evaluation of writing. I indicated earlier that one of the benefits for new teachers who use portfolios is that they have time to gain confidence in their ability to evaluate writing. They do not have to assign a grade to a paper after they have only been teaching a few weeks; they have time to learn to evaluate before they assign grades which, whether we like it or not, matter enormously to students. New teachers are relieved, at least temporarily, from worrying about whether they are being too harsh or too generous, whether they are fair in their assessment of student work. In the practicum, we can discuss how we would assess a particular piece of writing, what we would tell the student about its strengths and weaknesses, and how it might be revised. And we can talk about the grade we might give the paper, working out standards gradually over time, so when the instructor does grade, he or she is more confident. But portfolios, as we are beginning to discover, carry with them their own specific evaluation issues, issues which themselves provide opportunities for teachers to reflect on their practices. I have touched already on one issue: portfolios suggest that progress, development, and improvement in writing should be evaluated with as long a view as possible, and that a student's performance on an individual paper is less important than what the student has achieved over the course of the term.

For many teachers, this view may make sense, but it is nevertheless quite different from traditional views of evaluation in education which support the grading of individual assignments. Grading each assignment reinforces the hegemony of the classroom since each graded assignment emphasizes the power of the instructor, while portfolios have the potential to contribute to decentering the authority. But it is not that simple since the decision to assign only a single grade to the portfolio may also reinforce the instructor's authority because the portfolio grade is assigned at the end of the term, when students have no further opportunity to improve. And portfolio grading may increase students' anxiety about their grades instead of relieving it. While individual grades may lead students to give up if they are dissatisfied with their evaluation or become complacent if they are pleased, grades do give students familiar indicators of where they stand. So instructors who use portfolio evaluation face decisions about how best to keep students informed of their progress, how to reduce the number of dramatic surprises for students whose portfolio grade is lower than they expected it to be, and so on. In our practicum we discuss a variety of options, always emphasizing the importance of specific, clear, and detailed comments on early drafts, but also individual conferences, especially after the first paper and around the middle of the term to be sure students are reading and understanding comments accurately. Another option some teachers adopt is to offer students the opportunity to receive a tentative, unrecorded, grade on one piece of writing during the semester. Still others give their students unofficial midterm grades, again emphasizing the tentative nature of those grades.

A second evaluation issue, one I have only recently become aware of, is what I refer to as "psyching out the port. prof." Recently a student told me that the lore in his class was that the way to get a high grade in a portfolio course was to write poorly early in the semester so it would be easier to make significant improvements in the revisions for the portfolio. Now, there is a part of me which admires the cleverness with which students have found a way to turn their resistance to a required composition class into accommodation which works to their benefit. But I also am idealistic enough to want students to make honest efforts on their assignments, and I see this attitude provides both me and the teachers I work with a pedagogical problem to work out. Where does the problem here lie? Certainly in part it is institutional, since composition is one of the few university-wide requirements at most schools; a requirement which, regardless of how we view it, carries some historical baggage as gatekeeper or at least as a hurdle to be leaped before one gets to the serious work. And in part it is societal since we value measurable performance—grades and GPAs—over learning. The problem may also lie in our very notion of process—a notion which perhaps overprivileges revision, in which tangible signs of the process or particular concepts of revision are valued more than the result—the discourse the student produces. The comment from the student I referred to earlier and the following student's comment suggest that students find our insistence on revision to be one more teacher-mandated step in getting a good grade: "I think portfolios put more pressure on me to botch my papers so it looked like I revised. I didn't know how much I needed to scratch out to get a good grade" (Jill, quoted by Metzger and Bryant 1993, 284). These students' comments suggest that we may need to revise our conceptions of process and revision to account for writers' more idiosyncratic, yet successful approaches to both.

The final evaluation issue I want to raise is one which Kathleen Yancey has called "schmoozing." I think "schmoozing" is a variation of psyching out the port. prof. "Schmoozing" is a phenomenon of the reflective writing which is often submitted with a portfolio. According to researchers at Miami University, the reflective letters which are a required part of the placement portfolios used there "affect the rating situation in a powerful way" (Sommers et al. 1993, 11). Their speculation is that these letters lead to more reliable ratings of portfolios because the "raters feel better prepared to read the remainder of a portfolio after reading the reflective letters" and because "they bring the personal back into the scoring situation" (Sommers et al. 1993, 11). Later in this article, the authors refer to a concept they call "glow"—the positive effect a particularly strong piece of writing may have on the rating of the portfolio—and cite as an example a reflective letter that ended like this:

> Over the past few years, I've developed new attitudes toward writing, enjoying it rather than dreading it, and viewing each piece not as one completed but as a work-in-progress. There is always a more appropriate word (most often, the one that awakens me out of a sound sleep at 4 A.M. the day after the deadline), a better phrase, room for improvement. I find this stimulating, not frustrating. (Sommers et al. 1993, 21)

This is writing to warm the heart of a composition teacher, and as the Miami researchers point out, the rest of the portfolio "dropped off in quality" (Sommers et al. 1993, 21). They acknowledge that "it's not hard to surmise that the very strong impression made by the opening letter must have influenced the raters positively" (Sommers et al. 1993, 21). "Schmooze," I want to suggest, is the often indistinguishable evil twin of "glow," the telling-the-teacher-what-he-wants-to-hear that students may very well write in their reflective letters to set the stage for a positive evaluation. Individual teachers, no less than raters in placement or proficiency readings, must be sensitive to "glow" and "schmooze" (and, as the Miami researchers also point out, to the roller-coaster effect of uneven quality of individual pieces in a portfolio). I don't want to suggest that we discount or mistrust students' reflective writing; I mean that reflective letters, precisely because they reintroduce the personal, force us to recognize the subjective nature of our readings, always a particular concern for new teachers.[4] When portfolios become an integral part of our courses and programs, we need to consider their implications, their benefits, and the new issues they raise. For teachers of writing, experienced and new alike, portfolios encourage us to be, in Donald Schon's terms, "reflective practitioners." Our use of portfolios in the seminar has given us the opportunity—demanded, in fact—that we reflect upon how our concepts about teaching, process, evaluation, and grading are intertwined. It has encouraged us to consider how an approach to evaluating student work can contribute to changes in the power and authority relationships between teacher and students—and the extent to which those changes actually shift authority or only modify how students respond to it. Portfolios thus have become a means by which we can examine and revise our practices.

Notes

1. Portfolio evaluation has been part of our composition program since 1983 when I introduced portfolios in our basic writing course. Their use in this course is described in my "Portfolio Practice and Assessment for Collegiate Basic Writers" in Yancey, *Portfolios in the Writing Classroom*, pp. 89-101.
2. For an extended discussion, see my "Portfolios and the New Teacher of Writing," in Black et al., *New Directions in Portfolio Assessment*, pp. 219-229.
3. Belanoff and Elbow describe such an approach in "Using Portfolios to Increase Collaboration and Community in a Writing Program."
4. See Glenda Conway, "Portfolio Cover Letters, Students' Self-Presentation, and Teachers' Ethics" in Black et al., *New Directions in Portfolio Assessment*, pp. 83-92. Lester Faigley points out "the strong preference for autobiographical essays" and personal experience papers in the student writing contributed to Coles and Vopat's *What Makes Writing Good* by forty-eight professors of writing and linguistics. Faigley notes that these teachers cite what they identify as the "honesty," "truth," authentic voices, and strong sense of self in these essays ("Judging Writing, Judging Selves").

IV

Technology

20

Wedding the Technologies of Writing Portfolios and Computers

The Challenges of Electronic Classrooms

Gail E. Hawisher
Cynthia L. Selfe

WRITING PORTFOLIOS AND COMPUTERS COMPRISE TWO OF THE MORE recent teaching technologies introduced into late twentieth century English classes. In a relatively short time, these two technologies have spread to English classes at all levels and appear increasingly in the field's professional discussions. Not surprisingly, discussions of both technologies—in journals and other professional publications—are usually upbeat, heralding the innovations as revolutionary with the promise to improve dramatically students' learning and writing. Not surprisingly, each technology is seen also as a positive influence that will promote a social construction of knowledge in which teachers and students are all learners-in-progress, collaborating together to form new communities of learning.

But what *is* surprising are the striking similarities in the language used to extol each technology. Of computer networks we read that their "real strength [is] a shift in the way students think about their own writing shown by a greater ENGAGEMENT in writing tasks" (Batson 1988, 55, emphasis in the original) and that "[t]he computer-based collaborative approach attempts to re-empower text by emphasizing the student text itself instead of the instructor's evaluation" (Barker and Kemp 1990, 24). Correspondingly, of portfolios we learn that "[t]he experience [of using portfolios] changed the way we see our students as writers and as people. Because of our work with portfolios, we have altered the way we teach writing as well as the ways in which we talk to each other as members of an English department" (Bergamini 1993, 145). In an article entitled "Portfolios as a Vehicle for Student Empowerment and Teacher Change," we learn too that with the use of portfolios the teacher "was no longer center stage. [She] facilitated, answered questions, and joined reading and writing groups . . . the class had grabbed hold of the reins" (Weinbaum 1991, 213). Thus both technologies, we are told, are potentially transformative for English classes. Teachers who use these technologies—many educational experts maintain—are capable of changing classrooms into exciting intellectual spaces where students and their texts are privileged. Such instructional innovations, moreover, are extraordinary in that they help teachers reshape the social contexts of classrooms and departments, and subtly restructure the relationships among students, instructors, and the tasks at hand.

These comments—for both computers and portfolios—are hopeful and optimistic, capturing, we believe, what is best about the profession of English teaching: its strong commitment to positive educational change and a characteristic optimism about achieving instructional goals. Yet this same positive thinking can also be dangerous if its members want to think critically about portfolios and computers. As we have argued elsewhere exclusively of computers, the reliance on such laudatory language can serve to obscure problems that continue to characterize our classes despite our best intentions (Hawisher and Selfe 1991b). Computers, for example, at times sustain teaching approaches that contribute neither to good teaching nor learning in much the same way that portfolios can support perfunctory paper-collection procedures and evaluation systems that serve to reproduce existing class-based and race-based inequities within our educational system. We are thinking, for instance, of classrooms where computers serve the function primarily of grading and evaluating papers (Marling 1984; Jobst 1984), providing drill and practice grammar tutorials (Holdstein 1983; Falk 1985), and, in general, of reinforcing a back-to-basics mentality that supports traditional authority structures within educational settings (LeBlanc 1990). There are also English classes that employ writing portfolios as record-keeping devices that emphasize the number of assignments submitted and the kinds of errors students must avoid if they are to receive a good grade for their collective writing. Currently, some school districts and state educational systems (e.g., Vermont, Kentucky, and Indiana) are exploring options to use portfolios in efforts to set standards (that may ignore local constraints and goals) and in exit-examination systems (that may reflect district inequities without addressing their causes). The New Standards project, with its commitment to work with partner states on developing portfolios with performance-based standards for assessment, is yet another example of the use of portfolios for wide-scale assessment. It is possible, then, to introduce both these technologies into English classes with little changed except the method by which writing assignments are written and submitted.

We should note too that the enthusiastic discourse we have identified here is not limited to portfolios or computers. Similar claims over the years have been made for pedagogies using "process approaches," "peer groups," "journals," and "collaboration"—other instructional technologies that English teachers have turned to in the last twenty years in an attempt to improve the teaching and learning of literacy. We have all also heard comparable language extolling the National Writing Project and the Writing Across the Curriculum movement. In fact the optimistic discourse noted here has close connections with what Mike Rose has called the "myth of transience," that is, the belief that if, as English teachers, "we can just do *x* or *y*, the [literacy] problem will be solved—in five years, ten years, or a generation. . . . " (Rose 1985, 355). According to this argument, if the educational establishment would just institute a particularly promising innovation, the literacy crisis as defined by the public would begin to disappear and students would be able to read and write in ways prized by society. But, as Rose has noted, and he aims his criticism primarily at universities, this kind of thinking is also dangerous: the myth of transience usually prevents us from seeing multiple possibilities for reform and "serves to keep certain fundamental recognitions and thus certain fundamental changes at bay" (Rose 1985, 356). Thus the broad-based kinds of change that can and should be made in educational systems are often obscured by the introduction of new technologies, and the innovations themselves—because of our limited perspectives and uncritical acceptance—ultimately fail to bring about the necessary systemic-level changes in the values that undergird these same educational institutions and programs (Hawisher and Selfe 1993).

One site for change that such enthusiastic discourse serves poorly is teacher education programs, and we include here programs that educate college level teaching assistants as well as high school teachers. Many teacher education programs, in discussing the use of both portfolios and computers, provide teachers with the practical strategies for implementing such technologies without encouraging them to think through the educational issues and implications that accompany their effective integration. Using either portfolios or computers to support productive—if limited and local—educational reforms requires deep-seated changes that cannot be brought about by merely introducing teachers to innovative teaching technologies (Hawisher and Selfe 1993).

In this chapter, then, we would like to step back from an uncritical acceptance of promising educational innovations and offer a more tempered view of what we can and cannot expect from writing portfolios and computers, stressing the theoretical grounding and experiences teachers need if they are to succeed with the two technologies. We first define "electronic portfolios" and present an example of how one teacher uses them in a writing class. Following our discussion, we turn to the education of teachers and present three challenges to teacher training programs. Throughout the discussion, we caution that despite the potential for meaningful educational change often associated with portfolios and computers, the bringing together of the two does not necessarily double the benefits—in fact the combination may well double the liabilities.

Teaching Practices and Electronic Portfolios

We begin by uniting the two technologies in the term "electronic portfolio," which we define as an online collection of student work that will ultimately be evaluated by an audience of some type—either the student authors themselves; peer readers; teachers; parents; administrators; evaluation experts; or mixed audiences representing more than one of these groups. The kind of portfolio envisioned here reflects what Kathleen Yancey describes as "a working portfolio," that is, "an archive of work, collected over time, all of which counts for learning, but not all of which counts for assessment" (Yancey 1993b). We see the working portfolio, however, as finally resulting in what Yancey terms "a presentational portfolio," a collection that culls from the working portfolio exhibits pulled together for a specific purpose, in this case, the completion of a course. The electronic portfolio differs from its paper cousin primarily in that the portfolio materials are created and stored in a digitized form (e.g., on a floppy disk, on a compact disk, on a computer network), with students often collaborating electronically on projects and sharing their work with other students and the instructor during the course of a semester. That is not to say that the work in electronic portfolios is never printed out as hard copy but only to note that it is created, stored, and shared with others in a computer-based medium. Although, in most cases, the computer-based distribution will be local and probably limited to the student's teacher and classmates (e.g., the exchange of floppy disks and the exchange of files over a local-area network or LAN), it is also possible to set up such a system over a WAN (wide-area network) or the Internet (a collection of networks that spans the globe). With the Internet, other classes and teachers—as close as next door or as far away as another country—can also view and comment on the electronic portfolios.

To find out how teachers across the country use electronic portfolios, we queried an electronic discussion group, WAC-L, the Writing Across the Curriculum List, and in a very short time received several responses. Interestingly, the responses were from teachers with Appletalk and Macintosh technology. Portfolios seem to work transparently in Macintosh environments since the "folder" metaphor, which provides a ready-to-hand synonym for "portfolio," is already in place. By this, we do not mean to suggest electronic portfolios cannot be used with other computer systems; students can keep portfolios on individual disks using any kind of computer. The teachers who responded to our query, however, used computers for more than the creation and storage of documents; they also used the network to enable students to share their projects online. Macintosh environments make this easy, but other systems allow for the electronic sharing of texts as well.

Here we present one teacher's experience to demonstrate more clearly the positive ways electronic portfolios can function in English classes. Becky Howard's description of her use of electronic portfolios at Colgate University is particularly noteworthy, we believe, in that it is fairly simple to implement yet makes extensive use of computer technology. At Colgate, each writing instructor and student has an Appletalk local network "account," a folder in which they can store their work. These folders are secure in that they can be accessed only by the folder owner, his or her instructor, and the network administrator. Howard relies heavily on the network for her class on "Writing with Word Processing," which focuses primarily on revising. (Note that in focusing on revision, Howard uses the portfolios in yet another way. Portfolios become part of a pedagogy that emphasizes and showcases revision strategies.)

In describing her use of portfolios, she writes:

> students use their electronic folders as portfolios where they store their work—the assignments [she gives] them, their responses to each other's papers, and the

> papers they are writing for other classes. All of this constitutes work-in-progress; they revise work at their own discretion throughout the semester, regardless of whether it has already been submitted for a grade. This includes work submitted in other classes; in [her] Comp class they use papers assigned in other classes as laboratory opportunities for applying principles learned in [her class]. As they revise papers, the students keep old copies in their folders. At the end of the semester, they select what they consider their best work, not their best final products, but their best work as writers, the work that best demonstrates them as analysts, rethinkers, and revisers of their own writing and that of their classmates. They can select from work assigned in [her] class, work assigned for other classes, [as well as] their responses to classmates' papers. Having selected their best work, in all its drafts, they submit it to [her]—electronically, of course. Accompanying it is a road map explaining what each piece represents and why they chose it. This then constitutes 60-90 percent of their grade for the course, depending upon the vagaries of syllabus design from one semester to another. (email correspondence, 2-14-94, 8:19 A.M.)

For Becky Howard, the advantage of the electronic portfolio is that it allows her to have greater interaction with the students. As these students work, they can put drafts in a special electronic homework folder, which Howard checks daily. Because her students tend to work late at night, and she tends to work early in the morning, they leave material for her that she responds to, sometimes long after they go to bed. Then, when the students get up in the morning, Howard's response is waiting for them. Her use of electronic portfolios is in keeping with Yancey's definition of a "working portfolio" in which the portfolio's contents are always in a state of flux and under revision; finally, however, the students ready their portfolio for presentation and end-of-semester evaluation, choosing what they regard as their most successful efforts.

So what do teachers need to know about electronic portfolios that they cannot learn from other teachers' experiences such as Becky Howard's? What do they need to know that they have not already learned from their use of computers or portfolios as separate technologies? Quite a bit we think. Teachers who have used computer-based systems know that moving texts from hard copy to electronic form—essentially moving written communication from one medium to another—can result in major differences in the texts that students produce (Markel 1994), the processes they use to write (Heilker 1992), the structure of collaborative group tasks and the nature of collaboration itself (Forman 1992; Sirc and Reynolds 1990), and the style and tenor of written exchanges (Kremers 1988; Romano 1993; Regan 1994).

Given these observations, we also suspect that the change in medium can make a significant difference in the nature of electronic portfolio writing and, perhaps, in the way teachers use portfolios in their classes. For example, although Howard has been able to incorporate electronic portfolios seamlessly into her writing class, it is worth noting that the ease of communication via the network—her increased level of access to students and theirs to her, the elimination of some time and distance issues that can limit teaching in conventional classes, and the speed of electronic communication—may affect in subtle, and not so subtle ways, her approaches to teaching writing. Such a context could encourage both an emphasis on responding to students and an emphasis on discursive exchanges: students write, Howard responds, and students exchange drafts with each other. Such a context could make a qualitative change in her interactions with students and their interactions with one another.

But we suspect that for evaluation purposes—and for various pedagogical approaches as well—electronic portfolios also have some potential for making assessment *too easy*. With online networked portfolios, teachers can virtually inspect and monitor student writing without the student's knowledge; and, with some software, they can electronically copy papers to display to the rest of the class without the student's permission. Without thinking through the theoretical consequences, teachers can use electronic portfolios and the computer systems that support them to "keep tabs" on student work, to practice "surveillance" on individual writers and collaborative groups, and to create an oppressive setting that is not conducive to accomplished learning. Although we realize that such practices also come into play in traditional class settings, the supposed "efficiency" of computers in record keeping and surveillance tasks (Zuboff 1988; Marx and Sherizen 1989) can lead teachers to practices that they might otherwise eschew. Electronic versions of portfolios may encourage teachers unwittingly to collapse critical distinctions between learning and assessment. Because texts are easy to post and share in electronic environments, there is the temptation for teachers to *collect* at the expense of students' selecting and reflecting on their writing and learning.

Grant Wiggins, an assessment specialist, suggests, for example, that technology can support assessment efforts by providing the means of maintaining an ongoing data base of student performance. He writes, "We can use technology more efficiently. We can keep video and audio records and evaluate [students' progress] by sampling . . . efforts that have been stored electronically" (Wiggins 1991, 10). We would, however, hope that the profession thinks carefully about devising and developing such systems. To require students to keep a computer disk that follows them through all their years in school or to keep centralized computer records of students' work is fraught with problems that have not been considered carefully. Are students to carry with them every success and failure, especially their failures, from childhood to adolescence to adulthood? Will a disk or "computer file" become a prerequisite for admission to various academic programs? Perhaps our reaction waxes extreme, but decisions about who reads, who writes, and who can delete information in these "lifetime" portfolios are critical issues, and they have yet to be addressed. Instead the profession often exhibits a kind of thoughtlessness about technology or a kind of naive faith in it, both of which are problematic. It is our belief that electronic portfolios offer both opportunities and liabilities that hard copy formats do not. A major project for English teachers will be to develop a responsible professional vision—a vision grounded in sound composition theory and practice, and tempered by critical, informed, and humanistic perspectives on technology and teaching.

Challenges to Teachers and Those Who Would Teach Them

Although we have complicated the initial concept of electronic portfolios and their uses to some extent, we have not yet offered a realistic outline of what it will take to develop a responsible, professional vision of electronic portfolios. Several important and complex challenges suggest themselves immediately and we have listed three of them here. All of these comments are aimed at helping the profession reconsider its goals and approaches—rethinking what it means to teach and learn while developing critical perspectives on the new technologies. The challenges we identify are far from exhaustive, but they may help guide the profession's thinking about the education of teachers over the next five years, especially in relation to the use of electronic portfolios.

Challenge #1: The new technologies never stand still. They are constantly changing and as such require continuous learning on the part of teachers and those who would prepare English teaching professionals.

Electronic portfolios provide an excellent example of the remarkable changes that have occurred in software and hardware over the past couple of years. We have already mentioned, for example, how portfolios can be kept over a network for sharing and distributing various documents to teachers and other students. In addition, the portfolio documents can be more than just "papers"; they can, in fact, be comprised of artifacts created with graphics programs, hypertext software, and even animation and 3-D rendering programs. The students might well construct their portfolios in such a way that they combine text, visuals, and sound, ultimately creating multimedia portfolios. Moreover, students can use "conferencing" software to consult with other students and teachers as they work on their projects, eventually transforming their "working" online folders into presentational portfolios. These presentational portfolios, in turn, can be posted on the World Wide Web and linked in a global hypertext.

At the University of Illinois, Urbana-Champaign, the Center for Writing Studies has dedicated a capacious hard drive (3.2 gigabytes) to experiments with a combined Unix and Macintosh environment that will allow storing and accessing portfolios across the Internet. PacerForum software will also be used in conjunction with two other programs, *Replica* and *Acrobat*, which allows instructors to collect documents produced with different software programs and stores them in one file; in other words, as we mentioned, students can produce documents with graphics, word processing, even a spreadsheet, and arrange and store them in one file for presentation.

Figures 1 through 5 illustrate how students and teachers can create and exchange ideas through this electronic portfolio system. In Figure 1, there is the PacerForum interface with classes and groups over several parts of campus, along with a sample class, English 381 and Friends.

When students double click on the forum English 381 and Friends, they see Figure 2, a representation of the three particular class discussion groups: online portfolios, the violence of literacy, and a chat group. These are all electronic spaces set aside for the students to discuss and share possible portfolio documents. When one of the "tiles" is double-clicked, the tile opens up and there is a space where students can volunteer comments and also insert other documents. In Figure 3, for example, a Replica document has been inserted which, when clicked on, results in the illustration shown in Figure 4. (Obviously this is a document one of the authors has written, but the process we demonstrate here represents how students might create, send, discuss, and represent their work over the course of a semester.) As we noted, these electronic portfolios can easily become multimedia projects. In Figure 5, there is a "picture" and "sound" which can be added to students' other documents. Again by clicking on the icon, we can see or hear its contents. For our purposes, the sound might well be students introducing their portfolios by reflecting on how the various online documents represent

Figure 1
PacerForum Interface

Figure 2
Forums
within
the Class

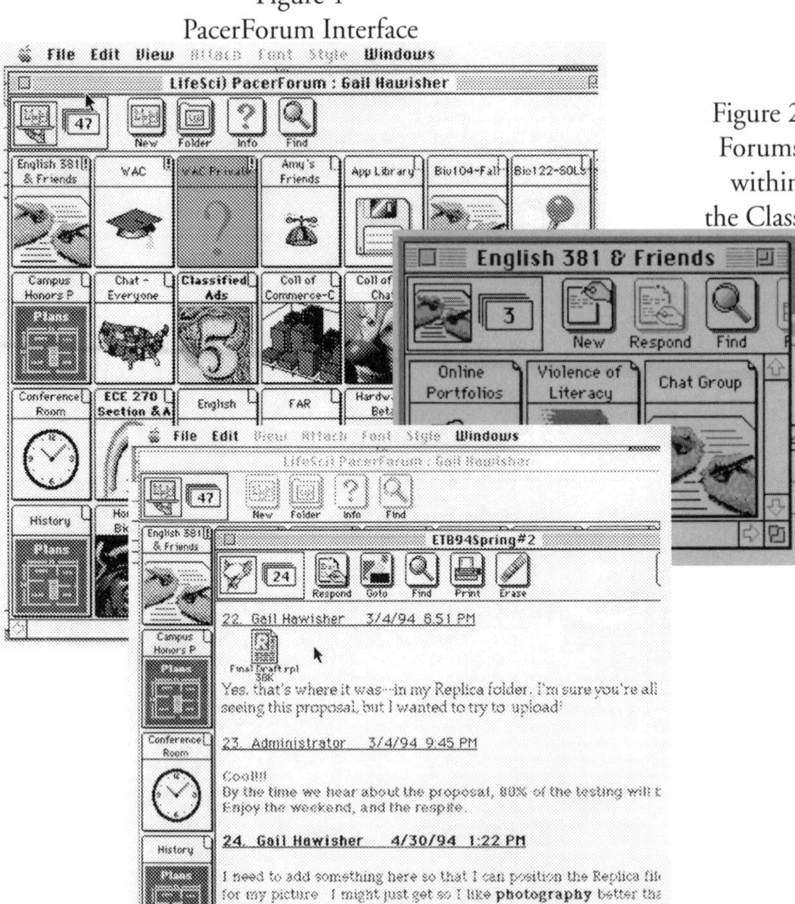

Figure 3
REPLICA Document

their interests and work in the course, what they were thinking about when they created them, and where they might lead in the future.

We think the software here presents one interesting and productive way in which teachers can use portfolios for classroom teaching and evaluation. One consideration, however, is to demonstrate how much preparation and learning is required before the teacher can work with the constellation of software and hardware mentioned here. Not that any of them are

Figure 4
Open REPLICA Document

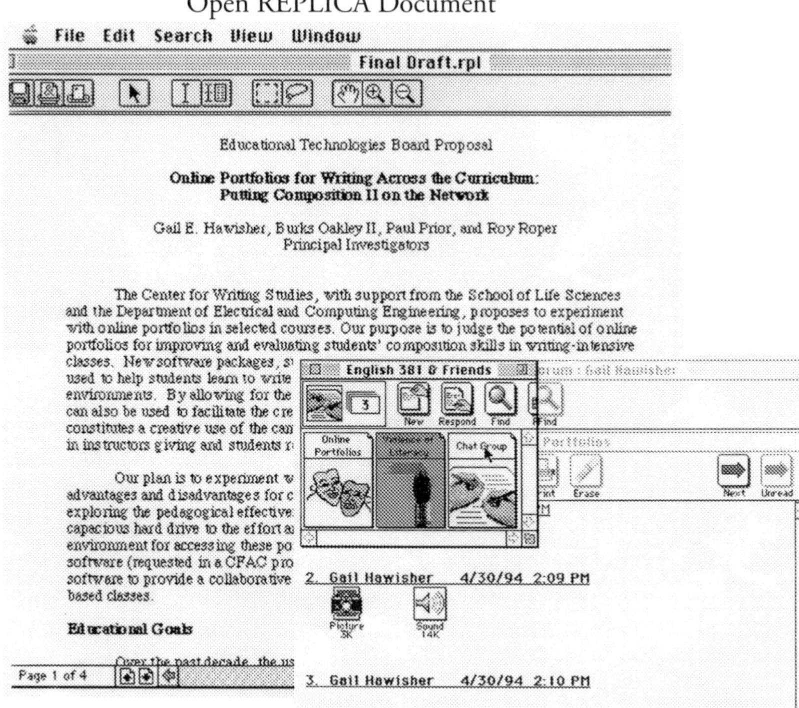

Figure 5
Graphics and Sound

particularly difficult, but any new software requires a great deal of time and preparation on the part of the English teacher. And it's often not until teachers have used the software extensively that they are really able to take advantage of its potential benefits and minimize its shortcomings.

As software changes, so will hardware. Even by 1989, Tom Forester, in *High Tech Society* had estimated that the power of computing technology was doubling for the same cost per unit every eighteen to twenty months. Today, many experts suspect this figure has dropped to fourteen months and is continuing a downward trend. And the change is evident in terms of breadth as well as pace. In the last several years, teachers have learned to deal with stand-alone personal computers, modems, synchronous and asynchronous networks, laptop computers, laser printers and laser disks,

CD-ROMs, video toasters, projection devices, and full-page and double-page displays—many of which are now being used in creating electronic portfolios. And, even more recently, English professionals are learning how to navigate the World Wide Web, an electronic space where students and instructors could construct a home page and introduce an entire class's individual portfolios to other students and classes throughout the world.

Challenge #2: Technology is not evenly distributed across schools and universities or even within given educational settings. The rapid changes contribute to creating among us those with easy access to innovative developments and those for whom access is difficult and sometimes nonexistent.

Unfortunately, the technological changes will not be easy to predict or to follow. Nor will they be distributed evenly among schools and universities across the country. In some schools—most predictably those who serve students who are privileged and white—teachers will already have access to every one of the devices we've mentioned and may even have access to technical training and expertise. In other schools—often those located in low socioeconomic areas with minimal tax bases and heavy populations of nonwhite students and students from non-English language backgrounds—teachers may have access only to the most minimal hardware and software, and they may be asked to master these in their spare time. What is true for teachers is also true for students—access to technology in this country depends to a great extent on socioeconomic status, class, race, and gender (see, for example, Jessup 1991; Gomez 1991a; LeBlanc 1994; Olson 1987; Ohmann 1985; and Pillar 1987).

For preservice teacher education programs, the implications of this rapid and uneven pace of technological development are disturbing indeed. Without a predictable base of technological support to aim at, programs will be hard pressed to prepare teachers to face realistic conditions. Does a preservice program dedicated to excellence, for example, prepare professionals to face a technologically rich learning environment, and thus risk failing to provide them the skills they may need to make effective use of a single computer on a crash cart shared by four teachers, or does it prepare them to face a technologically-impoverished environment, and thus risk failing to help them consider the implications of multimedia portfolios, access to the information superhighway, or hypertext document construction on the World Wide Web?

This tension at the level of preservice education, in turn, has placed increasing burdens on professional developmental programs that provide ongoing education responsive to local conditions. Professional developmental programs in public school systems, for example, given shrinking budgets and legislative constraints, are not always able to adapt. Nor are the in-service professional developmental programs at colleges and universities exempt from such pressures. At Michigan Technological University, the Department of Humanities has confronted teacher education issues in terms of staffing, funding, instructional strategies, and technology—all of which need coordination to make computer-supported work effective for portfolio development or any other large-scale literacy project. Although the department has had a sophisticated network to support teachers of writing for at least a decade (a classroom/lab with twenty-five Macintosh and twenty-five IBM computers, computers on every teacher's desk, a Unix-based department network that connects all machines, more than three gigabytes of storage for digital communications, access to the Internet, and a file system that supports electronic portfolio management), the department has only begun to understand how much help teachers need—even experienced and highly effective composition teachers—to make effective use of these facilities. To meet the needs of teachers who use computers to teach writing and other humanities classes, the department has employed a three-quarter time administrator for the Center for Computer-Assisted Language Instruction, a half-time faculty-computing support staff member, a full-time systems administrator, and a volunteer staff of fifty to sixty student consultants. It has, in addition, offered individualized instruction for faculty who want to integrate computers into their classes, provided student help for faculty using the computer-supported writing facilities, and begun weekly meetings of teachers who share strategies for teaching writing with computers, compiling electronic portfolios, and creating multimedia texts, among many other topics.

Even this partial catalogue of concerns suggests the range of issues that confront teachers of English who want to think in innovative ways about online portfolios. Many teachers, we know, after reading Rebecca Howard's description of her use of electronic portfolios and our own accounts of the possibilities at Michigan Tech and the University of Illinois wonder whether their schools or departments can indeed afford to make such investments in the hardware and software systems described and whether they have the resources to invest the time and support for faculty development that we've described here.

Challenge #3: It is too easy to see computers and writing portfolios as "tools." We need instead to view them as the richly embroidered artifacts of a culture, artifacts which ultimately embody the values and ideological directions of our society.

Viewed in this way, electronic portfolios provide an additional challenge. It is not enough for teachers to work to keep current of the latest software and hardware uses, but they must also develop the necessary theoretical and critical perspectives to accompany their new knowledge. When technology, as an artifact of our culture, is employed by teachers who lack a critical understanding of its nature or a conscious plan for its use, and when these teachers must function within an educational system that is itself an artifact of the political, social, and economic forces shaping our culture, the natural tendency of instruction is to support the status quo. This does not mean that the nature of writing or communications within portfolios will remain the same—we have already suggested how these might change dramatically.

What is likely to remain constant—unless we do a better job of educating teachers—is the social function of electronic portfolios within the overdetermined system of cultural, political, and economic formations that make up our educational system. Unless we develop a habit of thinking in new ways about technology and technologically-based texts, electronic portfolios are as likely to be used by teachers to support those practices we now see as reprehensible in our educational system (e.g., surveillance, competition, outdated assessment methods, and the continued oppression of women and students from underrepresented groups in our culture) as they are by teachers who employ those practices we see as positive (e.g., collaboration, the valuing of individual expression and creativity, and the productive exploration of difference). (See, for example, Cooper and Selfe 1990; Jessup 1991; Takayoshi 1994; Hawisher and Sullivan forthcoming).

In light of this realization, we can understand the importance of rethinking some of the approaches teachers now take to compiling, collecting, and evaluating student texts and coming at electronic portfolios from newly established critical perspectives. Some of the perspectives needed for this task can come from a broadly conceived program of humanistic studies for teachers—from cross-disciplinary approaches to social and cultural studies; science and technology studies; studies of postmodernism, Marxism, and radical democratic politics; of physics; and of feminism, among other perspectives. Each of these fields informs teachers at a general level about the relationships that bind people to one another in cultural groups, the language individuals use to express these relationships of society, and the intellectual tools used to give their language form and substance.

One of the complex issues that such perspectives from other fields will help us explore has to do with the security of electronic files and the ways in which these files are increasingly subject to electronic methods of surveillance (Zuboff 1988), certainly a direction we will want to avoid with online portfolios as we have mentioned earlier. Another issue has to do with the ways in which computer interfaces serve to reproduce the value our culture places on racism, sexism, capitalism, and monoculturalism (Kramarae 1988; Selfe and Selfe 1994; Winner 1986; Turkle 1995; Hawisher and Sullivan forthcoming) especially in educational settings—simply by the structure of the computer interfaces that students are forced to use. These interfaces, for example, now privilege an English-only, or English-by-default approach to education that many of us would not want to support in general terms. Even the PacerForum interface we present here is not without its biases. When we put together the figures accompanying this article, no clip art was readily available that featured women or other underrepresented groups working and collaborating together. Although most of the graphics *seem* innocuous enough, notice that a man in a business suit announces the "computer news" and also that a male clown introduces another forum. With the exception of the forum "Amy's Friends," ostensibly women and girls look as though they had little "say" in establishing the forums. The closest we could come to featuring women was in selecting the "sets of hands," safely androgynous we think although they are also very white. Our experience is a small example of how it is all too easy to reinforce social structures already in place in our society despite our best intentions. Unless the profession develops the necessary critical perspectives along with the requisite technical knowledge, we fear that teachers will continue to be hampered in their efforts to use technology equitably.

Conclusion

Finally, we think it important to note that these three major challenges mask a great many smaller complications—as many complications, indeed, as there are problems in our educational system at all levels. And we recognize that change connected to computer-supported literacy programs is often addressed with a special degree of conservatism. Not only are we asking colleagues to change their perspectives on teaching and learning with portfolios, but we are also asking that they inform their thinking with the promise of computers, yet another technology. Resistance and sometimes resentment to such dramatic calls for change in the culture of the classroom and schools should not be unexpected. But we consider it promising that the perspective we gain from exploring the unfamiliar landscape of these two technologies—computers and portfolios—also provides us with new ways to think about teaching.

In this context, we can offer a final, and important, suggestion for the profession to think about: teachers must continue to read, to experiment with technology but, more than anything perhaps, they need to speak up and talk with one another. This suggestion may sound like an easy task on the surface, but there are, as we all know, many factors in our educational system that serve to isolate teachers from one another. The cumulative effect of these factors—economic, political, and social—is to keep many teachers in their own classrooms and on their own campuses away from individuals in their discipline and in other disciplines; to bury some of our colleagues under mountains of paper work and extracurricular duties that shift attention away from pedagogy; to distract them from the consideration of theories that productively inform educational practices; and to eliminate, for many teachers, the option of attending conferences and exchanging ideas with other professionals.

Given the lack of experience and knowledge about electronic portfolios and their uses in English classrooms, teachers need to make—and be given—time to share their observations with other teachers, either locally or regionally through workshops, seminars, or campus and district newsletters, or on a wider basis through professional journals and national conferences. Until the profession begins to share the results we find, widely and systematically, we cannot begin productive comparisons, replications, or the large-scale collection and analysis of our experiments with electronic portfolios.

As Rose has argued, the problems with our educational system are not such that they will disappear magically with the enactment of a particular reform or, as we have claimed, with a particular innovative use of technology. We do know, however, that traditional portfolio projects encourage students to reflect on their learning, thereby giving them an opportunity to enhance their performance through evaluative feedback and review. Electronic portfolios have the added advantage of permitting students to share their work instantly with their instructors and other students over the network at any time of day or night, to "conference" asynchronously with other writers at will, and to revise assignments online as they progress through the semester. In small ways, then, the wedding of portfolios and computers can, in the hands of reflective and critically-minded teachers, begin to change the culture of our schools. We conclude with a statement from Kathleen Yancey which we have modified slightly. She writes:

> All of this discussion about . . . [computers] and portfolios is not to say that . . . [either of the two, combined or apart] can answer every need, or that they are "the answer." Rather, it is to say that [electronic] portfolios can help us as we seek to understand, describe, evaluate, and improve what we do. (Yancey 1993b)

Perhaps, for now, this request is all we can make of either electronic portfolios or ourselves.

21

A Hypertext Authoring Course, Portfolio Assessment, and Diversity

Gregory A. Wickliff

THE GOAL WAS TO PRODUCE A STUDENT-AUTHORED ELECTRONIC HYPERTEXT about issues of diversity at the University of North Carolina at Charlotte (UNCC) and to assess the course work by means of portfolios. The products included over one hundred and twenty linked screens of information, nine 100-page plus course portfolios, four one-hour long videotaped oral presentations, and three grades of "incomplete." The process entailed small group development of discrete electronic documents that were subsequently linked into a large common document. It was an ambitious and arduous task for many of the students. And yet the outcomes of this curricular experiment, as assessed by me and by my students, seem to warrant a claim of "success." That is the subject of this chapter—portfolio assessment of the design and value of a hypertext development course for advanced professional writing students. Here I will describe and critique my plans and materials for the course, the students' efforts, and the documented outcomes—especially the portfolios. I argue that a hypertext development course does have a place at an advanced level in a professional writing curriculum. Moreover, I contend that a course design that integrates discrete group-authored documents into a single large linked file series best serves the rhetorical (collaborative/ social constructionist) and political (democratic pluralist) aims that underpin much current hypertext development theory. I also argue that portfolio course assessment practices provide the best means of assessing students' work in authoring hypertexts while portfolios also support a curricular emphasis upon issues of diversity.

The Theory

I first argued for including a course in hypertext authoring in UNCC's Professional Writing curriculum because I was convinced of hypertext's potential for changing educational norms and classroom cultures. Theorists and practitioners of writing with computers have come to recognize the power of educational computing technology and the concept of hypertext. Edward Barrett, Jay David Bolter, Paul Delany, Nancy Kaplan, George Landow, and John Slatin among others have written of the ways that electronic hypertext challenges many print culture assumptions about texts and authoring. The very processes of authoring and reading are being redefined by online text, and hypertext technology proponents have even called into question the status of the published book (Bolter 1991; Landow 1992b; Coover 1992). Rhetorical critics now analyze the design of computer interfaces. Henrietta Shirk (1991b), Janet Eldred and Ron Fortune (1992) have analyzed structural metaphors that support specific hypertext systems, and they've written about the implications of those metaphors for constructing knowledge in an electronic rather than a print culture. Other rhetoricians (Bolter 1991; Landow; McDaid 1991) have argued that hypertext embodies and tests poststructural theories of textuality, narrative structure, and reader/writer relations because electronic reading tasks may be so much less sequential and hierarchical than work with some types of printed matter. Stuart Moulthrop has argued that there are clear political implications in cultivating an electronic discourse community within the larger print culture (Moulthrop 1991). Hypertext applications have also led to the creation of experimental interactive fictions and the development of new literary genres (Bolter 1992; Joyce 1988; Coover 1993; Moulthrop and Kaplan 1991). Computer classrooms used to teach writing have been redefined by the concepts of electronic hypertext and networking (Hawisher and LeBlanc 1992; Holdstein and Selfe 1990).

Professional Writing is a developing field and one that can accommodate the study of hypertext as an authoring technology (Sullivan and Porter 1993). Composition instructors have experimented with hypertext in limited ways (DiPardo and DiPardo 1990), and the potential of the medium has been widely acknowledged at all educational levels (McDaid 1991). But hypertext creates new challenges for training authors. The plurality of choices afforded by authoring electronic hypertext does not guarantee an effective document design, but instead, creates opportunities for confusion for the novice (Shirk 1991a). Yet hypertexts remain a viable option to many forms of print including reference manuals and tutorials, simulations, and textual databases. Hypertext structures have been used for presenting online instructions and help files, for employee training in Fortune 500 companies (Thé 1992), for educational course materials, and for interactive museum exhibits (Shneiderman et al. 1989). But each of these uses varies rhetorically. Authoring hypertext allows students to create electronic documents with types of variety, accessibility, and use that differ greatly from printed matter or word processor files.

Despite the claims of proponents, hypertext technology does not make the processes of reading or writing inherently easier, faster, or more natural. Reading and writing are complex learned skills in any medium. The challenge I faced as a teacher was to train students to become literate across several media and to do so in a context that was sensitive to "differences," both cultural and technological. This was a challenge I took quite seriously as I drew up plans for a course that was focused around hypertext development and that employed portfolio assessment.

I knew from experience that portfolio assessment would support my course goals well. Course portfolios that showcased polished products and that demonstrated development across the term through a series of exhibits would help to assuage students' anxieties about the need to rapidly develop computer skills and to publish a useful product. The portfolios would also provide me with a structured way to require reflection upon readings, exercises, and the overall project while also giving me a method of assessing the work of collaborating writers individually.

The Background

I came to the course with some background in hypertext authoring and several years of experience teaching technical communications courses. More specifically, I had taught hypertext authoring as a two- to three-week unit in advanced undergraduate computer-aided publishing classes for more than three years before designing an entire course around hypertext authoring (Wickliff and Tovey 1995). Those earlier efforts had been limited by the short time frame I afforded to a hypertext authoring assignment in a broader course syllabus. Instead of producing a fully working hypertext, my students were required to design an entire document structure, but

Yet another student already had worked with multimedia computing and used his journal to vent his frustrations with our computer classroom: "As I sit here typing this response on my 486-33 DX, I cannot help but be disappointed at the quality of computers we are going to use in our class project. I almost didn't take this class because it focuses on the Mac. I hate Macs. . . . If I can overcome my prejudice toward the outdated technology, I think this will be a very interesting class." He did, and it was, for all of us.

During our second class meeting, we began to probe through discussion the meanings of "diversity" and to raise issues of concern on campus—the underrepresentation of women and minorities among the faculty and administration, the retention of minorities on campus, the role of casual language in establishing cultural norms, the status of the disabled, religious freedom, the reception of older students by the campus youth, and the establishment of organizations for gays and lesbians. With a long list of these and related issues listed on the whiteboard, I collected the students' schedules and asked them to select topics they would like to write about. Then I formed groups of two to four students by their choice of topics with the provision that they have at least one free hour to meet outside of class each week. In retrospect, I see that on such a large project students need considerably more time than one hour per week to meet. (The dissolution of one group can be attributed primarily to the incompatible schedules of the group members and their failure to work out other, non face-to-face ways to exchange information.)

The students' reactions to working in small groups on the hypertext were positive. They saw their fellow group members as resources—visual artists, musicians, computer experts—and as members of other cultures—black, white, Jewish, Christian, older, younger. And, surprisingly enough, most groups moved quickly toward a written statement of their group goals: " 'Diversity at UNC Charlotte'—my group has decided to focus on three aspects of diversity. We are going to examine the policies at UNCC that support the ideas of diversity, the realization of these policies, and the perceptions of students. . . . For my section, I am going to create a questionnaire that will gauge exactly how students see the current state of diversity at UNCC."

Preparing Planning Materials

To formalize their plans, I required each group to submit a planning memo for their HyperCard stack, complete with a diagram of the stack structure, showing all the planned links between all the planned nodes (see figure 1).

Figure 1
Outline for a Hypertext on Issues of Diversity

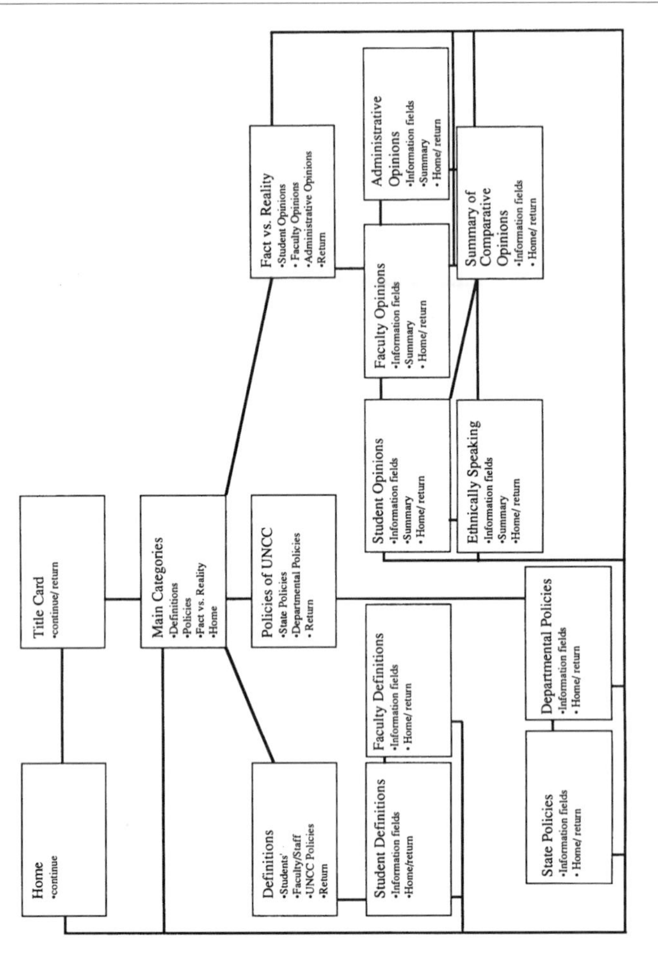

These "maps" of the stacks proved invaluable as students divided writing tasks and cross-linked the nodes of information later in the process, while their planning memos helped them clarify their general goals: "First, we need to reveal the diversity found on the UNC Charlotte campus. On the same level, we should address the dangers and problems found in categorizing people. On a second level, we need to educate diverse groups about cultural heritages and how groups are viewed from other vantage points (this discussion would get into stereotypes). Third, we need to show the benefits to everyone when we value all people equally."

The planning memos also helped groups clarify more specific document goals and led some students to discover things of permanent worth in the otherwise ephemeral world of the computer: "One thing is certain. I want the user to be able to interact with my stack. I would like to have a 'hard copy' that contains the responses to the questionnaires in a field that cannot be changed. On another card, I want a field where students can add their responses to the questions or to the comments gathered by the questionnaire. In this way, the text will never stop growing. I like that idea. In effect, my work will never end."

Other students' planning memos revealed they were more cynical about relinquishing partial ownership or authorship of the document to their readers: "I'm not sure if people should be able to contribute to the stack. It might do damage to others' work. Perhaps one should be able to leave sound recordings or messages, but only the author would allow that into the stack. That way the information can be reviewed for derogatory remarks."

Students were also required to sketch their first three cards using a technology in which they were already literate—pencil and paper. Some students went so far as to create nearly full-sized mock-ups of screens on five-by-seven–inch index cards. These and other preliminary materials I commented on in class and the students retained them for their own planning and portfolios.

Drafting at the Computer

Within four weeks time, the groups were working toward computer-aided drafts and were facing problems with programming and with managing the group tasks. The gap between the students' tele-visionary concepts and the limitations of the authoring tools and computing environment was a great one. "I don't like being limited to black and white. With color, the [drawing] tools would be perfectly useful. I also feel that the fill patterns are much too limited. I would like to add my own types of patterns. My last complaint deals more with HyperCard. Only being able to Undo your last action is a nightmare. Accidentally hit the fill bucket twice and you have big, big trouble."

One of my most experienced writers took charge of her group, assigned specific drafting and editing tasks to group members, all to no avail. In her written reflections, she made a prescient entry: "I must complain about the group approach. I have grave concerns that my team members are fading away. I, too, feel like it is very difficult to get started, but these guys don't seem to be working toward a common goal." Oddly enough, all three of her fellow group members dropped the course. She was forced to turn to another group already at work for support and to realize her stack goals with limited peer support.

And so the course went, week by week, and the students' hypertexts grew in design and complexity. As they became more confident with their authoring skills, they depended less and less upon the HyperCard exercises and grew more critical of unquestioning endorsements of hypertext as an authoring medium and of assertions of its superiority over print: "So he [Bolter] pooh-poohs print does he? Well, he seems to be doing an excellent job of building a linear argument on the wonder of the electronic text. He probably also considers himself an "authority' on electronic text. So, in essence, I could write Bolter and chide him for *printing* his information and opinions in ways that prevent the reader from interacting." Another student argued that an electronic culture would be slower to overcome print culture than Bolter seems to predict: "Bolter's book continues to attempt to prove his ideas about how hypertext is in the process of destroying all the basic ideas we have concerning text and author. . . . But Bolter's grand visions cannot occur until we have the common person in the street reading from a personal information device instead of a newspaper."

As the final month of the semester drew near, the students turned to the tasks of testing and revising their individual stacks. Students brought novice users into the classroom to work their HyperCard stacks and took notes on the problems and successes the users encountered. This proved quite valuable in guiding the students' revisions: "I am most pleased with the changes that I made after my user tests. As a result of those tests, I added the home icon, the intro screen, and changed the wording of the screens to keep the focus." The students continued to test and to revise their hypertexts up until the last day of classes, changing fonts for consistency, cropping and sizing graphics, repositioning text fields, and adding sounds and animated effects to their documents.

Presenting the Hypertextal Product

The final weeks of the course were given over to oral presentations of the students' final projects. Groups had one hour to summarize a vision of the rhetorical context for their hypertexts and to explain and defend their design choices before the rest of the class. This summative exercise set the tone for written self-evaluations included in the portfolios. Screen by screen, we saw the entire product of the class unfold, and began to take note of connections between our efforts—how issues of slang were related to issues of racial diversity, how historical underrepresentation was connected to contemporary student attitudes as revealed through survey research, and how official policies on diversity could be at the same time perceived as both too stringent and too permissive. The students were frank and critical in their assessments of each other, but they were also appreciative of the efforts involved in hypertext authoring and vocally impressed by the range of issues addressed by classwide product.

Our final class meeting was devoted to editing a parent HyperCard stack that would embrace and link together the efforts of the individual groups. "Diversity at UNC Charlotte" was the product (see figure 2). We decided to include the opening screen from each of the group stacks—"Racial Diversity," "Diversity in Language," "Policies of Diversity at UNC Charlotte," and "Changes, a Hyperfiction" as icons, and to make a space for "Credits and Critiques" of the product. Challenging in its tone, the parent stack was also designed to visually invoke the idea of diversity through the multiple font choices combined in the single word "Diversity." The parent stack was then tested, and an icon created for it that would make the entire product available over the local area network of the computer classroom.

Outcomes

The Course Portfolios

The course portfolios were, as a whole, a large and impressive demonstration of both the showcased final group products and the individual student's development across the semester. Divided into sections that include planning materials, sketches, computer-aided drafts, reflections, the final hypertext (on floppy diskette), and project and course assessment memos, the portfolios averaged over 100 pages. Bound in black, red, and green three-ring binders with colored tabs that marked section dividers, they collected together the bulk of the students' work over the fifteen week term. In the portfolios I found both unifying similarities (in the types of exhibits included) and useful differences, especially in the "final" assessment memos that highlighted the critical skills that the students developed: "I kept flipping from book to book, trying to get my arms around hypertext, and struggling with my desire to make chapter two follow chapter one and so on. At one point I had a revelation. I could see that I defined the text for this class myself. Indeed, it dawned on me that most of us have used educational material as a hypertext without ever realizing it." This was the type of structured reflection I had hoped this curricular experiment would inspire.

Figure 2
Opening Screens from Student-Authored Hypertext
"Diversity at UNC Charlotte"

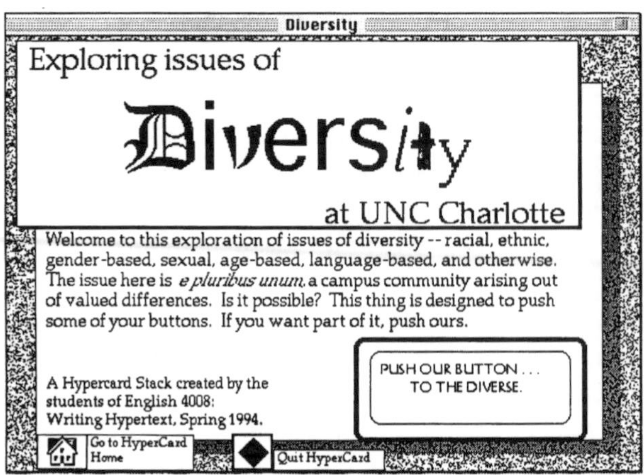

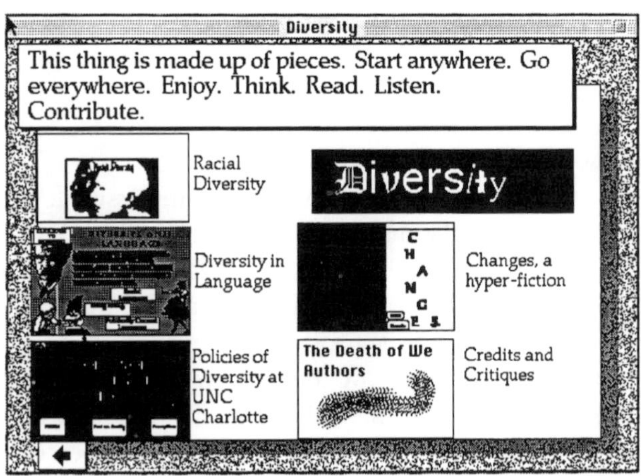

The student had argued convincingly that she had synthesized the content and the methods of the course. In otherwise similar portfolios, I chose to reward more highly this level of reflection in the formal assessment memos.

The quality of the students' three- to four-page assessment memos was, surprisingly, uniformly high. I found much to praise and reward in their commentaries. I had guided their reflections with a large set of orienting questions, and it was revealing to see which students responded most strongly to which issues:

> How did you define your audience for the HyperCard stack? What are the purposes of your stack (primary and secondary)? What areas of expertise did the members of your group bring to the stack? What are the guiding metaphors or images for the design of the overall stack? What are the key terms in your organization of the stack or its divisions? Why is each type of card designed the way it is? What visual and aural effects did you succeed in including in the stack, and what is the rationale for each? How would you assess the quality of the final product you have produced? What consistent processes or practices governed the work of the group? What writing processes worked well, and what did not? Would you select HyperCard as a medium for this writing project if you had it to do over again? Why or why not? What concepts from the reading did you find to be more and less useful in the creation of your own hypertext?"

One astute and honest student pondered her own feelings of ownership for the hypertext she had helped to author, and questioned in a public and theoretical way her responsibility to her readers:

> Apparently, then, I too am locked in the printed text world. As a writer of a HyperCard stack, feelings of ownership run strong. The possibilities of reader interaction excited me because of the potential of maintaining the reader's attention, but I also limited where the reader could directly influence the stack's contents. . . . Again, the question arises 'How holistic can a hypertext be when the writers limit the choices the reader may make?' . . . I learned to be aware of the limitations a writer puts on a reader regardless of the media.

This sort of self-awareness of language, media, and responsibility, prompted by structured written reflection, is perhaps the greatest product that such a course can foster among students. After working for weeks in hypertextual ways, the students all became more critical both of the limitations of print and of electronic documents. They developed new skills, giving them a measure of control over the electronic environment that steadily encroaches on their and our own work and living spaces. And, they prepared a document that is of use to an audience outside of the class itself—the successive generations of students and teachers working in our Macintosh computer classroom who just might be curious enough to double click on the networked icon "Diversity at UNC Charlotte."

I believe the student stack could be of great use to faculty teaching introductory composition courses in the computer classroom, especially to those who might be using a multicultural reader. If so, their students will be able to analyze and critique the information in this electronic document, and to add to it, and to comment on other students' additions and annotations. The limits to this program's future use include its size (over three megabytes of hard disk storage) and the great number of fonts used by the groups. The effect of its large size is to limit the life of the stack to users of our local area network. And since the classroom is not yet connected to the larger universitywide network, the size of its audience is extremely limited until such connections are made.

Graduate Student Papers

The graduate students in the course were also required to write a term paper on an aspect of electronic authoring that intrigued them. The papers became discussions of the contemporary electronic writing space—copyright law and digital media, usability testing for online documents, commercial applications of hypermedia, and a characterization of network writing spaces. Here, even more than in the reflective entries in the portfolios, the graduate students made perceptive critiques. In a discussion of copyright law and digital media, one student wrote that electronic texts were redefining the role of the author in ways that Michel Foucault had predicted—the author being considered not as a person but as a function in society. He also cited David Lange's claim that there will be "no moral rights of authors save one: that anyone who wishes will be free to play in the fields of the word" (Lange 1992, 151). But then he noted with irony that "Foucault's works are copyrighted and the first page of Lange's article announcing the end of an author's 'moral rights' contains the copyright symbol followed with 'by David Lange' " (Lange 1992, 139). He concludes by asserting that the author as owner of a copyright is an institution that will continue across media because of its economic and social roots, in American culture at least.

The Hypertext

The hypertext itself is an impressive student-authored product. It contains, among other things, some 120 screens of information, survey results from more than 100 students about issues of diversity and language, self-tabulating quizzes and ongoing surveys about policies of diversity on campus, music, narration, audio clips from contemporary films, animation, a short hyperfiction about a first year college student who wants "to belong," historical information, scanned photographs and images from recent newspapers (used with permission), bibliographies, and comment boxes. It is truly an engaging if at times incongruous product that does meet the standards that I set for it at the beginning of the course—it is a large working educational hypertext on the issues of diversity on campus that explores the limits of the hypertext authoring hardware and software that we used. And it cannot be conveyed well here, in print.

Conclusions

I believe designing and teaching a course in authoring hypertext is an investment in developing new kinds of critical sensibilities among students, an investment made possible by the flexible nature of portfolio assessment. An advanced Professional Writing course, driven by portfolio assessment that rewards both developmental and summative exhibits, is an appropriate setting for encouraging student authors to explore and critique new media. Perhaps this is hypertext's importance as an authoring medium, that it demands more kinds of skills than print alone. Hypertexts pull from other artful media, like video, that invoke images from many cultures; and structured portfolio assessment memos encourage students to be critical of design elements from several media and of elements of electronic culture itself. My students' work with hypertext shows that complex electronic documents can be at least as inclusive and pluralistic as print in form and theme. Their portfolios also demonstrate that work in this nascent medium can be assessed well. A hypertext course in a Professional Writing curriculum, when coupled with a portfolio approach to the course's assessment, provides a rich field for cultivating students' study of language, culture, and technology.

22

Down the Yellow Chip Road

Hypertext Portfolios in Oz[1]

Katherine M. Fischer

High Winds Predicted

I WAS NEVER QUITE SURE WHY I IDENTIFIED MY COLLEAGUE, BOB, FROM THE computer science department with the Tin Man from The Wizard of Oz. Sure, he often had his hands in a computer's innards just as his alloy counterpart seemed condemned to live inside that metal body. But Bob's head did not come to a point, he was certainly far from rusty when it came to teaching computer science, and this gentle professor was not lacking in heart. This identification only became clear when I received the notice from the academic dean announcing, "Professor Robert Adams will be available to assist with technology concerns for classes taught in the new Macintosh Classroom." This short memo whipped up the tornado that eventually would carry my creative writing students and me from our safe Paperland to the yellow chip road of electronic portfolios. In this chapter, you will skip down that road with Dorothy to examine writing produced by students in one college creative writing course and pick up the pebbles along the way, turning them over to discover how our experimentation with hypertextualizing portfolios resulted in collections far different from traditional print and word processed texts. Along the way, you will also meet a few witches, other travelers, and several guide figures, and you will receive both warning and advice about the journey.

Research on hypertext suggests that the software may be used in composition classes for student essay and research writing, and that novels like

Ulysses—read in hypertext—affect student learning in literature classes. Hypertext's ability to allow readers to switch from a primary text to footnotes and annotations gives students background on literary allusions; it also allows student writers to include bits of research for readers desiring such data. But in considering its use for a creative writing class, I was intrigued most by McDaid's prediction that in hypertext "we have an electronic medium that, in the hands of the poets, can be a precise and powerful technology that replaces passive viewing with active involvement, and that provides a means to achieve the connectivity and coherence leeched from modern culture by the primitive hybrid fusion of print and electronics" (McDaid 1991, 217). How would "hypertextualizing" creative writing break through the boundaries imposed by sequential and essentially linear forms of writing and bring us into the process of composing and reading in associative ways? What would hyper-writing do to traditional genres and the roles of reader and writer? And finally, how would the unpredictability of hypertextualizing entire portfolios affect student empowerment? Now with my colleague's technological expertise available, we were willing to risk leaving the farm—which had taken on a colorless and dusty appearance of late anyway.

Down on the Farm

Our creative writing class, offered mainly to sophomores, juniors, and seniors, attracted a varied population of fifteen students, some dedicated writers searching for improvement and an audience, some education majors fulfilling a requirement, and some students "getting English outta the way." During the first quarter of this semester-long course, students assembled traditional print portfolios showcasing their poetry, fiction, drama, and other writing along with their goals and metacognitive letters. Students drafted mainly in word processing, revised, printed, and assembled their writing in binders. Short fiction and drama selections were typically linear with beginnings, middles, and endings intact. Free verse and structured poetry varied but generally followed expected forms for the genre. Metacognitive "gateway" letters that introduced portfolio texts and reflected upon the writing process suggested that in some cases individual creations were arranged to syncopate short and long or serious and fanciful writings for the reader's sake; other students sequenced pieces from fair to best. Most, however, ignored any particular order. Students submitted their portfolios and met with me to evaluate how well they had met my portfolio requirements (which included a page count and specifics like "at least two poems, one short fiction") and how well they had accomplished their own writing goals. Together, we had safely minded the hogs and fed the chickens, but there was little doubt that ol' conventionally-minded Auntie Em was still determining the rules of what makes up a short story, what the elements of poetry are, and where the fences around the sty and coop belong.

Calm Before the Storm

Just after the midterm, I began removing the fence posts by introducing the hypertext portfolio project, explaining that while we would attempt to keep the writing foremost, we would use the technology as a means of encouraging more creative possibilities. Toto had indeed bitten Miss Gulch and Dorothy was on her way to Oz. Before Bob's initial visit, the students and I analyzed what we had always done and taken for granted: writing and reading in the linear tradition. We would run away from Kansas, but before going, we would take note of the fences, the doors, and the demarcations that might lead us to wonder along with Frost, "What I was walling in or walling out."

We examined how hyper-writing differed from word processing and how assembling hypertext portfolios would entail different concerns. Although Kerstin Severinson Eklundh noted that traditional texts are not really produced in strict linear fashion because of recursive composing and revising techniques, clearly the writer's intent is that such writing be read in a certain order; the students' prior writing supported this linearity in which there is a clear first page and a clear last. Print or word processed portfolios also anticipate that pieces will be read in their entirety and that all pieces will be read. Although writers may make connections between pieces in print portfolios and enhance individual creations by doing so, links between pieces are not intrinsically dictated by the medium; portfolio pieces may be considered separately and often have little to do with each other. Finally, the goal of word processing is to produce a print document even though the writing may be read on screen. Hyper-writing, on the other hand, may refrain from giving the reader a beginning or an ending. If the writer allows, the reader may access texts in various sequences. Hypertext may also present the reader with options to leap midtext or to avoid selections altogether. Hypertextualizing portfolio pieces, furthermore, requires that the writer provide metaphorical ways of moving from piece to piece because there are no paper pages to turn and because scrolling alone is not the norm.

Hypertext writing can be printed, but this works about as well as printing out storyboards for television commercials; it may help us see the basics, the blueprint, but it is not hypertext, itself. Because of the multiple ways of moving from piece to piece, and because the screen's physical attributes are part of the creation, hypertext "exists and can exist only online in computer" (Slatin 1989, 870).

Beginning with hypermedia examples already familiar to most in the class, we discussed interactive museum exhibits where visitors make touch screen selections to get background on various artifacts or historical events. We considered CD-ROM encyclopedias that offer, for example, a click on a button to view a video clip of the Hindenburg explosion, another button to find out more about how the Hindenburg was built, and yet another button-linking to an "interview" with the inventor Ferdinan von Zepplin. At any point, readers may also link to cross-referenced articles on famous inventors, German history, aerodynamics, fiction and poetry centering on air travel, famous historical explosions, or even hot air balloons. Some students were also aware of the hypermedia nature of the World Wide Web that allowed them to "surf" to various locations by clicking on "hot words" highlighted in the text.

Naturally, students asked what hypertext offers them as writers. And one of the most alluring answers is hypertext's siren call to free the writer and reader to imitate the associative connections natural to the workings of the human brain. "The purpose of computers," according to hypertext inventor Theodor Holm Nelson "is human freedom" (Nelson 1992, 44). In creating a term to describe this new writing, Nelson selected hyper because it "connotes extension and generality" (Nelson 1992, 49). I reminded students, too, that hypertext offered more choices to the reader as well as to the writer.

"The grammar of the screen" (Selfe 1989) is significantly different in hypertext than in word processing. The reader may manipulate screens to be scrolled or to be "flipped" to another screen by clicking the mouse on a linking space called a "button." Despite the multifarious nature of hypertext, however, only one screen appears visible on the monitor at a time. The button may actually appear as a rectangular button, as a picture, or as a "hot" (emboldened) word. This of course, contrasts with scrolling "pages" in word processing or turning paper pages, our orientations to writing prior to hypertext. Scrolling and page-turning encourage sequential movement through texts whereas hypertext's button-linking may support more varied, associative, and haphazard processes.

HyperCard 2.1 was the software that would whisk us into Oz. It allows the user to enter text on screens that take on the appearance of notebook pages, file folders, book pages, cards, or bordered windows. Like most hypertext tools, it also offers various other choices: pieces could be read backwards; they could be interrupted midroad allowing the reader to link to other pieces or to the metacognitive essay; different writings could be associatively linked by "hot" words; readers could select from a variety of endings; graphics and sound bits could augment text; and readers could be allowed to add their own writing to text fields. With multiple entryways into the yellow chip road and multiple ways home, we felt a sense of exhilaration. It was daunting, too, being faced with so many choices, truly what Johnson-Eilola called "a mix of vertigo and euphoria" (Johnson-Eilola 1994, 195) compared with the more stable and inflexible nature of print or word processing.

Twister in Sight

Our first task was to establish the linking metaphors that would make the boundaries of space between pieces disappear (Goldberg 1986). I suggested envisioning metaphorical structures as analogous to the film version of *The Wizard of Oz*. Dorothy is lifted out of Kansas by a tornado, a button-link. We discover near the end of the film that the Wizard also came to Oz from Kansas but by a different button, a hot air balloon. Dorothy alighted in Munchkinland; the Wizard plopped down in Emerald City. And so hypertext readers may enter the same portfolio in various ways and in various places. Regardless of the way in, upon arriving in hypertext, the reader is likely to exclaim, "I have a feeling we are not in Kansas anymore, Toto." Eventually, the road through hypertextualized pieces leads the reader to the crossroads where she is directed, "That way is very nice, or you could go this way. Of course, people do go both ways." At any moment, a witch may pop in from a rooftop, or a scarecrow who suspiciously resembles the farmhand back home may appear. One might enter a field of poppies where the road disappears altogether or be flown via winged monkeys to a dungeon where Auntie Em from Kansas shows up in a crystal ball. To top it all off, Dorothy discovers that she can click her heels (mouse?) at any time, whisper "There's no place like home," and return to the farm (which in hypermedia is "Home," the stack of origination).

After exhausting the metaphor, we invited Professor Adams into our class for his introduction to HyperCard seven weeks before the portfolios were due. Bob spent three classes showing students how to create screens of text and buttons, how to incorporate graphics, scan in sound and visual bits, and import text from word processed files. As follow-up to these sessions, Bob stopped by weekly to answer student questions and made himself available during office hours; the Tin Man did indeed have heart.

Following the Yellow Brick Road: Witches, Wing'd Monkeys, and Rust

During the last four weeks of the semester, students continued to work on creating pieces for their portfolios: drafting poems, short stories, scenes, and other writing as well as visiting one-to-one with me, with writing lab tutors, and with their writing groups to revise and develop voice, style, metaphor, variety and the like in their writing. We experienced the usual technological horrors. First, of course, we lost text only to find it playing hide-and-seek behind another part of the hypertext screen. Another time, one student's attempt to scan dog bark sounds into her exposé of the fire hydrant that bit dogs (after being possessed by the spirit of a dead mailman) sounded more like a duck than a dog. And when Anna's hot word button "Stomach" linked incorrectly to her poem about the gastronomic delights in a street scene of Mexico City, students ribbed her relentlessly, "Anna, how's that belly button?"[2]

Of far greater concern to me than the technological problems, however, was student persistence in working with the software linearly. Initial student reaction did not confirm Dryden's belief that the "implications of hypertext are more likely to perplex doggedly Guttenberg text-based scholars and teachers than to bother contemporary teenagers who have grown up with computerized choose-your-own-adventure video games" (Dryden 1994, 283-284). Indeed, students seemed stuck into old writing habits, much like the Tin Man appeared stock-still and rusted with his ax raised. Most began by creating button-links from piece to piece so that their portfolios would be nearly the same as if they were in print. By making these single buttons, student writers did not even allow their readers to return to the previous screen. In fact, using hypertext this way is even less flexible than print or word processing which at least allows readers to turn back to previous pages or to scroll back to earlier sections. I had not anticipated this allegiance to manipulating the text in intractable ways. Students seemed ensnared by what Bowden suggested are the limits of text-as-container in which writers corral their space and text, keeping out interference, as compared to text-as-process. Only Josh, a computer science major, and Cara, an extroverted adventurer, began from the outset to use multiple links in their portfolios.

Oil Can to the Rescue

Early in the process, Josh demonstrated his understanding of the need to employ underlying metaphors to assist the reader by creating a house metaphor linking his portfolio parts and selected appropriate writings. The "House Tour" button led to multiple ways of reading. Inside the "house" the reader discovered a floor plan allowing button-links to a bedroom, study, living room, hall, dining room, kitchen, garage, and even bathroom. The pieces available through each of these rooms fit his metaphor. The garage, for example, linked to three pieces: a poem, "The Sidewalk"; a haiku, "Garbage"; and another short piece, "Liver." The button "Metacognitive" took the reader to Josh's explanation that liver, in his opinion and in his poem, was just so much waste material and therefore deserved to be placed in the trash in the garage. He also explained that the "garage" writings attempted to satisfy his goal to write more concretely, and so he had put these texts in the "room" that had a concrete foundation. It would seem that in Josh's case, hypertextualizing his individual pieces brought him to "focus on connectedness," a trait Black et al. (1994b) say Carol Gilligan finds inherent in the female voice. The writing in Josh's earlier print portfolio had been less imaginative, much more literal, and without the connections and transitions to each other that were evident in his hyper-portfolio. Because of his computer science bent, he was immediately comfortable with HyperCard, more comfortable than he had been, perhaps, with the notion of writing "creatively." Josh's writing was liberated, it seems, by the technology. Using figurative language came easily once he realized the metaphorical structures necessary for supporting the technology. This is most evident in entering the "Hall" where we meet "The Accident," a short story that Josh explained is placed there because "the main character in the story is in a transitional phase of his life and must make choices just as a person must do when traveling down a hall faced with choices of which room to enter." In Josh's case, at least, hypertext made him capable of more abstract, complex thinking and composing which resulted in a more concrete, creative piece of writing.

Cara, recently returned from Japan and still under the spell of living abroad, used a journey motif to unite her portfolio pieces. As the reader enters the portfolio, she is handed a trip itinerary with open dates signaling that the traveler-reader will select sequence. From the "airport," we may fly to several locations. Multiple buttons also allow us to select an "in-flight movie," a "newspaper," or simply to relax with "headphones." Flying to Toronto, we land in Cara's poem, "Rain," after being cautioned to take our umbrellas off the plane with us by one of many mask characters, presumably a flight attendant. By "mask characters" I mean those created by writers to move readers from piece to piece within portfolios, thus becoming part of a bantam fiction with the sole purpose of making transitions. Although we did not discuss beforehand such characters, several students created these masks out of their perceived reader need for an escort through the electronic portfolio. Most fascinating in Cara's approach is the layers of fictions: the flight to Toronto is part of the airport fiction uniting portfolio pieces; this is overlaid by one of many mask characters cautioning us about our umbrellas. Under this is layered "Rain," a poem in its own right, but also an extension of the made-world of rainy Toronto. "Rain" is followed by another screen through which the tour guide, another mask character whose voice is evident throughout the portfolio, asks, "How was Canada, eh? It's a great place, even in the rain!" and then suggests we consider returning to the airport to catch the next flight to Rio De Janeiro or Sydney. The traveler-reader may view the in-flight movie on any of the flights; halfway through the "Exciting Adventures of Doug and Joanna," however, the flight attendant interrupts to inform us, "Oh, sorry, passengers, but we have an unscheduled landing and will be unable to finish our feature film for today. Please fasten your seat belts and observe the captain's warning lights." Cara never allows the reader to come to closure on the "movie." There is no ending. Her fiction violates the basic rules of the genre and so becomes, perhaps, more typical of postmodern writing and modern culture than the traditional forms of storytelling.

Yet, like successful disjunctive essays, Cara's overall portfolio gives a sense of wholeness despite the lack of linear connectedness. Her use of circuitous routes and a flexible interchange of different voices and fictions, along with her focus on connectedness and willingness to share text choices with the reader seem to coordinate with feminist theory. Cara found that "the electronic portfolio allowed me greater freedom to explore breaking the rules, to play, but to play in a very creative and meaningful way with my writing." In her student profile written the first day of class, Cara explained, "I've just returned from Japan. I've been out of school a year and I am really going to have problems buckling down to the structure. It is very difficult for me to be back in the states." One of the bonuses of the hypertext portfolio was that it encouraged the situated pedagogy suggested by Freire in which learning is placed in context with "students' cultures—their literacy, their themes, their present cognitive and affective levels, their aspirations, their daily lives" (Shor 1987, 24). The flexibility of hypertext allowed Cara to indulge her wanderlust spirit and recent travels.

On to the Emerald City: Searching for Brain, Heart, and Courage

As Josh and Cara shared their portfolios in process, they themselves served as button-links to the multitude of options writers might select; other students became dissatisfied with linear linking and came to see learning and writing as a social act (Yancey 1994c) and interaction. Jack decided to link his pieces by forming the portfolio into a rock and roll tour. Readers could join the rock group *Smashing Pumpkins* that linked to Jack's poem, "Tornado," or button-link *Nirvana* connecting to his idyllic pastoral poem, "Snow Capped Portrait." The reader found Jack's portfolio goals by clicking on "The Who," and his metacognitive clip explained that "who, what, where, when, why, and how were all contained in the goals of the portfolio." Although Jack's portfolio, without mask characters and without as many button-links, may not be considered as multifaceted as Cara's, it made use of his own culture: one rich in hypermedia with MTV videos and rock concerts embedded with light shows, screen projections, and singer-masks alongside the music itself.

Hypertext's ability to act somewhat like footnotes do in print, allowing the reader to leap to explanatory material and adjacent texts, supported another student's multicultural writing needs. Anna, a bilingual member of the class, inserted "hot" word buttons on Spanish phrases for readers who required English translation rather than "having to include the English on the same page that gives into the idea that English is the only important language in America and that I have to apologize somehow for writing in Spanish, even in this piece taking place in Mexico." The English-only reader coming upon "Que Dios te bendiga" could find the translation without the text being corrupted.

A few weeks after landing in Oz and being exposed to the new "normalcy" of associative linking, students took greater risks experimenting with hypertext's nonlinear capabilities, particularly those that required a heightened sense of reader. Tom's short story stops before ending and directs the reader, "Go ahead! You decide the ending. Will everything work out? How? Do you want to introduce another character or perform *deus ex machina* ? Write your own ending for this story in the empty field given on this page." Again with a nod to postmodern and feminist sensibilities, Becka further blurred the lines between reader and writer by allowing the reader not only to jump randomly from piece to piece midstream in texts and at the end but also to go backwards. Like McDaid, she determined there would be no one right way to read the text. Buttons allowing returns to previous screens let "the reader get back if she missed something." As an admitted recursive reader, Becka offered this flexibility. Her poem, "Alone in the Dark," linked in ways permitting the reader to view stanzas in any order. "I hoped reading stanzas in haphazard order would allow for a more abstract reading. I wrote those stanzas so that two different readings could result—one that built in intensity, and one that came together only in reading the final stanza (regardless of which one that would be). I think it worked."

Writers not only gave sequencing choices to their readers but also allowed readers to make shifts in tone and mood. Laurie's portfolio opened to the journal entries of a clinically paranoid woman in "Four Days of Paranoid Delusions." The entries bring the reader deeper and deeper into the mind of a seriously deranged character whose chantings grow increasingly dark along with her regressing mental state. "I knew that some of my portfolio was quite dark," Laurie explained, "so I offered 'save yourself' buttons so readers could leap and get to humorous pieces." Her buttons linked to "Deathscopes," ludicrous horoscopes rendering dire predictions and various ways to "escape" through suicide. "I wrote the 'Deathscopes,'" Laurie explained, "so the advice given was so bad that it would become grotesque, and the grotesque would actually lead to the absurd, and then it could be funny." By allowing the reader to hop from the journal entries to the darkly humorous poems of "Deathscopes," Laurie's reader may select comic relief resulting in one sort of reading, or choose becoming more deeply embroiled in the paranoid woman character's mental collapse without relief, resulting in an entirely different reading. Readers also could choose to jump back from "Deathscopes" into "Four Days" or to a poem, "Star Trekking," which links arabesquely in content with the suicidal nature of the "Deathscopes" as the persona realizes his lifelong wish to become the "savior on the bridge, the Terminator of Tribbles." Again, the reader may shift the tone by selecting button-links and thus become co-creator of the overall mood resulting from various readings of the text—how seriously, comically, or intensely it may come across.

Perhaps the greatest dissolution of boundaries between reader and writer occurs in Ellen's writing, "Fragments," where the reader may pick any of several enticing file folders giving background information on characters, just as one might stumble upon personnel files for employees. The reader may either sneak through these folders before reading the short story or jump right into the story's action and pop out again at anytime to peek inside the character files and better understand what motivates "Meghan" and "Ally" and "Alex" to act as they do. Mixing together various kinds of creative writings in this way calls into consideration the concept of genre. Wendy Bishop suggests that genre "refers to the form a piece of writing takes and the underlying structure and rules that appear to make it 'one game' and not another. We expect certain forms to have certain general characteristics" (Bishop 1991, 223-24). However, in portfolios like Ellen's, genre is unpredictable—at times, juxtaposed but, more often, intermeshed; hypertextualizing often results in a new "blended genre" where each reading may change the brew. Part way through "Fragments," the reader may opt to finish reading the story in dramatic script format, to continue with the narrative, or to select a poem that relates the same tone and mood as the plot but that is not essentially plot driven. Other buttons also let readers shift point of view from Alex's first person to an objective third or to Meghan's perspective. Different readers obviously may encounter vastly different readings of "Fragments" depending on their own choices. In defining genre Bishop further points out that "we may easily abstract the underlying rules of poems, stories, and dramas. We can do this because our games and our rules are socially constructed, agreed upon by our community or by the communities we wish to join" (Bishop 1991, 224). In hypertext, however, the social construction is at once so complete and so individualized by each new reader and each new situation that predictability vanishes (Jon Olson, personal communication, June 9, 1995). Every reading will result in a different blended genre. It seems that reader-response is inherent in hypertextualized portfolios.

Beyond the Poppy Fields

Hypertextualizing the portfolio makes writers far more aware of audience than they usually are because they are constantly faced with what choices to offer their readers and how far to go in releasing their ownership of their writing. Often during the process of entering their work into HyperCard, students remarked, "I don't want to offer a button there because I want the reader to go directly to the next piece," or "I want to make sure the reader has several options at this point." Hypertext writing makes writers acutely aware of Elbow's call to accommodate the reader's needs. Students' concerns about audience surfaced dramatically in our follow-up interviews. Their comments suggest that hypertext writing leads students to recognize naturally the importance of isolating and illustrating parts of the text for the sake of the reader (Romano 1994) and to appreciate the overall need to carefully organize work even though it may appear to come in hodgepodge nodes and chunks. They also became aware that the smaller frame intensified the impact of their texts (Landow 1992a). Although readers are more empowered by choices, student writers were acutely aware of their ability to offer those choices:

Teacher: Tell me about some of the choices you made in regard to your readers when processing your portfolios hypertextually.

Jack: I asked a lot of people from the class to read parts of mine to see if it "worked" before I ever handed it in. I wanted to test drive the buttons but also to see how others reacted to the writing and the choices I gave them.

Becka: In some pieces I allowed scrolling which I thought was a smoother way to read. But others were meant to come in smaller chunks of meaning, so I separated them onto separate screens. On "The Bus Drive" I had the readers scroll to a certain point where I wanted more of a break in their reading. Then they'd find a button which would require them to flip the page.

Laurie: I think readers who scroll have a tendency to read quickly because they want to read with the same rhythm at which they scroll. When I wanted to slow them down, I spread out the text with button-links.

Cara: I was always aware of how the reader could get bored sitting at a computer screen, so I tried to use graphics and tour guides who would interrupt now and again, sort of calling readers back to attention.

Ellen: When I didn't want the reader to have a choice, I didn't give him one. The choices I gave were the ones I'd have liked to give readers anyway but are often not possible in print or in word processing unless I expect him to flip back and forth with a bunch of paper.

Becka: I kept mine wide open so readers could get to anything from any place. Different people have different tastes. If a reader preferred to skip out of a long piece to a shorter one, that was fine with me.

Laurie: In a magazine I don't read every single article and if I begin a story and don't want to finish it, I don't. Magazines offer many of the same choices I tried to offer in my portfolio. The reader could go back and forth and flip around.

Teacher: How would you feel about readers reading only some of your pieces and then pronouncing the portfolio "poor" or "inadequate" or "unimaginative."

Josh: Well that might bother me at first, but I'd get over it.

Tina: I wouldn't like that. I'd want to shout at that reader, "Yeah, but that is your fault that the reading was so crummy. You left out half the good stuff."

Ellen: I work at MusicLand and it's sort of like living in hypertext. We'll get the videotape of *The Lion King* at the store, and then the audio tapes and CDs of it pour in and sing-along tapes and big cardboard cutouts, and then over at the toy store in the mall they are selling *Lion King* animals and Walgreens will be selling *Lion King* T-shirts. The shopper or reader decides which elements she wants to buy or read. Who knows what makes it good or bad? It just is whatever assortment is put together at any given time.

Laurie: It would be OK with me. I mean it's really no different than if someone reads only a few of the stories in a short story collection and then says it's a lousy anthology. Is that a fair reading? I know there would be other readers making other choices deciding it was pretty good.

Teacher: Suppose we published our portfolios on the World Wide Web where hackers could get in and change your text or add whole new stanzas. And your name would be there on the by-line. How would you feel about authorship shared to this extent?

Becka: I don't know if I want my writing that available. If a hacker gets into it and puts his name on the whole thing, then what? It would depend on who the reader-writer was. But if it was a serious writer, even one who completely changed the direction of my original piece, I think that would be interesting. If it was just someone who didn't care, who was just typing away . . . well, I don't know, but even then it could be really interesting. It would really take it out of my control, but that might not be a bad thing.

Laurie: I could really see doing that with a children's story so the reader or audience could be very actively involved in creating it.

Tom: No way. Not if my name is still on it.

Reining In A Horse of a Different Color

When the phrase "Surrender Dorothy" is replaced by surrendering some control over the text, who has responsibility for the trip through Oz? Miss Gulch, who threatened to have Toto put down for biting her, thus causing Dorothy to run away? Toto, who did the biting? The tornado that carried the house? The window that blew in, clunking Dorothy on the head and perhaps sending her off to Oz dreamland? Or Dorothy, herself, through her own need to find a life more satisfying than the one Kansas countryside offered? I discovered that most students became quite relaxed about sharing authorship with readers and relinquishing the inflexibility of inviolable short stories or poems. Certainly, every reader's response to a set of texts differs given the reader's biases, experiences, and so forth. But in the hypertext produced by these students, readers actually make decisions about genre selection, point of view, sequence, shifts in tone, and voice. Realizing the reader's influence on the text means "that readers can no longer judge the text without judging their own contributions" (Bolter 1992, 34).

In addition to their raised consciousness about the evaporating line between reader and writer in hypertext, students also became more aware of the appearance of texts. Although they had read poems and stories from each other's screens earlier in the semester, hypertext could effectively be read only on screen, as noted earlier. In some cases, graphics available in HyperCard stirred them to create certain pieces: "When I saw that juggler icon, I just knew I wanted to do a piece about clowns," reported Judy. Occasionally, graphics led students to select certain pieces over others as did Molly: "When I saw that haywire computer, it made me think of including my poem, 'I Hate Computers.'" Many students spent hours scanning in photographs and drawings to augment their writing. In attending to what Paul Valery called "the presence of absence" (Grumbach 1994, 24), Becka noted, "I think the white background was important to some of my pieces. I chose the background that looked like a book page for the haiku because I wanted a certain amount of blank space around those words. The regular text field would not have given enough and the full-page screen would have given too much."

This student's concern with the visual also provided one of the oddest occurrences on our trip to the Emerald City. One afternoon in the Macintosh classroom I found two students printing out their entire hypertextualized portfolios, screen by screen. Both explained that they needed to proofread (HyperCard does not include a spellchecker), and both said they needed to see the entire set of screens laid out because in the computer they could only see one screen at a time. I found it curious that as nonlinear as hypertextualizing allows us to be, it still limits viewers to one screen at a time, and these students had found the paper printout to be more multidimensional than the software version itself, by presenting the viewer with all screens simultaneously.

Melting the Wicked Witch

Finally, students submitted their portfolios with some trepidation. They were far less confident than they had been in turning in the paper portfolios in the first quarter, presumably because those were a known product. Their clinging to the security of print and linearity displayed itself in various ways. Several students included paper listings of the contents to ensure that as reader-evaluator, I read everything. Some entered only parts of their longer fiction in hypertext and submitted the rest in paper, apologizing "it was just too much stuff for someone to read off a screen." A couple turned in the entire portfolio printed out screen by screen in hypertext, "just in case the disk doesn't work." Most disks were submitted with a stick'em note attached telling me which icon to click on to open the portfolios. The students didn't quite trust that the yellow chip road could return them to Kansas. And I was a bit shaky myself because in Oz there seems to be more than simple north, south, east, and west to contend with.

My own journey through Oz similarly found me clutching the security blanket of practices I'd used to evaluate linear, paper portfolios in the past. I felt compelled to travel as many roads as possible through each of their portfolios to come away with the greatest number of readings available. Because writers intended adjacent paper submissions to be part of the total portfolio, I read them thoroughly along with each hypertext portfolio several times. Even the strictly linear portfolios (there were three of these) received multiple readings. I took notes on individual pieces (although I was unable to compartmentalize many writings that had been so thoroughly mixed) and on how they were linked. Broad's question of "how might we account meaningfully for both consensus and diversity among our evaluations of student writing?" (Broad 1994, 263) when grading portfolios was sidestepped because the guidelines that had served well in grading paper portfolios did not work for hyper-portfolio assessment. Requirements like "Portfolios must include at least two poems, one short fiction, and one scene" had to be set aside because of the blended genre nature of the writing. Pieces were so intrinsically linked and interwoven that grading individual pieces was impossible and actually would have violated the nature of the medium. Additionally, there is no page-counting in hypertext. Furthermore, hypertextualizing the portfolios led to other unexpected creations: mask characters, linking mini-fictions, and extensive metaphorical transitions. How could these be assessed? Earlier in the process, students had asked me if I would be giving two grades, one for writing and one for technology. This, also, was impossible, perhaps for the very same reasons Marshall McLuhan suggested "the medium is the message." When multiple links promote metaphorical connections and influence meaning, style, and tone, the two cannot be separated once stirred together. I felt like Dorothy asking for the way home without knowing how the ruby slippers could be activated. I turned again to the students' goals and metacognitive evaluations. I evaluated their own assessments and then met with them individually to negotiate the portfolio grade. In all cases but one (in which a student firmly believed that effort rather than outcome should be rewarded), students and I came to agreement. This was the ultimate example, quite by accident, of experiencing Freire's liberating education in which teachers are unable to "measure fulfillment of predetermined objectives" (Wallerstein 1987, 41). Auntie Em was so unfamiliar with these new creatures that she had no fences or rubrics to contain them.

"Pay No Attention to that Man Behind the Curtain!"

On the last day of class, students booted up their hyper-portfolios and we spent the hour playing "musical computers," moving from monitor to monitor reading each other's writing. I had not done as adequate a job preparing them to become hypertext readers as I had hypertext writers. Hypertext reading took far more time than I had anticipated because machines stalled, buttons occasionally failed to link, and readers needed time to make decisions. "Because it was the first time I'd read hypertexts, other than my own," Ellen pointed out afterward, "I kept wondering as I read, 'How'd she do that?' I was so fascinated by the technology it was hard for me to concentrate on just reading." Telling students to ignore the bells and whistles to focus on the writing was as effective as telling the Tin Man, Scarecrow, Lion, Toto, and Dorothy to "pay no attention to that man behind the curtain." One of the unexpected benefits, however, was that many students felt "reading in hypertext, maybe because of the graphics and buttons and frequent choices offered, was not boring the way reading pages and pages off a word processed screen would be." Technological failure also proved bothersome when "some of the buttons didn't link. It was like pages being stuck in a book but worse because in hypertext you can't slice through the paper and get to the next page." Perhaps the greatest indication of both the success and failure of the portfolios is echoed by Becka's perspective of the reading session. "I was disappointed in those portfolios which were linear. I found it frustrating and kept thinking 'Why use hypertext for this?

This would be better off in print.' " By becoming a hypertext writer, she had become a reader who would "demand control over text" (Bernhardt 1993, 173).

The Next Trip to Oz

Overall, the project was successful but could be improved in several ways, not the least of which would be attending more carefully to circumstances stirring students' affective responses. Because we spent so much time learning the technology near the end of the quarter, some students felt "all we ever did was look at computers all the time!" At the same time students also reported that although they favored the convenience of producing paper portfolios ("I could do it in my room anytime of the night."), 80 percent preferred the results of the electronic portfolios for reasons as varied as "allowing me more flexibility" to "the portfolio appears more professional" to "hypertext gave me more ideas which shaped my writing." Much of the frustration with technology and the feeling that creativity was being sublimated to HyperCard software might be lessened by introducing hypertext concepts and technology at the beginning of the semester. It may have been more palatable, too, to assign single pieces of writing to be hypertextualized and build up to hypertextualizing the whole portfolio although this is a rather linear way to deal with associative kinds of writing. In this way students would learn the software along with its capabilities earlier in the process and perhaps feel far less threatened by the removal of those restrictive but comfortable linear practices.

Although most students were comfortable with Professor Adams's initial introduction to the software, students wanted printed step-by-step instructions. Fortunately, Bob not only proved he had a heart by extending office hours for consulting with students, and the courage of a lion by agreeing to teach HyperCard in a writing class, but he also revealed he had a brain by sequencing lessons in the software carefully and keeping the pace moderate. Given my own discomfort with technology, if I had taught the technological side of this project, students would never have left the Munchkins' land: I don't like it, but I'll learn it so I can reach the Emerald City. As it was, Bob, a former music teacher with acute sensitivity to aesthetics, astutely perceived the need for technology to support rather than to unseat the creative writing process. This was a crucial part of the success of the project. Bob and I were comfortable piggybacking on each other's teaching during class presentation to satisfy the demands of both writing and software. Nonetheless, although technological know-how was accessible, the technology presented more of a problem.

From the beginning, I was concerned that access to technology not become yet another boundary replacing those we had eliminated by engaging in nonlinear writing. I gave students more in-class time to hypertextualize their work but assumed they would spend time out of class writing and revising. With firmer deadlines in other classes so near the end of the year, I assumed incorrectly. Campus computers loaded with HyperCard became less and less available as term end approached. Both problems could be relieved by introducing the technology earlier and by moving back the submission date for portfolios. Yet even with these adjustments, access remains a concern; some students have their own computers with hypertext software whereas others must depend on campus facilities already strained by growing demands on computers. With students who commute ninety miles or who are housebound with young children, access problems like those for materials on reserve in the campus library surface as obstacles. There are no easy solutions.

If only Dorothy had known that water could melt the Wicked Witch of the West rather than merely stumbling upon this by accident! And how these writers would have benefited also from being taught earlier how to read hypertextually. Because this was our first pilgrimage out of Linearland, examples of previous student hyper-portfolios were lacking. I learned about *Afternoon*, Michael Joyce's hypertext novel, and others of its kind too late to have copies available for students to view. But I would have been wary of using high tech, professionally produced hypertext disks anyway because students might have felt overwhelmed. The lack of examples had the advantage of freeing students to use the medium without models restricting their prospects. Overall, though, nonlinear reading and writing is so foreign to anyone schooled in more conventional print that the lack of models was more a drawback than a benefit. Neal Lerner (personal communication, May 25, 1995) suggested that students may come to a fuller understanding of how hypertext reading differs from sequential, nonrecursive reading by asking students to read hyper-portfolios aloud exercising "verbal protocols" (Flower et al. 1986). Not only reading aloud the text on the screen, but also remarking verbally upon the button-links available and those being selected would enable students to more completely understand the multifarious nature of associative writing. For first readings, the World Wide Web might offer simple button choices and could be easily accessed by students in a computer-assisted classroom. This might also be achieved by modeling aloud hypertext reading while projecting a portfolio on an overhead, allowing students to see the variety of choices the reader makes and the variety of hypertexts one might encounter. Learning more fully about reading hypertext early in the process would inevitably lead to an even more heightened sense of reader, writer, and co-author. As mentioned earlier, because readers have the ability to co-create the text, I would encourage students to discuss their parts as readers. Realizing now how important audience is in completing the act of writing, particularly in hypertext, I would allow for one class preparing readers and at least two class periods for reading portfolios.

There's No Place Like . . .

By hot air balloon, tornado, or ruby slippers, I will again journey to the Button-Linkland of hypertext with future classes. Although hypertext currently seems to be used more for literature classes reading texts like Hamlet (allowing students to see movie clips of the production or view other editions of Shakespeare's texts or scan a drawing of the Globe) or for writing classes (enabling students to more clearly organize and present their research when writing term papers), our experience suggests that it may serve as a powerful tool in the creative arts. With the blurring of lines between reader and writer, hypertext offers new dimensions to both. Because the software also encourages the use of metaphor, visual space and graphics, and multifarious ways of linking, it offers creative writers options not available in print or word processed writing. The greater emphasis on student empowerment at the cost of teacher authority that results from hypertextualizing the portfolio verifies Cynthia Selfe's belief that "what we lose, our students surely gain"(1994). The imaginative use of language stirred by thinking, writing, and reading associatively liberated in hypertext from many of the boundaries of linearity is enough to make me again click along with Dorothy saying, "There's no place like hypertext, there's no place like hypertext."

Notes

1. Reprinted with permission of Ablex Publishing, from *Computers and Composition* Special Issue: Electronic Portfolios, v13.2:169-185.
2. Pseudonyms are used for all students referred to specifically in this article.

23

Reflections on Reading and Evaluating Electronic Portfolios

Kristine L. Blair
Pamela Takayoshi

WITH THE SHIFT FROM PRODUCT TO PROCESS APPROACHES IN TEACHING writing has come the shift from indirect to direct procedures in evaluating writing quality. As a result, portfolios have become a widely accepted evaluation method which focuses on process over product, often assessing the development of written proficiency over time. Within classroom contexts, the form and function of portfolios are generally determined by teachers or administrators hoping to assess the written proficiency of students through the evaluation of academic essays. While students may have control over which essays go into their portfolios, their control over the form and purpose of their portfolios is limited in such an instance. However, the role students play in determining the form and function of portfolios may be influenced by the increasingly prevalent and important role of computer technologies in support of writing instruction. In this chapter, we reflect on the potentials and implications of what we have come to term the "electronic portfolio," a HyperCard project in which one student created an on-line (as opposed to hard copy) portfolio of her course work.[1]

Portfolios created and read electronically can differ from traditional hard copy portfolios in a number of ways. Comprised of more than static words on the page, electronic portfolios can include images, graphics, sound, and motion. Rather than constructing a set, linear path through numbered pages, electronic portfolios offer multiple paths readers might follow, depending on which direction they chose to go. Portfolios created and read electronically may thus blur boundaries between writer and reader by allowing readers to play more active roles in the construction of the text. As we will indicate in this chapter, such fundamental differences in the writing and reading of electronic portfolios necessitate changes in the ways we conceive of and evaluate these "radical departures from our linear notions of text" (Hawisher and Selfe 1991a, 173). Through an examination of one student's electronic portfolio, we argue that electronic portfolios may support and encourage the development of reflection and understanding in student writers about their writing processes, the relationship between the parts of those processes, and the fluidity of writing processes. These potential benefits pose several problems for evaluation, however, for electronic portfolios broaden notions of literacy as something at once visual, verbal, and aural. In order to support student writers negotiating these changes and develop evaluation strategies which respond to these changes, teachers must recognize the ways these changes effect their own notions of textuality and literacy. By exploring the example of an electronic student portfolio we received in a Computer-Aided Publishing class, we show how our own notions of textuality were revealed in our grappling to evaluate this new text form.

Hypertext

Many writing theorists consider hypertext to be a new form of writing which writers and readers must approach with different sets of conventions and rules for usage than those used with traditional printed texts. Part of this is a result of the physical nature of working in hypertext. Existing only online, hypertexts exist as an alternative to linear, sequential texts which are organized and predetermined for readers by writers. Hypertext might be thought of as a text of multiplicity: it is multilinear (readers must choose from multiple options which direction to take their reading), it is multivocal (with the opportunity for readers to add to the hypertext so that readers who follow will have previous readers' ideas and comments), and it is multisequential (with different readers sequencing the text differently depending on their individual choices). Hypertext is truly electronic text, since print versions destroy the fluidity of its multiplicity. As John Slatin puts it, "Hypertext is very different from more traditional forms of text. . . . Both word processing and desktop publishing have as their goal the production of conventional printed documents, whereas hypertext exists and can exist only on-line, only in the computer" (Slatin 1989, 870).

Many computers-and-composition specialists (Moulthrop and Kaplan 1994; Charney 1994; Smith 1994; Dryden 1994) share a belief that hypertext brings with it a new potential for radically altering notions and acts of reading and writing. Hypertext, Johndan Johnson-Eilola writes, holds the potential for theorists and teachers to "remap their conceptions of literacy, to reconsider the complex, interdependent nature of the ties between technology, society, and the individual in the acts of writing, reading, and thinking" (Johnson-Eilola 1994, 204). Thus hypertext allows theorists and educators, through its newness, to see composition issues illuminated in new ways. Sherry Turkle, arguing that "the mechanical engines of computers have been grounding the radically nonmechanical philosophy of postmodernism" (Turkle 1995, 17) describes a student who dropped out of her postmodern theory course because Derrida was too difficult for him to comprehend. Turkle ran into this student semesters later to discover that he felt he now understood Derrida as a result of using hypertext on his roommate's computer. Turkle writes, "the student's story shows how technology is bringing a set of ideas associated with postmodernism—in this case, ideas about the instability of meanings and knowable truths—into everyday life" (Turkle 1995, 18). Much in the way hypertext made postmodern theories visible to Turkle's former student, hypertext makes recursive, fluid reading and writing processes visible. While Davida Charney points out some limitations of hypertext which future developers must consider[2], she also holds this progressive belief in the illuminating effect of technology: "Hypertext has the potential to change fundamentally how we write, how we read, how we teach these skills, and even how we conceive of text itself" (Charney 1994, 239). Johnson-Eilola and Charney assume the radical newness of hypertext as a media, a newness that they argue will and does have a tremendous impact on the ways we write, read, and think, and thus, they teach these processes. The changes these theorists foresee for writing instruction as a result of hypermedia point also to the changes we must make in evaluation practices. How do we evaluate these new writing and reading processes? Should we respond to hypermedia and electronic writing according to the same standards we use for printed texts? If hypertext blurs the roles of reader and writer, how should our grading criteria account for our increased involvement in the creation of hypertext? Questions such as these arose for the two of us when we read portfolios at the end of a Computer-Aided Publishing course we taught.

Teaching Electronic Writing

Sullivan has described one effect of electronic writing as giving students and writers the possibility of "taking control of the page." In an age of desktop publishing software, sophisticated word-and-graphic-processing software suites, and laser printers, the published page is more directly under the writer's control. This increased control places new demands on writers and has serious implications for writing instruction as writers "must become sensitive to how pages look, attuned to how readers will see pages, and able to negotiate a look for pages that supports the aims of texts. Such activities add a new dimension to writing and call for pedagogy supporting the process of seeing the page" (Sullivan 1991, 56). These issues and questions played a role in decisions about our pedagogical goals and curriculum in Computer-Aided Publishing. For us, technology was a tool which students could use to take control of the page and their own design processes. Taking control of the page meant two things for us as teachers of this course: giving students theoretical knowledge necessary to design effective documents and encouraging in students positive, self-reliant attitudes toward technology. Further, we wanted students to see the interdependence of these two goals and to see them as existing in a dialectical relationship. Without theoretical knowledge, students would not be able to design effective pages simply because they knew how to use the technology and page design programs. Nor would effective documents come without a sense of control over the technology in order to make it support the document design goals students set for themselves. While textbooks and readings introduced students to page design theories, the application of those theories to real design situations and the teaching of technology pushed us to develop new classroom strategies and activities. At the heart of this task was a desire to encourage students to understand the application of technology not as learning every facet of individual software programs, a one-time acquisition process, but rather, as an ongoing, continually evolving process. Leaving our class, we wanted students to have the skills necessary for them to adapt when faced with new technologies in new situations and to have the confidence to know they could figure out unfamiliar technologies.

To support this learning attitude toward technology as a process, we asked student teams to be responsible for learning and teaching to the rest of the class the software applications students would be required to use in their designs. Teams provided brief software presentations and supported those presentations with individual attention to students as they worked on their designs in class using the applications. Anticipating a lack of familiarity with HyperCard, we taught the HyperCard section of the Design Studio, providing students with sample HyperCard stacks, documentation, and discussion to assist them in this process of creating nontraditional texts in this nontraditional learning environment. All of these presentations were designed to encourage the attitudes of self-reliance, creative problem-solving, and confidence in exploration which we feel are necessary qualities for students moving into design situations outside our classroom. These pedagogical desires contributed to the shape of the assignments. Instead of structuring the class around exercises in using the technology combined with exercises in applying design theory, we asked that students use the technology to support their theoretical understandings of design principles. Given the nature of the course goals, we wanted to create a classroom environment in which students took control of their learning processes and felt comfortable taking risks and experimenting both with the design principles and the technologies. In support of these pedagogical goals, we arranged the course around two themes: 1) a Design Studio in which students learned computer applications and applied them to their own designs, and 2) a Speakers' Bureau in which student teams first arranged for a professional to speak to the class about computer-aided publishing and then engaged in a series of design assignments—business cards and logos, business letters, newspaper ads, and flyers—supporting the speaker. While the projects were grounded in work place communication situations and asked that students demonstrate responses to different design situations within the rhetorical process, we allowed for individuals to fashion their own responses to those requirements. For the Design Studio, for example, one student designed her wedding invitations while another student produced a flyer protesting a beauty contest on campus.

Students were required to submit a portfolio of work at the end of the semester which included two designs from the Design Studio portion of the course and a HyperCard stack. We asked that students put together the portfolio for our evaluation of their semester's work, but we also discussed the ways this portfolio might function outside the classroom context as a demonstration of their design abilities and a collection of their own work for potential job interviews and employers. One student, Patti, combined these requirements (the two designs and the HyperCard stack) by making her mandatory HyperCard design a portfolio containing her two other design efforts. Through her unique approach, Patti demonstrated for us pedagogical potentials for electronic portfolios we had not seen, but she also raised several questions about the evaluation of this nonprint text.

Patti's Portfolio and Its Implications for Electronic Portfolios

Overall, the construction of Patti's HyperCard portfolio is not unlike the construction of a prospective employee portfolio. It opens with an introductory welcome to her portfolio, followed with a copy of her resume, and then particular samples of her design work that she has copied into her HyperCard program. Technically, Patti's portfolio is competent though not outstanding—the nodes are connected in a straightforward fashion, and the scripting of the stack demonstrates only a basic level of knowledge about the working of HyperCard. Although we evaluated Patti's HyperCard portfolio favorably in terms of its originality, demonstration of knowledge, and ability to meet both informative and persuasive aims, while reading her portfolio it became clear to us that the construction of electronic portfolios requires a blend of print, pictures, and sound to achieve rhetorical effectiveness. In part, Patti was aware of this requirement. For example, although she did not include sound on her HyperCard portfolio, she acknowledged that sound messages would have complemented her welcoming tone and her designs by providing an explanation of the designs' rhetorical contexts. This failure to push the limits of rhetorical effectiveness was not a conceptual failure on Patti's part; rather, it might be seen as an instance of the demands this medium makes on new users who must learn how to use the technology to support their design goals (by the point in the semester when Patti realized she wanted sound, she had run out of time to teach herself).

On another level, though, the simplicity of Patti's portfolio indicates that the potential benefits HyperCard (and new technologies in general) offers students also create additional demands upon students' conceptual powers. For example, although hypertext theorists share a belief it is the nonlinear nature of hypertext which makes it revolutionary, Patti's HyperCard portfolio was very linear. In Patti's portfolio, users move throughout the document unidirectionally in an order set by Patti. The author in this case never relinquishes control of the user's ability to access information, nor does she allow for a multidirectional, multilinear reading. One advantage of HyperCard, as scholars such as Bolter and Landow have noted, is its ability to create a nonlinear environment that allows the user to control the perspective of the information being presented in the hyperdocument and as a result to gain more control over her own reading and learning processes. Of course, there are limits to this claim, for even as Landow acknowledges, hypertext is sometimes used to merely reinforce existing hierarchical patterns of knowledge. Some texts put into hypertext format are only glorified versions of the hard copy text. With numerous scholarly secondary sources linked to the original text, some hypertexts serve to reinforce a belief in reading and writing as a knowledge transmission act, with readers reading in order to collect the knowledge writers merely organize and transfer to readers. As Patti's hypertext portfolio indicates, the potential for nonlinearity and nonhierarchical communication does not mean that HyperCard can't be used in traditional linear ways. Hypertext in and of itself does not displace traditional notions of textuality, including notions of linearity that limit the potential benefits to the use of such electronic texts.

What is impressive about Patti's electronic portfolio is that the parts of the portfolio were not just put together in one folder, but they were conceptually connected in a way that demonstrated her knowledge of their relationship with one another beyond the evaluation situation. Conceptually, though, the sophistication of her HyperCard stack both impressed us and forced us to think about the implications of this new medium for portfolio reading and evaluation. In embedding two of her designs within a third design—the required HyperCard stack—Patti recognized the extent to which hypertext could help fulfill a rhetorical need, in this case creating a portfolio of classroom work for use by both teachers and prospective employers. Additionally, Patti made these decisions about her electronic portfolio on her own. To paraphrase Sullivan, Patti had "taken control of the portfolio" and made the technology support her own conceptual goals. She answered our call for students to demonstrate a solid knowledge of course content (design principles and a use of technology), but further, she creatively and thoughtfully used the technology to support self-defined project goals based in those principles. Conceptually, she demonstrated an understanding of the effectiveness of technology in supporting her rhetorical goals and a willingness to engage with the portfolio at a level beyond the required classroom evaluation. Patti's electronic portfolio allowed her to have control over the organization of her portfolio. Working in HyperCard, Patti was forced by the technology to think about the relationship between the parts of her portfolio. The technology required that she consciously write the links between the parts, and thus, connect them in some sort of order. Patti could not just dump them into a three-ring binder with no organizational strategy. In this way, the design and implementation of a HyperCard presentation demanded the kind of reflection and metacognitive awareness we shared as a theoretical goal for using portfolios.

As teachers reading an electronic portfolio for the first time, we were not prepared to deal with these requirements of the new medium, in part because of a lingering conception of student portfolios as written documents organized in a traditional academic format and aimed at one audience, the evaluator. While we were prepared for the use of electronic media in creating documents, it was only after the assignments were completed and the portfolios were submitted that we realized our evaluation must take place electronically. The HyperCard portfolio, for example, would have to be read electronically in order to see what the writer had intended in using this medium. This, in turn, required that we change our ways of engaging with text. In a sense, we became more than mere graders of the work; we became actual users of the work, a real-life audience interacting with the document. Our standards for grading had to shift not only to account for the expanded capabilities of this medium but also to account for its different conceptual requirements. How well did the parts relate to one another? Were the parts arranged in a way that reflected some concept on the writer's part of the text as a whole? Did the text reflect audience awareness on the writer's part; did she account for the ways readers would approach her text? Patti had gone beyond our expectations for the assignment and required us to develop different evaluative criteria, a situation which teachers working in these environments must be prepared to address. Patti's work in hypertext represents a student's control over the form and function of her portfolio, linking visuals and text in a way to suit her professional and academic needs as well as to gain further access to an emerging technology that changes the way both students and teachers think about writing.

Evaluating Electronic Portfolios

Electronic portfolios offer several benefits for student writers: 1) they accommodate an expanded notion of literacy which incorporates words, images, graphics, sound, and motion; 2) they allow and encourage myriad ways of organizing thinking: "Hypertext's metaphor is, after all . . . a web which acknowledges the myriad of associative, syllogistic, sequential, and metatextual connections between words, phrases, paragraphs, and episodes" (Douglas 1992, 15); and 3) electronic portfolios support pedagogical goals of students' control over the organization of their portfolios and the kind of metacognitive awareness often associated with the reflective material found in traditional writers' portfolios.

John Slatin conceives of hypertext as "[a] new medium [which] involves both a new practice and a new rhetoric, a new body of theory" (Slatin 1989, 70). As we discovered in reading and assessing Patti's electronic portfolio, a new medium and rhetoric must also involve new approaches to evaluation. Indeed, while demonstrating some of the potential strengths of this forum for students, Patti's portfolio also posed interesting problems for us as evaluators. At a fundamental level, hypertext requires new ways of reading. Davida Charney believes that "[h]ypertext has the potential to change fundamentally how we write, how we read, how we teach these skills, and even how we conceive of text itself" (Charney 1994, 239). Even theorists who do not necessarily see hypertext as a new text form acknowledge that hypertext *does* require readers to develop new reading and writing conventions. David Dobrin, for example, agrees that users will need to learn new strategies to be literate in the hypertextual medium although he does not see hypertext as a new text: "Hypertext is . . . made unique by the text conventions it has, conventions that guide the reader's attention and allow him or her to navigate through the text. . . . you have to teach how the conventions work, and, once you do, you've taught people to be literate in hypertext" (Dobrin 1994, 308). Both Charney and Dobrin agree that hypertext requires new understandings of conventions and new reading strategies to negotiate those conventions. Certainly, as our reading conventions and strategies change, our evaluation conventions and strategies must change too.

Part of this changing evaluation process must include an awareness of the ways teachers must negotiate shifting roles as readers in the hypertextual environment. As readers of hypertext, we become co-writers. The text becomes our version of the text, depending on which direction we take our reading and on how much the writer involves us in our role as reader and coproducer. Thus, our evaluation becomes wrapped up in our creation of the portfolio as we make choices in our reading. With the hypertext portfolio, the blurring of roles of reader and writer significantly blurs the evaluation process as well. The teacher/evaluator no longer evaluates only the individual writer and static text, she also must acknowledge the role her own reading processes and conceptions of the text play in that evaluation. In evaluating hypertext, it is not possible to ignore the role of the reader in the construction and meaning-making of the text.

As we mentioned in the beginning of this chapter, however, this blurring together of writing and reading may prove to be a strength of hypertext for writers and readers in writing classes. Along with this blurring of the acts of writing and reading comes a similar blurring of the dichotomy of process and product. As Johndan Johnson-Eilola points out, computers were originally introduced as a support for process-based pedagogy. However,

> the move from written page to the more malleable computer memory/display often serves only to make the dichotomy between process and product more pronounced than when the intermediate product was pen and paper rather than virtual text. . . . [T]he virtual, fluid computer text is never delivered because, in most cases, the text will be frozen into print as a final step of the sculpting. (1992, 100)

For many students, seeing a clean, laser-printed copy of their draft often seals it with a certain finality, as though the physical product signifies the end of the process. Patti, on the other hand, submitted her portfolio in hard copy and on a disk. Given the nature of HyperCard stacks, however, we decided that those portions of the portfolios (and in Patti's case, her whole portfolio) needed to be read online. In this way, Patti's portfolio involved us as evaluators in a nonstatic text in ways which we had not previously experienced. Even within process-centered pedagogies, evaluation strategies are largely based upon final products turned in at the end of the semester. In our own process-based classrooms, for example, we had written into the syllabus a requirement that students submit process work (invention notes, drafts, responses from peers, revision plans) with final versions. But we suspect that the hard copy form of these stages in the process served to mark that stage for students as completed and discrete from the writing process as a whole. Electronic writing, on the other hand, emphasizes the fluidity of writing processes and constructs a vision of writing as an ongoing process—"a seamless flow of prose which culminates in a final piece"—with the resulting effect that "the segmented stages that have contributed to our linear writing paradigm of prewriting, writing, and rewriting begin to dissolve in the electronic classroom" (Sullivan 1991, 48). In this dissolving of processes lies an example of how changes in technology necessitate changes in theory. The shift in how "draft" is defined in electronic writing processes indicates the level at which evaluation methods might need to shift as well. The ability to follow the stages of writing by reading drafts and examining them in relation to one another is a key element of process-based pedagogies and portfolio evaluation. What happens when those drafts are not clearly marked in the way we used to understand them?

The "first draft" and the "second draft" or the "revised, final version" all suggest that there is some process students go through to end up with a series of products which culminate in one bigger, more important final product. The fluidity between invention notes, a rough draft of a paper, and the version turned in for a grade is emphasized in an electronic environment where students can cut and paste and carry over from one document to another easily. Within an electronic portfolio, these issues might be addressed by the metacognitive aspect of portfolio evaluation—students might be required to write a self-evaluation of their processes and the relationship between the process work and the final versions. Within the context of theorists who argue for electronic writing's potential to break down the dichotomies between process and product (Johnson-Eilola 1992) and to create a seamless flow of prose (Sullivan 1991), however, this might be seen as further entrenching old ways of looking at writing rather than capturing the potentially new visions electronic writing offers and seeing computers as agents of change. As Sullivan points out, "one reason the dominant forces have not confronted the consequences of electronic writing for composition theory (and its teaching) can be traced to the accommodation strategies used by advocates of computers in the English curriculum. . . . most computer-writing discussions have sought to fit electronic writing into currently accepted writing theories" (Sullivan 1991, 45).

Considering computers as agents of change and electronic writing's revision of some of the ways we have conceived of writing contributes to different requirements for electronic portfolios. Rather than having students bind together the multiple stages of writing which led to the final, revised version, students in an electronic environment might be asked to submit portfolios like the one Patti submitted—electronic portfolios in which technology supports and emphasizes the connections between process work and final versions. Students might be asked to put together HyperCard portfolios where the versions are not ranked hierarchically (with the drafts marked first version, second version, final version, and so on) but where the writings are linked together according to their relationship with one another. For example, in Patti's portfolio, she reconceived our requirements for the semester's end portfolio by rearranging the implied hierarchy of the HyperCard stack and her Design Studio submissions; she did not treat the HyperCard and Design Studio as at the same level of importance in relation to the other submissions in her portfolio, but she subsumed the Design Studio submissions into the HyperCard stack. The HyperCard stack became the organizing principle into which she fit the other designs as samples of her design ability. Similarly, students in composition classes might use a HyperCard stack as an organizing principle for their semester's writing. Rather than linearly connecting the stages of writing (prewriting, followed by drafts in numerical succession, followed by the final version), students might start at some other point than the end (the final version) and organize by some other format than a linear, temporal one. A student might start with the first draft, for example, and draw links between that writing and invention notes which influenced it, revised versions of sections of the writing, and responses by teacher and students to segments of the writing. Students might even draw connections between different submissions to the portfolio—between a first paper written for the course and a final paper which share similar ideas or approaches. As teachers using portfolios, we have sometimes found it difficult to assess the relationship between the drafts and the final versions. While students submit drafts and final versions in physical proximity to one another and write self-reflective memos about the process of producing the paper, it's not always clear exactly what the writer saw the parts contributing to the final version. Engaging students in electronic portfolios requires that students have a conscious conception of the relationship of the parts of the portfolio and that they make that relationship a structural part of the portfolio. By emphasizing processes over products and by requiring student self-reflectivity, electronic portfolios capture the potential electronic writing offers for supporting goals of portfolio evaluation.

In the process of evaluating Patti's portfolio, our own definitions of textuality in general and portfolios in particular were challenged, and we were forced to revise those definitions to better suit this situation. Patti's text reflected back to us our own constructs of text, writer, and reader—constructs based in print literacy and its attendant theories. As we found in this process, for teachers to develop evaluation strategies and approaches based in electronic writing, they must first shift their conceptions of text, writing, reading, readers, and writers.

From this position, we feel two questions need pondering: Are the potential benefits of hypertext promising enough to balance the investment such a shift necessitates? Are teachers and administrators prepared to make teacher training a form of technological training, introducing not just writing theory but technological literacy? It is important to emphasize in discussions which raise these questions that the shift from traditional written notions of literacy to these more technological notions of literacy is an evolving one. If we think of the use of electronic portfolios and other such electronic documents merely as tools for teachers in assessing student work, then the result is clearly not going to be worth the investment of time and resources. However, if we recognize in electronic portfolios the potential for modeling literacy acts in ways which overcome the limitations of the print medium, then the call for evolving, shifting conceptions of evaluation is seen as better capturing the complex ways people read, write, and engage with text. The value in such a shift becomes evident when we view electronic portfolios as tools for students to increase their knowledge of the rhetoric of electronic environments and to develop literacies that are inclusive of the workplace contexts in which formats other than the academic essay and audiences other than the teacher prevail.

Notes

1. The reflections we offer here on "electronic portfolios" are the result of working with a student portfolio which was produced and read using Apple Computer's HyperCard application which allows users to link text and incorporate sound and images. There are software applications available now which assist in the putting together and keeping track of student portfolios which are different than hypertext. For the purposes of this essay, our interest lies in the potentials and problems posed by electronic portfolios which incorporate multiple media.
2. Charney argues that future developers of hypertext must consider the ways changes in reading processes demanded by the new medium inhibit as well as encourage readers. The new text form may make it difficult for some readers to make sense of the text or to find needed information there.

24

Portfolios, WAC, Email, and Assessment

An Inquiry on Portnet

Michael Allen
William Condon
Marcia Dickson
Cheryl Forbes
George Meese
Kathleen Blake Yancey

Portnet and Portfolios: Michael Allen

"PORTNET" IS A GROUP OF POSTSECONDARY PORTFOLIO TEACHER-RESEARCHers across the country who exchange, evaluate, and discuss each other's portfolios. It began in October 1992 at Miami University's "New Directions in Portfolios" conference, as a way of examining an argument against portfolio assessment: that since there is no "normed" or standardized portfolio, portfolio programs are too local and thus too individualized. While they are interesting classroom pedagogy, portfolios lack the validity—but more particularly the reliability—needed for assessment purposes. At the Miami conference, Michael Allen asked several participants if they would send five to ten portfolios to be read by outside readers, and if they would read others' portfolios as well, to explore differences in scores and programs. Although surprised at the level of interest he found, he was also warned by a friend, Sandra Murphy, who said (approximately), "Since every program is different, you'll be lucky to get 50 percent agreement in scores." Initially, then, Portnet was established to explore these issues of portfolio localization and difference, and to see just how different portfolios and portfolio programs are. If portfolio programs are "too" local and "too" different, we reasoned, then "outside" readers would have difficulty understanding and evaluating different portfolios.

In the summer of 1993, nine participants sent five portfolios, plus scores and accompanying contextual material—a description of the program or course, rubrics or scoring guides, and sample scored portfolios, if available—to Michael, who kept the scores and sent the rest of the package on to two outside readers. Over the summer, participants read when they could. When they sent their scores, they often forwarded other responses: long analyses of the different program; objections to the program's requirements; concerns about the fairness of their scores. When two outside readings were complete, the scores were posted on an email mailing list called "Portnet."

The results of this initial reading were surprising. The sets of portfolios fell into two groups: 1) program portfolios scored locally by a reader other than the course instructor (entrance, first year, longitudinal, etc.); and 2) classroom portfolios graded by the course instructor. For the program portfolios, agreement among local and outside readers was high: 82.5 percent. For the classroom portfolios, agreement was low: 26.5 percent. These results suggested several hypotheses. First, experience in reading program portfolios seemed to allow readers to "take off our own hats and put another's hat on"; even when outside readers expressed objections to program elements, they could read the portfolios according to local standards. Second, classroom portfolios seemed encased in local context such that agreement among raters was much more difficult to accomplish. Third, more readings, and experiments with outside readings, were necessary.

Jeff Sommers, of Miami University, Middletown, suggested that we read a portfolio and discuss it over email before reaching an evaluation. This experiment transformed Portnet from a place where we *talked about* the project, portfolios, and assessment to a new scene *for* writing assessment. Through snail mail, Jeff sent us a Miami entrance portfolio; he asked us to read it and reach a tentative evaluation, then discuss it on Portnet for three days, sending him a private email message with a score at the end of the third day. Despite some technological glitches (missing messages and the crash of the Ohio State email system, which supports Portnet, on the last day), the email session was fascinating for those involved: over fifty messages with much variety in style and tone; a discussion which quickly left the portfolio (we felt an early consensus on the score) for larger issues in portfolios (e.g. how we read reflective letters); and nearly total agreement in scores (3,3,3,3,3,2 on a 6 point scale). The email session was a new experience in writing assessment, providing a privacy for discussion and fostering analysis in ways other assessment venues did not: on email, no one could interrupt our development of ideas; on email, we heard others' ideas more fully developed; on email, we were less constrained by time or local hidden agendas (however, also on email, we lacked the looks and familiar gestures of colleagues); and finally, on email, we reached near consensus on a midrange portfolio, which "conventional wisdom" holds is the range of portfolio that defies agreement.

Clearly, we would do another email evaluation, this time on a portfolio supplied by Kathleen Yancey, of the University of North Carolina at Charlotte: an across-the-curriculum portfolio from an Economics class. As with the Miami portfolio, we were forwarded the portfolio in advance and asked to read it and make a tentative evaluation using the local rubric, then to discuss it for four days before sending Kathleen a final grade. This time, more of us participated: Michael Allen (Ohio State, Mansfield); Bill Condon (University of Michigan); Marcia Dickson (Ohio State, Marion); Cheryl Forbes (Hobart and William Smith Colleges); George Meese (Eckerd College); Jeff Sommers (Miami University, Middletown); and Kathleen Yancey. This essay, then, begins with some background information on the portfolio and continues as a collaborative reflection of our findings after that second email session.

The Global Port: Kathleen Yancey

The portfolio I chose to share was composed by a student in an honors class on my campus. The class, Honors 1702, is an undergraduate class in global economics, with varying emphases: on economic theories; on the relationship between first and third world countries; on practical solutions that first-world peoples (i.e., students) can employ to address economic problems like diminishing resources and inequitable distribution of resources; and on student development of multiple perspectives. It is not, however, an advanced course; it usually attracts first and second year students. Nor is it quantitative in methodology. Nor, as I discovered, was it a WAC course; that is, when my colleague asked me to work with her, I said yes because I wanted to see how a writing-intensive portfolio on my campus might work. But as we examined the syllabus together, and as we discussed the criteria for the portfolio (e.g., understanding of economic systems), and as we thought about the trade-offs the portfolio would require, we decided that it would replace the final exam, thus contributing one-seventh of the student's final grade. It became clear, to me at least, that this portfolio was another kind of portfolio. It relied on writing, true enough, and the class was writing-intensive, but it relied on conceptual understanding and application, too. In a word, this was more than a writing portfolio. That's what I thought, anyway, and I wondered what my colleagues across the country would think.

A second reason that I wanted to share this portfolio was that the student who composed it had, I thought, created some interesting entries and used an interesting arrangement. She used the metaphor of a puzzle to talk about her learning. She included responses to her work—journal entries and a midterm, for instance—that showed her thinking in response to the comments made by the instructor. She included the reflective essay at the *end* of the portfolio, and I wondered what if any difference it made to put that entry at the end, after the "evidence." In other words, this student had made this model of portfolio come alive, and I wanted reaction to that as well: to the model my colleague, her student, and I had developed as well as to this enactment of it.

And perhaps too I wanted confirmation: that the score we awarded it would look like the scores from others.

Reading the Global Port and Reacting, too: Take One: Cheryl Forbes

My date book for Monday May 16, 1994 contains three entries: "Portnet discussion, 2:45 Sharna Fabiano WC, 10:45 Kristen." On May 17 I find these entries: "Portnet discussion, dinner w/ toni and susanne—my house; 4:00 SAOP meeting." And on May 18 "scoring/Portnet; Christy 3:00 re Alvarez." Anyone finding my date book would understand all the entries but those with the word "Portnet" in them. Seven letters—a lucky number, I hear—that signify intellectual roller coastering, rapid finger-slapping on my keyboard, and intensive email discussions that had the effect of mainlining caffeine and carbos. All in real time and info time. I had to up my email ante twice to accommodate the messages.

Kathleen's WAC portfolio took us all by surprise. Her brief introduction and the sweeping syllabus from the professor who taught the course caused some of us—me included—to assume that we had an upper level advanced portfolio. And so we read accordingly, and disappointingly. We—or should I say I—had missed the clues we needed: like the number of the course, like the discipline of the course, like the age of the writer, like our own fear of the subject—economics, broadly defined. What did we know about that? humanities types, one and all.

We bashed the writer and the portfolio. We bashed ourselves. We tried to keep pace with each other, even though we weren't face to face. Just as I ended a session, another provocative message appeared, and so I would begin again, thinking faster than my fingers could type but fearing that I was typing faster than my mind could think.

And once again, the rich, complex, challenging, ambiguous, ambitious, unaccountable act of reading overwhelmed me. Sure, we came to some agreements, and sure, Kathi kept us in a state of tenuous balance. When we threatened to head for a precipice, her "yes, buts," "aren't you forgettings?" and "but don't you thinks" let us live a little longer. She became the advocate for the writer, the portfolio, the professor, the course, and the context which she has convinced us every portfolio writer needs when outside evaluation occurs—like a defense attorney or a parent.

Which returns me to the act of reading and all the acts of reading I do when no advocate is around. Who, then, acts as advocate if not the text, or portfolio, itself? Or the writer? Do all texts need advocates? Or, better still, what rhetorical strategies help a text defend itself? What might hinder such a defense? For me, more is at stake in outside portfolio assessment than whether an outside group can reliably and validly read. Or, I should say, that's the least of what is at stake—the least of what I can learn.

Our email scoring session of this WAC portfolio forced me to consider how I read, what was important to me as I read, why I made the decisions that I did as I read, why my colleagues seemed so wrongheaded at times and why I was so wrongheaded at others; in short, it focused my attention on the *rhetoric* of reading. Which then returned me to the rhetoric of the writer at hand and to asking how the rhetorics of reading and writing intersect. Our Portnet discussion became a manifestation of this intersection, at the same time that we were discussing how our reading fit with the writer's writing. It's a matter of reading a noninteractive text interactively—or to invoke Bakhtin, all texts are dialogic and should be so read, even (or especially) email texts about portfolios.

For every question about my own rhetorical reading choices, then, I asked two about the writer's rhetorical choices. Why did she—we all assumed it was a she—choose *her* particular order, why the reflective letter at the end? What language showed that she had changed her mind about world population or the United States's use of resources? What kind of relationship with her professor and her text did her responses reveal? Why did she move between personal and distanced discourse? What tensions did her revisions reveal? What rhetorical strategies might have played portfolio advocate better?

I couldn't go to the writer and ask her these questions, any more than I can stop midsentence and shout a word to Joan Didion or Cynthia Ozik. I could only ask my colleagues. I could only ask, "Does my asking make sense?"

Reading and Reacting: Take Two: Michael Allen

I very much felt a contrast between the two email evaluation sessions. The first one concerned a Miami portfolio, from a program I'm somewhat familiar with, and with a purpose I'm very familiar with: placing incoming students.

The second session involved a WAC portfolio from an Economics class—something I'm not familiar with. I felt the information accompanying the portfolio, while it seemed appropriate (syllabus, rubric, and some description of the course), did not let me into the context enough; I always felt on the outside, trying to make sense, first of how I was to evaluate the portfolio, but later, of the portfolio itself. How much should I rely on the rubric? How much should the "honors" label count? The rubric seemed to ask for fairly sophisticated thinking and writing; maybe I should take the "honors" label seriously and expect to learn something from the portfolio? But because I was unfamiliar with this kind of portfolio, I was ready to be persuaded to review and revise my evaluation. This openness to persuasion led, however, to even more questions about this portfolio and how to evaluate it.

As Kathi started acting as an advocate for the portfolio, I listened hard. Early on, she listed three things she liked about the portfolio: the metaphor which governed it (the globe as puzzle pieces); the responses to midterm and journal comments; and the engagement with ideas in these responses.

Later, Kathi wrote, "A classroom portfolio is much more complicated (than a placement portfolio), much easier to critique, and much harder to honor, is what I've come to think." That's a good way to put it: how does an outside reader honor what is from a local context that perhaps can never be articulated well enough?

As the evaluation went on, Cheryl suggested that we needed a statement from the teacher about the class and its performance, a reflection from her that told us what was actually accomplished in the course. The rubric and syllabus alone set up an "ideal" context; the classroom experience may establish a different context, a "hidden" rubric which the teacher has in her head as she evaluates a portfolio, but which the outside reader cannot see. Maybe the class as a whole fell short of the teacher's plans and expectations; maybe within the context of the class, essays/portfolios were better than the course syllabus and rubric would lead one to expect. This difference became obvious as I noted the grades the teacher gave some of the portfolio's essays. I would have graded them lower, given the course syllabus and rubric.

But I was not the classroom teacher; I did not have a clear sense of the full context. Given the difference between the classroom context and what an outside reader misses—cannot see—of that context, should there even be outside reading of classroom portfolios? Maybe there are uses of portfolios which are more intimate, less public, and therefore an outside reading—while it may be an interesting event for outside readers such as us—is simply inappropriate. Maybe there is, in the process of a program portfolio's formation (e.g. the Miami portfolio) an articulation of issues and criteria with outside reading in mind. A program portfolio is designed to be read by an "outside reader"—an instructor outside the classroom. That design seems to be easily transferable to other outside readers, be they in Florida or Michigan. In order to be fair, an outside reader needs to be given ways into a portfolio, an invitation which arises not only from the rubric and program apparatus, but also from the writer's orientation toward two audiences: the classroom teacher and an outside reader.

My anxiety about being fair came not only from my unfamiliarity with an economics portfolio but from the lack of invitation I felt as an outside reader reading a classroom portfolio.

Email, Community and Time: Marcia Dickson

Can ten different readers, from ten different schools, develop an assessment community with a common context over something as cold as a computer network? It seems unlikely. In my experience, communities grow from spontaneous give-and-take discussion, frequent "do-you-mean?" questions, or "let's-cut-to-the-chase" interactions. In email communities that spontaneity disappears; correspondents read, respond, and wait for answers all alone at their computers.

These acts of reading and writing are far from spontaneous. In fact, the sheer number of email entries a participant must slog through can be a major detriment to community bonding. For instance, when printed out as individual messages, the posts generated by Portnet for the WAC evaluation described in the introduction to this article numbered over two hundred pages. Some posts were merely a line or two, but others were three or four printed pages of comments. Oddly enough, the short messages presented more problems to me than the lengthy ones. Because email messages come over the wire in a random fashion, interspersed with messages from students and other correspondents, these tidbit missives often seemed to come out of nowhere. I nearly always had to create a context for these abbreviated messages before I could make meaning from them. Needless to say, I sometimes had to hold four or five conversations in my mind at a time. After experiencing this intellectual overload, I'm no longer surprised to hear members of larger electronic mail groups claim that the commitment of time that their networks demanded forced them to drop out.

In theory, email should create more time. But even though readers can chug along at their own paces, individual paces may not always be in sync. For example, my participation in the first Portnet reading was hectic but manageable; the posts were fewer, the issues clearer, the demands of my local community under control. The second reading, however, led me to desperation. I was desperate for time. Because of my teaching and professional schedule, any email communication had to wait until evening—late evening. My commitment to Portnet faltered somewhat the first time I turned on my computer at eleven o'clock P.M. and discovered more than forty Portnet messages waiting for me. The next night over eighty Portnet messages appeared on the screen. Slipped in between Portnet questions were more than twenty posts from my students—asking for help on papers—and another ten from local colleagues on various matters. Needless to say, under those circumstances, I began to doubt that this was a community I should have joined.

But wait. As sour as this experience may sound (I've just reread), I'm not arguing that there can be no community over the wires or that the hassle isn't worth the outcome. Quite the contrary. There are other types of time involved in developing community, time which proves quite valuable and extremely positive. Despite the problems, I've learned a lot. The Portnet community has provided valuable insights into what other members of our profession believe constitutes good writing and good evaluation. Moreover, my interaction with these ten good people has caused me to rethink various aspects of my own writing program. This technological experience has even convinced me that under certain conditions portfolios can be read accurately by outside readers. But the Portnet project has also convinced me that teachers and evaluators need to take considerably more time to explore their assumptions about everything from student writing to the purpose of writing courses.

No community can be built by short, sporadic conversations. And Portnet has helped me see that this is as true of face-to-face communities as it is of electronic ones. Ironically, that lack of spontaneity I abhor in email messages contributes to the effective creation of context and community. The short spontaneous electronic messages, despite their resemblance to real conversational dialogue, were the least effective for me. I could attribute this fact to the lack of context or the assumed context that can exist on the information highway, but it's not really much different from the problems which arise when our spontaneous conversations are built on the assumption that our local colleagues know what we're talking about and accept our conclusions.

The Portnet community hasn't perfected the art of electronic assessment yet. To build on the benefits of email and minimize its defects, I'd suggest we change our present system: take longer to discuss portfolios, read more portfolios from the same school or classroom, and write each other frequently, allowing time—a week or even two—to digest ideas before we decide on final scores. I believe that this sort of continuous yet studied conversation will bring our very diverse attitudes about writing much closer together. Will it help us to find that mythical perfect national standard for writing? No. That's still a myth. However, this well-spent time can keep us from teaching, grading, and/or evaluating in a vacuum, and that serves both our profession and our students.

CMC and Portfolio Assessment: William Condon

Although electronic mail was not part of the original scope for the Portnet project, its use in scoring two portfolios revealed that computer-mediated communication (CMC) can play a powerful role in large-scale portfolio assessment. Granted, since both CMC and portfolios are in their early stages, we should proceed with caution as we attempt to meld them, but the early indications, based on what we know about how to perform a reliable writing assessment and about how CMC can expand and extend communities, are promising.

Portnet's first two experiences with email scoring sessions suggest that CMC can provide both a medium for readers from distant places to communicate effectively with each other and a forum within which those readers can have more than the usual opportunities to talk with each other about matters of importance in achieving agreement on portfolio readings—in other words, in achieving reliability: the context for the portfolio, the readers' criteria, the meaning and consequences of different score levels, and so forth. CMC seems to provide support for just the sort of reading community that is most likely to agree, over time, on outcomes.

Basically, there are two ways to achieve reliability among readers, and these methods echo the two primary movements in writing instruction: product and process. First, a program may focus on agreement of scores—the product of the reading. This kind of program typically supplies "anchor" samples that have been carefully chosen to represent certain score levels, and readers are trained to read to those samples. If a reader cannot understand why the anchor illustrates a certain level, or if s/he cannot consistently match other samples to the anchors, then s/he is removed, dismissed, or given some other task that does not involve scoring samples. This method is the standard in holistic scoring of timed samples. The second method works in almost the opposite way. Instead of focusing on scores, readers spend time bringing their reading processes into line with each other. They read and discuss samples with an eye toward developing and refining a shared sense of values and criteria for scoring. In other words, this method fosters a reading community in which reliability grows out of the readers' abilities to communicate with each other and to grow closer in terms of the way they approach samples (see Decker et al. 1992).

This second method seems best suited for reading portfolios since portfolios tend to be so complex and so varied, both internally and among samples, that anchor portfolios less effectively illustrate a particular score level. In other words, if the sample is rigidly controlled, then the anchor method is likely to work, since the range of possibilities for what writers can include is severely limited. However, the more open the sample is, the less likely we are to find anchors that adequately illustrate each score level. The reading process needs to respond to this heightened complexity, which necessarily accompanies the portfolio's heightened face validity. No longer can readers simply look to the major characteristics of anchors; instead, readers need to share their internal as well as external criteria with each other, to discuss what they notice, and, as they read and score sample portfolios, to talk about their scores and their scoring practices with an eye toward developing a consensus that can last as they read other samples.

CMC can support the process of developing communities that place a priority on sharing a complex set of values that support decisions made by individuals. In an electronic mail group like Portnet, for example, each member of the group can "speak" as much and as often as s/he wishes, and as long as the other members of the group are conscientious about reading their email, each member will be attended to as often as s/he speaks. In addition, even though we know each other to varying degrees, communicating via electronic mail exerts a leveling influence on the group, giving it an attractive egalitarian flavor. No one voice can dominate; no one member's input can necessarily have more import than another's. All the talk helps forge a community, helps us find our evaluative center, and helps us come to know each other. In the end, at the deadline, each of us makes her or his decision alone. In other words, this process avoids the weakest aspect of CMC: while it is a powerful tool for discussion, it is not particularly apt for reaching group consensus for decision-making. CMC supports the community-building activities so necessary for scoring portfolios, but it also leaves readers the space to exercise their judgment as members of the reading community.

Portfolio Assessment and the Well-Educated Men and Women: George Meese

Portfolio evaluation has been instituted for many purposes, but primarily to give evaluators a rich sample of discourse to judge and to spread the evaluative acts among several people, with the hope of improving the fairness of summative evaluation. In a typical preportfolio situation, a college would rely on composition courses or a single-shot timed essay to assure every graduate's competency in written discourse, but such choices reduce the foundation for judgment to one teacher's opinion of a whole course's assignments or to several people's opinion of a single, unrepresentative document. (Timed essay tests are unlike most other written work, and thus, low in validity.)

When an institution sets up a program for evaluating writing by portfolio, a "community" of experienced women and men get to pass judgment on the student's representation of her or his best work. At our college, we originally wanted to allow faculty to make judgments while fully aware of contexts: in this community of learners, is this student's composition successful in this particular situation, for these particular purposes, and at this level of developmental sophistication? Our vision of good writing assessment has not been to ask, "Can I defend my judgment to the student's family or friends?"; the student is in college to meet the standards of a collegiate community, and if Mom and Dad want to set criteria, they can join the faculty. We believe that this community is a fundamentally different institution than other human endeavors, and that our assessment of writing needs to embrace originality of thinking and expression. Our portfolio system seeks to include professors' local purposes for discourse in all fields, as well as highly experimental forays by the students themselves, in or out of class, and thus we do not write detailed specifications for portfolios that would serve only the writing pedagogues among us.

When Michael Allen offered the Portnet opportunity at the Miami University conference, I wanted to test our program's presuppositions against the evaluative perspectives of folks outside our community. If composition really is radically contextual, wouldn't outside scoring be problematic, and maybe impossible? In the first round of Portnet scoring (before the email phase), I behaved defensively, saying, "Those of us who are assessing ought to know what the purposes are . . . A portfolio at Eckerd College is *not* just like any other school's unless we share very similar philosophies of what senior undergraduate level academic discourse ought to look like, and differences due to purposes should bother only those who think all colleges ought to be roughly the same. We don't." After many more iterations of Portnet evaluations and email conversations, I've had to modify my composition theory to accord with actual practice. While the production of successful collegiate texts is indeed radically contextual (especially for the more sophisticated tasks in major field papers), experienced evaluators from outside the generative community can make reliable assessments.

How is this possible? Our Portnet experiment in external evaluation included program descriptions that helped the readers imagine themselves within the system of evaluation at the home institution. The encouraging agreements we achieved (above 82 percent on all the instances of competency/summative evaluations) might depend on the quality of the program descriptions: to the degree that the outsiders are able to imagine themselves in the matrix of assumptions of the home institution's evaluators, the resultant judgments correlate. Portnet's modest sample sizes and necessarily restricted design do not support broad claims, but the experience strongly suggests that evaluators try to play out a role consistent with both the institution's purposes and, when context-setting introductions are present in a portfolio, with the student's professed purposes as well.

Another phenomenon may influence correlations between home and external evaluations. When students graduate from college, most deans or presidents mark the occasion with the expression, "Welcome to the community of educated men and women." This is no accidental locution, but a commendation with significant social import. It is possible our good correlations of scores over Portnet are part of a real, larger community of judgment that shares more commonality than the limited, partial psychometrics of earlier composition evaluation. In other words, when the sample is sufficiently rich, and the evaluators have clarified their purposes, it is possible to render reliable judgments with strong external agreement. Further, the acts of judgment are far more complex, yet more simple in expression, than previous constructions of "writing competency." It is possible that when we say, "This student's portfolio has demonstrated competency in writing," we are also saying, "This student has performed as a member of the community of educated women and men."

A Final Take: Kathleen Yancey

My national colleagues valued the model of the portfolio my local colleague and I had designed; that pleased me. My local colleague and I valued the student's work more highly than Portnet did; that disappointed me. But on reflection, I think it shouldn't have. English professors critique more rigorously when the material belongs to someone else; as Peter Elbow has noted, our education has rewarded us for exercising such critical judgment.

But through the reading, talking about, and scoring of this single portfolio—over email—we learned:

> *about assumptions* and about how embedded they are. Honors on one campus, for instance, isn't honors on another; a number like 1706 might be an advanced level and might not. Even when the subject matter of the portfolio is outside our area of expertise (especially when it is the work of a first or second year student), many of us feel comfortable evaluating it;
>
> *about the role that reflection can play*. Reflection is important for the *student*, who learns through the review of her work and the articulation of what that review produced; for the *teacher*, who might comment on what actually transpired in the class and use that to help her improve her teaching, and also about how this reflection would help outside readers; for the *readers*, who balance the tacit with what is known as they reflect on what they found in the portfolio as opposed to what they expected;

about the role of email in assessment in research. Through email discussion groups, teachers and researchers can come together to read portfolios from each other's campuses, can critique the models, can assess the work, and can make suggestions for improvement. How we do this is still being determined, but some factors seem evident: a stable, informed group; a clear focus; an agreed upon protocol; and a leader who facilitates without dominating.

and about how we read fairly/reliably/appropriately without being directed by anchors and benchmarks and a training process. Again, we don't have all the answers here, but we are beginning to see some of the items:

1) *program/course descriptions*: level of the course and its aims, with a syllabus if possible; rationale; conditions of compilation; and a rubric.
2) *demographic information about the school* Some of these items, however, can lead to false assumptions, so some of them may need "qualifiers" or "amendments": an honors student on my campus might not be admitted at some of the other institutions represented here, for instance.
3) *some explanation as to what actually happened in the class/program exemplified in the portfolio* As teachers, we sometimes promise more in our syllabus than we actually are able to deliver, or we deliver differently than we expected. These kinds of data need to be supplied as well, and during the reading process.
4) *an advocate* It's true that texts need to act as advocates for themselves, but within a reading process like the one described here, where no one is really vested in the outcome and where being critical can be its own reward, having someone commit to being the advocate simply insures that all perspectives will be represented, that the readers are asked to advocate for our own points of view in the same ways that the students are asked to do.

In other words, without our quite being aware of it, we've created a lab where we can learn about our work and the context where it takes place: what it means to teach writing, both inside the writing class and beyond; what it means when we say reflection; what we actually do when we read; what kind of response we might make to a student; what goes into a program and why; and how to work together in an electronic context. Like portfolios, this lab is messy, with borders that are permeated by other borders, with more questions than answers, with potential not fully realized, nor, I think, quite understood yet.

As important, I think, are the processes involved in Portnet. What we have shared here of it is in its way a vignette, a very small tableaux of what it feels like to read together, to compare notes about portfolios and writing and reading and teaching and values and discourse, and then to write together. In the process, as Cheryl noted, we can find ourselves surprised at how wrongheaded some of our colleagues on Portnet are, and then surprised at our own wrongheadedness. In sum, our community is informed by difference as much as by consensus, and given who we are, that's no surprise, really, either. Some of us teach at elite institutions where students arrive with high SATs if not financial legacies; others of us teach at open admission schools. Some of us believe passionately in the value of external assessment and its power to enhance teaching; others would just as soon slay the assessment dragon. Some of us find email easily the equal (and in some cases the superior) of real life; others see it as a pale and inadequate reflection of face-to-face interaction. It is through explaining, exploring, and defending these differences—more than through agreeing, perhaps—that we learn.

And we continue to explore, believing too, that it is in the exploration as much as in what is found we—and our students—learn.

Works Cited

Apple Computer, Inc. 1990. *Global Warming*. Computer software. Sacramento, CA: Econet.

Applebee, Arthur. 1986. Problems in Process Approaches: Toward a Reconceptualization of Process Instruction. *The Teaching of Writing (85th Yearbook of the National Society for the Study of Education, Part II)*, ed. Anthony Petrosky and David Bartholomae. Chicago: University of Chicago Press: 95-113.

———. 1993. *Literature in the Secondary School: Studies of Curriculum and Instruction in the United States*. Urbana, IL: NCTE

ASCD (Association for Supervision and Curriculum Development). 1992. *Redesigning Assessment: Portfolios*. Videocassette. Alexandria, VA.

Atwell, Nancie. 1987. *In the Middle: Writing, Reading, and Learning with Adolescents*. Portsmouth, NH: Heinemann-Boynton/Cook.

Baker, Nancy W. 1993. The Effects of Portfolio-Based Instruction on Composition Students' Final Examination Scores, Course Grades, and Attitudes toward Writing. *Research in the Teaching of English* 27: 155-174.

Barker, Thomas T. and Fred O. Kemp. 1990. Network Theory: A Postmodern Pedagogy for the Writing Classroom. *Computers and Community*, ed. Carolyn Handa. Portsmouth, NH: Boynton/Cook: 1-27.

Barrett, Edward, ed. 1988. *Text, Context, and HyperText: Writing with and for the Computer.* Cambridge, MA: MIT Press.

———, ed. 1989. *The Society of Text: Hypertext, Hypermedia and the Social Construction of Information.* Cambridge, MA: MIT Press.

———, ed. 1992. *Sociomedia: Multimedia, Hypermedia, and the Social Construction of Knowledge.* Cambridge, MA: MIT Presss.

Batson, Trent. 1988. The ENFI Project: A Networked Classroom Approach to Writing Instruction. *Academic Computing*: 32-33.

Belanoff, Pat. 1994. Portfolios and Literacy: Why? *New Directions in Portfolio Assessment: Reflective Practice, Critical Theory, and Large-scale Scoring*, ed. Laurel Black, Donald A. Daiker, Jeffrey Sommers, and Gail Stygall. Portsmouth, NH: Boynton/Cook, Heinemann: 13-24.

———, and Marcia Dickson, ed. 1991. *Portfolios: Process and Product.* Portsmouth, NH: Boynton/Cook.

———, and Peter Elbow. 1991. Using Portfolios to Increase Collaboration and Community in a Writing Program. *Writing Program Administration* 9.3 (Spring 1986): 27-40. Rpt. in *Portfolios: Process and Product*, ed. Pat Belanoff and Marcia Dickson. Portsmouth NH: Heinemann, Boynton/Cook.

Bergamini, Jan. 1993. An English Department Portfolio Project. *Teachers' Voices: Portfolios in the Classroom*, ed. Mary Ann Smith and Miriam Ylvisaker. Berkeley: National Writing Project: 145-159.

Berlak, Howard. 1992. Toward the Development of a New Science of Educational Testing and Assessment. *Toward a New Science of Educational Testing and Assessment*, ed. Howard Berlak et al. Albany, NY: SUNY Press.

Berlin, James. 1987. *Rhetoric and Reality: Writing Instruction in American Colleges, 1900-1985*. Carbondale, IL: Southern Illinois University Press.

———. 1994. The Subversions of the Portfolio. *New Directions in Portfolio Assessment: Reflective Practice, Critical Theory, and Large-scale Scoring*, ed. Laurel Black, Donald A. Daiker, Jeffrey Sommers, and Gail Stygall. Portsmouth, NH: Boynton/Cook, Heinemann: 56-67.

Bernhardt, Stephen A. 1993. The Shape of Text To Come: The Texture of Print On Screens. *College Composition and Communication* 44: 151–175.

Bishop, Wendy. 1991. Going up the Creek without a Canoe: Using Portfolios to Train New Teachers of College Writing. *Portfolios: Process and Product*, ed. Pat Belanoff and Marcia Dickson. Portsmouth, NH: Boynton/Cook, Heinemann: 215-227.

———. 1992. *Working Words*. London: Mayfield.

Bissex, Glenda L. 1985. Watching Young Writers. *Observing the Language Learner*, ed. A. Jagger and M. Trika Smith-Burke. Newark, DE.

Black, Laurel, Donald A. Daiker, Jeffrey Sommers, and Gail Stygall, eds. 1994a. *New Directions in Portfolio Assessment: Reflective Practice, Critical Theory, and Large-Scale Scoring*. Portsmouth, NH: Boynton/Cook, Heinemann.

———. 1994b. Writing Like a Woman and Being Rewarded for It: Gender, Assessment, and Reflective Letters from Miami University's Student Portfolios. *New Directions in Portfolio Assessment: Reflective Practice, Critical Theory, and Large-scale Scoring*, ed. Laurel Black, Donald A. Daiker, Jeffrey Sommers, and Gail Stygall. Portsmouth, NH: Boynton/Cook, Heinemann: 235–248.

Blanton, William E., Max S. Thompson, and Sara O. Zimmerman. 1993. The Application of Technologies to Student Teaching. *The Arachnet Electronic Journal on Virtual Culture* 1.

Bolter, Jay David. 1990. *Writing Space: The Computer in the History of Literacy*. Hillsdale, NJ: Lawrence Erlbaum.

———. 1991. *The Computer, Hypertext, and the History of Writing*. Hillsdale, NJ: Lawrence Erlbaum.

———. 1992. Literature in the Electronic Writing Space. *Literacy Online: The Promise (and Peril) of Reading and Writing With Computers*, ed. Myron C. Tuman. Pittsburgh: University of Pittsburgh Press: 19–42.

Boomer, Garth, ed. 1982. *Negotiating the Curriculum: A Teacher-Student Partnership*. Sydney: Ashton-Scholastic.

Bowden, Darsie. 1993. The Limits of Containment: Text-as-container in Composition Studies. *College Composition and Communication* 44: 364–379.

Brandts, Lois. 1993. A First Grade Perspective. *Teachers' Voices: Portfolios in the Classroom*, ed. Mary Ann Smith and Miriam Ylvisaker. Berkeley: National Writing Project: 108-109, 115.

Britton, James N., T. Burgess, N. Martin, A. McLeod, and H. Rosen. 1975. *The Development of Writing Abilities (11-18)*. London: Macmillan Education Ltd.

Broad, Robert. 1994. 'Portfolio Scoring': A Contradiction in Terms. *New Directions in Portfolio Assessment: Reflective Practice, Critical Theory, and Large-scale Scoring*, ed. Laurel Black, Donald A. Daiker, Jeffrey Sommers, and Gail Stygall. Portsmouth, NH: Boynton/Cook, Heinemann: 263-76.

Bryk, A.S., and Hermanson, K.M. 1993. Educational Indicator Systems: Observations on Their Structure, Interpretation, and Use. *Review of Research in Education* 19: 451-484.

Burke, Kenneth. 1945. *Grammar of Motives*. Berkeley: University of California Press.

Burnham, Chris. 1986. Portfolio Evaluation: Room to Breathe and Grow. *Training the New Teacher of College Composition*, ed. Charles W. Bridges. Urbana, IL: NCTE: 125-138.

Calfee, Robert, and Elfrieda Hiebert. 1987. The Teacher's Role in Using Assessment to Improve Learning. *Assessment in the Service of Learning*, ed. Eileen E. Freeman. Princeton, NJ: Educational Testing Service: 45-63.

Calkins, Lucy McCormick. 1983. *Lessons From A Child: On the Teaching and Learning of Writing*. Portsmouth, NH: Heinemann Educational Books.

Callahan, Susan. 1994. "Trying to Dance in the Glass Slipper: Portfolios and Accountability." Paper presented at the Conference on College Composition and Communication. Nashville, TN.

———. 1995. Portfolio Expectations: Possibilities and Limits. *Assessing Writing* 2: 117-152.

Camp, Roberta. 1985. The Writing Folder in Post-Secondary Assessment. *Directions and Misdirections in English Education*, ed. Peter J. A. Evans. Ottawa, Canada: Canadian Council of Teachers of English.

———.1992. Portfolio Reflections in Middle and Secondary School Classrooms. *Portfolios in the Writing Classroom: An Introduction*, ed. Kathleen Blake Yancey. Urbana, IL: NCTE: 61-79.

———. 1993a. Changing the Model for the Direct Assessment of Writing. *Validating Holistic Scoring for Writing Assessment: Theoretical and Empirical Foundations*, ed.Michael M. Williamson and Brian Huot. Cresskill, NJ: Hampton.

———. 1993b. The Place of Portfolios in Our Changing Views of Writing Assessment. *Construction Versus Choice in Cognitive Measurement: Issues in Constructed Response, Performance Testing, and Portfolio Assessment*, ed. R. E. Bennett and W. C. Ward. Hillsdale, NJ: Lawrence Erlbaum: 183-212.

Chancer, Joni. 1993. The Teacher's Role in Portfolio Assessment. *Teachers' Voices: Portfolios in the Classroom*, ed. Mary Ann Smith and Miriam Ylvisaker. Berkeley: National Writing Project: 41-42.

Charney, Davida. 1994. The Effect of Hypertext on Processes of Reading and Writing. *Literacy and Computers: The Complications of Teaching and Learning with Technology*, ed. Cynthia L. Selfe and Susan Hilligoss. New York: MLA: 238-263.

Cherry, Roger, and Paul Meyer. 1993. Reliability Issues in Holistic Assessment. *Validating Holistic Scoring for Writing Assessment: Theoretical and Empirical Foundations*, ed. Michael M. Williamson and Brian Huot. Cresskill, NJ: Hampton.

CLAS (California Learning Assessment System). 1994. Dimensions of Learning.

Clay, Marie M. 1966. Emergent Reading Behavior. Diss. University of Auckland.

———. 1972. *Reading: The Patterning of Complex Behavior*. Auckland, NZ: Heinemann Educational Books.

———. 1975. *What Did I Write?* Auckland, NZ: Heinemann Educational Books.

———. 1985. *The Early Detection of Reading Difficulties: A Diagnostic Survey with Recovery Procedures*. 3rd ed. Auckland, NZ: Heinemann.

Clift, Renee. 1991. Learning To Teach English—Maybe: A Study of Knowledge Development. *Journal of Teacher Education* 42.5: 357-372.

Cochran-Smith, Marilyn. 1991. Learning to Teach Against the Grain. *Harvard Educational Review* 61: 279-310.

Condon, William, and Liz Hamp-Lyons. 1994. Maintaining a Portfolio-Based Writing Assessment: Research That Informs Program Development. *New Directions in Portfolio Assessment: Reflective Practice, Critical Theory, and Large-scale Scoring*, ed. Laurel Black,

Donald A. Daiker, Jeffrey Sommers, and Gail Stygall. Portsmouth, NH: Boynton/Cook, Heinemann: 277-285.

Conway, Glenda. 1994. Portfolio Cover Letters, Students' Self-Representation, and Teachers' Ethics. *New Directions in Portfolio Assessment: Reflective Practice, Critical Theory, and Large-scale Scoring*, ed. Laurel Black, Donald A. Daiker, Jeffrey Sommers, and Gail Stygall. Portsmouth, NH: Boynton/Cook, Heinemann: 83-92.

Cooper, Marilyn M., and Cynthia L. Selfe. 1990. Computer Conferences and Learning: Authority, Resistance, and Internally Persuasive Discourse. *College English* 52.8: 847-869.

Coover, Robert. 1992. The End of Books. *New York Times Book Review* 21: 1, 23-25.

———. 1993. Hyperfiction: Novels for the Computer. *New York Times Book Review* 29 A: 1, 8-12.

Corbett, H. Dickson, and Bruce L. Wilson. 1991. *Testing, Reform, and Rebellion.* Norwood, NJ: Ablex.

Cronbach, Lee J. 1989. Five Perspectives on Validity Argument. *Test Validity*, ed. Harold Wainer. Hillside, NJ: Lawrence Erlbaum.

Csikszentmihalyi, Mihaly. 1990. *Flow: The Psychology of Optimal Experience.* New York: Harper and Row.

———, and Reed Larson. 1984. *Being Adolescent: Conflict and Growth in the Teenage Years.* New York: Basic Books.

———, Kevin Rathunde, Samuel Whalen, with contributions by Maria Wong. 1993. *Talented Teenagers: The Roots of Success and Failure.* Cambridge, UK: Cambridge University Press.

Culp, George H., and G. Morgan Watkins. 1993. *The Educator's Guide to HyperCard and HyperTalk.* Boston: Allyn and Bacon.

Darling-Hammond, Linda. 1989. Accountability for Professional Practice. *Teacher's College Record* 91: 59-80.

———. 1990. Instructional Policy into Practice: The Power of the Bottom Over the Top. *Educational Evaluation and Policy Analysis* 12.3: 339-347.

———, and Jon Snyder. 1992. Reframing Accountability: Creating Learner-Centered Schools. *The Changing Contexts of Teaching (Ninety-first Yearbook of the National Society for the Study of Education)*, ed. Ann Lieberman. Chicago: University of Chicago Press: 11-36.

———, and Jacqueline Ancess. 1994. *Graduation by Portfolio at Central Park East Secondary School.* New York: National Center for Restructuring Education, Schools and Teaching: 7-8.

Decker, Emily, George Cooper, and Susanmarie Harrington. 1992. Crossing Institutional Boundaries: Developing an Entrance Portfolio Assessment to Improve Writing Instruction. *Journal of Teaching Writing* 12.1: 83-104.

Deen, Mary Kay. 1993. Portfolios as Discovery. *Teachers' Voices: Portfolios in the Classroom*, ed. Mary Ann Smith and Miriam Ylvisaker. Berkeley: National Writing Project: 52, 57-58.

Delany, Paul, and George P. Landow. 1991. *Hypermedia and Literary Studies.* Cambridge, MA: MIT Press.

Despain, LaRene, and Thomas L. Hilgers. 1992. Readers' Responses to the Rating of Non-Uniform Portfolios: Are There Limits of Portfolios' Utility? *Writing Program Administration* 16.1-2 (Fall/Winter): 24-37.

Dewey, John. 1963. *Experience and Education.* New York: Collier Books.

DiPardo, Anne, and Mike Dipardo. 1990. Towards the Metapersonal Essay: Exploring the Potential of Hypertext in the Composition Class. *Computers and Composition* 7.3: 7-22.

Dixon, John. 1975. *Growth Through English.* 3rd ed. London: Oxford University Press.

Dobrin, David N. 1994. Hype and Hypertext. *Literacy and Computers: The Complications of Teaching and Learning with Technology*, ed. Cynthia L. Selfe and Susan Hilligoss. New York: MLA: 305–315.

Door-Bremme, D., and J. Herman. 1986. *Assessing Student Achievement: A Profile of Classroom Practices*. Los Angeles, CA: Center for the Study of Evaluation.

Douglas, J. Yellowlees. 1992. What Hypertexts Can Do that Print Texts Cannot. *Reader* 28: 1–22.

Dryden, L. M. 1994. Literature, Student-Centered Classrooms, and Hypermedia Environments. *Literacy and Computers: The Complications of Teaching and Learning with Technology*, ed. Cynthia L. Selfe and Susan Hilligoss. New York: MLA: 282–304.

Edgerton, Russell, Pat Hutchings, and Kathleen Quinlan. 1991. *The Teaching Portfolio: Capturing the Scholarship in Teaching*. Washington, DC: American Association of Higher Education.

Elbow, Peter. 1994. Will the Virtues of Portfolios Blind Us to Their Potential Dangers? *New Directions in Portfolio Assessment: Reflective Practice, Critical Theory, and Large-scale Scoring*, ed. Laurel Black, Donald A. Daiker, Jeffrey Sommers, and Gail Stygall. Portsmouth, NH: Boynton/Cook, Heinemann: 40-55.

———. 1996. Writing Assessment in the Twenty-first Century: A Utopian View. *Composition in the 21st Century: Crisis and Change*, ed. Lynn Z. Bloom, Donald A. Daiker, and Edward M. White. Carbondale, IL: Southern Illinois University Press: 83-100.

———, and Pat Belanoff. 1991. SUNY: Portfolio-Based Evaluation Program. *New Methods in College Writing Programs: Theory into Practice*, ed. Paul Connolly and Teresa Vilardi. NY: MLA, 1986. Rpt. in *Portfolios: Process and Product*, ed. Pat Belanoff and Marcia Dickson. Portsmouth NH: Heinemann, Boynton/Cook: 3-16.

———, and Kathleen Blake Yancey. 1994. On the Nature of Holistic Scoring: An Inquiry Composed on Email. *Assessing Writing* 1: 91-108.

Eldred, Janet. 1989. Computers, Composition, and the Social View. *Critical Perspectives on Computers and Composition Studies*, ed. Gail E. Hawisher and Cynthia L. Selfe. New York: Teachers College Press: 201-218.

———, and Ron Fortune. 1992. Exploring the Implications of Metaphors for Computer Networks and Hypermedia. *Re-imagining Computers and Composition: Teaching and Research in the Virtual Age*, ed. Gail Hawisher and Paul LeBlanc. Portsmouth, NH: Boynton/Cook: 58-73.

Emig, Janet. 1983. *The Web of Meaning: Essays on Writing, Teaching, Learning, and Thinking*, ed. Dixie Goswami and Maureen Butler. Upper Montclair, NJ: Boynton/Cook Publishers.

Fader, Daniel. 1986. Writing Samples and Virtues. *Writing Assessment: Issues and Strategies*, ed. Karen L. Greenberg, Harvey S. Weiner, and Richard A. Donovan. New York: Longman.

Faigley, Lester. 1989. Judging Writing, Judging Selves. *College Composition and Communication* 40: 395-412.

Feiman-Nemser, S., and M. Buchman. 1985. Pitfalls of Experience in Teacher Education. *Teachers College Record* 87: 53-65.

Fajans, Elizabeth, and Mary Falk. 1993. Against the Tyranny of Paraphrase: Talking Back to Texts. *Cornell Law Review* 78: 163-205.

Falk, C.J. 1985. English Skills Tutorials for Sentence Combining Practice. *Computers and Composition.* 2.4: 2-4.

Ferreiro, E. 1984. The Underlying Logic of Literacy Development. *Awakening to Literacy*, ed. H. Goelman, A. A. Oberg, and F. Smith. Portsmouth, NH: Heinemann.

Flower, Linda, John R. Hayes, Linda Carey, Karen Shriver, and James Stratman. 1986.

Detection, Diagnosis, and the Strategies of Revision. *College Composition and Communication* 37: 16–55.

Forman, Janis. 1992. *New Visions of Collaborative Writing*. Portsmouth, NH: Boynton/Cook, Heinemann.

Forester, Tom. 1989. *High Tech Society: The Story of the Information Technology Revolution*. Cambridge, MA: MIT Press.

Foster, Jack D. 1991. The Role of Accountability in Kentucky's Education Reform Act of 1990. *Educational Leadership* 48.5: 34-36.

Foster, Teree E. 1993. But Is It *Law*? Using Literature to Penetrate Societal Representations of Women. *Journal of Legal Education* 43: 133-148.

Foucault, Michel. 1977. *Discipline and Punish*. NY: Vintage Books.

The Foxfire Approach: Perspectives and Core Practices. *Hands On: A Journal for Teachers* (Spring): 3-4.

Frazier, D. M., & Paulson, F. L. 1992. How Portfolios Motivate Reluctant Writers. *Educational Leadership* 49.8: 62-65.

Frederiksen, Norman. 1984. The Real Test Bias. *American Psychologist*: 193-202.

Gallehr, D.R. 1993. Portfolio Assessment in the College Writing Classroom. *Process and Portfolios in Writing Instruction*, ed. Kendall Gill. Urbana, IL: NCTE.

Gemmette, Elizabeth Villiers. 1989. Law and Literature: An Unnecessarily Suspect Class in the Liberal Arts Component of the Law School Curriculum. *Valparaiso University Law Review* 23: 267-340.

Gentry, J. Richard. 1981. Learning to Spell Developmentally. *The Reading Teacher* 34: 378-381.

Gere, Anne Ruggles. 1987. *Writing Groups: History, Theory, and Implications*. Carbondale, IL: Southern Illinois University Press.

———, Deborah Williams Minter, and Deborah Keller-Cohen. 1995. Learning Literacies. *College English* 57: 669-687.

Giroux, Henry A. 1989. *Teachers as Intellectuals: Toward a Critical Pedagogy of Learning*. Granby, MA: Bergin & Garvey.

Goldberg, Natalie. 1986. *Writing Down the Bones*. Boston: Shambhala.

Goldenberg, Claude. 1995. (Re-)Constructing Constructivism. *CAIP Quarterly* 7.2: 3.

Golub, Jeff, ed. 1988. *Focus on Collaborative Learning: Classroom Practices in Teaching English*. Urbana, IL: NCTE.

Gomez, Mary Louise. 1991. The Equitable Teaching of Composition. *Evolving Perspectives on Computers and Composition Studies: Questions for the 1990s*, ed. Gail E. Hawisher and Cynthia L. Selfe. Urbana, IL: NCTE: 318-335.

Gomez, Mary Louise, M. Elizabeth Graue, and Marianne N. Bloch. 1991 Reassessing Portfolio Assessment: Rhetoric and Reality. *Language Arts* 68: 620-628.

Goodman, J. 1985. What Students Learn From Early Field Experiences: A Case Study And Critical Analysis. *Journal of Teacher Education* 36: 42-48.

Goodman, Yetta. 1984. The Development of Initial Literacy. *Awakening to Literacy*, ed. H. Goelman, A. A. Oberg, and F. Smith. Portsmouth, NH: Heinemann.

Goswami, Dixie, and Peter R. Stillman, eds. 1987. *Reclaiming the Classroom: Teacher Research as an Agency for Change*. Portsmouth, NH: Boynton/Cook.

Graff, Gerald. 1987. *Professing Literature: An Institutional History*. Chicago: University of Chicago Press.

Graves, Donald H. 1992. Help Students Learn to Read Their Portfolios. *Portfolio Portraits*, ed. Donald H. Graves and Bonnie S. Sunstein. Portsmouth, NH: Heinemann.

———. 1994. *A Fresh Look at Writing*. Portsmouth, NH: Heinemann.

———, and Sunstein, Bonnie, eds. 1992. *Portfolio Portraits*. Portsmouth NH: Heinemann.

Greenblatt, Stephen. 1985. Shakespeare and the Exorcists. *After Strange Texts: The Role of Theory in the Study of Literature*, ed. Gregory S. Jay and David L. Miller. University, AL: University of Alabama Press: 101-123.

———. 1988. *Shakespearean Negotiations: The Circulation of Social Energy in Renaissance England.* Berkeley: University of California Press.

Guba, Egon, and Yvonna Lincoln. 1989. *Fourth Generation Evaluation.* Newbury Park, CA: Sage.

Grumbach, Doris. 1994. *Fifty Days of Solitude.* Boston: Beacon.

Haertel, Edward, and Robert C. Calfee. 1983. School Achievement: Thinking About What to Test. *Journal of Educational Measurement* 20:119-132.

Hain, Bonnie. 1991. Portfolios and the M.A. in English. *Portfolios: Process and Product*, ed. Pat Belanoff and Marcia Dickson. Portsmouth NH: Boynton/Cook: 93-98.

Hamp-Lyons, Liz and William Condon. 1993. Questioning Assumptions about Portfolio-Based Assessment. *College Composition and Communication* 44: 176-190.

Harrison, Susan. 1995. Portfolios Across the Curriculum. *Writing Program Administration* 19 (Fall/Winter): 38-49.

Hawisher, Gail, and Cynthia L. Selfe. 1991a. Introduction to Part Three. *Evolving Perspectives on Computers and Composition Studies: Questions for the 1990s*, ed. Gail E. Hawisher and Cynthia L. Selfe. Urbana, IL: NCTE 173–175.

———, and Cynthia L. Selfe. 1991b The Rhetoric of Technology and the Electronic Writing Class. *College Composition and Communication.* 42: 55-65.

———, and Cynthia L. Selfe. 1993. Tradition and Change in Computer-Supported Writing Environments: A Call for Action. *Theoretical and Critical Perspectives on Teacher Change*, ed. Phyllis Kahaney, Joseph Janangelo, and Linda A. M. Perry. Norwood, NJ: Ablex: 155-186.

———, and Paul LeBlanc, eds. 1992. *Re-Imagining Computers and Composition: Teaching and Research in the Virtual Age.* Portsmouth, NH: Boynton/Cook.

———, and Patricia Sullivan. Forthcoming. Women on the Networks: Searching for Presence in Online Discussions. *Feminism and Composition*, ed. Lynn Worsham and Susan Jarratt. New York: MLA.

Hayakawa, S. I. 1962. Learning to Think and to Write: Semantics in Freshman English. *College Composition and Communication* 13: 5-8.

Heiges, J. M. 1994. "Replacing a Doctoral Candidacy Examination with a Portfolio: The Trade-offs." NCTE Portfolios, Reflection, and Teacher Research Conference. Baltimore.

Heiges, J. M. 1992. "Should Portfolio Assessment Be Used in Graduate Education?" Paper presented at New Directions in Portfolio Assessment Conference. Miami University, Oxford, OH.

Heilker, Paul. 1992. Revision Worship and the Computer as Audience. *Computers and Composition.* 9.3: 59-69.

Hewitt, Geof. 1995. *A Portfolio Primer.* Portsmouth, NH: Heinemann.

Holdstein, Deborah. 1983. The WRITEWELL Series. *Computers and Composition* 1: 7.

Holdstein, Deborah H., and Cynthia L. Selfe, eds. 1990. *Computers and Writing: Theory, Research, Practice.* New York: MLA.

Hollingsworth, Sandra. 1989. Prior Beliefs and Cognitive Change in Learning To Teach. *American Educational Research Journal* 26.2: 160-189.

Howard, Kathryn. 1993. Portfolio Culture in Pittsburgh. *Fire in the Eyes of Youth*, ed. Randolph Jennings. St. Paul: Occasional Press: 89-102.

Howard, Rebecca. (1994, February 14). Online Portfolios [email to Gail E. Hawisher], [Online]. Available email: HAWISHER@UIUC.EDU.

Huot, Brian. 1994. A Survey of College and University Placement Practices. *Writing Program*

Administration 17: 49-67.

Huling-Austin, L. 1986. What Can and Cannot Reasonably Be Expected From Teacher Induction Programs. *Journal of Teacher Education* 7.1: 2-5.

Jamentz, Catherine. 1994. Will Performance Assessment Improve Student Performance? *California Curriculum News Report* 19.3: 1,7.

Jessup, Emily. 1991. Feminism and Computers in Composition Instruction. *Evolving Perspectives on Computers and Composition Studies: Questions for the 1990s*, ed. Gail E. Hawisher and Cynthia L. Selfe. Urbana, IL: NCTE: 336-355.

Jobst, Jack. 1984. Computer-Assisted Grading of Essays and Reports. *Computers and Composition* 1.2: 5.

Johnson-Eilola, Johndan. 1992. Review Essay. Structure and Space: *Writing Space* and StorySpace. *Computers and Composition* 9.2: 95–129.

———. 1994. Reading and Writing in Hypertext: Vertigo and Euphoria. *Literacy and Computers: The Complications of Teaching and Learning with Technology*, ed. Cynthia L. Selfe and Susan Hilligoss. New York: MLA.: 195–219.

Johnston, Peter. 1989. Constructive Evaluation and the Improvement of Teaching and Learning. *Teachers College Record* 90: 509-528.

Joyce, Michael. 1988. Siren Shapes: Exploratory and Constructive Hypertexts. *Academic Computing* 3.4: 10-42.

Juska, Jane. 1993. No More One-Shots. *Teachers' Voices: Portfolios in the Classroom*, ed. Mary Ann Smith and Miriam Ylvisaker. Berkeley: National Writing Project: 63-64.

Kaplan, Nancy and Stuart Moulthrop. 1990. Other Ways of Seeing. *Computers and Composition* 7.3: 89-102.

Kentucky Office of Management Information Services. *Profiles of Kentucky Public Schools*, Fiscal Year l991-1992. Frankfort, KY: Kentucky Department of Education.

Kirby, Dan, and Carol Kuykendall. 1991. *Mind Matters: Teaching for Thinking*. Portsmouth, NH: Boynton/Cook.

Kneeshaw, David. 1992. Writing Portfolios in Secondary Schools. *Portfolios in the Writing Classroom: An Introduction*, ed. Kathleen Blake Yancey. Urbana, IL: NCTE: 80-89.

Knoblauch, C.H., and Lil Brannon. 1984. *Rhetorical Traditions and the Teaching of Writing*. Upper Montclair, NJ: Boynton/Cook.

Koretz, Daniel. 1992. *The Vermont Portfolio Assessment Program: Interim Report on Implementation and Impact*. Santa Monica, CA: Rand Institute on Education and Training, National Center for Research on Evaluation, Standards and Student Testing.

———. 1994. *The Vermont Portfolio Assessment Program: Findings and Implications*. Washington, DC: RAND.

———, Richard L. Linn, Susan B. Dunbar, and Lorrie A. Shepard. 1991. "The Effects of High Stakes Testing on Achievement: Preliminary Findings About Generalization Across Tests." Paper presented at the Annual Meeting of the American Educational Research Association. Chicago.

Koretz, Daniel M., B. Stecher, and E. Deibert. 1993. The Reliability of Scores from the 1992 Vermont Portfolio Assessment Program (Technical Report No. 355). Los Angeles: University of California, Center for the Study of Evaluation.

Kramarae, Cheris, ed. 1988. *Technology and Women's Voices: Keeping in Touch*. New York: Routledge & Kegan Paul.

Kremers, Marshall. 1988. Adams Sherman Hill Meets ENFI: An Inquiry and a Retrospective. *Computers and Composition* 5.3: 69-77.

Kunz, Chris, Edwin R. Hazen, Steven J. Jamar, and Mauree J. Arrigo. 1993. Collaboration. *The Second Draft: Bulletin of the Legal Writing Institute* 8.2: 6-7.

Landow, George P. 1992a. Hypertext, Metatext, and the Electronic Canon. *Literacy Online:*

The Promise (and Peril) of Reading and Writing With Computers, ed. Myron C. Tuman. Pittsburgh: University of Pittsburgh Press: 67–94.

———. 1992b. *Hypertext: The Convergence of Contemporary Critical Theory and Technology.* Baltimore: Johns Hopkins University Press.

———, and Paul Delany. 1993. *The Digital Word: Text-Based Computing in the Humanities.* Cambridge, MA: MIT Press.

Lange, David. 1992. At Play in the Fields of the Word: Copyright and the Construction of Authorship in the Post-Literate Millennium. *Law and Contemporary Problems* 55.2: 139-151.

LeBlanc, Paul J. 1990. Competing Ideologies in Software Design for Computer-Aided Composition. *Computers and Composition* 7.2: 8-19.

———. 1994. The Politics of Literacy and Technology in Secondary School Classrooms. *Literacy and Computers: The Complications of Teaching and Learning with Technology*, ed. Cynthia L. Selfe and Susan Hilligoss. New York: MLA.

LeClercq, Terri. 1993. I Use Them! Law School Portfolios. *Newsletter of the Association of American Law Schools Section on Legal Writing, Reasoning, and Research* 93: 3.

Little, Judith Warren. 1993. Teachers' Professional Development in a Climate of Educational Reform. *Educational Evaluation and Policy Analysis* 15.2: 129-151.

Linn, Robert L. 1994. Performance Assessment: Policy Promises and Technical Measurement Standards. *Educational Researcher* 23.9: 4-14.

Lovett, Carl, and Art Young. 1994. Portfolios in the Disciplines: Sharing Knowledge in the Contact Zone. *New Directions in Portfolio Assessment: Reflective Practice, Critical Theory, and Large-scale Scoring*, ed. Laurel Black, Donald A. Daiker, Jeffrey Sommers, and Gail Stygall. Portsmouth, NH: Boynton/Cook, Heinemann: 334-346.

Lucas, Catharine. 1988. Toward Ecological Evaluation. *The Quarterly of the National Writing Project and the Center for the Study of Writing* 10.1: 1-17.

———. 1992. Introduction: Writing Portfolios–Changes and Challenges. *Portfolios in the Writing Classroom: An Introduction*, ed. Kathleen Blake Yancey. Urbana, Illinois: NCTE: 1-11.

Macrorie, Ken. 1991. The Freewriting Relationship. *Nothing Begins with N: New Investigations of Freewriting*, ed. Pat Belanoff, Peter Elbow, and Sheryl Fontaine. Carbondale: Southern Illinois University Press: 173-88.

Madaus, George. 1988. The Influence of Testing on the Curriculum. *Critical Issues in Curriculum (87th Yearbook of the National Society for the Study of Education, Part I)*, ed. L. Tanner. Chicago: University of Chicago Press: 83-121.

Markel, Mike. 1994. Behaviors, Attitudes, and Outcomes: A Study of Word Processing and Writing Quality among Experienced Word-Processing Students. *Computers and Composition* 11.1: 49-58.

Marling, William. 1984. Grading Essays on a Microcomputer. *College English* 46: 797-810.

Martin, Megan. 1994. Research Results Say YES! to Portfolios in Science: California's Golden State Examinations. *California Curriculum News Report* 19.3: 4.

Martin, Megan, George Miller, and Jane Delgado. 1993. Preliminary Research Results of Portfolio Assessment: California's Golden State Examinations in Science. *Research Report.* California Learning Assessment System. Sacramento, CA.

Marx, G. T., and S. Sherizen. 1989. Monitoring on the Job. *Computers in the Human Context: Information Technology, Productivity, and People*, ed. T. Forester. Cambridge, MA: MIT Press: 397-406.

Mason, J. 1984. Early Reading from a Developmental Perspective. *Handbook of Reading Research*, ed. P. D. Pearson. New York: Longman.

Mayers, Tim. 1996. From Page to Screen (and Back): Portfolios, Daedalus, and the

"Transitional Classroom." *Computers and Composition*, Special Issue on Electronic Portfolios: 47-55.

Mayher, John S. 1990. *Uncommon Sense: Theoretical Practice in Language Education.* Portsmouth, NH: Heinemann/Boynton/Cook.

McClelland. D. C. 1973. Testing for Competence Rather Than for Intelligence. *American Psychologist* 28: 1-14.

McDaid, John. 1991. Toward an Ecology of Hypermedia. *Evolving Perspectives on Computers and Composition Studies: Questions for the 1990s*, ed. Gail E. Hawisher and Cynthia L. Selfe. Urbana, IL: NCTE: 203-223.

McDonnell, Loraine. 1994. Assessment Policy as Persuasion and Regulation. *American Journal of Education* 102: 394-413.

Mcknight, Cliff, Andrew Dillon, and John Richardson. 1991. *Hypertext in Context.* Cambridge: Cambridge University Press.

McNeil, L. M. 1988. Contradictions of Control, Part 3: Contradictions of Reform. *Phi Delta Kappan* 69: 478-485.

Messick, Samuel. 1989. Meaning and Values in Test Validation: The Science and Ethics of Assessment. *Educational Researcher* 18.2: 5-11.

———. 1994. The Interplay of Evidence and Consequences in the Validation of Performance Assessments. *Educational Researcher* 23.2: 13-23.

Metzger, Elizabeth, and Lizbeth Bryant. 1993. Portfolio Assessment: Pedagogy, Power, and the Student. *Teaching English in the Two-Year College* 20: 279-288.

Miller, Susan, ed. 1989. *The Written World: Reading and Writing in Social Contexts.* New York: Harper and Row.

Mishler, Elliot G. 1979. Meaning in Context: Is There Any Other Kind? *Harvard Educational Review,* 49.1: 1-19.

Mitchell, Ruth. 1992. *Testing for Learning: How New Approaches to Evaluation Can Improve American Schools.* New York: Macmillan.

Moffett, James. 1968a. *A Student Centered Language Arts Curriculum: Grades K-13.* Boston: Houghton Mifflin.

———. 1968b. *Teaching the Universe of Discourse.* Boston: Houghton-Mifflin.

———. 1991. *Active Voice: A Writing Program Across the Curriculum.* Upper Montclair, NJ: Boynton/Cook.

———. 1992. *Detecting Growth in Language.* Portsmouth, NH: Boynton/Cook.

Morris, Barbra S. 1983. The English Composition Board at the University of Michigan. *Literacy for Life: The Demand for Reading and Writing*, ed. Richard W. Bailey and Robin Melanie Fosheim. New York: MLA.

Morrow, Leslie Mandel. 1989. *Literacy Development in the Early Years.* Englewood Cliffs, NJ: Prentice Hall.

Moss, Pamela A. 1992. Shifting Conceptions of Validity in Educational Measurement: Implications for Performance Assessment. *Review of Educational Research* 62: 229-258.

———. 1994a. Can There be Validity Without Reliability? *Educational Researcher* 23.2: 5-12.

———. 1994b. Validity in High Stakes Writing Assessment: Problems and Possibilities. *Assessing Writing* 1: 109-128.

Moulthrop, Stuart. *1991.* The Politics of Hypertext. *Evolving Perspectives on Computers and Composition Studies: Questions for the 1990s*, ed. Gail Hawisher and Cynthia Selfe. Urbana, IL: NCTE: 253-271.

Moulthrop, Stuart, and Nancy Kaplan. 1991. Something to Imagine: Literature, Composition, and Interactive Fiction. *Computers and Composition* 9.1: 7-23.

———. 1994. They Became What They Beheld: The Futility of Resistance in the Space of

Electronic Writing. *Literacy and Computers: The Complications of Teaching and Learning with Technology*, ed. Cynthia L. Selfe and Susan Hilligoss. New York: MLA: 220–237.

Murphy, Sandra. 1994a. "Portfolio Networks: Linking Assessments at Local, State, and National Levels." Paper presented at NCTE Convention, Orlando, FL.

———. 1994b. Portfolios and Curriculum Reform: Patterns in Practice. *Assessing Writing* 1.2: 175-206.

———, and Mary Ann Smith. 1990. Talking about Portfolios. *The Quarterly of the National Writing Project and Center for the Study of Writing* 12 (1990): 1-3; 24-27.

———. 1991. *Writing Portfolios: A Bridge from Teaching to Assessment.* Ontario, Canada: Pippin.

———. 1992. Looking into Portfolios. *Portfolios in the Writing Classroom: An Introduction*, ed. Kathleen Blake Yancey. Urbana, IL: NCTE: 49-61.

Myers, Miles, and David P. Pearson. 1996. Performance Assessment and the Literacy Unit of the National Standards Project. *Assessing Writing* 3.1: 4-27.

National Assessment of Educational Progress (NAEP). 1994. *Student Achievement in Core Subjects of the School Curriculum.* Washington, DC: US Department of Education.

Nelson, Jennie. 1995. Reading Classrooms as Text: Exploring Student Writers' Interpretive Practices. *College Composition and Communication* 46: 411-430.

Nelson, Theodor Holm. 1992. Opening Hypertext: A Memoir. *Literacy Online: The Promise (and Peril) of Reading and Writing With Computers*, ed. Myron C. Tuman. Pittsburgh: University of Pittsburgh Press: 43-57.

New Standards Takes a Close Look at Portfolios. 1993. *The Council Chronicle* 3.2: 1.

New Standards Project. 1994. *Student Portfolio Handbook: High School English Language Arts.* Field Trial Version. Pittsburgh: National Center on Education and the Economy.

O'Donnell, Roy. 1990. English Language Arts Teacher Education. *Handbook of Research on Teacher Education*, ed. W. Robert Houston. New York, Macmillan: 357-372.

Ohmann, Richard. 1985. Literacy, Technology, and Monopoly Capitalism. *College English* 47: 675-689.

Olson, C. Paul. 1987. Who Computes? *Critical Pedagogy and Cultural Power*, ed. D. Livingstone. South Hadley, MA: Bergin and Garvey: 179-204.

PacerForum. Pacer, 7911 Herschel Avenue, Suite 402, LaJolla, CA 92037.

Paulson, F. Leon., and Pearl R. Paulson. *Four Varieties of Self-Reflection.* Unpublished manuscript.

———. 1990. *How Do Portfolios Measure Up? A Cognitive Model for Assessing Portfolios.* (ED 324 329).

———. 1991. *The Making of a Portfolio.* (ED 334 251).

———. 1992. *Portfolios: A Perspective on Learning.* Videocassette. Portland, OR: Paulson & Paulson, Educational Consultants.

———, Pearl R. Paulson, and Carol A. Meyer. 1991. What Makes a Portfolio a Portfolio? *Educational Leadership* 48.5: 60-63.

Paulson, Pearl R., and F. Leon Paulson. 1991. Portfolios: Stories of Knowing. *Knowing: The Power of Stories (Claremont Reading Conference 55th Yearbook)*, ed. P. H. Dreyer. Claremont, CA: Center for Developmental Studies of the Claremont Graduate School: 294-303.

———, F. Leon Paulson, and D. M. Frazier. Sarah's Portfolio. Unpublished manuscript.

Phelps, Louise Wetherbee. 1989. Images of Student Writing: The Deep Structure of Teacher Response. *Writing and Response: Theory, Practice, and Research*, ed. Chris M. Anson. Urbana, IL: NCTE: 37-67.

Pearson, P. David, and Sheila Valencia. 1987. Assessment, Accountability, and Professional Prerogative. *Research in Literacy: Merging Perspectives (Thirty-sixth Yearbook of the*

National Reading Conference): 3-16.

Piller, Charles. 1987. Separate Realities: The Creation of the Technological Underclass in America's Public Schools. *MacWorld*: 218-230.

Pratt, Mary Louise. 1991. Arts of the Contact Zone. *Profession 91*. New York: MLA: 33-40.

A Preliminary Study of the Feasibility and Utility for National Policy of Instructional "Good Practice" Indicators in Undergraduate Education. 1994. U.S. Department of Education; Office of Educational Research and Improvement. NCES 94-437.

Regan, Alison. 1994. Type Normal Like the Rest of Us: Writing, Power, and Homophobia in the Networked Composition Classroom. *Computers and Composition* 10.4: 11-23.

Reidy, Edward. 1992. All about Assessment. *EdNews.* Frankfort: Kentucky Department of Education: 3-14.

Resnick, Lauren B., and David Resnick. 1992. Assessing the Thinking Curriculum: New Tools for Educational Reform. *Changing Assessments: Alternative Views of Aptitude, Achievement and Instruction*, ed. Byron R. Gifford and Mary C. O'Connor. Boston: Klewer.

Reynolds, David S. 1988. *Beneath the American Renaissance: The Subversive Imagination in the Age of Emerson and Melville.* Cambridge: Harvard University Press.

Reynolds, Joan. 1995. Unpublished manuscript.

Richardson-Koehler, V. 1988. Barriers to Effective Supervision of Student Teaching. *Journal of Teacher Education* 39: 28-34.

Riedl, R. 1989. Patterns in Computer-Mediated Discussions. *Mindweave: Communication, Computers, and Distance Education*, ed. R. Mason and A Kaye. Oxford: Pergamon Press: 215-220.

Rief, Linda. 1990. Finding the Value in Evaluation: Self-assessment in a Middle School Classroom. *Educational Leadership* 47.6: 24-29.

———. 1992. *Seeking Diversity: Language Arts with Adolescents.* Portsmouth, NH: Heinemann.

Rideout, J. Christopher, and Jill Ramsfield. 1994. Legal Writing: A Revised View. *Washington Law Review* 69: 35-99.

Roe, Mary. 1991. "Portfolios: from Mandate to Implementation." Paper presented at the 41st Annual Meeting of the National Reading Conference. (ED 343 103).

Roemer, Marjorie Godlin. 1991. What We Talk about When We Talk about School Reform. *Harvard Educational Review* 61.4: 434-48.

Romano, Susan. 1993. The Egalitarianism Narrative: Whose Story? Which Yardstick? *Computers and Composition* 10.3: 5-28.

Romano, Tom. 1994. Removing the Blindfold: Portfolios in Fiction Writing Classes. *New Directions in Portfolio Assessment: Reflective Practice, Critical Theory, and Large-scale Scoring*, ed. Laurel Black, Donald A. Daiker, Jeffrey Sommers, and Gail Stygall. Portsmouth, NH: Boynton/Cook, Heinemann: 73–82.

Replica. Farallon. (10-pack $500.)

Rose, Mike. 1985. The Language of Exclusion: Writing Instruction at the University. *College English* 47: 341-359.

Roussea, Ann. 1993. From the Inside Out. Unpublished manuscript.

Salzillo, F., and A. Van Fleet. 1977. Student Teaching and Teacher Education: A Sociological Model for Change. *Journal of Teacher Education* 28: 27-31.

Schlechty, Phillip, and Anne W. Joslin. 1986. Images of Schools. *Rethinking School Improvement: Research, Craft, and Concept*, ed. Anne Lieberman. New York: Teachers College Press.

Schneiderman, Ben, Dorothy Brethauer, Catherine Plaisant, and Richard Potter. 1989. Evaluating Three Museum Installations of a Hypertext System. *Journal of the American Society for Information Science* 40 (3): 172-182.

Schon, Donald A. 1987. *Educating the Reflective Practitioner: Toward a New Design for Teaching and Learning in the Professions.* San Francisco: Jossey-Bass.

Scott, Patrick. 1991. Step by Step: The Development in British Schools of Assessment by Portfolio. *Portfolios: Process and Product,* ed. Pat Belanoff and Marcia Dickson. Portsmouth, NH: Heineman, Boynton/Cook: 80-92.

Selfe, Cynthia L. 1989. Redefining Literacy: The Multilayered Grammars of Computers. *Critical Perspectives on Computers and Composition Instruction,* ed. Cynthia L. Selfe and Gail E. Hawisher. New York: Teachers College Press: 13-15.

———. 1994. "Portfolios, Technology, and the World." Paper presented at NCTE Portfolios, Technology, and the World Conference, Indianapolis.

——— and Richard Selfe. 1994. The Politics of the Interface: Power and Its Exercise in Electronic Contact Zones. *College Composition and Communication* 45.4: 480-504.

Severinson Eklundh, Kerstin. 1994. Linear and Nonlinear Strategies in Computer-based Writing. *Computers and Composition* 11: 203–216.

Sewell, Lauren. 1994. "Portfolio Pedagogy and Teacher Reflexivity." Paper presented at NCTE Portfolios, Reflection, and Teacher Research Conference. Baltimore.

Sheingold, Karen, Joan I. Heller, and Susan T. Paulukonis. 1994. *Actively Seeking Evidence: Teacher Change through Assessment Development.* (Technical Report No. 94-04). Princeton New Jersey: ETS, Center for Performance Assessment: 1-34.

Shepard, Lorrie A. 1991. Will National Tests Improve Student Learning? *Phi Delta Kappan* 73: 232-238.

Shirk, Henrietta Nickels. 1991a. "Hyper" Rhetoric: Reflections on Teaching Hypertext. *The Technical Writing Teacher* 18: 189-200.

———. 1991b. Hypertext and Composition Studies. *Evolving Perspectives on Computers and Composition Studies: Questions for the 1990s,* ed. Gail Hawisher and Cynthia Selfe. Urbana, IL: NCTE: 177-202.

Shor, Ira. 1987. Educating the Educators: A Freirean Approach to the Crisis in Teacher Education. *Freire for the Classroom: A Sourcebook for Liberatory Teaching,* ed. Ira Shor. Portsmouth, NH: Heinemann, Boynton/Cook: 7-32.

Short, K., and G. Hartmann. 1992. Hearing Students' Voices: The Role of Reflection in Learning. *Teachers Networking: The Whole Language Newsletter* 11.3: 1-6.

Shulman, Lee S. 1987. Knowledge and Teaching: Foundations of the New Reform. *Harvard Educational Review* 57.1: 1-22.

———. 1996. "Course Anatomy: The Dissection and Transformation of Knowledge." Paper presented at American Assocation of Higher Education Conference on Faculty Roles and Rewards. Atlanta.

Sirc, Geoffrey, and Tom Reynolds. 1990. The Face of Collaboration in the Networked Writing Classroom. *Computers and Composition* 7.4: 53-70.

Slatin, John M. 1990. Reading Hypertext: Order and Coherence in a New Medium. *College English* 52: 870-883.

Smith, Catherine F. 1991. Reconceiving Hypertext. *Evolving Perspectives on Computers and Composition Studies: Questions for the 1990s,* ed. Gail Hawisher and Cynthia Selfe. Urbana, IL: NCTE: 224-252.

———. 1994. Hypertextual Thinking. *Literacy and Computers: The Complications of Teaching and Learning with Technology,* ed. Cynthia L. Selfe and Susan Hilligoss. New York: MLA: 264-281.

Smith, Mary L. 1991. Put to the Test: The Effects of External Testing on Teachers. *Educational Researcher* 20.5: 8-11.

Sommers, Jeffrey, Laurel Black, Donald A. Daiker, and Gail Stygall. 1993. The Challenge of Rating Portfolios: What WPAs Can Expect. *Writing Program Administration* 17.1-2: 7-29.

Spaulding, Elizabeth. 1995. The New Standards Project and English Language Arts Portfolios: A Report on Process and Progress. *The Clearing House*: 219-223.

Stake, R. 1967. The Countenance of Educational Evaluation. *Teachers College Record* 68.7: 523-540.

Stone, Sandra J. 1995. Portfolios: Interactive, Dynamic Instructional Tool. *Childhood Education* 71.4: 232-234.

———. 1996. *Creating the Multiage Classroom.* Glenview, IL: GoodYear Books/Scott Foresman.

Stotsky, Sandra. 1992. From the Editor. *Research in the Teaching of English* 26: 245-248.

Sullivan, Patricia A. 1991. Taking Control of the Page: Electronic Writing and Word Publishing. *Evolving Perspectives on Computers and Composition Studies. Questions for the 1990s*, ed. Gail E. Hawisher and Cynthia L. Selfe. Urbana, IL: NCTE: 43-64.

Sullivan, Patricia A., and James E. Porter. 1993. Remapping Curricular Geography: Professional Writing in/and English. *Journal of Business and Technical Communication* 7: 389-422.

Sulzby, Elizabeth. 1986. Writing and Reading: Signs of Oral and Written Language Organization in the Young Child. *Emergent Literacy: Writing and Reading*, ed. William H. Teale and Elizabeth Sulzby. Norwood, NJ: Ablex.

———. 1988. Appendix 2.1: Forms of Writing and Rereading Example List. *Reading and Writing Connections*, ed. J. Mason. Boston: Allyn and Bacon.

———, J. Barnhart, and J. A. Hieshima. 1988. Forms of Writing and Rereading from Writing: A Preliminary Report. *Reading and Writing Connections*, ed. J. Mason. Boston: Allyn and Bacon.

Takayoshi, Pamela. 1994. Building New Networks From the Old: Women's Experiences With Electronic Communications. *Computers and Composition* 11: 21-35.

Thé, Lee. 1992. PCs Tool Up For Hypertext. *Datamation* 38.3: 35-36.

Thomas, M. Wynn. 1987. *The Lunar Light of Whitman's Poetry.* Cambridge: Harvard University Press.

Tierney, Robert J., Mark A. Carter, and Laura E. Desai. 1991. *Portfolio Assessment in the Reading-Writing Classroom.* Norwood, MA: Christopher-Gordon Publishers, Inc.

Turkle, Sherry. 1984. *The Second Self: Computers and the Human Spirit.* New York, NY: Simon and Schuster.

———. 1995. *Life on the Screen: Identity in the Age of the Internet.* New York: Simon and Schuster.

U.S. Department of Labor. 1991. *What Work Requires of School.* Washington, DC: U.S. Government Printing Office.

Valencia, S. W., and R. Calfee. 1991. The Development and Use of Literacy Portfolios for Students, Classes, and Teachers. *Applied Measurement in Education* 4.4: 333-345.

Van Buren I.S.D (Independent School District). Undated. *Student-Directed Portfolios: Bridging the Gap.* Videocassette. Laurence, MI.

Vavrus, Linda. 1990. Put Portfolios to the Test. *Instructor*: 48-53.

Wallerstein, Nina. 1987. Problem-posing Education: Freire's Method for Transformation. *Freire for the Classroom: A Sourcebook for Liberatory Teaching*, ed. Ira Shor. Portsmouth, NH: Heinemann: 33-44.

Walvoord, Barbara, and Lucille McCarthy. 1990. *Thinking and Writing in College: A Naturalistic Study of Students in Four Disciplines.* Urbana, IL: NCTE.

Weinbaum, Kerry. 1991. Portfolios as a Vehicle for Student Empowerment and Teacher Change. *Portfolios: Process and Product*, ed. Pat Belanoff and Marcia Dickson. Portsmouth, NH: Boynton Cook: 206-214.

Weiser, Irwin. 1992. Portfolio Practice and Assessment for Collegiate Basic Writers. *Portfolios in the Writing Classroom: An Introduction*, ed. Kathleen Blake Yancey. Urbana, IL: NCTE: 89-101.

———. 1994. Portfolios and the New Teacher of Writing. *New Directions in Portfolio Assessment: Reflective Practice, Critical Theory, and Large-scale Scoring*, ed. Laurel Black, Donald A. Daiker, Jeffrey Sommers, and Gail Stygall. Portsmouth, NH: Boynton/Cook, Heinemann: 219-230.

Wells, P. 1991. Putting America to the Test. *Agenda* 1: 52-57.

White, Edward M. 1985. *Teaching and Assessing Writing: Recent Advances in Understanding, Evaluating, and Improving Student Performance*. San Francisco: Jossey-Bass.

———. 1993. Holistic Scoring: Past Triumphs and Future Challenges. *Validating Holistic Scoring for Writing Assessment: Theoretical and Empirical Foundations*, ed. Michael M. Williamson and Brian Huot. Cresskill, NJ: Hampton.

———. 1994. Issues and Problems in Writing Assessment. *Assessing Writing* 1.1: 11-28.

White, James Boyd. 1982. Law as Language: Reading Law and Reading Literature. *Texas Law Review* 60: 415-445.

———. 1985. *Heracles's Bow: Essays on the Rhetoric and Poetics of the Law*. Madison: University of Wisconsin Press.

Whitman, Walt. 1982. A Backward Glance O'er Travel'd Roads. *Walt Whitman: Complete Poetry and Collected Prose*, ed. Justin Kaplan. New York: Literary Classics of the United States.

Wickliff, Gregory and Janice Tovey. 1995. Hypertext in a Professional Writing Course. *Technical Communications Quarterly* 4.1: 47-61.

Wiggins, Grant. 1989. A True Test: Toward More Authentic and Equitable Assessment. *Phi Delta Kappan* 70: 703-13.

———. 1991. quoted by Gwen Solomon in Electronic Portfolios. *Electronic Learning*: 10.

———. 1992. Creating Tests Worth Taking. *Educational Leadership* 49.8: 26-33.

———. 1993a. *Assessing Student Performance*. San Francisco: Jossey Bass.

———. 1993b Assessment: Authenticity, Context, and Validity. *Phi Delta Kappan*: 200-214.

Williams, William Carlos. 1964. Appendix. How To Write. *The Poems of William Carlos Williams*, ed Linda Welshimer Wagner. Middletown CT: Wesleyan University Press.

Williamson, Michael M. 1992. The Worship of Efficiency: Untangling Theoretical and Practical Considerations in Writing Assessment. *Assessing Writing* 1.2: 147-174.

Wilson, Tish. 1992. Personal Interview. 21 April.

Wimsatt, W. K., and Monroe C. Beardsley. 1954. The Intentional Fallacy. *The Verbal Icon: Studies in the Meaning of Poetry*, ed.W. K. Wimsatt. Lexington, KY: The University of Kentucky Press: 3-18.

Winner, Langdon. 1986. *The Whale and the Reactor: A Search for Limits in an Age of High Technology*. Chicago, IL: The University of Chicago Press.

Witte, Stephen. P., and Jennifer Flach. 1994. Notes Toward an Assessment of Advanced Students Ability to Communicate. *Assessing Writing* 2.1: 207-246.

Wolf, Dennie Palmer. 1993. Assessment as an Episode of Learning. *Construction Versus Choice in Cognitive Measurement: Issues in Constructed Response, Performance Testing, and Portfolio Assessment*, ed. R.E. Bennett and W.C. Ward. Hillsdale, NJ: Lawrence Erlbaum Associates: 213-239.

———. 1987. Opening Up Assessment. *Educational Leadership* 45: 24-29.

———. 1989. Portfolio Assessment: Sampling Student Work. *Educational Leadership* 46: 35-39.

———, Eunice Ann Greer, and Joanna Lieberman. 1995. Portfolio Cultures: Literate Cultures. *Voices from the Middle* 2.1: 4.

———, Paul G. LeMahieu, and JoAnne Eresh. 1992. Good Measure: Assessment as a Tool for Educational Reform. *Educational Leadership* 49: 8-13.

Wolfgang, Charles H., and T. S. Sanders. 1981. Defending Young Children's Play as the Ladder to Literacy. *Theory into Practice* 20.2: 116-120.

Yancey, Kathleen Blake, ed. 1992a. *Portfolios in the Writing Classroom: An Introduction.* Urbana, IL: NCTE.

———. 1992b. Portfolios in the Writing Classroom: A Final Reflection. *Portfolios in the Writing Classroom: An Introduction*, ed. Kathleen Blake Yancey. Urbana: NCTE: 102-116.

———. 1992c. Teachers' Stories: Notes Toward a Portfolio Pedagogy. *Portfolios in the Writing Classroom: An Introduction*, ed. Kathleen Blake Yancey. Urbana: NCTE: 12-20.

———. 1992d. "The Scholarship of Our Practice and the Teaching Portfolio: A New Kind of Celebration." NCTE Annual Convention. Louisville, KY.

———. 1993a. "Exploring Together: Designing and Reading with Portfolio Rubrics." Workshop at NCTE Annual Convention. Pittsburgh.

———. 1993b. Portfolios and Program Assessment. Unpublished manuscript.

———. 1994a. Address. Portfolio Conference at Virginia Commonwealth University, Richmond, VA.

———. 1994b. Make Haste Slowly: Graduate Teaching Assistants and Portfolios. *New Directions in Portfolio Assessment: Reflective Practice, Critical Theory, and Large-scale Scoring*, ed. Laurel Black, Donald A. Daiker, Jeffrey Sommers, and Gail Stygall. Portsmouth, NH: Boynton/Cook, Heinemann: 210-218.

———. 1994c. "Portfolios, Technology, and the World." Paper presented at NCTE Portfolios, Technology, and the World Conference, Indianapolis.

Zaharlick, Amy, and Judith L. Green. 1991. Ethnographic Research. *Handbook of Research On the Teaching of the English Language Arts*, ed. James Flood et al. New York: Macmillan: 205-225.

Zeichner, Kenneth M. 1990. Changing Directions in the Practicum: Looking Ahead to the 1990s. *Journal of Education for Teaching* 16: 105-132.

Zemelman, Steve, Harvey Daniels, and Arthur Hyde. 1993. *Best Practice: New Standards for Teaching and Learning in America's Schools*. Portsmouth, NH: Heinemann.

Zuboff, Shoshana. 1988. *In the Age of the Smart Machine: The Future of Work and Power.* New York, NY: Basic Books, Inc.

About the Editors

KATHLEEN BLAKE YANCEY is Associate Professor of English at The University of North Carolina at Charlotte, where she teaches undergraduate courses in first year and advanced writing, in tutoring and teaching writing, and in writing and technology; and graduate courses in rhetorical theory and writing assessment. Her earlier books include the edited collections *Portfolios in the Writing Classroom: An Introduction* (NCTE, 1992) and *Voices on Voice: Perspectives, Definitions, Inquiry* (NCTE, 1994). With Brian Huot, she founded and edits the journal *Assessing Writing*. Her current projects include work in the rhetoric of reflection and in the dialectical relationship between literacy and technology.

IRWIN WEISER is Associate Professor of English at Purdue University, where he teaches a practicum in the teaching of composition for first year teaching assistants. Having recently completed a long term as Director of Composition, he is teaching full-time again: graduate courses in the Rhetoric and Composition program and undergraduate writing courses. In addition to his chapters in *New Directions in Portfolio Assessment* and *Portfolios in the Writing Classroom*, he has recently published articles on teacher preparation, cultural studies, and the assessment of teaching.

About the Contributors

MICHAEL S. ALLEN teaches writing and literature at The Ohio State University at Mansfield, and other writing classes at North Central Technical College. In 1992, Allen asked ten college faculty attending Miami University's "New Directions in Portfolio Assessment" conference if they would be interested in exchanging and evaluating portfolios from their classrooms, and Portnet was formed. Soon Portnet was evaluating portfolios online; Mike developed a strong new interest in electronic communication and texts. He has published several articles, most recently in *Assessing Writing* and in the *Journal of Teaching Writing*, and he also led an external validation of the Missouri Western State University graduation portfolio for technical writing majors.

CHERYL AUSE and GERILEE NICASTRO continue to experiment with portfolios at their respective schools. The Bonneville-Cottonwood portfolio connection is ongoing as well: currently, Ause and Nicastro are working together on a district committee to develop performance assessment tasks for reading and writing. Gerilee has taught for twenty-four years, Cheryl for twenty years. Cheryl is also a contributor to *Peer Response Groups in Action* (Boynton/Cook, 1993), a collection of work which focuses on collaborative writing in the classroom.

KRISTINE BLAIR is Assistant Professor of English at Bowling Green State University. She teaches undergraduate and graduate courses in composition theory and pedagogy, the majority of them in electronic settings. Her work with Pamela Takayoshi began while they were graduate students in Purdue's program in rhetoric and composition. Currently, she and Takayoshi are co-editing the collection *Feminist Cyberscapes: Essays on Gender in Electronic Spaces*. Blair's current research addresses the ability to extend cultural studies pedagogies to all levels and sites of the English curriculum, including computerized writing classrooms.

C. BETH BURCH is Assistant Professor at Binghamton University, SUNY, where she teaches courses in English education, English, and education and is responsible for the Master of Arts in Teaching English program. She has just finished writing a first year rhetoric on writing in the portfolio classroom. Her publications include *Students Write* (with Leonora Woodman), *Laura and Jim and What they Taught Me About the Gap Between Educational Theory and Practice* (with Dona Kagan), articles in *Portfolio News, Studies in American Jewish Literature,* and *The Oxford Companion to Women's Writing*, among others. Her current research projects focus on portfolios and reflection and on Jewish women writers.

SUSAN CALLAHAN became aware of the role writing portfolios were expected to play in school reform while teaching basic writing at Kentucky State University. Since her previous teaching experience included work with at-risk middle and high school students as well as returning adults who had not been successful in traditional classrooms, she hoped the assessment portfolios would encourage high quality writing experiences for all students. She currently teaches advanced composition, writing theory, and pedagogy to preservice secondary teachers at Northern Illinois University. She has an article on portfolio theory in a recent issue of *Assessing Writing* and is planning a follow-up study at Pine View.

WILLIAM CONDON, formerly the Director of the University of Michigan's English Composition Board, now directs the Washington State University Writing Program. Condon is active in the area of portfolio-based writing assessment. His publications include "Readers' Responses to Portfolios" in *College Composition and Communication*, and "Maintaining a Portfolio-Based Writing Assessment: Research that Informs Program Development," in *New Directions in Portfolio Assessment.* He and Liz Hamp-Lyons have co-written a book about portfolio-based assessment (forthcoming, Hampton Press).

SUSAN R. DAILEY is Writing Specialist and Assistant Professor of Legal Writing at Quinnipiac College School of Law in Hamden, Connecticut. She holds a Ph.D. from Catholic University, and before joining the Law School faculty, she taught writing and literature in college English and basic studies programs. In addition to working with student writing portfolios, she has developed a teacher portfolio project for faculty involved in teaching legal writing. Her articles have appeared in *The Leaflet* and *The Second Draft: Bulletin of the Legal Writing Institute.*

ROBERT LEIGH DAVIS is Assistant Professor of English at Wittenberg University in Springfield, Ohio, where he teaches undergraduate courses in composition, literary theory, and American literature. He was awarded Wittenberg's Omicron Delta Kappa Excellence in Teaching Award in 1996 and is author of *Whitman and the Romance of Medicine* (University of California Press, forthcoming). For the past four years, he has directed Wittenberg's writing program.

MARCIA DICKSON teaches composition at The Ohio State University at Marion, where she is Associate Professor of English. Although her area of expertise is basic writing instruction, she uses portfolios for all of her composition and literature courses, and as a member of the Portnet project, she collaborates over the wires about portfolio assessment. Her publications include *Portfolios:Process and Product*, co-edited with Pat Belanoff, and *It's Not Like That Here: Teaching Reading and Writing to Novice Writers* (Boynton/Cook).

PETER ELBOW and PAT BELANOFF have been writing collaboratively about portfolios for over ten years. This collaboration began at the University at Stony Brook and led to the establishment there of the first major university portfolio system in the country. That collaboration also led to two textbooks, *A Community of Writers* and *Sharing and Responding*, both now in second editions. Sharing drafts and trading feedback continued after Peter moved to the University of Massachusetts at Amherst. Peter's other books, *Writing Without Teachers*, *Writing With Power*, and *Embracing Contraries*, focus on the interactions of classroom practices and their philosophic and theoretical underpinnings. His most recent book, *What Is English?*, is a personal report of and response to the 1994 English Coalition Conference. Pat edited, with Marcia Dickson, the collection of essays *Portfolios: Process and Product*, which has served as the source of a variety of portfolio projects throughout the country. Pat has also authored a grammar book, *The Right Handbook*, now in its second edition. Peter serves on the executive board of CCCC; Pat currently is chair of the CCCC Assessment Committee. Both now also serve as Directors of the writing programs at their institutions.

KATHERINE FISCHER teaches courses in creative writing, science fiction, poetry, introduction to literature, essay writing, and nature writing at Clarke College in Dubuque, Iowa; she also serves as the director of the writing lab and coordinator for computer-assisted writing classes. She has published articles about teaching writing and literature, and most recently, about using computer technology to teach writing and literature. She has also had poetry published in various small presses and journals.

CHERYL FORBES teaches writing and rhetoric at Hobart and William Smith Colleges in Geneva, New York. Her recent articles include "Fifth Business: Typography and the Act of Reading" in *Writing on the Edge* and "Cowriting, Overwriting, and Overriding in Portfolio Land Online" in *Computers and Composition, Special Issue on the Electronic Portfolio*. She has an article on African-American women's voices in a forthcoming book, *Women's Words, Women's Worlds* (Mayfield) and has just finished an article, "Discerning Domesticities: Critical Narrative and Composition" for *Feminism and Empirical Writing Research: Emerging Perspectives in Rhetoric and Composition* (forthcoming, Boynton/Cook).

GAIL E. HAWISHER is Professor of English and Director of the Center for Writing Studies at the University of Illinois, Urbana-Champaign. She has served on the NCTE College Editorial Board and is currently Assistant Chair of NCTE's College Section. Her published work includes the co-edited collections *Critical Perspectives on Computers and Composition Instruction*; *On Literacy and Its*

Teaching; *Evolving Perspectives on Computers and Composition Studies: Questions for the 1990s*; and *Re-Imagining Computers and Composition: Teaching and Research in the Virtual Age*. She has published widely in composition studies in such journals as *Research in the Teaching of English*, *College English*, and *Written Communication*. With Cynthia Selfe, she also edits *Computers and Composition*. Her most recent projects are the co-authored "Women on the Networks: Searching for E-Spaces of Their Own" and *Computers and the Teaching of Writing in American Higher Education, 1979-1994: A History*.

Janice M. Heiges, an Associate Professor of Composition at Northern Virginia Community College, Loudon campus, teaches a variety of writing courses, including developmental, business, and technical writing. Introduced to portfolios in 1990, she has been using portfolios in all of her classes. In 1994, while completing a doctoral degree on student attitudes towards portfolios, she successfully pursued substituting a portfolio for the doctoral comprehensive examination. During the past four years, she has made presentations about portfolios at regional and national conferences. Recently, she has published a monograph entitled "Using Portfolios in the English 111 Classroom."

Brian Huot and Michael M. Williamson are, respectively, Associate Professor of English at the University of Louisville and Professor of English at Indiana University of Pennsylvania. Brian has published research and theory on writing assessment in *College Composition and Communication* and *Review of Research in Education*, as well as in other journals and books. He is co-editor, with Kathleen Yancey, of the journal *Assessing Writing*. Mike and Brian have been working collaboratively on writing assessment for some time. Together, they edited *Validating Holistic Scoring for Writing Assessment: Theoretical and Empirical Foundations*.

George P. E. Meese is director of the Writing Excellence Program at Eckerd College in St. Petersburg, Florida, where he instituted a campuswide writing competency portfolio system in 1988. He is a charter member of the Portnet research group, with a continuing interest in making writing assessment serve at least three stakeholders: each student's learning; our faculty colleagues' curricular purposes; and our institutions' different missions. His other interests include undergraduate learning-through-writing, developmental factors in learning, John Hawkes's fiction, value theory, applied ethics, and cross-cultural studies, especially Asian and western aesthetics.

Sandra Murphy is Professor and Director of the Center for Cooperative Research and Extension Services for Schools (CRESS) in the Division of Education at the University of California, Davis. She teaches graduate-level courses on the teaching of reading and writing and has taught high school English and freshman composition. She co-authored *Designing Writing Tasks for the Assessment of Writing* (with Leo Ruth) and *Writing Portfolios: A Bridge from*

Teaching to Assessment (with Mary Ann Smith) and has written several articles on the acquisition of literacy and the assessment of writing.

Charlotte W. O'Brien is currently the Coordinator of Curriculum Services for the Missouri Department of Elementary and Secondary Education, where she is overseeing the development of curriculum frameworks in response to the Missouri (Show-Me) Standards. When her chapter for this collection was first drafted, she was the English/language arts supervisor for the department. In that capacity, she was responsible for the development of the Missouri Writing Assessment, an extended writing experience incorporating process writing in large-scale assessment. She has taught at elementary, secondary, undergraduate, and graduate levels and written articles for state and national publications.

Pearl R. Paulson is the special education director for Gladstone School District in Oregon. Her interest in portfolios began when she was looking for ways to celebrate students' diversity as well as document their progress. Portfolios became a venue for studying the integration of learning, an interest she and her husband have long shared.

F. Leon Paulson is an assessment specialist for the Multnomah Education District in Portland, Oregon. His primary interest is cognitive processes and their implications for instruction. Leon became interested in portfolios because the approach encourages students to develop their skills in self-assessment.

Mary Perry has taught in both Louisiana and Texas, in middle and high schools, and served as a writing specialist for the Fort Worth Independent School District from 1988 to 1993. Currently residing in Austin, she consults with school district personnel about process writing, writing across the curriculum, portfolios, project-based instruction, performance tasks, and school-to-work transition.

Thomas Philion is Assistant Professor in the Department of English at the University of Illinois at Chicago and Assistant Director of the Secondary English Teacher Education Program. His publications consist of articles in *English Journal*, *Illinois English Bulletin*, and the NCTE collection *Focus on Reflecting and Connecting*. A former middle school teacher, he is involved in research and development projects, with urban educators, encompassing computers, collaborative learning, and reading pedagogy.

Cynthia L. Selfe serves as Professor of Composition and Communication and the Chair of the Humanities Department at Michigan Technological University. When she's not working on Michigan Tech business, Selfe serves as the current Program Chair for the CCCC (1997). She has also chaired the College Section of the NCTE and served as a founding member and Chair of that organization's Assembly of Computers in English. She has been a member of the Executive Committee of the CCCC, and the Committee on Computers